ELEMENTS OF THE EURO AREA

Global Finance Series

Edited by
John J. Kirton, University of Toronto, Canada, Michele Fratianni, Indiana University, U.S.A. and Paolo Savona, LUISS Guido Carli University, Italy

The intensifying globalisation of the twenty-first century has brought a myriad of new managerial and political challenges for governing international finance. The return of synchronous global slowdown, mounting developed country debt, and new economy volatility have overturned established economic certainties. Proliferating financial crises, transnational terrorism, currency consolidation, and increasing demands that international finance should better serve public goods such as social and environmental security have all arisen to compound the problem.

The new public and private international institutions that are emerging to govern global finance have only just begun to comprehend and respond to this new world. Embracing international financial flows and foreign direct investment, in both the private and public sector dimensions, this series focuses on the challenges and opportunities faced by firms, national governments, and international institutions, and their roles in creating a new system of global finance.

Also in the series

Sustaining Global Growth and Development
G7 and IMF Governance
Edited by Michele Fratianni, Paolo Savona and John J. Kirton
ISBN 0 7546 3529 5

Governing Global Finance
New Challenges, G7 and IMF Contributions
Edited by Michele Fratianni, Paolo Savona and John J. Kirton
ISBN 0 7546 0880 8

Global Financial Crime
Terrorism, Money Laundering and Offshore Centres
Edited by Donato Masciandaro
ISBN 0 7546 3707 7

Elements of the Euro Area
Integrating Financial Markets

Edited by

JESPER BERG
Danmarks Nationalbank, Denmark

MAURO GRANDE
European Central Bank, Germany

FRANCESCO PAOLO MONGELLI
European Central Bank, Germany

Routledge
Taylor & Francis Group
LONDON AND NEW YORK

First published 2005 by Ashgate Publishing

Reissued 2018 by Routledge
2 Park Square, Milton Park, Abingdon, Oxon, OX14 4RN
711 Third Avenue, New York, NY 10017, USA

Routledge is an imprint of the Taylor & Francis Group, an informa business

First issued in paperback 2018

A Library of Congress record exists under LC control number: 2004025947

ISBN 13: 978-0-815-38876-0 (hbk)
ISBN 13: 978-1-138-61955-5 (pbk)
ISBN 13: 978-1-351-15912-8 (ebk)

Contents

Preface and Acknowledgements

The motivation for this book came from the observation that there is relatively scarce information on the changes that are brought about by the introduction of the euro and, in particular, concerning the ongoing transformation of euro area financial systems. By bringing together, and making available, a set of comprehensive data, analysis and research on diverse features of euro area financial systems, this book intends to serve as a source of reference.

While the book reflects the input of many colleagues at the European System of Central Banks (ESCB), without whom it would never have materialized, it does not necessarily reflect the views of the ESCB, and the European Central Bank in particular. Any error or omission is our responsibility as editors.

Credit for the completion of this book is due to many people, of whom only a few can be mentioned here. Our Executive Board Members, Professors Otmar Issing and Tommaso Padoa-Schioppa, have allowed us to devote resources to transforming diverse analytical pieces of work into a hopefully coherent and informative volume on some elements of financial integration in the euro area. Many of our colleagues have provided comments and support, including Klaus Masuch, Sergio Nicoletti, Francesco Drudi, Nuno Cassola, Huw Pill, Caroline Willeke, Sinead Lennon, Tuomas Välimäki, Alain Vandepeute, Denis Blenck, and Manfred Kremer. Chapter 2 has benefited from comments and suggestions from Yoshikazu Morimoto (Bank of Japan) and Mark Wynne (Federal Reserve Bank of Dallas). In particular, we are indebted to Hans-Joachim Kl'ckers who has contributed to improving the clarity of the book. He has also done his best to avoid any unintended message. Jesper Berg, now at the Danmarks Nationalbank, has worked on this book while at the European Central Bank. Annette Hochberger has put in a great effort in editing all the chapters.

The work behind diverse chapters originated in joint projects with others. Chapter 1 (Some International Comparisons of the Economic and Financial Structure of the Euro Area) draws heavily – but also extends – on some initial sections of the book, *The Monetary Policy of the ECB* (ECB, 2004). Chapter 5 (How are Euro Area Financial Structures Changing?) is an extension and an update of the *Report on Financial Structures* (ECB, 2002). Chapter 6 (What Effects is EMU having on the Integration of Financial Services?) builds on an earlier Occasional Paper of the ECB (Inês Cabral et al., 2002, *Banking Integration in the Euro Area*), while Chapter 7 (Integration of the Money Market in the Euro Area) draws on a recently published ECB Occasional Paper. The space available here makes it impossible to give due credit to all those who have contributed to these joint projects.

Thanks are also due to John Kirton, Michele Fratianni and Paolo Savona for inviting us to submit this volume, to an anonymous referee for making constructive remarks that have strengthened this volume, and to those involved in several aspects of the production at the publishing house.

This book is intended for the advanced undergraduate student as well as the professional observer of developments in financial markets. It contains the most comprehensive overview available today of developments in the integration of financial markets in the euro area.

The book can be read on its own, also as an introduction to more specific studies. In the latter context, it should also be of benefit for graduate students. The first part of the book is deliberately drafted to bring those without prior knowledge of institutional features and/or the study of financial integration up to date. Those readers who are already familiar with these aspects may proceed directly to the subsequent parts of the book.

The book deals mostly with the European experience, and with the initiatives pursued by diverse European authorities over the last 40–50 years. In fact, the European path toward financial integration is providing several lessons on the role played by institutions – and integrating and harmonizing previously separated national financial institutions – and financial and non-financial 'barriers' – including national habits and preferences. There are also several comparisons with the US and Japan. However, the latter countries did not need to face such a daunting, and extended, policy challenge.

A common theme linking the contributions in this volume is that they all provide a snapshot of diverse segments of the financial markets – and the institutions, market forces, and policies – shaping them. At the same time one needs to keep into consideration that all these elements are rapidly re-shaping the financial markets of the euro area.

List of Contributors

Lieven Baele is currently assistant professor at Tilburg University. He holds a PhD from Ghent University (2003). His research interests cover various fields in international finance and econometrics, with a special focus on (measuring) financial integration and international financial shock transmission, optimal portfolio allocation, the interaction between bank strategy and risk, as well as in the evolution of Central and Eastern European capital markets. He has published his work in the Journal of Financial and Quantitative Analysis, the Oxford Review of Economic Policy, and the ECB Occasional Paper series. He worked on several occasions as a consultant for the ECB in matters related to European financial integration. He is also a member of a European Commission research group investigating the effects of further financial integration on the propagation of shocks.

Gabe de Bondt is Principal Economist in the Capital Markets and Financial Structure Division of the Directorate Monetary Policy of the European Central Bank. Prior to joining the ECB, he was Economist at the Research Department of De Nederlandsche Bank, obtained a fellowship from the Bank for International Settlements, and completed his Ph.D. at the University of Amsterdam. His doctoral work – which has been published as a book – dealt with financial structures and monetary policy transmission in European countries. His research in the field of financial markets, finance, banking, and monetary economics has appeared in numerous journals.

Jesper Berg is Head of Market Operations at Danmarks Nationalbank. His responsibilities include the day to day management of the bank's foreign exchange reserves and domestic bond portfolio, the execution of the bank's foreign exchange and monetary policy, as well as the execution of the government's debt management policy. He was previously Head of Division, Capital Markets and Financial Structure Division, in the ECBs Directorate Monetary Policy, and has also worked as an Economist in the IMF's Policy Development and Review Department. He holds a degree as Cand. Polit. from University of Copenhagen.

Tom Bernhardsen is a Senior Adviser in the Monetary Policy Department of Norges Bank (the central bank of Norway). His duties include analysis of monetary policy in Norway, notably issues regarding exchange rate and interest rate developments. In 2002–2003 he was employed as a national central bank expert in the Monetary Policy Department of the ECB. His responsibilities included analysis of money market rates and preparing briefing notes for the Board. He holds a degree as Cand. Oecon.

(Candidatus Oeconomiae) and a Ph.D (Doctor Rerum Politicarum) (both in macroeconomics) from the University of Oslo and a degree as Lic. Oec. International (Lizentiat der Internationalen Wirtschaftsbeziehungen) from the University of Konstanz.

Frank Dierick is Principal Expert at the ECB's Financial Supervision Division and is especially involved in work regarding the regulation and supervision of credit institutions. Before joining the ECB, he worked at the Belgian Banking and Finance Commission in the departments responsible for supervisory policy and off-site banking supervision. He holds degrees in economics and law from the Free University Brussels and a masters degree in finance from the London Business School.

Steen Ejerskov is Adviser in Money and Banking Statistics at Danmarks Nationalbank and Monetary Policy Adviser for the IMF at the Central Bank of Egypt. He was previously Senior Economist in the Monetary Policy Stance Division in the ECB's Directorate Monetary Policy. He has conducted empirical and theoretical research in the areas of financial economics and the conduct of monetary policy, focussing in recent years on monetary policy implementation and the structure of money markets. He holds a M.Sc.Econ. from the University of Aarhus and Université Louis Pasteur of Strasbourg.

Annalisa Ferrando is Senior Economist in the Capital markets and Financial Structure Division, Directorate Monetary Policy at the European Central Bank. Her responsibilities include the monitoring and assessment from a monetary policy perspective of the degree of financial market integration in the euro area. Before joining the ECB, she worked at the Research Department of Banca d'Italia in the macroeconometric modeling unit and in the money and banking statistics division. She also worked as national expert at the European Commission. She holds a degree in Economics from the University of Venice and an M.Phil. in Economics from Oxford University.

Dieter Gerdesmeier is a Principal Economist in the Monetary Policy Stance Division of the Directorate Monetary Policy at the European Central Bank. His responsibilities include theoretical and empirical work in the areas of monetary analysis, the transmission mechanism of monetary policy and the interplay of monetary policy, especially central bank behaviour and financial markets. He previously worked in the Deutsche Bundesbank and is the author of a number of publications in various fields. Dieter Gerdesmeier holds a doctoral degree in economics from the University of Basel (Switzerland). He also teaches at the Hochschule fuer Bankwirtschaft in Frankfurt and at the Technische Universität of Karlsruhe.

Mauro Grande is Head of Financial Stability and Supervision at the European Central Bank. The area is responsible for the functions of the Eurosystem in the fields of financial stability and prudential supervision of financial institutions, including the monitoring and assessment of the stability of the euro area financial system, the provision of advice to the design of regulatory and supervisory requirements and the promotion of co-operation between central banks and supervisory authorities. Before joining the European Monetary Institute, the predecessor of the ECB, he worked at Banca d'Italia in different areas of the banking and financial supervision departments. He also worked as national expert at the European Commission in the field of financial services. He holds a degree in economics and banking from University of Siena.

Jung-Duk Lichtenberger is Senior Economist-Statistician in the Capital Markets and Financial Structures Division in the ECB's Directorate Monetary Policy. His responsibilities include the assessment of structural features of the financial markets in the euro area and monitoring developments from the perspective of monetary policy. Before joining the European Central Bank, he worked for the European Mortgage Federation in Brussels focusing on economic and statistical issues related to mortgage banking and capital markets as well as for a private investment bank. He holds a degree in economics, in engineering business management and an M.B.A.

Angela Maddaloni is Economist in the Capital Markets and Financial Structure Division, in the ECB's Directorate Monetary Policy. Her main responsibilities include the monitoring and assessment of developments in global financial markets from a monetary policy perspective. She also participated in several research projects concerning the structure and development of the euro area financial system, including the implications for financial stability. She holds a Ph.D. in Financial Economics from Columbia University in New York.

Francesco Paolo Mongelli is Adviser of the Directorate General Economics at the European Central Bank. His responsibilities include co-ordinating the analytical agenda of DG-E, overseeing the ECB Occasional Paper Series, and organising selected workshops and meetings. He is also a member of the Editorial Board of the ECB Working Paper Series. Before joining the ECB he worked at the International Monetary Fund in different areas including the Policy Development and Review Department and the Office of the Managing Director. He holds a Ph.D. from The Johns Hopkins University of Baltimore and teaches at the Johann Wolfgang Goethe University of Frankfurt.

Christoffer Kok Sørensen is Economist in the Capital Markets and Financial Structure Division of the Directorate Monetary Policy at the European Central Bank. His main responsibilities include analysing structural developments in the financial system, banking in particular, from a monetary policy perspective. Before joining the ECB he worked at Danmarks Nationalbank, in the areas of banking and statistics. He holds a degree in Economics from Aarhus University and Université Paris I Sorbonne-Panthèon and a degree in Finance from Copenhagen Business School.

Jukka Vesala is Deputy Director General in the Finnish Financial Supervision Authority. He is in charge of the Prudential Supervision Department, whose tasks include the on and off-site monitoring of banks' and investment firms' financial condition, risks and capital adequacy, and analysis of financial industry developments. He was previously employed, inter alia, as a Principal Expert in the Financial

Stability Division of the ECB and research economist in the Bank of Finland. He has also beenthe Secretary of the ESCB Banking Supervision Committee. He holds a doctoral degree from the Helsinki School of Economics. He has published articles in the fields of integration and competition in European banking markets and issues related to supervision and public safety nets, technological change in banking and payments industry, and market discipline and the use of market information for financial stability monitoring and supervisory purposes.

List of Tables

List of Figures

Introduction, Summary and Some Final Remarks

Jesper Berg, Mauro Grande and Francesco Paolo Mongelli

On the last day of 1998 the exchange rates of eleven European countries were irrevocably fixed. On 1 January 1999 the *euro* was established as the single currency of these countries and the European Central Bank started operating and managing the single monetary policy. Greece then joined on 1 January 2002. This represents the first time in history in which a large group of sovereign countries chose to relinquish their national currencies in order to share a new single currency. One of the largest common economic and financial areas in the world thus received an added impetus.

Monetary unification among European countries has required more than 25 years from the first efforts of exchange rate stabilization in the 1970s following the demise of the Bretton Woods system. However, the broader process of European integration that has now led to the European Economic and Monetary Union (EMU) had started already in the 1950s.[1] The singularity of the euro area lies in the fact that it consists of sovereign countries maintaining a control of, amongst others, their national fiscal and structural policies but accepting a common economic policy framework. Furthermore, the number of members of the European Union, and countries sharing the euro, will increase in the future.

About six years after the introduction of the euro, it is legitimate to start asking what impact the new currency and the single monetary policy have had on European integration, both directly and indirectly. To assess such an impact one needs to take into consideration the diverse roles of the euro. The euro as *'unit of account and means of payment'* is fostering cross-border transparency and competition and promoting progress towards a single European market, i.e., economic integration and the effective establishment of the 'four freedoms': that is, the free movement of goods, services (including financial services), labour and capital. The euro as a trigger for *'financial innovation'*, in combination with the gradual progress toward

1 As a background, the European process of integration started with the European Steel and Coal Community of 1952 and the Treaty of Rome in 1957 among the six founding members of the EEC: these were Belgium, France, Germany, Italy, Luxembourg and the Netherlands. The number of countries then rose over time. The common agricultural policy was adopted in 1965, the customs union was established in 1968, the Single Market Programme was launched in 1985, the Single European Act followed in 1986 (leading to an increase in the shared competencies, and the centralization of several regulatory functions), a European System of Central Banks was set up in June 1998, and the single monetary policy was launched on 1 January 1999.

the single market for financial services, is contributing to reshape euro area capital markets. The euro is also having an effect outside its geographical borders, given its wider international role with respect to any of its constituent currencies in many respects. The euro as an *'irrevocably fixed exchange rate'* among euro area countries has removed intra-euro area nominal exchange rate uncertainty. This has reduced transaction costs, fostering trade and strengthening the internal market. This has in turn lowered investment risks, promoted cross-area foreign direct investments, and enhanced resource allocation. The above roles are of course connected. Last, the euro is also having a direct and indirect impact on macroeconomic linkages and economic policy making, at both a national and supranational level.

Against this background of the euro as a catalyzing factor in so many areas, the *specific goal of this book* is to contribute to the analysis of the ongoing transformation of the euro area financial system, for which there is still scarce data and assessment *as a whole*. Hence, this book intends to serve as a *stocktaking exercise* and as a *source of reference* for some of the ongoing research that is conducted both in the Eurosystem at large, and outside it. To that end, the book brings together, and renders available, a set of comprehensive research and analysis on the diverse features of euro area financial systems.

Broadly speaking there are a number of reasons for focusing on financial markets and understanding their evolution. First, as argued in more detail in the next section, this is an area that is close to the interest and expertise of central banks that deal with financial markets on an ongoing basis. Understanding financial systems is important to gauge the effects of the transmission of the single monetary policy across euro area countries. A change in the policy-controlled interest rate has an effect on market interest rates and prices of financial assets. These are in turn transmitted to the rest of the economy, affecting spending decisions and ultimately the inflation rate. The magnitude and speed of the pass-through of monetary impulses depend on various features of the financial system such as the importance and role of banks and capital markets respectively, the maturity structure of non-financial sector financing and the prevalence of variable and fixed interest rate contracts. Second, deeper financial market integration is essential for the success of EMU in many ways. Integrated and efficient money markets permit the smooth operation and transmission of monetary policy. Integration of equity and bond markets should, amongst other factors, foster an efficient allocation of resources and increased international risk sharing across the euro area and beyond, and ease the smoothing of transitory shocks.[2] Third, the euro can constitute a force that speeds up and completes EU integration in financial services, bringing about significant benefits to the users of financial services.

2 For example, an increase of cross-country asset holdings within the euro area would mitigate the effects of asymmetric shocks among euro area countries through the diversification of their income sources. This can operate through *income insurance* when residents of a country hold claims to dividends, interests and rental revenue in other countries. Such *ex ante* insurance allows the smoothing of both temporary and permanent shocks as long as output is imperfectly correlated. Country residents can also *adjust their wealth portfolio* in response to income fluctuations by buying and selling assets and borrowing and lending on international credit markets.

Strictly speaking, central banks are at the same time a component of the financial system and also operate through it, as well as via the rest of the economy: e.g., by transmitting monetary impulses. This also explains why central banks analyse and monitor ongoing developments in the financial system at large and the rest of the economy. Against this background, the book is organized into nine chapters that together constitute four parts. The *first part of the book*, Chapters 1–4, provides the reader with certain basic information that is useful for setting the subsequent parts into some context. This information covers the main economic and financial characteristics of the euro area in comparison with the US and Japan (Chapter 1), a comparison of some features of the Eurosystem, the US Federal Reserve System and the Bank of Japan (Chapter 2), the methodology used when analysing financial integration (Chapter 3), and the legal framework supporting financial integration (Chapter 4). The *second part of the book*, Chapter 5, describes the euro area financial structure before and after introduction of the euro, examining the changes involved. The *third part of the book*, Chapters 6–8, contains a more detailed analysis of integration across financial services and markets. Finally, the *fourth part of the book*, Chapter 9, refers to one of the cores of the European Central Bank's (ECB's) interest in assessing financial market developments: the integration of the transmission process.

Three caveats are in order. The first is that the book focuses principally on financial intermediaries and financial markets and deals to a lesser extent with developments in and challenges to the EU framework for financial regulation, supervision and stability. Whereas the importance of this topic is clearly acknowledged, the range of issues concerned is so wide that its analysis would deserve a book on its own. A brief snapshot of the main issues is however provided at the end of this section. The second caveat is that, given that the introduction of the euro occurred only so recently, data availability prevents us from being more than tentative in drawing some first lessons: a more complete picture will require more time to emerge. The third caveat is that many factors other than the introduction of the euro (such as new technologies, lower communication costs and product standardization) are also influencing financial markets and they need to be duly recognized. Several sections of the book present some very new material that has been painstakingly assembled and that is not available on a comparable basis for many non-euro area countries. This limits the possibility for widespread international comparisons of the euro area and the Eurosystem with the US and the Federal Reserve System, and even more so with Japan and the Bank of Japan. Hence, this book represents a 'window', and a source of references, on the integration of financial markets in the euro area.

In the book we adopt the following classifications with regard to institutions and instruments. Concerning financial intermediaries we distinguish between *monetary and financial institutions* (MFIs), including banks, mortgage credit institutions and money market funds;[3] *other financial institutions* (OFIs), including investment funds and other financial auxiliaries that are not characterized as banks; and ICPFs, including insurance companies and pension funds. Concerning financial markets we

3 Some argue that money market funds (MMFs) belong to financial 'markets' and not 'intermediaries', since the extent of intermediation provided by them is rather limited. However, according to the ECB definitions, MMFs belong to the 'money creating' sector, that is MFIs, and in the ECB statistics are treated as intermediaries.

distinguish between *money markets* (a further distinction is due between the unsecured and secured (repo) money market); *bond markets*) and (a further distinction is between the short-term (commercial paper market) and long-term bond markets). It is also relevant to distinguish between the markets for government bonds, MFI issued bonds and corporate bonds; and *stock markets*: a further distinction is between traded/quoted shares and non-traded/non-quoted shares (plus private equities). One could argue that non-traded shares and private equity do not belong to the 'markets', since these typically do not have the features of traditional marketable instruments (such as a continuously available market price). However, in this book these instruments are included as financial market instruments.

Part I Some Background Information and International Comparisons

In Chapter 1, Jung-Duk Lichtenberger describes some key economic and financial features of the euro area and sets them into a broader perspective by making a comparison with the US and Japan. The euro area as a whole is the second largest economy in the world and more open than those of the US and Japan. The structures of production are quite similar, and in all three economies the service sector accounts for the largest share of total output. However, the euro area exhibits a higher share of public sector services than the US and Japan, while the US exhibits a higher share of financial intermediation services than Japan and the euro area. Over the last decade the three economies posted a very different development in consumer prices, labour markets, public finance, and trade with other countries. In terms of price stability the euro area has performed relatively well both in the run-up to EMU and since the introduction of the euro compared with the US and Japan. By contrast economic growth in the euro area has been lower than in the US (but slightly higher than in Japan), and the unemployment rate has been higher than in the US and Japan over the same period. Jung-Duk Lichtenberger then compares a few characteristics of the financial structure, where there are some notable differences. The proportion of assets and liabilities broken down into the 'direct' channel (e.g., debt securities and shares) and the 'indirect' financing channel (namely banks and other financial intermediaries such as insurance corporations and pension funds) in the euro area lies halfway between the more market-oriented US financial system and the largely bank-dominated Japanese financial system.

In Chapter 2, Dieter Gerdesmeier, Jung-Duk Lichtenberger and Francesco Paolo Mongelli present and compare some of the main features of the Eurosystem, the US Federal Reserve System (Fed) and the Bank of Japan (BoJ). This comparison highlights some similarities, as well as differences, between the recently set-up Eurosystem – that is responsible for the single monetary policy of the euro area only since January 1999 – and the more established Fed and BoJ. The institutional arrangements of the Eurosystem resemble those of the Federal Reserve System in the US. For example, the 12 National Central Banks (NCBs) of the members of the euro area play a role similar to the 12 regional Federal Reserve Banks. The chapter also reviews and compares the main provisions to secure the independence of the central banks, their accountability and transparency, and last their monetary policy strategy and implementation. All in all, the Eurosystem is more decentralized than the Fed as more tasks are left to NCBs. The Board of Governors of the Fed also has more control over the functioning of the rest of the Fed, than the ECB over the Eurosystem. The Bank of Japan operates instead in a more centralized fashion. This chapter also clarifies the main reasons for the interest of central banks in financial markets. In fact, central banks are at the same time a component of the financial system and also operate through it: e.g., to transmit monetary impulses to the rest of the economy.

The next contribution lays out diverse measures of financial integration (both direct and indirect) that underline most of the analysis in many of the subsequent chapters of this book. Different, and at times complementary, approaches to financial integration exist. In Chapter 3, Annalisa Ferrando and Jukka Vesala postulate that, in a normative sense, financial integration is a situation where there are no barriers that discriminate between economic agents on the basis of their location in their access to funds and investment of capital. However, a positive approach, building on industrial economics, is needed to construct quantitative indicators of integration drawing on data on market prices and quantities. Ideally, the authors argue, the clearest indicators of financial integration should be obtained by applying the law of one price (on the basis of market prices, or returns). However, a large number of financial assets and services do not lend themselves to applying the law-of-one-price – either due to heterogeneity across assets and service providers, or lack of high quality data. In such cases, quantity-based measures provide some indirect indicators of integration. Adopting a demand-side viewpoint, quantity-based indicators (such as a reduction in 'home bias') can be motivated by portfolio theory. Adopting a supply-side viewpoint, quantity-based indicators can be motivated by the theory of contestable markets. Last, the relationship between the concepts of financial integration, competition and efficiency is clarified. The principal merit of this chapter is to rationalize and then present diverse indicators of financial integration that are used in different parts of the book (such as of government bonds and money markets, corporate bond markets, and equity markets), and discuss the relation between integration, competition and efficiency. The authors argue that the assessment of the actual degree (or deepening) of financial integration across diverse financial market segments is necessarily based on an eclectic analysis that permits varying degrees of conclusiveness. Hence, the sobering message of the chapter is that great care must be given not to over-interpret any finding and to jointly interpret different direct and indirect indicators of financial integration. This chapter is mainly confined to the euro area, due to the fact that in the US and Japan 'domestic' financial integration has already been achieved.

In Chapter 4, Frank Dierick deals with one of the most complex facets of the process of European financial integration: The removal of obstacles to the optimal exploitation of the economies of scale and scope that such integration would render possible. The chapter only deals with the European experience – and the initiatives pursued by the EU public authorities over the last 40–50 years – as the US and Japan did not need to face such a daunting, and extended, policy challenge. The chapter first reviews the major institutional steps that have been taken since the Treaty of Rome (1957) to foster financial integration, including the Single Market Programme (SMP), the Financial Services Action Plan (FSAP) and the Economic and Monetary Union (EMU). It then presents the most important EU institutions and committees that are involved in the process of integration, including the European Parliament, Council, Commission and Court of Justice. The main legislative tools and procedures that are used by these institutions are presented next. The main European regulatory measures that have been taken over the past years in the different financial sectors (banking, securities and insurance) are then addressed. The arrangements for regulation and supervision of these sectors, presently undergoing major changes, are also discussed. In the area of competition policy, and (in particular) mergers and state aid control, Community initiatives are having an important impact on the process of integration as is demonstrated in the latter part of the chapter. The chapter concludes with a brief overview of the most recent legal initiatives to foster financial integration.

Part II Changes in the Financial Structure

In Chapter 5, Angela Maddaloni and Christoffer Kok Sørensen examine the developments of the financial structures in the euro area over the 1995 to 2002 period and compare them with the financial structures of the US and Japan. Several salient features of the euro area's financial structures emerge. First, in the euro area, the main financing flows are from households to non-financial corporations and governments. Capital flows in and out of the euro area have been relatively balanced over recent years. Financial intermediaries play a major role in collecting and allocating funds in the euro area. Second, the euro area financial system is well developed and diversified. Intermediated instruments (i.e. financial instruments offered by financial intermediaries) and non-intermediated ones (i.e. typical market instruments like shares and bonds) are equally important both as investments and as financing tools. Third, among the financial intermediaries, monetary financial institutions are the principal collectors of funds, but other types of financial intermediaries, such as investment funds, insurance corporations and pension funds, have become more important in recent years. Fourth, euro area economies are generally dominated by small and medium-sized enterprises. Partly because of this feature, non-quoted shares, other forms of private equity, and bank loans are extensively used as means of financing. At the same time, debt securities financing, which has historically played a minor role for euro area corporations, has become more important – especially relative to shares – since the start of Stage Three of Economic and Monetary Union. Fifth, the bond market has undergone a series of structural changes over the past few years. Changes have been particularly pronounced with regard to market liquidity, tick sizes, the behaviour of sovereign issuers, growth in the corporate bond market, more closely integrated pan-European trading possibilities and, finally, what seems to be a certain degree of specialization in some market segments (maturity, economic sectors) among countries in the euro area.

Part III Elements of Integration across Financial Services and Markets

As indicated at the start of this introduction, a number of chapters analyse integration across financial services and markets. In Chapter 6, Frank Dierick and Jukka Vesala focus on the evolution of integration in the markets for financial services in the euro area, and its constituent countries, over time. This includes the capital market-related investment banking and asset management services provided by banks and securities firms, and retail financial services provided by banks, securities firms and insurance companies. Most of the systematic empirical evidence on European financial integration relates to the financial markets, while there is less evidence on the financial products and services provided to corporate and personal clients. This chapter concentrates on filling this gap in information. To this end, it relies on an extensive set of available data from official statistics, commercial databases and ad hoc sources. The chapter postulates that in the area of financial services it is often impossible to gauge the effective level of integration only on the basis of tests of the law-of-one-price, owing to a lack of data and wide differences in financial products.

In Chapter 7, Tom Bernhardsen and Steen Ejerskov present some stylized facts about the euro area money market and provide an assessment of its degree of integration. Among the various segments of the financial markets, this market has perhaps been the one experiencing the most direct impact of the introduction of the euro. Funds traded between banks in the individual legacy currencies became a homogenous good literally overnight on 1 January 1999, with prices in the market represented by a single yield curve for the entire euro area anchored by one short-term monetary policy rate. Previously diverse procedures of the NCBs for implementing monetary policy and supplying reserves in the money market were substituted by a single operational framework. The chapter describes all the main elements of the money market, including the operational framework of the Eurosystem, the overnight market, and the money market instruments and derivatives. The main factors affecting the volatility of money market rates and the risk premia in the money market are also described. The chapter shows that the euro money market is generally characterized by a high degree of efficiency and integration, both in the primary and secondary markets. The prevailing evidence suggests that the money market is currently reinforcing its implicit two-tiered structure, with large wholesaling banks specializing in primary market participation and cross-border trading, and a second tier of smaller banks with primarily local business. Furthermore, money market structures still exhibit some national heterogeneity. A further development of the money market infrastructure, such as common payment and settlement systems, may provide a boost to the cross-border activity.

In Chapter 8, Lieven Baele and Annalisa Ferrando examine the process of integration of the different euro area bond and equity markets. These markets have witnessed substantial growth over the last decade, not only in the total amounts outstanding, but also in the number of new issues and listings. In addition, evidence suggests that bonds and stocks are now more homogeneously priced than before. Euro area government bond yields converged dramatically in the run-up to the single currency. This reflected the similarly large convergence in economic fundamentals. Further economic and especially monetary integration resulted in a strong convergence of inflation expectations across the various euro area economies, while exchange rate risk, previously an important element for some government bonds, vanished entirely with the introduction of the single currency in 1999. The authors also argue that full integration of the government bond market has not yet been achieved. While the level of convergence in yields is impressive, integration in euro area government bond markets is not complete, in the sense that yields of government bonds with similar, or in some cases identical, credit risk and maturity have not entirely converged. The chapter then turns to the spectacular development of the relatively young euro area corporate bond market. Before 1998, this market was dominated by debt issued by highly rated (financial) corporations, whereas after that date industrial corporations increasingly found their way to the corporate bond market. This is reflected in the dramatic growth in the lower-rated A and BBB market segments since then. Together with its development, the liquidity of the market for lower rated bonds also improved. However, despite the impressive growth rates recorded over the last years, the euro area corporate bond market continues to be much smaller than in the US and Japan, both in terms of absolute value and relative to the size of the economy. Next, the authors report three (indirect) measures of equity market integration. Each suggests that euro area equity markets are now more integrated than before. First, since the end of 2000, the advantages of sector diversification have for the first time in the last 30 years surpassed those of geographical diversification. Second, equity returns in the various euro area equity markets appear to be more and more determined by common news factors. Third, there is strong evidence that the home bias in the equity holdings of insurance corporations as well as investment and pension funds has decreased considerably over the last few years. The authors argue that while integration has increased, there still exist a number of important barriers to further integration.

Part IV A Case Study: The Integration of Transmission Processes

The perspective of this last contribution differs from that of the preceding ones as it analyses the effects of financial integration instead of aiming to measure it. In Chapter 9, Gabe de Bondt shows how changes in the financial structure, the banking system and the money, bond and equity markets in the euro area, as described in the previous chapters, have had an impact on the linkages between the price of debt finance and monetary policy. The focus is put on the price of the two main forms of debt, namely loans – usually from banks – and publicly traded debt securities issued by non-financial corporations. It is shown that the price and therefore the availability of debt finance play an important role in the monetary policy transmission process. Monetary policy can influence private consumption and investment directly by altering the liquidity or financial constraints as well as indirectly via various channels, for instance via the pass-through of official interest rate changes to the prices of bank-based debt finance or via a premium on external finance, the so-called balance sheet channel. The main message of this chapter – admittedly tentative given the short history of Stage Three of EMU, but shown to be robust across different empirical methods – is that the speed and nature of some linkages between external finance premia (EFP) and monetary policy at the euro area level seem to have changed since the single currency. In particular, the monetary policy transmission mechanisms in the euro area seem to have strengthened and deepened in Stage Three of EMU.

As already noted, this book provides a snapshot of diverse features of euro area financial systems. Such features change over time, since financial markets and institutions are in a continuous process of transformation, as is the economic environment. All this needs to be continuously analysed and monitored. Whereas the book is mainly backward-looking in its focus, references are spread across the chapters to some important future challenges relating to the process of financial integration in the euro area.

A first relevant aspect relates to the ability of the current EU framework for financial regulation, supervision and stability to cope with the challenges of a more integrated financial system. As mentioned above, this is a topic which for its extension and importance would require an effort on its own. Here a short summary is given of just the main developments in order to provide the reader with a general sense of the main directions of public action in this field. Broadly speaking, several measures have been taken by public authorities since the introduction of the euro, and these go in the direction of reinforcing the current institutional set-up.

In the field of financial regulation, it should be recognized that an extensive part of the relevant rules for financial institutions and markets at the national level was already laid down at the EU level (as shown in Chapter 4). Therefore the main challenge in this area is not so much further harmonization of legislative provisions, but rather the existence of an effective legislative process, which allows for a timely and efficient adaptation of the regulatory framework for financial institutions and markets. The key initiative in this respect is represented by the adoption of the so-called Lamfalussy approach which was first introduced in the securities sector in 2001 and then extended in 2004 to banking and insurance. This approach is based on the simple notion that EU legislation on technical aspects should be approved with a sort of simplified procedure. This is pursued by formally dividing Community legislation in two tiers, the so-called Level 1 legislation containing the general framework principles and the Level 2 legislation containing the technical rules. Whereas the Level 1 legislation continues to be adopted by the European Council and the European Parliament (co-decision procedure), the Level 2 legislation is adopted via a simplified procedure by the European Commission following a vote taking place in newly established regulatory committees in which Finance Ministries are represented. There are four regulatory committees, notably the European Banking Committee (EBC), the European Securities Committee (ESC), the European Insurance and Occupational Pensions Committee (EIOPC) and the Financial Conglomerates Committees (FCC). Whereas it is premature, given the short experience, to assess the full impact of the new approach, the results achieved so far in the securities sector are certainly positive and provide an encouraging example for the other financial sectors. An important element which has contributed to date to the effective implementation of the Lamfalussy approach in the securities sector is the existence of a formal monitoring by an independent group of experts (inter-institutional monitoring group) which releases periodically a report on the degree of implementation of the framework.

In the area of financial supervision, with particular regard to the prudential dimension, the main challenge relates to the need to maintain effectiveness of the supervisory action on financial groups which operate more and more on a cross-border basis, while at the same time keeping their compliance costs within reasonable limits. This challenge clearly calls for reinforcing substantially the cooperation and coordination among the supervisors who are responsible for the various layers of a financial group as well as for pursuing consistency in supervisory approaches on a cross-border basis. The latter is also invoked in relation to the implementation of the new framework for capital adequacy for credit risk agreed in 2004 by the Basel Committee on Banking Supervision, which will be transposed in the EU through Community legislation. Also in this area the Lamfalussy framework is expected to play a decisive role since it envisaged the establishment of sectoral supervisory committees (the so-called Level 3 committees): one of the main objectives of these committees is indeed the pursuit of supervisory convergence. The three committees, notably the Committee of European Banking Supervisors (CEBS), the Committee of European Securities Regulators (CESR) and the Committee of European Insurance and Occupational Pensions Supervisors (CEIOPS), located respectively in London, Paris and Frankfurt, have been established at different dates and are fully operational. There are strong expectations that they will make substantive progress in delivering supervisory convergence, and in curbing pressures towards the establishment of a single European supervisor (pressures which would mount inevitably in case of failure of their efforts).

In the field of financial stability, progress is under way both on crisis prevention and crisis management under the aegis of the Economic and Financial Committee (EFC), the Financial Services Committee (FSC) and the ECB/ESCB. The EFC, composed of representatives of Finance Ministries and NCBs, has taken up a role in the EU similar to that of the Financial Stability Forum at the G–10 level. In particular, the EFC promotes discussions on financial vulnerabilities in the EU, regulatory and supervisory developments as well as financial crisis management arrangements. The EFC is expected to provide a strong impulse toward the strengthening of cooperation and coordination among all relevant authorities (central banks, supervisory agencies, finance ministries) in normal circumstances and in times of crisis. In the latter respect, discussions are prepared by the FSC, composed of representatives of Finance Ministries, which addresses strategic policy issues relating to financial services mainly from a cross-sector and cross-institution perspective. The ECB and the ESCB on their part have developed a monitoring activity of financial stability in the euro area/EU. This activity aims at identifying sources of vulnerabilities for the financial system as a whole and at making an evaluation of the degree of its resilience to potential shocks. This analysis complements the financial stability assessment, which is normally conducted by NCBs at the domestic level. The ECB/ESCB initiative is an important step, which should contribute to better understanding the increased cross-border dimension of systemic risk associated with enhanced financial integration. In the area of crisis management, since the introduction of the single currency the Eurosystem has clarified the arrangements for the provision of emergency liquidity assistance (ELA) in the euro area. The guiding principle is that the provision of ELA remains under the responsibility of NCBs with the prior involvement of the decision-making bodies of the ECB in case the envisaged operation can have an impact on the overall liquidity situation in the euro area. An important contribution to enhance crisis management arrangements in the EU has been the multilateral memorandum of understanding agreed in 2003 by the ECB, the EU NCBs and the EU banking supervisory authorities on principles for the cooperation and exchange of information among them in financial crisis situations. This agreement, extended in 2004 to the new member states, represents a basis for a possible extension to other relevant authorities.

All these initiatives are summarized in the table below. All in all, the existence of appropriate institutional mechanisms and the progress so far achieved enable a broadly positive assessment of the ability of the EU framework for financial regula-

Table I.1 Summary of initiatives for financial regulation, supervision and stability

Area	*Main initiatives*	*Main players*
Financial regulation	Lamfalussy approach with a distinction between Level 1 (general principles) and Level 2 (technical rules) legislation	European Council, European Parliament, European Commission, FSC, Level 2 sectoral regulatory committees (EBC, ESC, EIOPC, FCC)
Prudential supervision	Lamfalussy approach with the establishment of the Level 3 committees in charge of pursuing supervisory convergence	FSC, Level 3 sectoral supervisory committees (CEBS, CESR, CEIOPS)
Financial stability monitoring	– Overall monitoring of financial vulnerabilities in the EU – Monitoring of the stability of the euro area/EU financial system – Monitoring of the stability of national financial systems	EFC ECB/ESCB NCBs, supervisory authorities
Crisis management	– Monitoring of crisis management arrangements – MoU on cooperation among central banks and supervisory authorities in crisis situations – Framework for granting ELA in the euro area	EFC, FSC ECB, NCBs, supervisory authorities ECB, NCBs

tion, supervision and stability to cope effectively with the challenges brought by increased financial integration.

A second important challenge for the future is the process of consolidation of the financial market infrastructure. Further consolidation in the area of securities clearing and settlement should provide economic benefits, but it is also a process that should be essentially in the hands of the private sector. However, those who would bear the costs of integration in financial market infrastructure are not necessarily the same as those who would derive most benefits from it. Additionally, there may be trade-offs between short-term and long-term gains (whereby some major participants in the short term in fact benefit from fragmentation), and there might be vested national interests to be overcome. In such cases, collective action on a market-wide scale might have to be undertaken, which requires an active role of Europe-wide industry associations in all segments of the financial system, where such coordination can take place.

Part I
Some Background Information and International Comparisons

Chapter 1

Some International Comparisons of the Economic and Financial Structure of the Euro Area

Jung-Duk Lichtenberger

Introduction

This chapter provides an overview of selected features of the economic and financial structures of the euro area and sets them into perspective with the situations prevailing in the US and Japan. The main features of the real economy are considered first, focusing on output, consumer prices, labour markets, public finance and trade with other countries. One of the essential components of an economic system is the financial market because it enables the channelling funds from those who have a net surplus to those who require funds for investment and consumption. The following section therefore highlights a few key characteristics of the financial structure. It describes the 'direct' channel, namely debt securities and shares, and the 'indirect' channel, namely banks and other financial intermediaries such as insurance corporations and pension funds. Appendix 1.1 presents an overview of the selected indicators of the economic and financial structure in the euro area, the US and Japan that are used in this chapter.[1]

The Economic Environment

This section describes some of the key macroeconomic features of the euro area and sets them into a broader perspective by making a comparison with the US and Japan.

Gross Domestic Product and Economic Growth

The euro area gross domestic product (GDP) amounted to €7.3 trillion in 2003. The euro area is thereby the second largest economy in the world measured in terms of GDP

1 It should be emphasized however at the outset that comparisons across countries should be made with care because of differences in national definitions and data availability. The main focus of this chapter is to provide broad indications on the basis of commonly-used measures and to compare changes over time within one economic area rather than across economic areas.

with a 16 per cent share of world GDP in 2003 (see Figure 1.1), which places it behind the US with a share of 21 per cent, and ahead of Japan with a share of 7 per cent. Taken together, the US, the euro area and Japan account for nearly half of total world GDP.

The structure of production in the euro area closely resembles that in the US and Japan (see Figure 1.2). In all three economies the service sector accounts for the largest share of total output in 2003. This share amounted to 71 per cent of GDP in the euro area, which is somewhat below the figure for the US (80 per cent of GDP) and broadly equal to the situation prevailing in Japan. It is also notable that the share of services in total output has increased over the last ten years in all three economies, with a corresponding decline in the share of industry and agriculture, fishing and forestry. In the euro area, as is the case in the US and in Japan, the industrial sector accounts for the second largest share of total output. Given the highly developed nature of these economies, the share of agriculture, fishing and forestry is relatively small in all three. In the euro area, this share amounted to 2.3 per cent of total output in 2003, which is higher than in the US (0.8 per cent) and Japan (1.3 per cent).

The importance of financial intermediation[2] within the services sector amounted to 8.2 per cent in the euro area in 2002 (see Figure 1.3), slightly higher than in 1995 (7.8 per cent). The contribution of this sector to value added and the increase in its

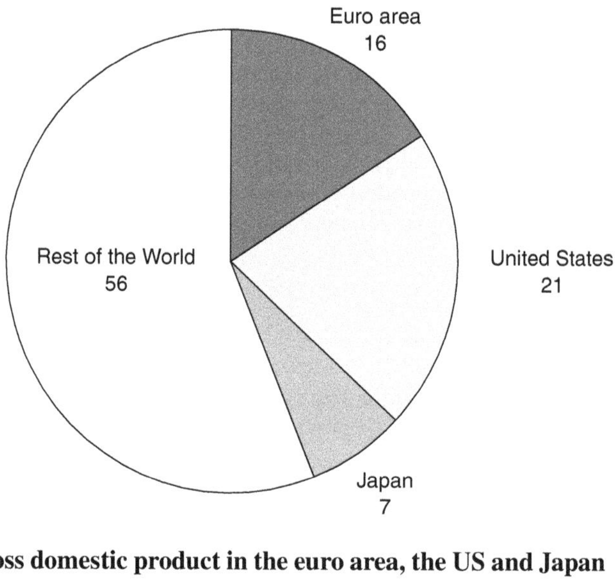

Figure 1.1 Gross domestic product in the euro area, the US and Japan

Note: Percentage of world GDP, 2003.
Sources: ECB, Federal Reserve, Bank of Japan.

2 Financial intermediation refers to monetary intermediation and other financial intermediation as well as insurance and pension funding (except compulsory social security) and other activities auxiliary to financial intermediation.

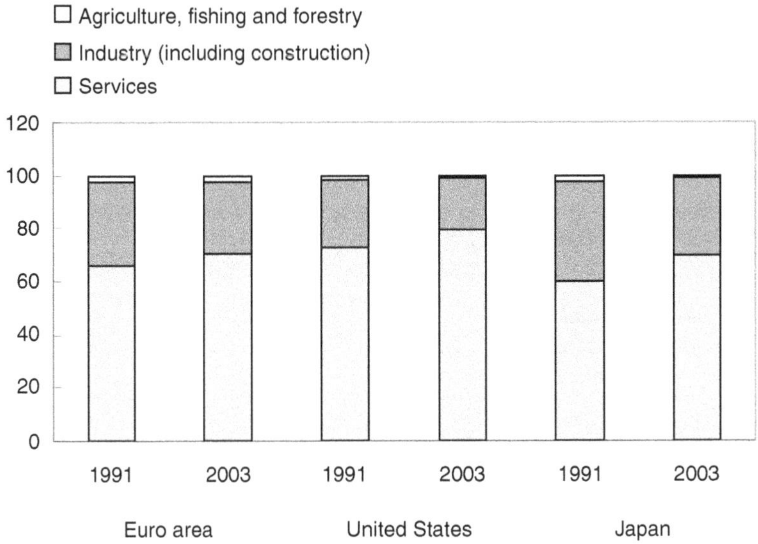

Figure 1.2 Sectors of production in the euro area, the US and Japan

Note: Gross value added, in percentages of total.
Sources: Eurostat, national sources.

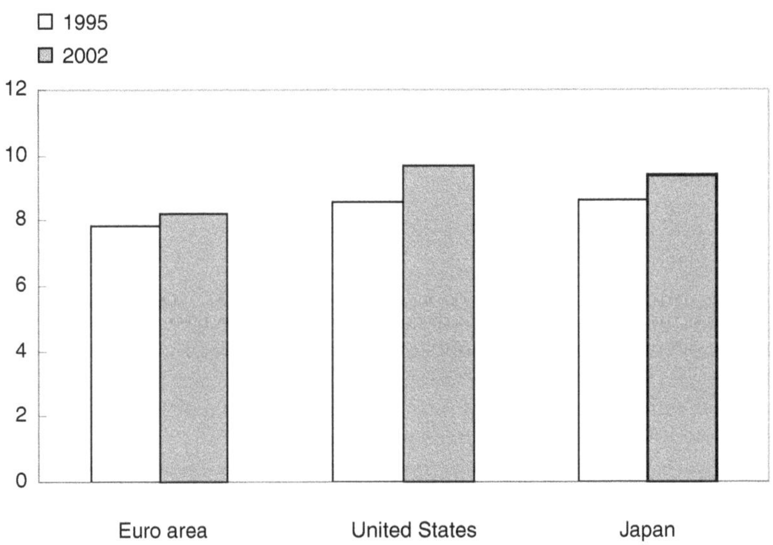

Figure 1.3 Financial intermediation in the euro area, the US and Japan

Note: Gross value added, in percentages of total services.
Sources: OECD, Eurostat, national sources, author's calculations, partly estimated.

relative importance between 1995 and 2002 is somewhat lower than in the US and in Japan. In the former, the share of financial intermediation accounted for 9.7 per cent of the services sector in 2002, compared with 8.6 per cent in 1995. In Japan, this ratio amounted to 9.4 and 8.7 per cent in 2002 and 1995, respectively.

As regards economic growth, the euro area economy grew at an annual rate of 2.0 per cent on average over the last decades since 1980 (see Figure 1.4). During the same period, the US economy grew at an average annual rate of 3.0 per cent, that is, one percentage point higher than the euro area. Economic growth in Japan, on average since 1980, amounted to 2.5 per cent.

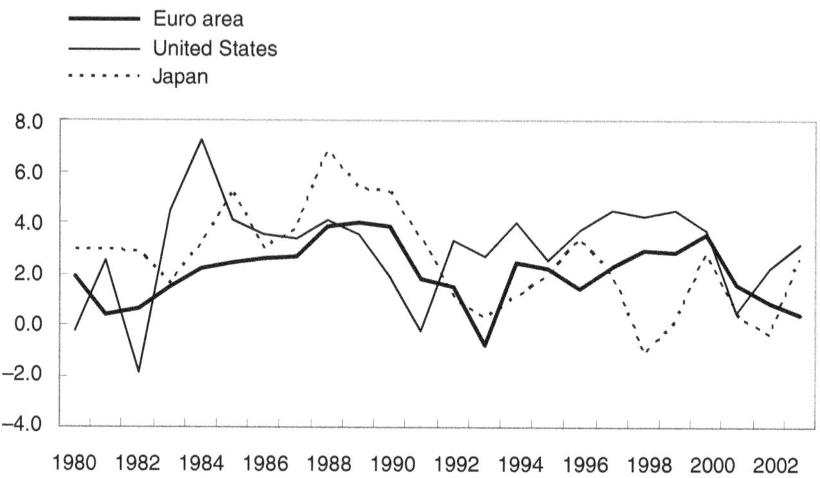

Figure 1.4 Real GDP growth in the euro area, the US and Japan

Note: Annual percentage changes, 1980–2003.
Sources: Eurostat.

Consumer Prices

The inflation rate in the euro area amounted to 4.7 per cent, on average, since 1980 (see Figure 1.5). Inflation fell rapidly during the 1980s from 13.8 per cent in 1980 to 5.2 per cent in 1989. Thereafter in the run-up to Economic and Monetary Union, the inflation rate fell further at a steady rate. The average annual inflation rate in the euro area between 1999 and 2003 amounted to 2.0 per cent.

By comparison, the average inflation rate in the US since 1980 amounted to 4.0 per cent, which is broadly at the same level as in the euro area. During the period starting in 1999, average US inflation stood at 2.4 per cent. The Japanese average inflation rate over the last decades since 1980 amounted to only 1.5 per cent, which is considerably lower compared with both the euro area and the US. The Japanese economy has been faced with deflation since late 1990s; the inflation rate stood at –0.6 per cent on average since the beginning of 1999.

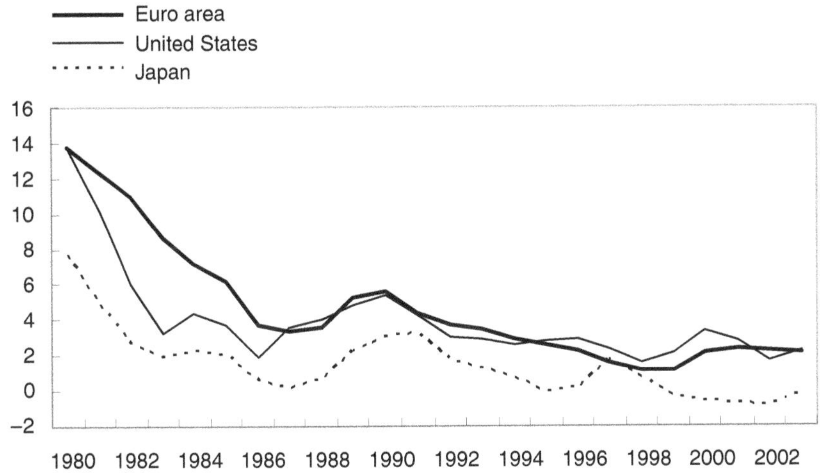

Figure 1.5 Consumer price inflation in the euro area, the US and Japan

Notes: Annual percentage changes from 1980–2003. The Harmonized Index of Consumer Prices (HICP) for the euro area is available as of 1990. For the purposes of historical publication, as from 1980, measures for consumer price changes in the euro area are approximated by data for the European Union (excluding Austria, Finland and Sweden) published by the OECD.
Sources: Eurostat, OECD.

Labour Market

The unemployment rate in the euro area amounted to 9.1 per cent of the labour force on average over the last decades since 1980 (see Figure 1.6). Although having come down since its last peaks during the mid-1990s, the unemployment rate in the euro area remains markedly higher than in the US and in Japan. In these two countries, the unemployment rates amounted to 6.3 per cent and 3.2 per cent respectively, on average, since 1980. The institutional aspects of labour markets, such as job protection legislation, unemployment benefit systems, the wage formation process and the taxation of labour, among others, play a significant role in determining economic developments. For instance, structural rigidities in labour markets reduce the speed at which an economy adjusts to adverse economic shocks. Structural rigidities are therefore typically associated with relatively high and persistent unemployment rates. Moreover, rigidities in the labour market tend to limit the pace at which an economy can grow without fuelling inflationary pressures.

Public Finance

Government expenditure exceeded government revenue in the euro area throughout the period from 1980 to 2003 (see Figure 1.7). Accordingly, the general government

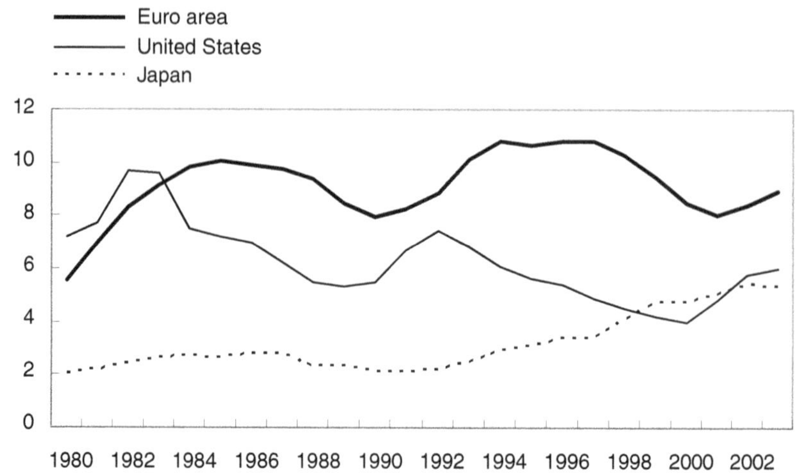

Figure 1.6 Unemployment rate in the euro area, the US and Japan

Note: As a percentage of the labour force, 1980–2003.
Sources: European Commission.

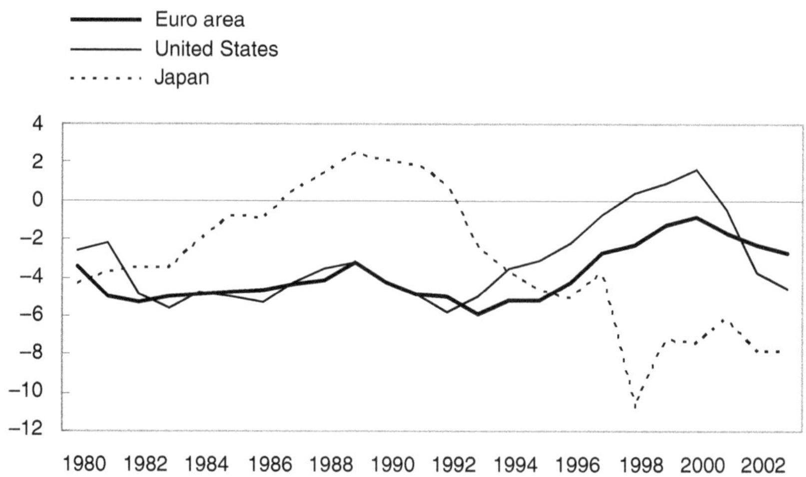

Figure 1.7 Government fiscal position in the euro area, the US and Japan

Note: As a percentage of GDP, 1980–2003 (latest figure for Japan is 2002).
Sources: Eurostat, IMF.

budget balance recorded a deficit in each year throughout that period. On average, between 1980 and 2003, this deficit amounted to –3.9 per cent of GDP. The evolution of the fiscal position in the US was broadly similar to the euro area up to the early 1990s. Thereafter, the fiscal deficit in the US decreased and in the period 1998–2000 the US experienced budget surpluses. The government deficit in the US on average amounted to –3.2 per cent of GDP between 1980 and 2003. In contrast, the evolution of the fiscal position in Japan, subject to relatively large swings, has been markedly different in the euro area and in the US. The fiscal deficit in Japan decreased steadily throughout the first half of the 1980s and the fiscal position experienced surpluses during 1987–1992. This period was followed by a sharp deterioration of the fiscal position. The government deficit in Japan amounted to –3.2 per cent of GDP, on average, since 1980.

In the euro area, the general government gross debt reached a peak of around 75 per cent of GDP in 1996 and 1997, after having risen rapidly over the previous decades. Thereafter, it has fallen somewhat to reach around 70 per cent of GDP in 2003 (see Figure 1.8). The general government gross debt-to-GDP ratio in the US was lower, at 48 per cent in 2003. In Japan, the ratio stood at 141 per cent (in 2002) and has risen sharply since 1991.

External Trade

With regard to external trade, exports and imports of goods and services for the euro area amounted to around 18 per cent of GDP in 2003. This positions the euro area

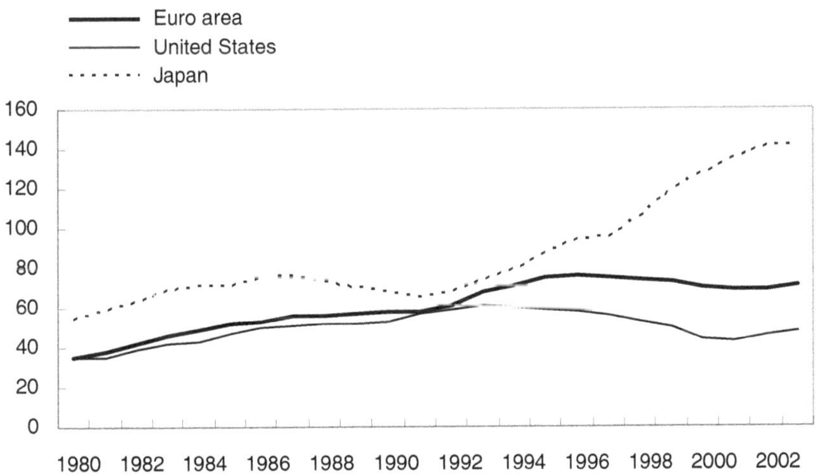

Figure 1.8 Government gross debt outstanding in the euro area, the US and Japan

Note: As a percentage of GDP, 1980–2003.

Sources: European Commission, OECD, Federal Reserve, Bureau of Economic Analysis, author's calculations.

economy as a far more open one than the economies of either the US or Japan (see Figure 1.9).

As to the composition of trade, goods account for around three-quarters of both euro area imports and euro area exports. Within the goods category, machinery and transport equipment made up almost half of exports in 2003. They also constituted the largest share of euro area goods imports. The second largest component was that of other manufactured articles, which had broadly the same share in both imports and exports. In 2003, chemicals accounted for 15.2 per cent of goods exports but only 10.0 per cent of imports, while, by contrast, the shares of raw materials and energy were considerably larger for imports than for exports. This shows that, in net terms the euro area tends to import raw materials and intermediate goods and to export processed goods. This in turn reflects the international division of labour and the limited availability of raw materials in the euro area.

Turning to the geographical distribution of euro area trade, the UK and the US are the two largest trading partners of the euro area. Based on average trading flows over the period 1995–2003, the sum of their weights is above 30 per cent. They were followed by Switzerland, Japan and Sweden, with trade weights of 6.3 per cent, 5.2 per cent and 4.1 per cent respectively.

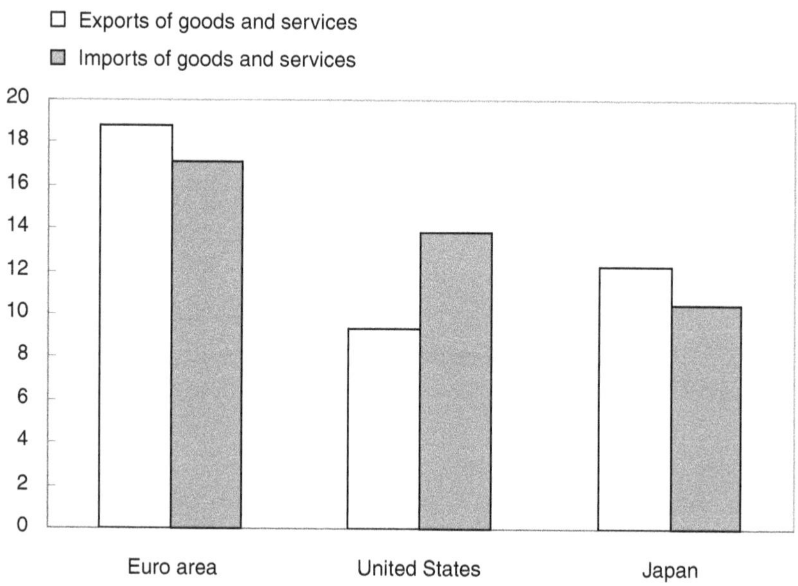

Figure 1.9 Exports and imports in the euro area, the US and Japan

Note: As a percentage of GDP, 2003.
Sources: Eurostat, national sources.

Financial Markets

The financial system performs the essential economic function of channelling funds from those who have excess funds (because they spend less than their income) to those who require funds (because they spend more than their income). Funds flow from lenders to borrowers via two routes. Direct or market-based finance means that debtors borrow funds directly from lenders in financial markets by selling them financial instruments, also called securities, such as bonds, short-term papers and shares. Indirect or bank-based finance is characterized by financial intermediaries playing an additional role in the channelling of funds.[3] Financial intermediaries refer to monetary financial institutions (MFIs) and other financial intermediaries such as insurance corporations and pension funds.

There are notable differences in the importance of these two financing routes in the euro area, the US and in Japan. In Chapter 5 of this volume, it is shown that the proportion of assets and liabilities broken down into direct and indirect finance in the euro area seems to lie halfway in-between the more market-oriented US financial system and the largely bank-dominated Japanese financial system.

Debt Securities Market

The market for debt securities includes both short-term and long-term instruments. 'Short-term' usually means securities with an original maturity of one year or less and is often referred to as the money market.[4] The short-term segment of the debt securities market commonly includes treasury bills (issues by government), commercial papers (issues by firms) and certificates of deposit (issues by banks), although there are national differences (EFMLG, 2002). Debt securities with a longer original maturity or with optional maturity dates, the latest of which is more than one year away, or with indefinite maturity dates, are usually considered as long-term. This segment of the debt securities is also known as the 'bond market' and commonly includes government bonds and corporate bonds, the latter being issued by both

3 Direct and indirect finance can also be referred to as *disintermediation* and *intermediation*, respectively.

4 The money market in its widest definition refers to a primary and a secondary market (ECB, 2002). The primary money market refers to the supply of reserves by a central bank to the money market through open market operations. The secondary money market is commonly divided into three parts: the cash market, the market for derivatives and the market for short-term securities. The most important 'cash' segment of the euro area money market is the market for unsecured deposits, in which banks exchange short-term liquidity without the guarantee of collateral. There are two important reference rates for the unsecured money market, the EONIA (Euro Overnight Index Average) and the EURIBOR (Euro Interbank Offered Rate), which together provide uniform price references for maturities from overnight to one year. The other main cash segments of the money market are the repo market and the market for swaps against foreign currencies. These markets are known as secured markets, since lending is done against assets acting as collateral. The derivatives segment of the money market includes primarily the interest rate swap markets and futures markets. The most active instruments in these markets are the EONIA swaps and EURIBOR futures (see also Chapter 7).

financial corporations (primarily banks and special purpose vehicles) and non-financial corporations. The outstanding total of the short-term and long-term debt securities issued by euro area residents amounted to €8.7 trillion at the end of 2003. The bond market is by far the larger segment of the debt securities market, reaching 90 per cent of the outstanding amount of debt securities issued by euro area residents at the end of 2003. As regards the currency, more than 90 per cent of the outstanding amount of debt securities issued by euro area residents at the end of 2003 were denominated in euro.

Financing through issuance of debt securities is smaller in the euro area than in the US and Japan. At the end of 2003 the outstanding amounts correspond to 110 per cent of GDP in the euro area, compared with 154 per cent and 175 per cent of GDP in the US and Japan respectively (see also Chapter 5). The high figure for Japan can be explained primarily by the strong growth in government debt securities that has been observed in the context of a prolonged period of weak economic growth since the early 1990s. Looking at the corporate sector, the outstanding amount of debt securities issued by non-financial corporations in the euro area was around 7 per cent of GDP at the end of 2003, while it totalled around 22 per cent and 16 per cent of GDP in the US and Japan respectively. In the euro area, most of the debt securities are issued by the government and financial corporations, which contrasts with the situation prevailing in the US and Japan. The euro area government debt securities market is much smaller than in Japan and the financial debt securities market is smaller than in the US. The corporate debt securities market in the euro area is smaller compared with both countries.

Despite being relatively small, the euro area corporate debt securities market has largely outpaced the growth in this sector in the US and Japan since the introduction of the euro. As regards issues by non-financial corporations, the average annual growth rate in the euro area between January 1999 and December 2003 was higher than in the US and Japan by around 10 percentage points (see Figure 1.10). This contrasts with the situation prevailing before the introduction of the euro when the growth rate of non-financial corporate debt securities was considerably lower in the euro area compared with both the US and Japan. Much of the growth in the euro area since the introduction of the euro can be explained by the fact that issuers started to have a euro area-wide perspective and benefited from easier access to the larger institutional investor base, in particular the ability to issue on a major scale. In addition, the ongoing process of corporate restructuring in the euro area resulted in strong demand for funds to finance mergers and acquisition activity (de Bondt and Lichtenberger, 2003).

The rapid growth of debt securities issues by financial corporations has enabled the euro area market to grow at the same rate as in the US. In both cases, the average annual growth rate since the introduction of the euro stood at around 10 per cent. This contrasts with the situation prevailing before the introduction of the euro when the growth rate for the euro area market (4.9 per cent) was on average nearly a third of the growth for the US market (12.6 per cent). By comparison, the growth of this sector in Japan is much lower than in the euro area and the US for the entire period ranging from January 1995 to December 2003. Much of the euro area growth for financial debt securities since the introduction of the euro has been driven by non-monetary financial corporations. Issuance by this latter sector has tended to be

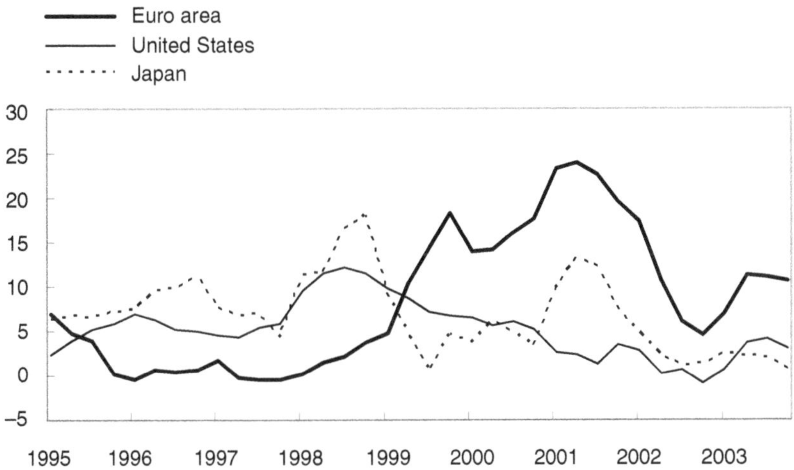

(A) Issues by non-financial corporations

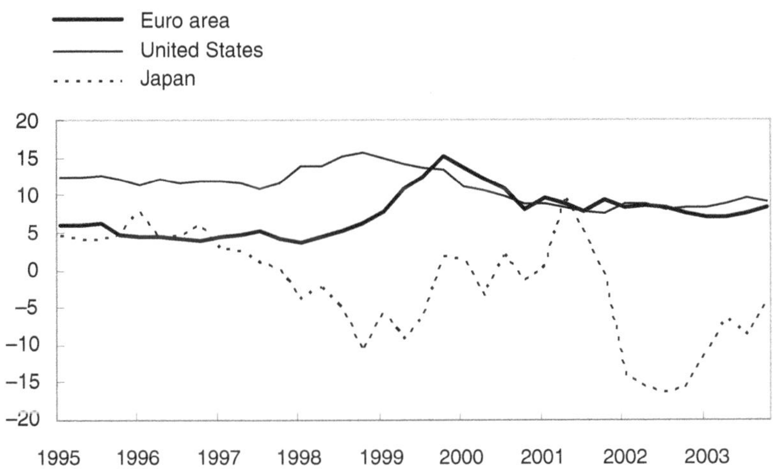

(B) Issues by financial corporations

Figure 1.10 Growth rates of corporate debt securities in the euro area, the US and Japan

Notes: Annual percentage changes, 1995–2003.
Sources: ECB, BIS, author's calculations.

concentrated in a few countries whose tax systems offer corporations a cheaper source of funding via special purpose vehicles helping them to raise capital on the corporate securities market (ECB, 2003).

Despite the significant growth in the euro area corporate debt securities market, some market segments, such as those for debt with a low credit rating or unrated debt, have remained relatively underdeveloped. Compared with the US, relatively few euro area corporations had credit ratings by 2002, and this restricted their access to the corporate bond market.

With regard to the government bond market, one of its main features is that it provides a measure for long-term interest rates in the economy. It is common to use the ten-year government bond yield as a benchmark for the cost of long-term capital. Considering the developments since January 1994, Figure 1.11 illustrates that these yields in the euro area have been on average lower since the introduction of the euro than before. The average yield between January 1999 and December 2003 amounted to 4.9 per cent, which compares with an average yield of 7.0 per cent for the period from January 1994 to December 1998. The yields in the euro area are similar to those in the US, in particular since the introduction of the euro. The differences have been relatively small, amounting to on average 50 basis points in absolute terms since January 1999. The yields in Japan have been consistently lower than in the euro area and in the US. They have fallen steadily from 3.3 per cent in January 1994 to 0.6 per cent in June 2003 and have thereafter started to increase slightly to reach 1.4 per cent in December 2003.

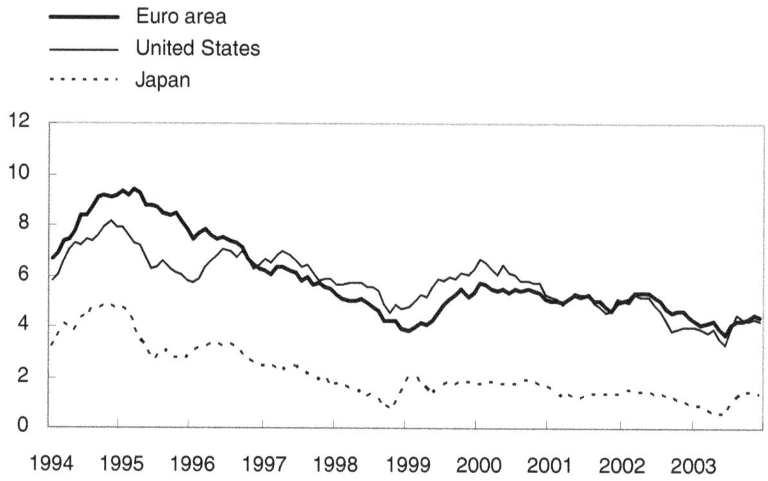

Figure 1.11 Ten-year government bond yields in the euro area, the US and Japan

Notes: Up to December 1998, euro area yields are calculated on the basis of harmonized national government bond yields weighted by GDP; thereafter, the weights are the nominal outstanding amounts of government bonds in each maturity band; period averages, nominal yields.

Sources: Reuters, ECB, Federal Reserve and Bank of Japan.

Equity Market

A commonly used indicator of the importance of the equity market is the market capitalization of stocks in terms of GDP. The euro area stock market capitalization increased from 21 per cent of GDP at the end of 1990 to 45 per cent of GDP at the end of 2003 (see Figure 1.12). However, the stock market capitalization was as high as 88 per cent of GDP at the end of 2000. These movements in stock market capitalization were caused by a period of strong increases in stock prices up to early 2000, which was then followed by a significant fall. Total stock market capitalization in the euro area remains significantly smaller than in the US. The gap between stock market capitalization in terms of GDP in the US and the euro area even widened from around 30 percentage points in 1990 to around 81 percentage points in 2003. By contrast, in Japan the stock market capitalization declined from 90 per cent of GDP in 1990 to 62 per cent of GDP in 2003, mostly reflecting significant falls in stock prices over this period.

An alternative indication of the importance of the equity market is provided by statistics on the number of listed companies. In the euro area this number grew from 4,276 at the end of 1990 to 6,670 at the end of 2003 (see Figure 1.13). As a comparison, the number of listed companies in the US and Japan at the end of 2003 was 6,159 and 2,206 respectively.

Since the introduction of the euro there have been many initiatives to form alliances or merge the activities of stock exchanges of individual euro area countries. Stock market participants also increasingly seem to be taking into account the economic factors common to the euro area as a whole. One clear indicator for the increasing integration of euro area stock markets is the widespread focus on a range of euro area-wide stock market indices, such as the Dow Jones EURO STOXX index.

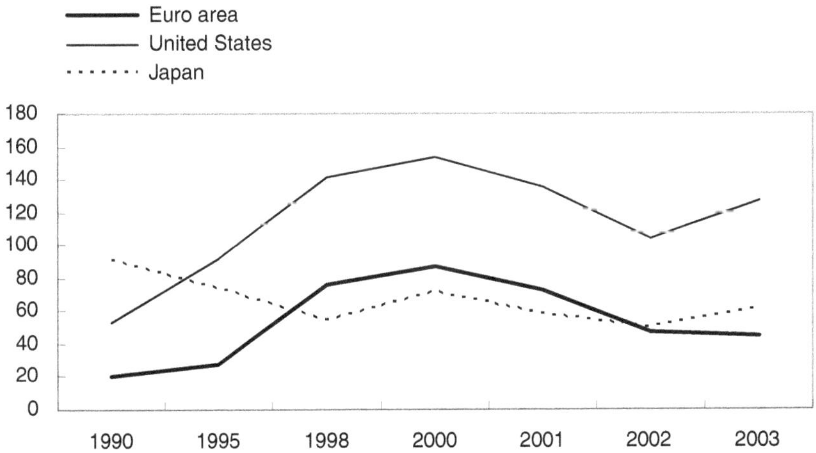

Figure 1.12 Stock market capitalization in the euro area, the US and Japan

Note: Percentage of GDP.
Source: World Federation of Exchanges.

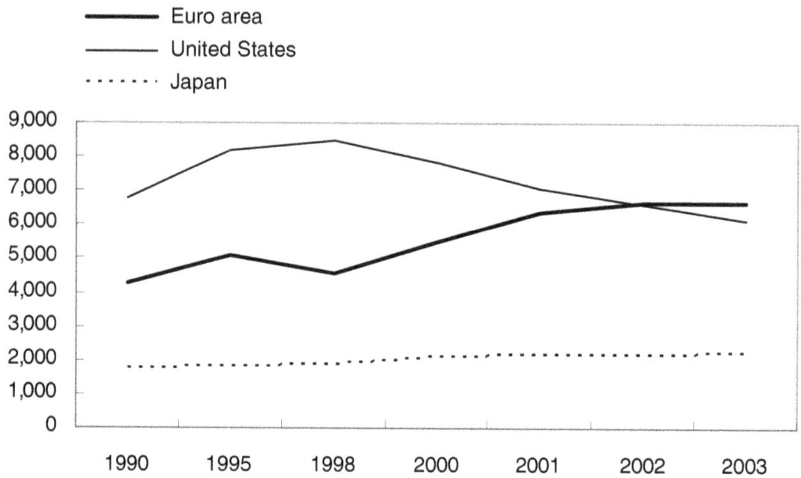

Figure 1.13 Number of domestic and foreign companies listed on stock markets in euro area countries, the US and Japan

Source: World Federation of Exchanges.

Bank Intermediation

The main financial intermediaries in the euro area are monetary financial institutions[5] which numbered 8,269 at the end of 2003 (see Figure 1.14). This reflects the large number of savings and cooperative banks – often operating only at a local level – and specialized credit institutions in several countries. The number of MFIs declined markedly between 1998 and 2003, reflecting the ongoing consolidation process in the European banking industry. The trend towards consolidation in the credit institution sector is a response to changing market conditions, driven by a number of factors, such as technological developments, deregulation, liberalization and globalization. The introduction of the euro has probably fueled these developments by creating more transparency across national borders.

The total number of banks in the US (excluding credit unions) and in Japan amounted to 10,285 and 2,228 respectively in 2003. Measured relative to population size, there are 2.7 MFIs per 100,000 inhabitants in the euro area, which is a lower proportion than in the US (3.5 banks per 100,000 inhabitants) but higher than in Japan (1.7 banks per 100,000 inhabitants).

5 'Monetary financial institution' (MFI) refers to credit institutions, money market funds and other institutions (such as central banks). The term has been created because an increasing number of non-credit institutions, notably money market funds, perform activities and offer products that were traditionally the preserve of banks. At the end of 2003, credit institutions accounted for 80 per cent of all euro area MFIs and the remaining 20 per cent were primarily money market funds.

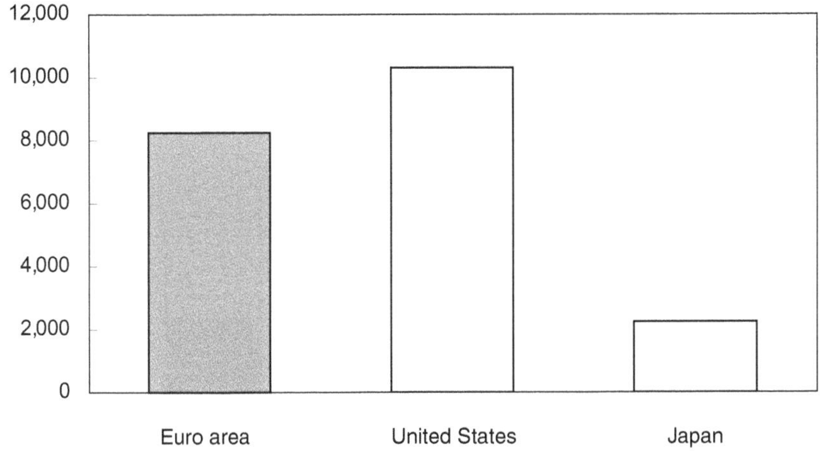

Figure 1.14 Number of banks in the euro area, the US and Japan at end-2003

Note: Banks refer to monetary financial institutions for the euro area and depository financial institutions (including trust accounts of domestically-licensed banks) in Japan. For the US, banks refer to depository institutions, money market funds and the Federal Reserve System. Data on depositary institutions include commercial banks and savings institutions insured by the Federal Deposit Insurance Corporation, and exclude the around 12,000 credit unions. The latter represented around 5 per cent of total financial assets of depository institutions at the end of 2003.

Sources: ECB, Federal Reserve, Bank of Japan, Investment Company Institute, Federal Deposit Insurance Corporation.

Bank deposits in the euro area amounted to 85 per cent of GDP at end-2003 (see Figure 1.15), which is higher than in the US (48 per cent of GDP) and lower than in Japan (120 per cent of GDP). At the same time, bank loans in the euro area totalled 110 per cent of GDP, while for the US and Japan this ratio was 51 per cent and 119 per cent respectively. These figures indicate the importance of financial intermediation executed by banks in the euro area, in particular when compared with the US.

Other Financial Intermediaries

Indirect finance to the public and private sectors is not only provided by MFIs, but also by other financial intermediaries such as insurance corporations and pension funds, financial auxiliaries, mutual funds, securities and derivatives dealers as well as financial corporations engaged in lending. One of the key differences compared with credit institutions is the lack of deposits on the liabilities side of the balance sheets of these institutions. In the euro area, these other financial intermediaries – despite having become increasingly active in the 1990s – still play a minor role compared with MFIs. At the end of 2003 the assets of insurance companies, mutual funds and pension funds in the euro area were equivalent to 95 per cent of GDP, while the assets of MFIs equalled 201 per cent of GDP. In the US and Japan, the assets of insurance

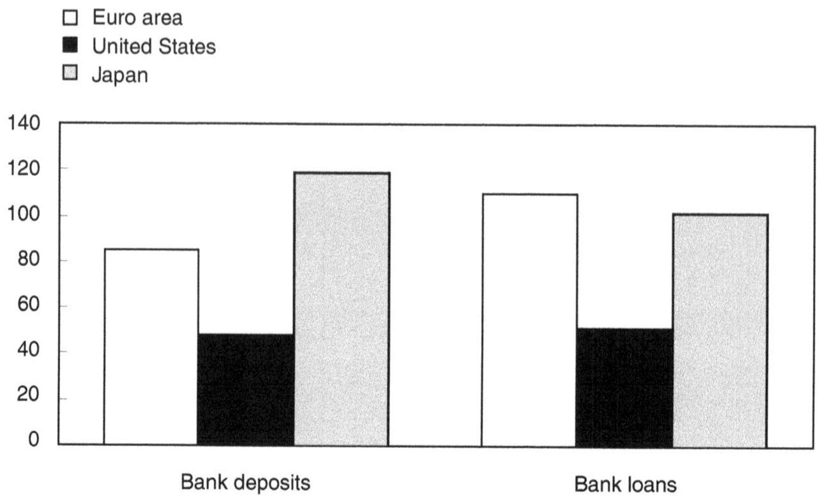

Figure 1.15 Bank deposits and loans in the euro area, the US and Japan at end-2003

Note: As a percentage of GDP.
Source: ECB, Federal Reserve and Bank of Japan.

corporations, pension funds and investment funds amounted to 144 per cent and 98 per cent of GDP respectively (see Figure 1.16). In particular insurance corporations and pension funds are more active in the US and Japan.

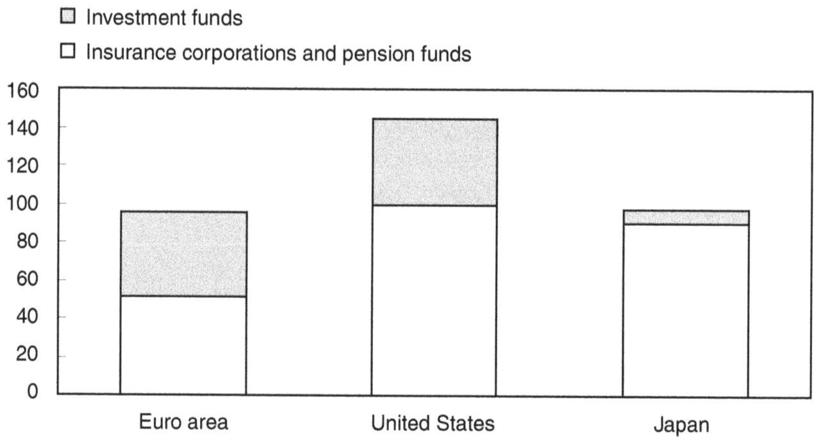

Figure 1.16 Assets of other main financial intermediaries in the euro area, the US and Japan at end-2003

Note: As a percentage of GDP.
Source: ECB, Federal Reserve and Bank of Japan.

Conclusions

The euro area is the second largest economy in the world and more open than the US and Japan. This chapter has reviewed a number of selected economic indicators, including output, consumer prices, labour markets, public finance and external trade in order to provide a broad indication of the situation prevailing in the euro area from a broader international perspective. However, comparisons across countries or economic areas should be made with caution because of differences in definitions and data availability.

As to the financial structure of the euro area, it is usually considered to lie halfway between the market-based US financial system and the largely bank-dominated Japanese financial system. One notable development in the euro area since the introduction of the euro has been the rapid growth of corporate debt securities issuance primarily driven by industry consolidation.

References

Amel, F. (1996), 'Trends in the Structure of Federally Insured Depository Institutions, 1984–1994', *Federal Reserve Bulletin*, 82(1), pp. 1–15.

Bondt, G.J. de and Lichtenberger, J.-D. (2003), 'The Euro Area Corporate Bond Market: Where Do We Stand Since the Introduction of the Euro?', *European Business Organisation Law Review*, 4: 517–539.

European Central Bank (1999), 'The Balance Sheets of the Monetary Financial Institutions of the Euro Area in Early 1999', *Monthly Bulletin*, August, pp. 55–69.

European Central Bank (2002), *Report on Financial Structures*, October.

European Central Bank (2003), 'Recent Developments in Financial Structures of the Euro Area', *Monthly Bulletin*, October, pp. 39–52.

European Central Bank (2004), *'The Monetary Policy of the ECB', Chapter 2.*

European Commission (1998), *Services in Europe, Panorama of the European Union*, Eurostat.

European Commission (2000a), *Economic portrait of the European Union 1999, Panorama of the European Union*, Eurostat.

European Commission (2000b), *Europe in Figures*, fifth edition, Eurostat.

European Commission (2003), *Quarterly panorama of European business statistics, Panorama of the European Union*, Eurostat.

European Financial Market Lawyers Group (EFMLG, 2002), 'The Money Market: Legal Aspects of Short-term Debt Securities', September.

The Federal Reserve Bank of St. Louis (2003), *National Economic Trends*, September.

Investment Company Institute (2004), *Mutual Fund Fact Book: A guide to trends and statistics in the mutual fund industry.*

Policy Research Institute (2003), *Ministry of Finance of Japan, Monthly Finance Review*, No. 364, November.

Organisation for Economic Co-operation and Development (2001), *OECD Historical Statistics 1970–2000.*

Appendix 1.1 Selected indicators of the economic and financial structure in the euro area, the US and Japan

2003	Unit	Euro area	United States	Japan
I. ECONOMIC ENVIRONMENT				
Gross domestic product				
Share of world GDP	% of total	15.9	21.1	7.0
Valued added by economic activity				
Agriculture, fishing and forestry	% of total	2.3	0.8	1.3
Industry (incl. construction)	% of total	27.0	19.7	29.1
Services, of which:	% of total	70.8	79.5	69.6
Financial intermediation*	% of services	8.2	9.7	9.4
Real GDP growth	annual percentage change	0.4	3.1	2.6
Consumer price inflation	annual percentage change	2.1	2.2	–0.3
Unemployment rate	% of labour force	8.9	6.0	5.3
Government finance				
Budget surplus (+) or deficit (–)	% of GDP	–2.7	–4.6	–7.9*
Gross debt outstanding	% of GDP	70.6	47.9	141.3*
External trade				
Exports of goods and services	% of GDP	18.8	9.3	12.2
Imports of goods and services	% of GDP	17.1	13.8	10.5
II. FINANCIAL MARKETS				
Debt securities issued				
by non-financial corporations	annual percentage change	10.7	3.1	0.7
by financial corporations	annual percentage change	8.4	9.2	–4.6
Government bond yields (10-year)	percentage per annum	4.4	4.3	1.4
Stock market				
Market capitalization	% of GDP	45.2	126.7	61.6
Number of companies listed	total	6,670	6,159	2,206
Financial intermediation				
Number of banks	total	8,269	10,285	2,229
Number of banks	per 100,000 population	2.7	3.5	1.7
Bank deposits	% of GDP	85.4	47.8	120.1
Bank loans	% of GDP	109.5	51.4	118.7
Assets of other fin. intermediaries	% of GDP	94.9	144.5	97.5

Sources: European Commission, IMF, OECD, BIS, ECB, Federal Reserve, Bank of Japan, Bureau of Economic Analysis, World Federation of Exchanges, Reuters.
Note: *2002 figure and partly estimated.

Chapter 2

A Brief Comparison of the Eurosystem, the US Federal Reserve System, and the Bank of Japan

Dieter Gerdesmeier, Jung-Duk Lichtenberger
and Francesco Paolo Mongelli

Introduction

Following a comparison of the economic and financial environment of the euro area, the US and Japan, this chapter provides a brief comparison of some key features of the Eurosystem, that is, the central banking system of the euro area, the Federal Reserve System in the US, and the Bank of Japan. Several similarities as well as differences between the three central banks are highlighted. The motivation for including this comparison in this book is that central banks are a part of the financial system and also operate through it (e.g. for the transmission of monetary impulses to the rest of the economy). Central banks also play an important role in the evolution of financial markets. To our knowledge this is the first systematic comparison of the three institutions.

The three central banks were established at different points in time and their structures also reflect different historical conditions as well as national characteristics. The Bank of Japan was established in 1882, the Federal Reserve System in 1914 and the Eurosystem became operational in 1998.[1]

The euro area is unique among single currency areas. Twelve sovereign nations have not only adopted a single currency, the euro, but have also created a supranational institution, the European Central Bank that is (to our knowledge) the youngest member of the central bank community.

The chapter is organized as follows. We first compare the main features of the institutional structure of the three central banks. We then turn to their monetary policy objectives, and describe the main provisions to guarantee their independence and secure their accountability and transparency. After this we briefly compare their monetary policy strategies and the implementation of monetary policy. Finally, we present some further elements differentiating the Eurosystem from the Federal Reserve and the Bank of Japan, and conclude with some remarks.

1 The National Central Banks of the Eurosystem were of course established much earlier; for example, Banque de France in 1800, De Nederlandsche Bank in 1814, Banque Nationale de Belgique in 1850, Banco de España in 1856, Banca d'Italia in 1893 and the Bundesbank in 1957.

Main Features of the Institutional Structures

The Treaty contains the institutional arrangements for the conduct of monetary policy in the European Economic and Monetary Union (EMU).[2] The Treaty also provides the legal basis for the formation of the European System of Central Banks (ESCB), which comprises the European Central Bank and the national central banks (NCBs) of the 15 Member States of the European Union (EU). The term 'Eurosystem' was created to denote a subset of the ESCB, comprising the ECB and the NCBs of EU Member States that have adopted the euro (currently 12 countries, see Figure 2.1). The governing bodies of the Eurosystem are the Governing Council and the Executive Board. The Executive Board consists of the President, the Vice-President and four board members. Its main task is to implement the decisions of the Governing Council. The latter consists of the Executive Board members plus currently 12 governors. Each Governing Council member has one vote (see Figure 2.2).[3]

The institutional arrangements of the Eurosystem resemble in some ways those of the US Federal Reserve System (Wynne, 1999, see Figures 2.3 and 2.4). In principle, the ECB has a role similar to that of the Federal Reserve's Board of Governors in Washington D.C. and the 12 NCBs of the Eurosystem play a role similar to the 12 regional Federal Reserve Banks in the US. The President of the ECB chairs the Governing Council meetings, and in essence holds a position comparable to that of the Chairman of the Federal Reserve's Board of Governors. In the euro area, the Governing Council is responsible for formulating monetary policy. In the US this task is carried out by the Federal Open Market Committee (FOMC).

While there are many similarities in the structures of the Eurosystem and the Federal Reserve System, there are also differences. All NCB governors of the

---

2 The Treaty refers to the Treaty establishing the European Community that was signed in Rome on 25 March 1957 – and is often referred to as the 'Treaty of Rome' – and entered into force on 1 January 1958. It established the European Economic Community (EEC) that subsequently became the European Community (EC). The Treaty on European Union (EU) – that is often referred to as the 'Maastricht Treaty' – was signed on 7 February 1992 and entered into force on 1 November 1993. The EU Treaty amended the previous EC Treaty and established the European Union. The 'Treaty of Amsterdam', which was signed on 2 October 1997 and entered into force on 1 May 1999, amended both the EC and EU Treaties. Equally, the 'Treaty of Nice', which was signed on 26 February 2001 and entered into force on 1 February 2003, also amended both the EC and EU Treaties.

3 The Governing Council will also need to take decisions in a timely and efficient manner in an enlarged euro area (ECB, 2004). To this end, prior to the accession of ten additional countries to the EU on 1 May 2004, on 21 March 2003 the European Council approved an amendment to the Statute of the ESCB which provides for an adjustment of the voting modalities in the Governing Council. This decision was submitted to all Member States for ratification in accordance with their respective constitutional requirements. According to the new voting scheme, the six members of the Executive Board will maintain a permanent voting right, but the voting rights of NCB Governors will be subject to a rotation scheme once the number of euro area countries exceeds 15. However, all Governors will participate in all meetings of the Governing Council, irrespective of whether they hold a voting right at the time.

Figure 2.1 The euro area

Source: Pollard (2003).

Note: The 12 EU Member States that adopted the euro (as at end 2003) are Belgium, Germany, Greece, Spain, France, Ireland, Italy, Luxembourg, the Netherlands, Austria, Portugal and Finland. More information on national central banks, including information on national branches, is available on their respective websites, which can all be accessed via the website of the ECB (www.ecb.int).

Eurosystem have a vote in all policy decisions of the Governing Council, whereas with the exception of the President of the Federal Reserve Bank of New York (FRBNY), Reserve Bank presidents participate in FOMC votes every two or three years. Furthermore, the voting mechanism is different. When taking decisions on monetary policy, the Governing Council as well as the FOMC act by simple majority. In practice, however, the Governing Council has so far practised consensus voting.

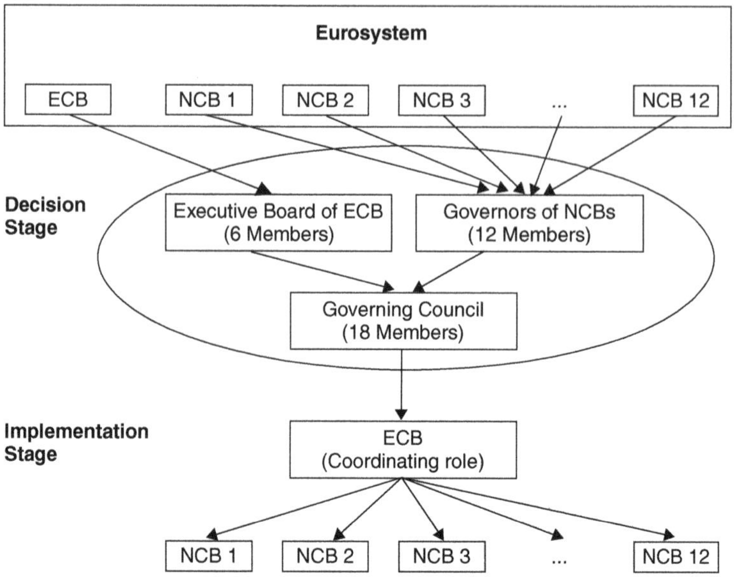

Figure 2.2 Organizational framework of the Eurosystem

Note: NCB refers to the national central banks of the 12 euro area countries.

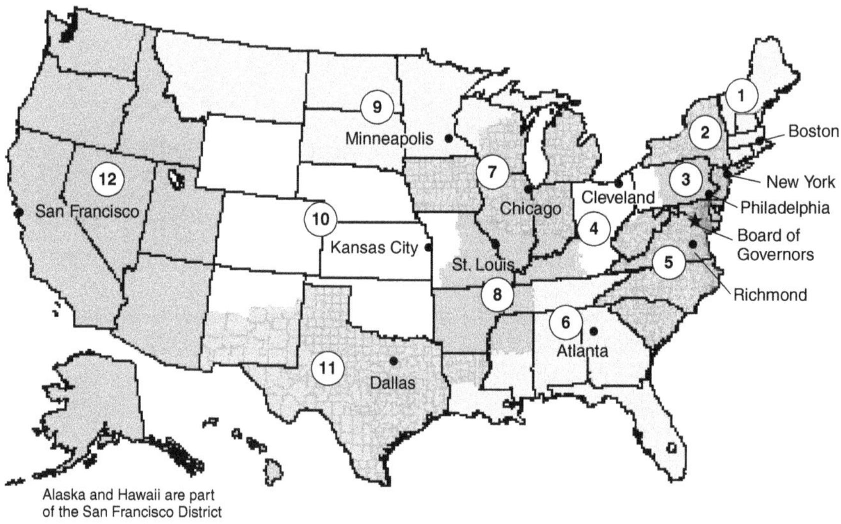

Figure 2.3 The Federal Reserve System

Source: Pollard (2003).

Note: The regional Federal Reserve Banks themselves have branches. For example, the Dallas Federal Reserve has branches in San Antonio, Houston and El Paso. The purpose of these branches is to provide cash and check services. More information on the regional Federal Reserve Banks is available on their respective websites, which can all be accessed via the website of the Federal Reserve Board (www.federalreserve.gov).

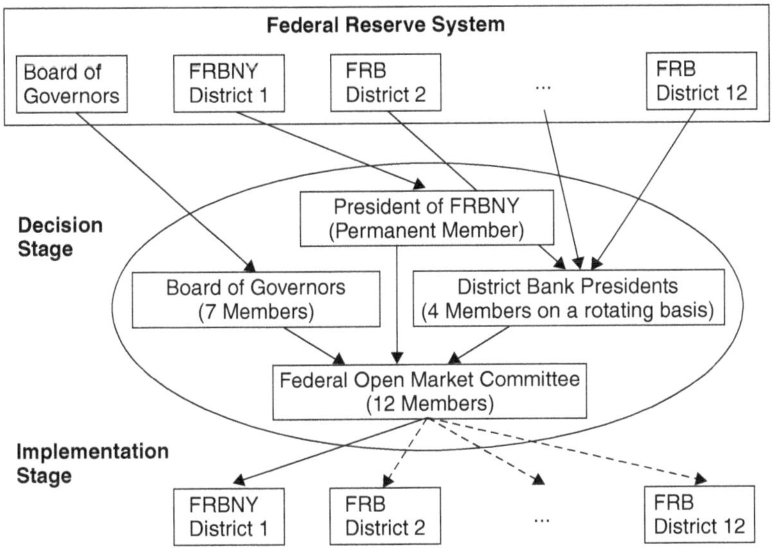

Note: FRBs are the regional Federal Reserve Banks of the 12 districts.
——▸ The solid line in the implementation stage denotes the fact that the Fed New York is entrusted with the conduct of open market operations.
- - -▸ The dashed line in the implementation stage denotes that fact that the Board of Directors of each Fed Bank sets the discount rate (subject to the approval of the Board of Governors).

Figure 2.4 Organizational framework of the Federal Reserve System

Source: Pollard (2003).

The highest decision-making body of the Bank of Japan is the Policy Board (see Figures 2.5 and 2.6). The Policy Board comprises the Governor, two Deputy Governors, and six appointed members. These nine Policy Board members are each appointed for 5 years by the Cabinet and approved by the Diet. The Chairman of the Policy Board is elected by the Policy Board members among themselves. As of September 2000, the Governor of the Bank has been elected Chairman of the Policy Board. The Policy Board takes its decisions by a majority vote.

As regards the implementation stage, the Bank of Japan carries out its business operations through its head office in Tokyo, 33 branches (B), 13 local offices (LOs) and several overseas representative offices. The Financial Markets Department at the head office conducts daily market operations and intervenes in the foreign exchange markets. The tasks of the domestic branches include the conduct of (1) business operations relating to currency issue and (2) banking operations such as discounting of bills, extension of loans, purchases and sales of bills and services related to deposit accounts, treasury funds and Japanese government bonds. The local offices handle some of the business operations of the head office or branches.

In addition to the monetary policy function, all three central banks perform other functions and tasks (see Table 2.1 for details). Several are common to all three central

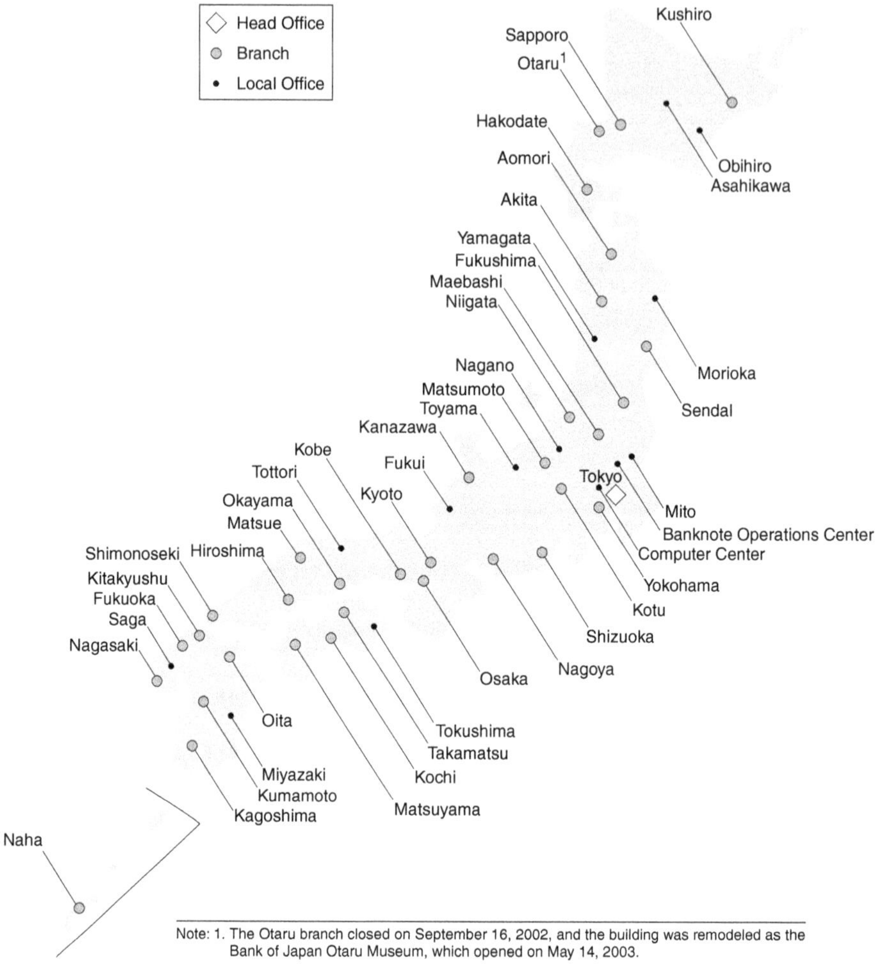

Note: 1. The Otaru branch closed on September 16, 2002, and the building was remodeled as the Bank of Japan Otaru Museum, which opened on May 14, 2003.

Figure 2.5 The Bank of Japan

Source: Bank of Japan (www.boj.or.jp).

banks, including the issuance of banknotes, the operation of the payment system, the collection of statistical information and the holding of foreign exchange reserves. These functions are clearly of crucial importance for monetary policy and thus are, in practice, often assigned to the monetary authorities.

The assignment of some other functions and tasks varies considerably across the three central banks. This is due, amongst others, to diverse factors that are not addressed here. One of these tasks worth mentioning is the responsibility for banking supervision and financial stability. Although the tasks of examination of depository institutions are delegated to the twelve Federal Reserve Banks, the determination of

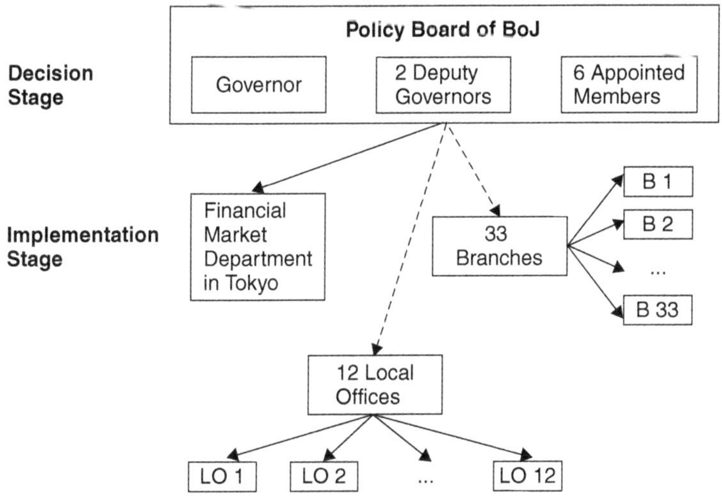

Figure 2.6 Organizational framework of the Bank of Japan

Source: BoJ (2003).

the general bank supervision policy is performed by the Federal Reserve Board in a centralized manner. In the euro area, instead, only some national central banks are involved in national supervision policies. The Bank of Japan supervises banks on a contractual basis. In order to receive emergency liquidity assistance, banks must provide the BoJ with regular information about their balance sheet and the BoJ can inspect them. The formal supervision of banks for financial stability purposes is carried out by the supervisory agency.

Monetary Policy Objectives

The Treaty (see Footnote 2) states that 'the primary objective of the ESCB shall be to maintain price stability' and that, 'without prejudice to the objective of price stability, the ESCB shall support the general economic policies in the (European) Community with a view to contributing to the achievement of the objectives of the (European) Community....'.[4] These objectives of the Community are, *inter alia*, 'a high level of employment..., sustainable and non-inflationary growth, a high degree of competitiveness and convergence of economic performance'. The Treaty thus establishes a clear hierarchy of objectives for the ECB and assigns overriding importance to price stability (see Table 2.2).

The ESCB's mandate to pursue price stability compares with the Federal Reserve's mandate of multiple objectives: 'The Board of Governors of the Federal

4 The Treaty refers to the ESCB rather than to the Eurosystem, since it was drawn up on the premise that eventually all EU Member States would adopt the euro.

Table 2.1 Comparison of the Eurosystem, the US Federal Reserve System and the Bank of Japan (I): Selected features and tasks

	Federal Reserve System	Eurosystem	Bank of Japan
Institutional structure	The Federal Reserve System comprises the Board of Governors (Washington D.C.) and 12 Federal Reserve Banks (including their 25 branches).	The Eurosystem comprises the European Central Bank (Frankfurt/ Germany) and 12 National Central Banks (including branches).	The Bank of Japan is not a system. Its head office is located in Tokyo. There are 33 branches and 13 local offices.
Define and implement monetary policy	Yes	Yes	Yes
Issue banknotes	Yes	Yes	Yes
Conduct foreign exchange operations	Yes	Yes	Yes
Hold and manage official reserves	Yes	Yes	Yes
Act as the fiscal agent for the government	Yes	NCBs	Yes
Promote stability of financial system	Yes	Yes	Yes
Supervise banks	Yes	Some NCBs	On a contractual basis
Promote the smooth operation of the payments system	Yes	Yes	Yes
Collect statistical information	Yes	Yes	Yes
Participate in international monetary institutions	Yes	Yes	Yes

Source: Pollard (2003), BOJ (2003), ECB (2004).
Note: NCBs refers to national central banks of the Eurosystem.

Reserve System and the Federal Open Market Committee shall maintain long-run growth of the monetary and credit aggregates commensurate with the country's long-run potential to increase production, so as to promote effectively the goals of maximum employment, stable prices and moderate long-term interest rates (Federal Reserve Act, Section 2A.1).' It has been argued that the Federal Reserve System has traditionally placed more emphasis on achieving price stability compared with its multiple objectives and in recent years there have been calls for a clearer price stability mandate for the Federal Reserve System (Wynne 1999).

Article 1 of the Bank of Japan Law stipulates that one of the objectives of the Bank of Japan is to issue banknotes and conduct monetary policy, the latter being referred

Table 2.2 A comparison of the Eurosystem, the Federal Reserve System and the Bank of Japan (II): Elements of the monetary policy framework

	Eurosystem	**Federal Reserve System**	**Bank of Japan**
Monetary policy decision-making body	Governing Council, comprising 18 members: the ECB Executive Board (6 members) and the governors of the 12 NCBs	Federal Open Market Committee, comprising 12 members: the Board of Governors (7 members), the president of the New York Fed and 4 other Reserve Bank presidents (rotating)	Policy Board (9 members)
Monetary policy objective(s)	Price stability is the primary objective	Multiple objectives, to promote maximimum employment, stable prices and moderate long-term interest rates	Price stability
Independence from political influence	Yes	Yes	Yes
Accountability	Reports/presentations to European Parliament, the Commission and EU Council	Reports/testimony to Congress	Reports/ testimony to Diet
Transparency	Immediate press conference	Immediate announcement and minutes	Immediate announcement and minutes
Monetary policy strategy	Formal strategy	Risk-management approach	Multi-indicator approch with, in principle, special weight on money
Monetary policy implementation	Decentralized (operations conducted by the Eurosystem)	Centralized (operations conducted by New York Reserve Bank)	Centralized

Sources: ECB, Federal Reserve, Bank of Japan, Bank for International Settlements.

to in the BoJ Law as 'currency and monetary control'. Article 2 of the BoJ Law further specifies that monetary policy shall pursue price stability to ensure the sound development of the national economy. The second objective of the Bank of Japan is to ensure smooth and stable operation of the payment and settlement system through measures such as acting as lender of last resort so as to maintain financial system stability (Bank of Japan, 2004).

Independence of the Central Bank

Central bank independence is a multilayered concept with several constituent elements, including personal independence (e.g. appointment process and duration of mandate), financial independence (e.g. setting of budget) and functional independence (e.g. implementation of monetary policy decisions). By all these elements, the Eurosystem is considered to be one of the most independent central bank systems in the world.

As regards the Eurosystem, the Treaty lays down the important principle of central bank independence. Article 108 of the Treaty establishes a central bank system that is independent from political influence. There are also other provisions to safeguard the independence of the Eurosystem and the decision-making bodies of the ECB. For instance, the ECB's financial arrangements are kept separate from the financial interests of the European Community. The ECB has its own budget, and its capital is subscribed and paid up by the euro area national central banks. Long terms of office for the members of the Governing Council and a rule stipulating that members of the Executive Board cannot be reappointed, also contribute to minimizing potential political influence on individual members of the decision-making bodies. Furthermore, the Eurosystem's independence is strengthened by the Treaty prohibition of any provision of central bank credit to the public sector. The Eurosystem is also functionally independent. The ECB has at its disposal all instruments and competencies necessary for the conduct of an efficient monetary policy and is authorized to decide autonomously how and when to use them. Moreover, the ECB has the right to adopt binding regulations to the extent necessary to carry out the tasks of the ESCB and in certain other cases as laid down in specific acts of the EU Council.

While the Federal Reserve System enjoys significant independence, it has been argued that it is somewhat lower than for the Eurosystem (see, for example, Wynne 1999). The US Constitution gives the right to 'coin money and regulate the value thereof' to the Congress. While the Congress has delegated this responsibility to the Federal Reserve, it could, in principle, revoke it at any time.[5]

5 It is worth mentioning that in the case of the US, foreign exchange policy is fully in the hands of the Treasury Department. In Japan, foreign exchange interventions are decided by the finance ministry. The Bank of Japan undertakes these interventions as an agent of the government using government funds. As far as the euro area is concerned, Article 111 of the Treaty gives the Council (acting either on a recommendation from the Commission and after consulting the ECB or on a recommendation from the ECB) the right to formulate 'general orientations for exchange rate policy'. At the same time, the Treaty also contains provisions ensuring that the pursuit of the objective of price stability is fully respected by the single exchange rate policy (ECB 2004).

The intent of US Congress in shaping the Federal Reserve Act was also to keep politics out of monetary policy. There are a number of provisions to safeguard the independence of the Federal Reserve. For example, the Federal Reserve is independent of other branches and agencies of government. It is self-financed and therefore is not subject to the congressional budgetary process.

The terms of the members of the Board of Governors span multiple presidential and congressional terms. The seven members of the Board of Governors of the Federal Reserve System are nominated by the US President and confirmed by the Senate. A full term is fourteen years. A member who serves a full term may not be reappointed. A member who completes an unexpired portion of a term may be reappointed. Hence, the actual term for a member of the Board could be much longer. If a member resigns prior to the end of the term of office, the new member is appointed to serve the remainder of the term and then can be appointed to a full fourteen-year term. The Chairman and Vice-Chairman of the Board are chosen by the US President from among the sitting Governors and must be confirmed by the Senate. They serve terms of four years and may be reappointed as Chairman or Vice-Chairman until their terms as Governors expire.

The Bank of Japan Law was revised in 1997 to secure independence of the bank. The law states that 'the Bank of Japan's autonomy regarding currency and monetary control shall be respected.' To ensure such independence, members of the Policy Board cannot be dismissed for holding opinions at variance with the government, and the government cannot order the Bank to undertake any particular policy action or to conduct any particular business operation. At the same time it is important that the Bank's monetary policy is consistent with the government's basic economic policy framework. Therefore the Bank of Japan shall 'always maintain close contact with the government and exchange views sufficiently.' The Bank of Japan Law also allows representatives of the government to attend Monetary Policy Meetings of the Policy Board, to give their views and submit proposals, or request that the Board postpone a vote on monetary policy measures until the next meeting. However, the government representatives have no votes in the monetary policy decisions.

Accountability and Transparency

To retain legitimacy, an independent central bank must be accountable to democratic institutions, as well as the general public, for its actions in the pursuit of its mandate. Correspondingly, the ECB is accountable first and foremost to the citizens of the EU, from whom the Treaty's legitimacy derives, and more formally to the European Parliament (ECB 2004). The Treaty lays down a number of reporting requirements for the ECB – for example, the presentation of an Annual Report to the European Parliament, the Commission and the EU Council – and establishes regular presentations to the European Parliament to ensure accountability.

Similar reports to legislature are carried out in the US and Japan. The Federal Reserve's ultimate accountability is to Congress, which at any time can amend the Federal Reserve Act. Legislation requires that the 'Fed' reports annually on its activities to the Speaker of the House of Representatives, and twice annually on its plans for monetary policy to the banking committees of Congress. Fed officials also testify before Congress when requested. The Bank of Japan publishes an outline of its business operations (BoJ, 2004). A report on currency and monetary control is submitted to the Diet twice a year and the Governor or a designated representative appears before Diet committees, on request, to explain the Bank of Japan's policies, business operations and balance sheet conditions.

A concept closely related to, but yet distinct from accountability, is that of transparency. Ultimately, all efforts to enhance transparency are aimed at ensuring that monetary policy is better understood by the public, as well as the various institutions to which central banks are accountable. This would foster both monetary policy credibility and effectiveness. Winkler (2002) flags different constituting elements of transparency – including openness, clarity and information efficiency (see Figure 2.7). He cautions that an effective approach to communication requires that a balance be struck between being open about the complex nature of policy making and simplifying the presentation of this process in the interest of greater clarity.

Trichet (2004) points out that both the Eurosystem and the Fed place a strong emphasis on transparency of the decision-making process, on transparency of the analysis that is worked out by the responsible decision-making 'college', on explanations of the economic diagnosis to the public opinion and market participants, and on accountability vis-à-vis the Parliament of the Union. Furthermore, both explain their decisions in real time.[6]

An important role rests on the presentation of the ECB's monetary policy strategy and monetary policy implementation. The information can then be structured in such a way that it is accessible and can be understood by the public. Concerning clarity, the publication of a precise quantitative definition of price stability by the ECB – as opposed to the practice of the Fed – may be seen as a component of both transparency

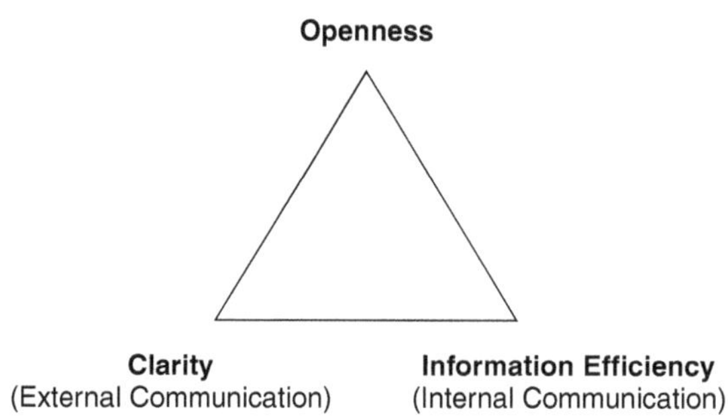

Figure 2.7 Facets of Central Bank transparency

Source: Winkler (2002), p. 417.

6 Both the ECB and the Fed are clear on being as comprehensive as possible in their analysis. They both incorporate in their analysis all possible pertinent information, all relevant forecasts and modelling exercises, including private sector views, whether economic or monetary.

and accountabilty of the ECB: it provides the public with a yardstick against which the performance of the ECB can be measured.

The Introductory Statement at each ECB press conference shortly after the first Governing Council meeting each month is a means to almost instantenously announce and explain the most recent monetary policy decision. Similarly, the current practice of the FOMC is to announce policy changes as soon as they are made. Immediately after each meeting, the FOMC issues a statement that a decision was taken to lower or raise rates, or merely noting that the meeting ended, if the decision is to leave rates unchanged. The FOMC publishes the minutes of each meeting around five to eight weeks after the meeting.

The Bank of Japan Law requires the Bank to 'endeavor to clarify to the public the content of its decisions, as well as its decision-making process.' In accordance with this provision, after each Monetary Policy Meeting (MPM), the Policy Board makes public the decisions reached at the MPM, including the guidelines for money market operations and the Bank's assessment of economic and financial developments. The Bank of Japan releases the minutes of the MPMs around one month after the meeting and will publish a detailed record of the discussions ten years after each meeting. Other matters decided at the Policy Board meetings are disclosed in the Monthly Report of the Policy Board of the Bank of Japan.

It has been argued that the publication of minutes makes the Fed and the BoJ more transparent than the ECB. In its own view, however, the ECB is very transparent and has helped to define the 'state of the art' of central banking in this domain (Trichet 2004). Nevertheless, the ECB has abstained from the publication of minutes for diverse reasons. First, it wanted to communicate to the public that the entity which decides is not a personality – or a group of personalities – but a college (i.e., a united team which benefits from its collegial wisdom). Second, the ECB did not want to convey the impression that it is a place to reconcile various national interests, represented by various national central bank governors. In fact, the Treaty clearly requires that decisions are taken in the interest of the euro area as a whole and to abstain from any kind of reasoning on the basis of a national vision. In the latter sense, the situation in the euro area is to be seen as being different from those of the US or Japan. In any case, the ECB publishes its 'diagnosis' in real time and provides a press conference so that all the arguments that have led to the decision are presented in full to the public. Several recent studies have shown the ECB to be highly predictable in its decisions, which is one of the major ultimate goals of transparency.

Monetary Policy Strategy

The main elements of the monetary policy strategy of the ECB are a quantitative definition of price stability and a comprehensive analysis of the risks to price stability (ECB 2004). In the pursuit of price stability, the ECB aims to maintain inflation rates below but close to 2 per cent over the medium term. The assessment of the different risks to price stability is based on two complementary analytical perspectives: economic analysis and monetary analysis. The economic analysis – focusing on the most immediate causes of inflation, such as cost developments and demand-supply imbalances – helps primarily to assess short to medium-term economic developments and consequently risks to price stability at that horizon. The monetary analysis – focusing on the ultimate monetary determinants of inflation – contains mainly information for assessing price trends at medium to long-term horizons. In this context, the monetary analysis serves mainly as a means of cross-checking, from a medium to long-term perspective, the short to medium-term indications from the economic analysis.

Due to the breakdown of the stability of money demand in the early 1990's, the Fed proceeded by pursuing a multi-indicator approach (Ruckriegel and Seitz 2002), attaching less importance to monetary aggregates but utilizing a broad range of financial and economic indicators in assessing its policy stance (Greenspan 1993). While some commentators have labelled this approach as 'just do it strategy' (Mishkin 2003), Fed officials have called this a 'stitch-in-time strategy' (Blinder 1995).

More recently, representatives of the Fed stressed that the Fed should neither be understood as an inflation-targeting central bank nor would the Fed regard simple rules as adequate (Greenspan 2004). Instead, a risk-management paradigm to monetary policy making was introduced (i.e. a strategy directed at 'maximizing the probabilities of achieving over time our goals of price stability and the maximum sustainable economic growth that we associate with it') and it was emphasized that such cost-benefit analysis was seen as an ongoing part of monetary policy decision making. Such an approach actually coincides with the fact that the Fed – like the ECB – have repeatedly stressed the importance of uncertainty on monetary policy decision making (Issing 2002, Greenspan 2004).

Like the ECB and the Federal Reserve System, the Bank of Japan (BoJ) has refused to adopt an inflation-targeting strategy. This does not denote a rejection of such a framework *per se*, but rather reflects doubts about the appropriateness in the current extraordinary state of the Japanese economy (Okina 1999). Indeed, over the last years, the BoJ has certainly been facing a period of historically unprecedented economic challenges. Since the latter half of the 1980s Japan's economy has experienced an extremely large swing following the emergence, expansion and bursting of asset price bubbles. This has lead to instabilities in money demand in the mid-1990s, a fact which is generally attributed to dramatic changes in firms' borrowing and financial institutions' lending behaviour. Following the increasingly aggressive monetary easing policy by the Bank of Japan and the related extremely low short-term interest rates, fund shifts between various financial assets occurred, thus spurring further instabilities in the relationship between the money stock and economic activity, leading to a loss in importance attached to monetary aggregates. This so-called 'zero-interest rate policy' was adopted with a view to avoiding further recession, putting a stop on deflation, and preventing the spread of anxieties over the financial system.[7] Given these distortions, the BoJ deemed it appropriate to look rather closely at the prices of various financial assets, real economic variables, price developments and also the fund-raising behaviour of firms and households (Bank of

7 Some observers have made use of the wording 'liquidity trap' for this situation. We are not aware whether the BoJ itself agrees to this description.

Japan 2003). Nevertheless, against the background of the relative 'uniqueness' of money as an indicator variable, the money stock is still regarded as an important and useful information variable and is monitored carefully by the Bank of Japan (Bank of Japan 2003). At the present stage, the question of how to deal with asset price movements in an appropriate way seems to be an issue of discussion (Okina and Shiratsuka 2002). Various studies have investigated this question, sometimes against the background of a Taylor rule framework. It remains uncertain, however, whether a more appropriate policy judgement would have been possible, if the BoJ had in addition explicitly taken asset price into account.[8]

Implementation of Monetary Policy

The two groups of operations available to the Eurosystem for the conduct of the single monetary policy are open market operations and standing facilities (ECB 2004). Open market operations play an important role in steering interest rates, signalling the stance of monetary policy and managing the liquidity situation in the money market. The main refinancing operations are the most important open market operations. For the purpose of controlling short-term interest rates in the money market and, in particular, restricting their volatiliy, the Eurosystem also offers two standing facilities to its counterparties, one for providing reserves (the marginal lending facility) and one for draining reserves (the deposit facility). The interest rates on these standing facilities normally provide a ceiling and a floor for the overnight rate in the money market. By setting the rates on the standing facilities, the Governing Council determines the corridor within which the overnight money market rate can fluctuate.

The three key interest rates for the euro area, i.e. the interest rate on the main refinancing operations, the rate on the deposit facility and the rate on the marginal lending facility, are illustrated in Figure 2.8. As regards the main refinancing operations, the Eurosystem may execute its tenders in the form of fixed rate or variable rate. Since June 2000, main refinancing operations have been conducted as variable rate tenders with a minimum bid rate. The differences between the standing facility rates and the rate on main refinancing operations were kept unchanged since April 1999 at +/– 1 percentage point.

In the US, the policy rate is the announced target level for overnight rate (federal funds rate). The FOMC directs open market operations to meet a specified target for the overnight federal funds rate (see Figure 2.9). The Federal Reserve does not offer facilities for draining reserves and also uses more discretion than the Eurosystem in providing funds for temporary liquidity needs of counterparties.

Under normal circumstances the main operating objective of open market operations conducted by the Bank of Japan is to keep the overnight rate (uncollateralized call money rate) in line with the target set at each MPM. In March 2001, the Bank of Japan adopted new procedures for money market operations whereby the balance of current accounts held by financial institutions at the Bank of Japan, instead of the overnight rate,

8 There are, of course, a number of remedies for the situation in Japan suggested in the literature. It would, however, lead us too far astray to touch upon this point. See, for instance, Bernanke (2003) for a recent assessment of the situation in Japan from the viewpoint of a Fed official.

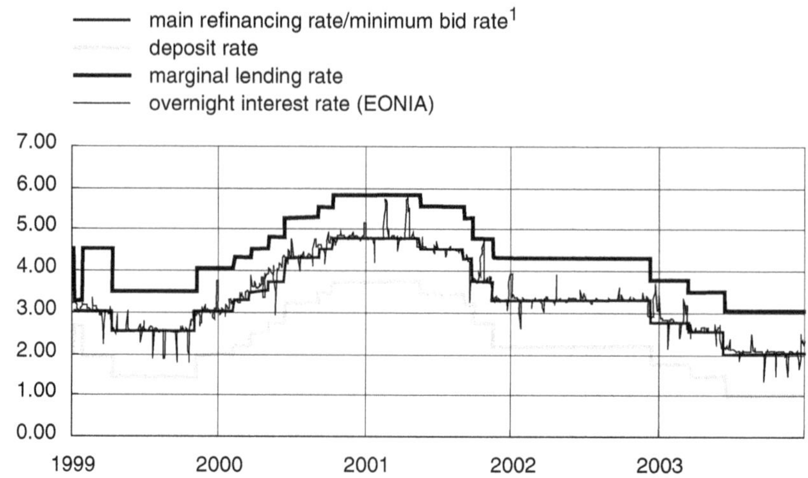

Figure 2.8 Key ECB interest rates and the overnight interest rate (percentages per annum, daily data)

Source: ECB.
Note: [1] As of 28 June 2000, pre-announced minimum bid rate in variable rate tenders; before rate on fixed rate tenders. The minimum bid rate refers to the minimum interest rate at which counterparties may place their bids.

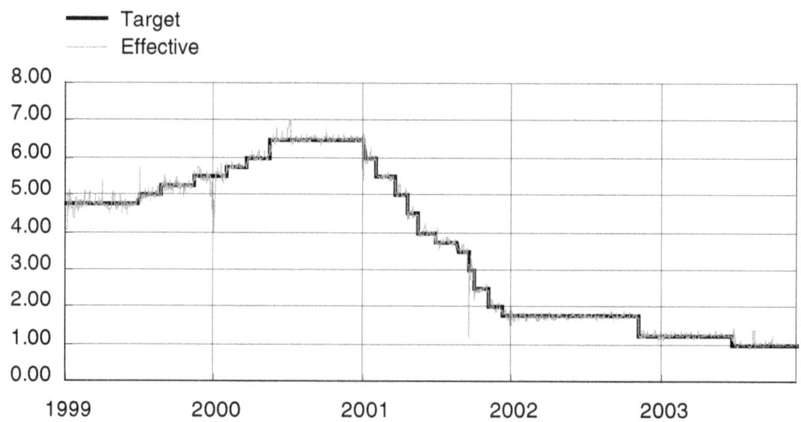

Figure 2.9 Federal funds rate: target and effective[1] (percentages per annum, daily data)

Source: Federal Reserve.
Note: [1] The effective federal funds rate is a weighted average of the reported rates at which different amounts of the day's trading through New York brokers occurs.

is set as the operating target (BoJ 2004, see also Figure 2.10). This shift from an interest rate to a quantitative target was motivated by the extraordinary circumstances facing the Japanese economy (see also Chapter 1). The Bank of Japan operates a standby lending facility, known as the Complementary Lending Facility, which is designed to complement market operations initiated by the Bank of Japan. This facility is analogous to the euro area marginal lending facility and provides a ceiling for the overnight rate.

The operational frameworks used by the Eurosystem, the Federal Reserve and the Bank of Japan for implementing monetary policy rely on similar fundamental characteristics. They allow the three central banks to clearly signal their monetary policy stance, even if the tools at work are different (Blenck et al., 2001). One common trend is a stronger market orientation in policy implementation, relying on open market operations often, though not exclusively, effected in the form of repurchase agreements. For example, the operational framework of the Eurosystem is based on the principles laid down in the Treaty, which states that the Eurosystem '[...] shall act in accordance with the principle of an open market economy with free competition, favouring an efficient allocation of resources [...]' (Article 105).

While the three central banks have in common some features of the general framework for implementing policy, there exist also many differences, which are, to some extent, a reflection of historical traditions and also explicit design choices. While it is beyond the scope of this chapter to review these differences in detail, an elaborate discussion of the implementation of monetary policy in the euro area and a comparison with other major central banks is provided in Chapter 7.[9] One difference worth noting is

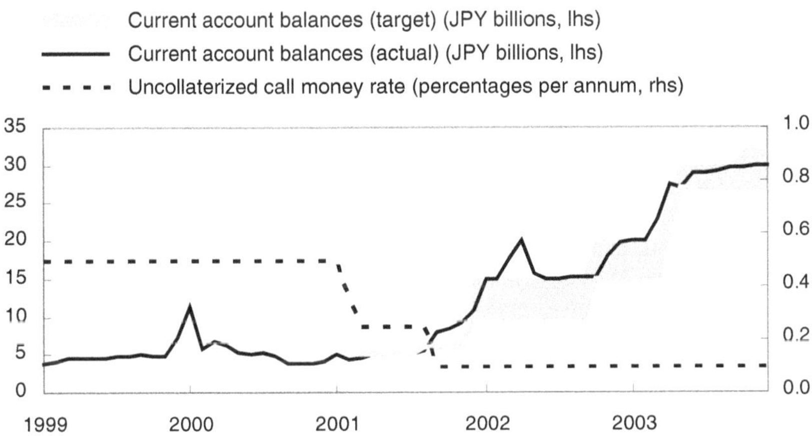

Figure 2.10 Bank of Japan policy rate and target range of banks' reserves[1,2]

Source: Bank of Japan.

Note: [1] Current account balances with the Bank of Japan. [2] From March to December 2001, target level; thereafter target range.

9 The interested reader can also refer to, for example, ECB (2004a), Bank of Japan (2004), Bank for International Settlements (2001).

the specificity of the Eurosystem to implement monetary policy with a decentralized approach. Accordingly, the Eurosystem's monetary policy operations are normally implemented through the NCBs, which means that the ECB coordinates the operations and the transactions are carried out by the NCBs. In the US, the Federal Reserve's practice is to conduct all operations through the New York Reserve Bank and, in Japan, operations are carried out by the headquarters in Tokyo.

Further Elements Differentiating the Eurosystem from the Federal Reserve System and the Bank of Japan

As already said, the monetary policy in the euro area is delegated to a new supranational European institution, the Eurosystem. While the 'transfer of sovereignty' in the monetary field has been successfully completed, other areas of economic policies such as fiscal and structural policies, still remain decentralized.[10] This puts the Eurosystem in a unique position vis-à-vis the other actors in the euro area as well as the European Union and its diverse institutions. In particular, a single monetary policy for the euro area is compatible with the other economic policies conducted at the national level, as long as the minimum set of common objectives, principles and rules established in the Treaty are followed in letter as well as in spirit. It goes without saying that the US Federal Reserve System and the Bank of Japan are not facing such challenges.

Central banks rely on financial markets to operate through it, for example, for the transmission of monetary impulses to the rest of the economy. This monetary policy transmission mechanism has been the subject of a vast amount of economic reseach over recent decades but various aspects of the complex interactions involved remain to be clarified. In this respect, the Eurosystem faces a level of uncertainty that may even be somewhat greater than that faced by many other central banks, given that the ECB took over responsibility for an entirely new currency area (ECB 2004). Moreover, the European financial landscape has changed dramatically over the past few years and the pace of change appears to have moved into a higher gear with the introduction of the euro (Gaspar et al., 2003). The Eurosystem provides active support to financial market integration, as part of the general efforts by EU policy-makers in this area. As is described in more detail in Chapter 4, contributions by the Eurosystem can take many forms such as direct action, acting as a catalyst for collective action or contributing to raising the awareness of the need for integration.

Some Final Remarks

This chapter has reviewed and compared several features of the Eurosystem, the US Federal Reserve System and the Bank of Japan. The central points of our comparison were the institutional structure, the monetary policy strategy, the monetary policy instruments, and operating procedures. While the institutional structure and the use

10 Although fiscal policies are subject to the provisions of the Stability and Growth Pact.

of instruments does not differ that much, the main tasks and the legal status are quite different.

It must be admitted that in its first years of existence, the Eurosystem has mastered a number of significant challenges. It has built up an extensive statistical infrastructure and set up a monetary policy framework for the euro area. Nevertheless, the process can by no means be seen as having come to a halt. Financial markets and institutions are in a continuous process of transformation and need to be analysed and monitored.

While, contrary to the Eurosystem, the US Federal Reserve System and the Bank of Japan have not been confronted with such exceptional challenges as the profound changes in the economic, financial and institutional environment, they have also been facing developments forcing them to act under considerable uncertainty.

In such a world of ongoing changes, the challenges facing central banks are considerable. So far, all three central banks have performed well. One can, therefore, trust that the three central banks will also master their tasks in the future.

References

Bank for International Settlements (2004), *74th Annual Report*, p. 22.

Bank of Japan (2000), 'Functions and Business Operations of the Bank of Japan', http//boj.or.jp.

Bank of Japan (2003), 'About the Bank of Japan', *Annual Review*, pp. 78–118, http//boj.or.jp.

Bank of Japan (2003), 'The Role of the Money Stock in Conducting Monetary Policy', *Quarterly Bulletin*, May 2003, http//boj.or.jp.

Bank of Japan (2004), *Functions and Operations of the Bank of Japan*, edited by the Institute for Monetary and Economic Studies.

Bernanke, B.S. (2003), 'Some Thoughts on Monetary Policy in Japan', Remarks before the Japan Society of Monetary Economics, Tokyo, May 31, 2003, http://www.federalreserve.gov.

Blenck, D., Hasko, H., Hilton, S. and Masaki, K. (2001), *The Main Features of the Monetary Policy Frameworks of the Bank of Japan, the Federal Reserve System and the Eurosystem*, BIS Papers No. 9, December, Bank for International Settlements, Basel.

European Central Bank (2003), 'The Outcome of the ECB's Evaluation of its Monetary Policy Strategy', *Monthly Bulletin*, June, pp. 79–92.

European Central Bank (2004), *The Monetary Policy of the ECB*, Second Edition.

European Central Bank (2004a), *The implementation of monetary policy in the euro area: General documentation on Euosystem monetary policy instruments and procedures*, February.

Gaspar, V., Hartmann, P., Sleijpen, O. (eds.) (2003), *The transformation of the European financial system*, Second ECB Central Banking Conference, European Central Bank, Frankfurt am Main, May.

Greenspan, A. (2003), 'Testimony to the Sub-Committee on Economic Growth and Credit Formation of the Committee on Banking. Finance and Urban Affairs of the US House of Representatives on 20/07/1993', http://www.federalreserve.gov.

Greenspan, A. (2004), 'Risk and Uncertainty in Monetary Policy', Remarks at the Meetings of the American Economic Association, San Diego California, January 3, 2004, http://www.federalreserve.gov.

Issing, O. (ed.), Angeloni, I., Gaspar, V., Klöckers, H.-J., Masuch, K., Nicoletti-Altimari, S., Rostagno, M. and Smets, F. (co-eds.) (2003), *Background Studies for the ECB's Evaluation of its Monetary Policy Strategy*, European Central Bank, Frankfurt am Main.

Issing, O. (2002), 'Monetary Policy in a World of Uncertainty', *Économie Internationale* 92, pp. 165–180.

Meyer, L.H. (1998), 'The Strategy of Monetary Policy', The Alan R. Holmes Lecture, Middlebury College, Middlebury, Vermont, March 16, 1998, http://www.federalreserve.gov.

Mishkin, F. (2003), *The Economics of Money, Banking and Financial Markets*, Sixth Edition, Pearson Education International.

Morgan Stanley Central Bank Directory (2003), Central Banking Publications Ltd, London.

Okina, K. (1999), 'Monetary Policy under Zero Inflation: A Response to Criticisms and Questions Regarding Monetary Policy, Monetary and Economic Studies', December, http//boj.or.jp.

Okina, K. and Shiratsuka, S. (2002), 'Asset Price Bubbles, Price Stability and Monetary Policy: Japan's Experience, Monetary and Economic Studies', October, http//boj.or.jp.

Pollard, P. (2003), 'A Look Inside Two Central Banks: The European Central Bank and the Federal Reserve', *Review of the Federal Reserve Bank of St. Louis*, January/February.

Ruckriegel, K. und Seitz, F. (2002), *The Eurosystem and the Federal Reserve System Compared: Facts and Challenges*, ZEI Working Paper B02.

Taylor, J.B. (1993a), *Discretion versus Policy Rules in Practice*, Carnegie Rochester Conference Series on Public Policy 39, S. 195–214.

Taylor, J.B. (1993b), 'A Historical Analysis of Monetary Policy Rules', in Taylor, J. (ed.), *Monetary Policy Rules*, University of Chicago Press, Chicago and London.

Trichet, J.-C. (2004), 'The Current State of the European Economy and the ECB's Monetary Policy Concept', Speech delivered at the International Financial Forum, Paris, Europlace, 9. July, http//www.ecb.int.

Winkler, B. (2002), 'Which Kind of Transparency? On the Need for Clarity in Monetary Policy-Making', *ifo Studien*, Jg. 48, Nr. 3, pp. 401–427.

Wynne, M. (1999), 'European System of Central Banks', *Federal Reserve Bank of Dallas Economic Review*, first quarter, pp. 2–14.

Chapter 3

Concepts and Measures of Financial Integration

Annalisa Ferrando and Jukka Vesala

Introduction

A notion of financial integration, which also underlies much of the policy discussion, is a situation where there are no barriers that discriminate economic agents on the basis of their location in their access to funds and investment of capital.[1] Having *equal,* or *symmetric*, access to larger financial markets for all participants in the EU single market would result in clear economic benefits. A larger financial market facilitates financial innovation and competition, which enhances risk sharing and efficient allocation of capital to investment opportunities. These effects, together with the benefits of deeper and more liquid financial markets (financial deepening), should also enhance economic growth. Recent research has found evidence that financial deepening, in particular, produces significant growth benefits.[2] Naturally, these benefits apply most substantially to previously less financially developed regions (see e.g. Giannetti et al., 2002).

This approach to defining financial integration leads one to look for any existing barriers that affect different regions *asymmetrically* in their access to financial markets when assessing how far integration has progressed. These barriers should then be addressed by policy measures.[3] While this *normative* approach is straightforward and useful for policy purposes, it might be impossible to list *all* relevant barriers and check whether they hold or not. On the other hand, focusing on the existing barriers does not give us a benchmark to assess whether we are at or close to full integration. For this purpose we need a *positive* approach, which draws on industrial economics and observable market data (prices and quantities). The positive analysis can point to segments of non-existent or slow integration where remaining barriers can be very relevant and, thus, it can also be helpful for a normative 'policy-centred' discussion.

1 See the ECB October 2003 *Monthly Bulletin* 'The integration of Europe's financial markets'. Note that this definition does not require favourable access, it only requires non-discriminatory access.
2 See e.g. Rousseau, 2002.
3 Literature suggests that one needs to pay very close attention that some regions are not hurt in the process and that equal conditions are attained. For instance, Allen and Gale (1997) show that when several regions with originally different kinds of financial systems open up to financial trades, not all regions necessarily benefit to the same extent.

This book is mainly confined to the *euro area*, whose regulatory framework is shared with the broader EU single market (see Chapter 4). It is often thought that all that really matters to achieve further integration in financial services is the single European market programme, not the single currency which only unites monetary policy and wholesale financial markets (such as money and currency markets) (see Chapter 7). Undoubtedly, the effects of the single market and the single currency on integration are difficult to separate. It is also true that the effects of the single market have not yet developed in full. However, it is also true that the multiplicity of currencies was a fundamental factor behind the preservation of the segmentation of the financial industry (Padoa-Schioppa, 2000) (see discussion below). Thus, one could see more profound integration in a single currency area, also outside wholesale financial markets.

The chapter is organized as follows. The next section introduces the positive industrial economics approach to defining financial integration, on which (most of) the analyses in this book are based. We do not present quantitative evidence in this chapter – our goal is to lay out the framework for studying financial integration. Then, we turn to the issue of more precisely measuring the progress in financial integration. We note and present measures, which are put in use in the different Chapters of this book. Finally, we discuss some links between the three concepts of integration, competition and efficiency, and offer some final remarks. This Chapter also serves as a brief review of the relevant literature that develops indicators of integration.

Positive Approaches to Financial Integration

The Law-of-One-Price

As for any goods or services, integration in financial markets is defined as a situation in which, out of previously segmented markets for a single good (or substitute goods), one coherent market is created. In industrial economics, markets are first and foremost considered integrated when the *law-of-one-price* holds, i.e. when the prices for a fully homogeneous product in question are the same irrespective of the geographical domicile of the seller or the buyer. The law may fail to hold because of factors such as transportation and transaction costs, consumer switching costs or other barriers to entry. These factors may maintain market segmentation and discourage *arbitrage* across the area that would force prices to converge.

The direct implication is that the *singleness* of prices provides the benchmark of full integration and that cross-sectional differences in prices signal incomplete integration. In this context, this mainly refers to cross-country differences. In addition, *convergence* in prices constitutes evidence of progress in integration. (Statistical) indicators can be put in use to directly analyse price deviations and convergence, while indirect evidence of integration can be obtained from the reaction of prices to specific events or from the way prices are determined in financial markets as argued more extensively below.

The law-of-one-price and, consequently, *price-based indicators* of integration should be used as far as possible as they provide the strongest and most clear-cut evidence of integration. The law-of-one-price can only be applied, first, when price comparisons are meaningful, which requires that the goods or services in question are *homogeneous* such that they should carry the same prices in integrated markets. This is sometimes, but by no means predominantly, the case in financial markets. Broadly speaking, many liquid financial instruments traded on regular market places can, in particular, fall into this category (such as money market instruments – Chapter 7, and debt and equity securities – Chapter 8), while non-traded assets and many services of financial institutions are significantly heterogeneous, both in wholesale and capital market as well as in retail fields (Chapter 6). The law-of-one-price can be, however, approximated also in the latter fields when the products are homogeneous.

The second condition for applying the law-of-one-price is that (adequately) comprehensive and *high quality price data* exist. The data available for studying financial integration in Europe are far from the ideal set a researcher would like to have at his or her disposal (in particular, when long time series are sought). Fortunately, some reliable sources of data exist, making it possible to write this book. Quoted market prices are quite easily available. For financial services, prices are most readily available for capital market related activities, as data on underwriting charges can be obtained from public databases, for example. The same holds for wholesale financial services such as interbank lending. For many retail financial services, data availability constrains the possibility to construct price-based indicators.

Application to financial market returns When analysing integration in the different segments of financial markets, 'prices' refer to the quoted market prices of assets, or, expressed alternatively, as *returns* to investors. The returns consist of the benchmark risk-free yield and a premium reflecting risk, but also secondary market liquidity conditions and other factors.

The *benchmark yield* is determined by the *risk-free* yield curve, which is different in different monetary policy jurisdictions and is affected by monetary policy and overall macroeconomic conditions. Hence, the introduction of the euro immediately harmonized one component of pricing – the risk-free yield curve (see Chapters 7 and 8) and thereby provided a major factor leading to harmonization of returns in the euro area. A common benchmark can also facilitate the comparison of returns by investors, and thus provide a further boost to integration and competition. A common currency can also circumvent practical hindrances to investment across borders, such as currency limits of institutional investors. These are major reasons why integration can go further in the euro area compared with the single market as a whole.

However, a single currency does not guarantee full and immediate integration, as we will see later on in this book. But as the risk-free benchmark yield is the same in the euro area, one can focus on the *premia* over and above risk-free yields, when measuring integration. Conversely, one might not even want to require common monetary policy and macroeconomic conditions to be preconditions for financial integration, which would be the case when analysing the EU single market (as long as the euro area and the EU do not coincide). Hence, one should indeed focus on the premia – or *yield spreads* – which depend on microeconomic factors, rather than on the total returns, which also reflect the macroeconomic conditions.

The key component of the overall premium is the *risk premium*, which the investor should receive. It depends on the probability of default of the issuer (public entity or a firm) and the variance of the interest/dividend streams to the investor. Liquidity is another intrinsic feature of financial instruments, which can result in differences in the return demanded by investors, as less liquid instruments, which are more difficult to sell further, will demand a higher return. By contrast, other possibly relevant factors, i.e. region- (or country-) specific factors, should not play out differently in different parts of the integrated area, where market conditions should be equal (according to the notion of a 'single' market). Hence, we can finally state that – applying the law-of-one-price – *in integrated markets, yield spreads (and total returns if the benchmark yields are the same) on comparable instruments, available throughout the area, should converge to the same level, provided that the risk and liquidity features of the instruments are identical.*[4]

This notion directly lends itself to devise indicators of integration (variation and convergence). It also allows constructing indirect indicators. Namely, in integrated markets, returns should not be affected by region-specific factors, but only the individual issuer risk characteristics. This implies, for example, that ratings, or individual probability of default estimates, should be the main determinants of bond yields and be part of stock returns, rather than country-specific factors. It also implies that securities' returns should be more correlated across industries than countries. Hence, a number of studies looking at these issues can also provide indications of integration (see below).

Finally, if there were no barriers to international investment, investors would be able to diversify against local shocks by holding assets from different countries. Then, local shocks should not constitute a source of systemic risk for the investors and affect, in turn, the asset returns (through 'fire sales', for instance). Hence, in fully integrated financial markets, returns on similarly risky assets should be influenced by common factors only.

Application to customer rates and charges As far as financial services are concerned, 'prices' can also refer to investment returns (e.g. deposit or mutual fund returns) or, alternatively, loan interest rates. In these cases, the above considerations related to financial market returns basically apply. The loan or deposit interest rate levels also reflect macroeconomic factors, while *margins* vis-à-vis the risk-free rates microeconomic factors (such as banks' market power and other pricing features like cross-subsidization across different financial services). While convergence in loan and deposit rates can be due to macroeconomic convergence – in particular, the creation of the single yield-curve in the euro area – a real indicator of integration is convergence in the margins. In integrated markets, the loan and deposit margins would be the same for similarly risky debtors (loan margins) and banks (deposit margins).

In several financial services, direct *service fees* are increasingly charged to customers, instead of pricing service costs into the interest margin. In these cases, the law-of-one-price can be applied directly like in other goods and services, provided that the product homogeneity and data availability conditions are met.

4 See, for example, Adam et al., 2002, and Bernard and Bisignano, 2002.

Other Approaches

As noted above, many financial products and services are heterogeneous, even tailored to the needs of individual clients. Indeed, *quality competition* – as distinguished from price competition – is very important in many financial services. Therefore, using the law-of-one-price and only looking at prices – even if comprehensive data were available – could be misleading.

When the law-of-one-price is not applicable, an alternative broad category of indicators, *quantity-based* measures, could be introduced. Such measures provide indirect indicators of integration. One is left with less satisfactory and conclusive, but nevertheless useful measures, which can be based on various theoretical approaches.

Portfolio diversification Adopting a *demand-side* viewpoint, quantity-based indicators can be motivated by *portfolio theory*. Notably, the portfolio composition according to domestic-foreign composition of financial assets provides a quantitative measure for the degree of integration. With integrated financial markets, investors should take advantage of new or improved foreign investment opportunities by increasing the international diversification of their portfolio across the single currency (or single market) area.

'*Home bias*' implies that domestic investors hold a substantially larger proportion of their wealth in domestic assets than standard portfolio theory (i.e. optimal risk diversification) would suggest.[5] In the absence of the home bias, investors would optimally diversify away domestic risk factors, such as individual country-specific macroeconomic developments, if costs to do so were not prohibitively high. In other words, the home bias should disappear when financial markets are perfectly integrated. In order to construct an indicator of the remaining home bias, the share of foreign over total assets invested by the domestic sector can be calculated and possibly compared to the benchmark value of full (or optimal) diversification. In this sense, data on cross-border flows on the acquisition of investment products and services, for instance, can be used to construct indicators of integration. One should note, however, that transaction costs could be prohibitive for retail investors to achieve optimal diversification, unless they invest in collective investment vehicles such as mutual funds.

Contestable markets Analysing the *supply-side*, quantity-based indicators can be motivated by the theory of *contestable markets*. In this vein, the cross-border establishment and acquisition of financial institutions, changes in the structure of local markets, and the share of foreign suppliers in the local markets can be used as signals of integration. These indicators are especially interesting, since in the field of retail financial services the suppliers often have to locate close to their customers. This is the case for retail bank loans, deposits, and many insurance and investment products.

5 In simplest terms, and following the Markowitz portfolio theory, optimal diversification means choosing efficient portfolio weights, which minimize the variance of portfolio returns. This would require diversifying away individual country risks (including exchange rate risks) by spreading investment across countries.

However, especially the quantitative 'supply-side' indicators need to be interpreted very prudently. For instance, an entry by a foreign bank via the purchase of an existing local bank does not necessarily imply integration, as the acquired bank may continue to operate as before in the local market, and the pricing conditions will not necessarily converge across local markets. An error to the other direction of downplaying integration could be to claim that integration would only emerge when cross-border mergers occur. This idea seems quite widespread. In areas where cross-border acquisition of services is possible, or where the establishment in foreign markets can occur also through other means than mergers and acquisitions, integration can progress further. Nevertheless, it is true that in many retail financial services mergers and acquisitions are still the fastest and most effective way of gaining clientele and presence in new markets.

The problem with all quantitative indicators is that they do not represent conclusive evidence of integration and are thus weaker indicators than the price-based ones, for which the law-of-one price provides an absolute benchmark of full integration. Another problem is that these indicators cannot be linked with specific products, as typically financial services providers are *multi-product* firms. Indeed, in the predominant European universal banking model, banks offer a wide range of products and services. Given the tendency to form financial conglomerates, this includes increasingly insurance products. On the other hand, the markets for different financial services may exhibit different degrees of integration, which calls for a breakdown of the analysis into product categories, as is done in this book.

The next section discusses in more detail possible measures of integration that follow from the conceptual considerations set out above. They also focus in particular on those indicators that will be used in the subsequent Chapters to describe specific markets (money, credit, bond and equity markets) as well as various financial services.

Indicators of Financial Integration

Government Bond and Money Markets

As discussed above, full financial integration in the euro area would imply that assets that are comparable and available throughout the various jurisdictions of the euro area and generate identical cash flows trade at the same price in all countries of the area. In money and government bond markets, assets are often sufficiently comparable to permit the measurement of price differences directly as an indicator of the degree of integration.[6] Ideally, one should compare local yields with the risk-free rate that would prevail in a perfectly integrated financial market of the Monetary Union. Since this rate is unobservable in practice and swap-markets do not provide a completely risk-free rate either, most studies have used the *spread between the yield on a local asset and a well-chosen benchmark asset* as the second-best alternative.[7]

6 See e.g. Adam et al. (2002) and Bernard and Bisignano (2002).
7 See Adam et al. (2002), Adajaouté and Danthine (2003), and Baele et al. (2003).

For instance, in the 10-year government bond market in the euro area, German bonds are considered by market participants to be the reference bonds. Consequently, it seems reasonable to measure integration by calculating the difference between local yields and the one in Germany. While in perfectly integrated markets the spread should be equal to zero, the time variation in the size of the spread serves as an indicator of how integration is proceeding in a particular country and market. However, it should be notice that differences in liquidity as well as in perceived credit risks may imply that spreads could be different from zero and different across specific instruments in integrated markets.

A second useful measure is the *cross-sectional dispersion in bond yields*. This is calculated as at each point in time by taking the standard deviation of yields, e.g. across euro area countries. There exists an inverse relationship between cross-sectional dispersions and correlations. When series are highly correlated, as they should be in integrated markets, yields will generally move in the same direction, and the instantaneous cross-sectional dispersion will be low. Alternatively, dispersion will be high when yields in different countries drift apart. A variant of this measure is based on the cross-sectional dispersion in the spread relative to a benchmark asset (which also works outside the Monetary Union) (see Chapter 8). The aim is also to eliminate the effects due to the observed fact that interest rate volatility tends to be positively related with the level of interest rates.

For euro money markets, the problem of defining the risk-free benchmark yield does not exist, as this is defined by the ECB policy rates concerning the shortest maturities (see Chapter 7). For banks' unsecured money market borrowing (through depos and swaps), an useful indicator of integration is *the variance of average spreads by countries*, which should tend to zero, as major banks' creditworthiness should not have major country-specific components in the euro area. This is in particular the case, because the major money market banks have substantial international operations. Arbitrage should ensure that the law-of-one price applies. In this area, the set-up of ECB monetary policy auctions, which provides for equal access throughout the area, creates a vehicle for integration of the money market (see Scalia and Ordine, 2003). The country-averages should be even closer together as far as secured repo-rates are concerned, as there is no risk vis-à-vis the borrowing bank's creditworthiness.

Corporate Bond Markets

In corporate bond markets, the degree of integration cannot be analysed by using yield differentials relative to a benchmark as such, because corporate bonds are generally not homogeneous enough to allow such comparisons. Corporate bonds typically differ in their cash flow structure, liquidity, industry sector and, most importantly, their credit rating, or available probability of default estimates. For this reason, useful measures of integration must be derived from *models* that control for these other determinants of the bond returns.

For instance, Baele et al. (2003) investigated whether yields, once corrected for differences in systematic risk and other characteristics, still depend on the country, in which the bond was issued (see further Chapter 8). The authors estimated the following equation:

$$S^{i}_{c,r}(\tau,t,z_t)=\alpha_t+\sum_{r=1}^{K}\gamma_{r,t}CR^{r}_{i,t}+\sum_{s=1}^{2}\delta_{s,t}S^{s}_{i,t}+\varphi_t z_t+\sum_{c=1}^{N}\beta_{c,t}C_{i,c,t}+e_{i,t} \tag{1}$$

where $S^{i}_{c,r}(\tau,t,z_t)$ is the yield spread for corporate bond i – issued in country c with τ years to maturity and with credit rating r – from a benchmark government bond with identical time to maturity. Other factors, which may influence the rate investors require to hold a corporate bond at time t, like the structure of cash flows or the bond's liquidity, are grouped into a vector z_t. Additionally, α is an intercept common to all corporate bonds, CRrit,t is a rating dummy which takes a value of one when corporate bond i belongs to rating category r at time t, and *Ssi,t* is a sector dummy which takes a value of one for financial corporations and zero for non-financials. The parameter vector φ groups the sensitivities of the various corporate bonds to the instruments contained in *zt*, namely time to maturity, liquidity, and coupon of the ith bond. *Ci,c,t* is a country dummy that equals one when corporate bond i belongs to country c at time t, and zero otherwise.

In an integrated corporate bond market, yield spreads, once corrected for systematic risk, should not depend on the country of issue. Consequently, a measure of the degree of integration in the corporate bond market is given by the *size of the coefficients of the various country dummies*. More precisely, a test for integration is to check whether the country parameters, $\beta_{c,t}$, are zero, or at least converge towards zero.

Equity Markets

As noted above, an important implication of integration is that the returns on similarly risky assets should only react to common factors across the euro area. This idea underlies indirect *news-based measures,* which aim at disentangling the effects of new information on different shocks from other market frictions. Bekaert and Harvey (1997) showed that the proportion of the local equity market variance that is explained by common news is positively related to the degree of financial integration.

Baele et al. (2003) estimated a (time varying) shock spillover model where the stock return for a particular country i, $R_{i,t}$, has an expected component $\mu_{i,t}$ and an unexpected part $\varepsilon_{i,t}$: $R_{i,t} = \mu_{i,t} + \varepsilon_{i,t}$. The local 'surprise' return $\varepsilon_{i,t}$ is decomposed into a local shock ($\varepsilon_{i,t}$), and a reaction to respectively euro area ($\varepsilon_{eu,t}$) and world news, where the latter is proxied by innovations in the US stock market ($\varepsilon_{us,t}$):

$$\varepsilon_{i,t}=e_{i,t}+\beta^{eu}_{i,t}\varepsilon_{eu,t}+\beta^{us}_{i,t}\varepsilon_{us,t} \tag{2}$$

While all countries share the same two factors, they are allowed to have different sensitivities, or $\beta_{eui,t}$ and $\beta_{usi,t}$, to common shocks. When markets become more integrated, one should expect euro area-wide risk factors to become more important, relative to purely local news. Consequently, *the beta coefficients are, ceteris paribus, expected to be higher in integrated than in segmented markets.* Additionally, an alternative measure of integration is based on the variance ratios, i.e. *the proportion of total domestic equity volatility explained by euro area and US shocks.*

The law-of-one-price also argues that, as equity markets become more integrated, the country-specific component in equity returns should decrease while the industry sector component should increase in importance. In this respect, a measure of integration is given by the *relative importance of the cross-sectional standard deviation in sector vis-à-vis country index returns*. A shift from country to sector diversification would mean that the cross-sectional dispersion in country returns would decrease below the dispersion in sector returns.[8] A large number of papers have examined the importance of country and industry effects in explaining equity returns by using the approach obtained from the portfolio theory.[9] The results of these studies, however, much depend on the specification of the asset-pricing model.

The above indicators for financial markets draw on observed (equilibrium) market prices and the law-of-one-price. However, quantity-based indicators can also be used as secondary measures of integration, such as the share of assets invested in bond and equity funds with a cross-border or European-wide investment strategy (see Adam et al., 2002).

Further important insight into the integration of the capital markets can be obtained by adopting the perspective of corporate finance services, i.e. the way firms obtain underwriting and other services related to their capital market operations (see Chapter 4). This approach is especially useful for corporate debt and equity issues, as the instruments could be weakly traded and heterogeneous in terms of risk. In an integrated market, the services facilitating firms' market access should be equally priced, given the risks accruing to the underwriting financial institution. Looking also at these issues – in addition to market prices – can bring in substantial further insight how the area-wide market functions and whether the access conditions to capital markets are symmetric.

Finally, the organization and functioning of the trading and settlement functions might reveal significant barriers to entry. High costs for foreign investors and issuers in their access to foreign trading and settlement systems could constitute a major obstacle to the integration of financial markets.

Financial Services

Data on banks' *underwriting fees* and *margins* on lending rates and deposit rates, and their convergence, can be computed and used as indicators of integration as discussed above (see Chapter 4). For most other retail financial services, data are often scarce to allow for the construction of comprehensive price-based measures of integration.

To the existing data, also an indicator called *sigma-convergence* can be applied. Sigma-convergence occurs if the cross-sectional (here cross-country) distribution of a variable decreases over time. The value for sigma-convergence (σ) for the euro area is obtained by running OLS regressions with the cross-country standard deviation

8 Adjaouté and Danthine (2003) measure the relative importance of country and sector effects by simply calculating the cross-sectoral dispersion in country and sector returns, respectively. The higher the cross-sectional dispersion, the lower the correlations, and the higher the diversification potential. Ferreira and Gamma (2002) use a different approach based on a decomposition of return volatility into sectoral and regional components.

9 See e.g. Beakaert and Harvey (1997) and Hardouvelis et al. (2002a and 2002b).

(std_{it}) of the interest rate considered as the dependent variable and the linear time trend (t) as the explanatory variable:

$$std_{i,t} = \alpha_0 + \sigma t + e_{i,t} \tag{3}$$

If the cross-sectional sigma-convergence falls to zero, full integration is achieved.

The studies analysing the *homogeneity of the transmission of the monetary policy impulses to bank lending and deposit rates* provide indirect evidence of the degree of integration, since in fully integrated markets competition conditions should be equalized. The reason is that the elasticity of the banks' rates vis-à-vis the changes in the monetary policy rates is determined by the degree of competition, such that the more competitive the banking system the faster the pass-though of the policy rates into banks' rates (see Vesala, 2001). A number of studies have looked at this transmission, also investigating the existing cross-country differences in the speed of the transmission.[10]

Given the substantial heterogeneity of many financial services, we are largely compelled to resort to the more ambiguous quantity-based indicators of integration. There are various types of indicators, which can be used for different financial services, also taking into account their specific features (see Chapter 4).

First, in the larger market, the capacity of international distribution could carry a heavier weight than before, eroding the franchises of national intermediaries previously operated in the distribution of products and services. For instance, the knowledge of local market conditions and investor bases may not be as big an advantage for domestic institutions. In an integrating market, the nationality of an intermediary and the client (issuer firm or a wholesale or retail investor) should become less important. Thus, *the importance of foreign intermediaries in capital market services or cross-border acquisition of financial services constitute indicators of integration.*

Second, *increasing portfolio diversification by institutional investors* (mutual and pension funds and insurance companies) *across borders* constitutes an indicator of integration and signals reducing home bias. In light of the portfolio theory, substantial shares of domestic assets in investors' portfolios cannot be justified in integrated markets with non-prohibitive transaction costs. The distribution of the assets of wholesale investment funds (mutual and pension funds) constitutes evidence of further integration as regards the capital market-related leg of the activity. It also gives indication of the portfolios of the retail investors, who increasingly invest via large collective investment vehicles, even though the retail interface with the final investor could still remain largely local. To the extent available, data on *the cross-border holdings of securities by households and firms* would naturally be useful indicators of integration.

Third, *cross-border branching by financial institutions* provides a supply-side indication of widening possibilities for local users of financial services. However, foreign branches of financial institutions so far often concentrate on corporate finance services, trading activities and private banking, rather than retail activities.

10 The ECB has lately published a series of working papers studying the monetary policy transmission. See, for instance, Angeloni et al. (2003) based on pre-EMU data and Angeloni and Ehrmann (2003) based on post-EMU data.

Retail businesses are much more difficult to enter; domestic banks enjoy substantial competitive advantages because of their widespread branch distribution networks. Thus, the most effective way of gaining access to the retail sector has been to merge with or acquire an existing local bank. For this reason, *the market share of foreign-owned institutions* and *the number and value of cross-border M&A's* can constitute useful indicators of integration.

Finally, technological changes in the financial industry, in particular *the spread and use of remote access options* to financial services can provide indications of integration. Such possibilities allow customers to by-pass their local service providers and allow competitive forces to push prices to converge. Consequently, if technology allows for a wider competition in a larger integrated market area, local branch delivery networks (Vesala, 2001) or local market concentration (Corvosier and Gropp 2001) should not determine banks' pricing.

Integration, Competition and Efficiency

Despite being two different concepts, integration and competition are linked in the sense that advancing integration is likely to generate more competition. Competition refers to the pricing behaviour of firms in a given market. Increasing competition implies that firms' profit margins decrease to the benefit of consumers. This can occur if the number of suppliers in the market increases (as in the standard Cournot oligopoly model), or if the threat of new entry becomes more realistic (as in the model of contestable markets).[11]

Integration implies that competition is extended from a particular market (the local level) to a larger set of markets (the European level), which generally leads to an increase in the number of competing firms. In addition, a higher degree of competition can be achieved through the increased ease of entry under the single market and single currency conditions. Indeed, reducing the barriers to entry and fostering integration has been pursued as a major policy objective because of the significant economic benefits of increased competition.[12]

Competition is most commonly measured against the benchmark of *perfect competition*, in which the number of firms operating in a market is high and price equals marginal cost. There are few studies which address the degree of competition in the European banking markets using the methods of empirical industrial economics.[13] It is rather difficult to implement this benchmark in financial services, again on account of product heterogeneity. The paradigm of contestable markets may be more appropriate, since it is applicable to differentiated products and recognizes that the extent of competition may be unrelated to the number of suppliers in a given market.

A *perfectly contestable market* is one in which there are no excessive barriers to entry or exit. If the barriers are not prohibitively high, incumbent firms will not be in

11 The literature on repeated games also recognizes the possibility of occasional price wars among the existing set of firms as part of a collusion enforcement mechanism.

12 See e.g. Obstfeld (1994), and Martin and Rey (2000).

13 See e.g. Corvoisier and Gropp (2001), and Bikker et al. (2000). Vesala (2001) presents a review of such methodologies.

a position to charge excessively high prices (above marginal cost) to customers, even in concentrated local markets, since this would attract new entry. Perfect contestability does not require actual entry, but simply the discipline exerted by potential competitors on the pricing behaviour of the established firms. However, any empirical evidence pointing to contestable markets must be interpreted prudently as a signal of greater competition, as consumers need to benefit from new entrants. This may not necessarily happen in all acquisitions of local firms by foreign financial institutions, for instance.

Increasing *efficiency* is related to more competition:[14] as is well known, competitive pressure forces suppliers to reduce costs in relation to the output produced (exploit scale economies and avoid waste). Competition also supports the dynamic innovation process in the financial industry, improving the allocation of funds and risk-sharing opportunities. Competition and efficiency are also the ultimate objectives of the policies supporting further integration.

In an environment such as the European one where countries present various degrees of financial development, it is often argued that there is scope for financial integration to increase flows of funds for investment opportunities in some regions. This should be the case whenever financial integration eases the access to investment opportunities in these regions, if they are relatively more productive than foreign ones. With additional funds flowing in, further financial development of these regions appears plausible, as discussed in Giannetti et al. (2002). There, the authors argue that the process of integration will not only increase competition within less developed regions, but also improve the efficiency of their financial systems, by reducing for instance the costs of intermediation.

Concluding Remarks

This Chapter has attempted to contrast the normative and positive approaches to defining integration, arguing that both have their places, but the positive approach is needed for actually judging whether we have achieved, or how far we are from full financial integration. Moreover, for this purpose only the law-of-one-price and the consequent indicators based on observable market prices can really be used.

However, a large number of financial assets and services do not lend themselves to applying the law-of-one-price – either due to heterogeneity across assets and service providers, or lack of high quality data. Therefore, a more comprehensive, even an eclectic, approach looking at market quantities and structures is also justified and useful. As discussed above, judging the integration in financial markets can be based to a relatively larger extent on the price-based measures, while in financial services on the more ambiguous quantity-based indicators.

When carrying out such an eclectic analysis, a wide range of data sources can be used case-by-case to make judgement of the degree of integration, with varying

14 Industrial economics distinguishes three major aspects of efficiency: scale efficiency, avoidance of waste ('X-efficiency'), and dynamic efficiency (referring to the dynamic innovation process in the market). Competition fosters all these aspects of efficiency.

degrees of conclusiveness. In doing so, close attention is also paid to the types of institutions providing financial services. However, great care must be given not to over-interpret the results and to jointly evaluate the different interpretations of the data, which is particularly needed in the case of supply-side indicators drawing on the ideas of the contestable markets theory.

References

Adam, K., T. Jappelli, A. Menichini, M. Padula, and M. Pagano (2002), *Analyse, Compare, and Apply Alternative Indicators and Monitoring Methodologies to Measure the Evolution of Capital Market Integration in the European Union*, Centre for Studies in Economics and Finance (CSEF), University of Salerno.

Adjaouté, K., and J.-P. Danthine (2003), 'European Financial Integration and Equity Returns: A Theory-Based Assessment', in Gaspar V., Hartmann P. and Sleijpen O. (eds) *The Transformation of the European Financial System*, Frankfurt, pp. 186–245.

Allen F. and D. Gale (1997), 'Financial Markets, Intermediaries and Intertemporal Smoothing', *Journal of Political Economy*, 105, 523–546.

Angeloni, I., A. Kashyap, B. Mojon and D. Terlizzese, (2003), 'The Output Composition Puzzle: a Difference in the Monetary Transmission Mechanism in the Euro Area and the U.S.', *Journal of Money Credit and Banking*.

Angeloni I. and M. Ehrmann (2003), *Monetary Policy Transmission in the Euro Area: Any Changes after EMU?*, ECB Working Paper, 240.

Baele, L., A. Ferrando, P. Hordahl, E. Krylova, and C. Monnet (2003), *Measuring the Integration of Euro Area Capital Markets*, forthcoming Occasional Paper, European Central Bank.

Bekaert, G., and C. R. Harvey (1997), 'Emerging Equity Market Volatility', *Journal of Financial Economics* 43, pp. 29–77.

Bernard, H. and J. Bisignano (2002), 'European Financial Market Integration: Concepts, Measurement, and Contribution to Growth', unpublished manuscript, BIS.

Bikker, J. and H. Groeneveld (2000), 'Competition and Concentration in the EU Banking Industry', *Kredit-und-Kapital*, 33 (1), pp. 62–98.

Cabral, I., F. Dierick, and J. Vesala (2002), *Banking Integration in the Euro Area*, ECB Occasional Paper Series, 6, December.

Corvosier, S. and R. Gropp (2001), *Bank Concentration and Retail Interest Rates*, ECB Working Paper, 72.

Ferreira, Miguel A. and Paulo M. Gama (2002), *The Developed Market's Stock Portfolio Volatility: An Investigation of Country and Sector Idiosyncratic Risk*, Working paper, ISCTE Business School (Lisbon) and University of Coimbra.

Giannetti M., L. Guiso, T. Jappelli, M. Padula and M. Pagano (2002), *Financial Market Integration, Corporate Financing and Economic Growth*, Economic Papers of the European Commission, n.179.

Hardouvelis, Gikas, Dimitrios Malliaropulos, and Richard Priestley (2000a), *EMU and European Stock Market Integration*, CEPR Discussion Paper No. 2124.

Hardouvelis, Gikas, Dimitrios Malliaropulos, and Richard Priestley (2000b), *The Impact of Globalization on the Equity Cost of Capital*, Working Paper.

London Economics (2002), *Quantification of the Macro-Economic Impact of Integration of EU Financial Markets*, Report for the European Commission's Directorate-General for the Internal Market.

Martin, P. and H. Rey (2000), 'Financial Integration and Asset Returns', *European Economic Review* 44, pp. 1327–1350.

Obstfeld, M. (1994), 'Risk-taking, Global Diversification, and Growth', *American Economic Review*, 84 (5), pp. 1310–1329.

Padoa-Schioppa, T. (2000), 'Is a Euroland Banking System already Emerging?', SUERF Marjolin Lecture, April.

Rousseau, P. (2002), *Historical Perspectives on Financial Development and Economic Growth*, NBER Working Paper 9333.

Scalia, A. and Ordine, M. (2002), 'New Evidence on Money Market Integration in the Euro Area: A Panel Data Study on Banks' Participation in the Eurosystem Auctions', mimeo, Banca d'Italia.

Vesala, J. (2001), 'Technological Transformation and Retail Banking Competition: Implications and Measurement', *Bank of Finland Studies*, E: 20.

Chapter 4

EU Policies to Support Financial Integration

Frank Dierick

Introduction

Chapter 3 has discussed how the achievement of financial integration implies the removal of financial and non-financial barriers to the optimal exploitation of the economies of scale and scope issuing from this integration. In this chapter we show how this process requires an effective interplay between market forces, collective action within the market to overcome coordination problems, and action by public authorities. The focus will be on the initiatives pursued by the EU public authorities to foster financial integration.

The chapter is organized as follows. The second section reviews the major institutional steps that have been taken since the Treaty of Rome to foster financial integration, such as the Single Market Programme, the Financial Services Action Plan and the Economic and Monetary Union. The third section turns then to the most important EU institutions and committees that are involved in the process of integration, while the fourth section reviews the legislative tools and procedures that are used by them to achieve their objectives. The fifth section briefly presents the main European regulatory measures that have been taken over the past years in the different financial sectors (banking, securities and insurance). The arrangements for regulation and supervision of these sectors are presently undergoing major changes, as is discussed in the sixth section. Also in the area of competition policy, and in particular that of merger and state aid control, Community initiatives have a major impact on the process of integration as is demonstrated in the seventh section. The chapter concludes with a brief overview of the most recent legal initiatives to foster financial integration.

Major Institutional Steps towards Financial Integration

The Period before the Single Market Programme

The starting point of the institutional process towards economic and financial integration is the Treaty of Rome (1957), which created the European Economic Community.[1] The Treaty provides for the progressive establishment of an internal

1 See also Footnote 2 of Chapter 2.

market within the Community, an area without internal frontiers and characterized by four basic freedoms: free movement of goods, persons, services and capital. It also created a set of institutions and legislative tools that are important in the process of financial integration, and which are discussed in more detail in the following two sections.[2]

All in all, relatively few additional steps were undertaken in the period before the Single Market Programme to foster financial integration. In the area of financial services there are foremost the First Banking Directive (1977), which established a list of common authorization criteria for a credit institution, and the Banks' Annual Accounts Directive (1986), which harmonized the financial disclosures by banks in their annual accounts. As capital markets are concerned, several directives were adopted related to listed companies (harmonization of listing conditions, disclosure requirements). In the insurance area, a first generation of directives realized the freedom of establishment.

The Single Market Programme

The Treaty of Rome already contained the basic principles for the creation of a single European market for financial services. In practice, however, the formation of the single market continued to be hampered by divergent national financial regulations. A major step in the further opening-up of cross-border competition was the Single European Act (1986) which provided for the completion of the single market by the end of 1992. A necessary condition for the development of a single market in financial services is the free movement of capital. The Capital Liberalization Directive (1988) therefore committed the Member States to the removal of controls over cross-border capital movements, such as exchange controls. Most Member States had to achieve this objective from 1 July 1990 onwards.

The single market for financial services relies on the building blocks of the single licence or passport, home country control and mutual recognition. Under these principles, a financial firm that is operating in another Member State (host country) is supervised by the authority in the country of origin where it has obtained its authorization (home country). A bank incorporated in a particular Member State may, directly or indirectly, provide services across EU borders on the basis of a single licence issued by the authority of its home country and under this authority's control. However, several areas, in particular those relating to consumer protection, competition and other conduct-of-business rules, continue to be covered by the host country's rules. In addition, the so-called 'general good' exception allows the host country to apply its own rules 'for imperative reasons relating to the general good'. This exception is subject to the conditions established by the Court of Justice. Home country control and mutual recognition can only work when the Member States' national laws reflect minimum common standards, which is achieved through minimum

2 The Treaty of Rome, now known as the Treaty establishing the European Community or the EC Treaty, has since 1992 become part of the wider Treaty on the European Union (EU). Over time, it has also undergone several amendments, in particular through the Single European Act (1986), the Treaty of Maastricht (1992), the Treaty of Amsterdam (1997) and, most recently, the Treaty of Nice (2001).

harmonization at the European level. A more detailed overview of the major legislative measures taken to support financial integration in the different financial sectors are mentioned in the fifth section.

Finally, there is an Agreement on the European Economic Area (1994), which permits the non-EU EEA countries (Iceland, Liechtenstein and Norway) to participate in certain aspects of the European integration, but without participating in certain political aspects. In this way, the legal rules governing financial integration in the twenty-five EU Member States are extended to three more European countries.

The Economic and Monetary Union (EMU)

With the Treaty of Maastricht (1992), a very significant step for the advancement of financial integration was taken as Member States agreed to establish an economic and monetary union (EMU) from 1999 onwards, including the setting-up of the European Central Bank (ECB). With this aim, a three-phase transition period, spread out over ten years, was introduced. Stage One (1990–93) provided for the freedom of capital flows and the coordination of national monetary policies. Stage Two (1994–98) called for the creation of the European Monetary Institute (EMI), which would prepare for what became later the European System of Central Banks (ESCB). Finally, Stage Three would lead to EMU (1999). The adoption of the euro enhanced price transparency, eliminated the need for foreign exchange transactions within the euro area, and led to broader, deeper and more liquid securities markets. In addition, it facilitated a reorganization of the Community financial infrastructure, such as payment and securities settlement systems.

The road towards the single European currency or euro had been mapped in the earlier Delors report (1989). This report started from the belief that the development of the single market necessitated more effective coordination of economic policy between national authorities. It also pointed out that with full freedom of capital movements and integrated financial markets, incompatible national policies would quickly translate into exchange rate tensions and put an undue burden on monetary policy.

The Financial Services Action Plan (FSAP)

Despite the successful implementation of the core directives, obstacles of various nature to the integration of financial services continued to exist. In 1999 the European Commission identified a number of areas in which action was required in order to complete financial integration. This took the form of the Financial Services Action Plan (FSAP), covering policy initiatives to be implemented by 2005 in the areas of financial law, regulation and supervision, and taxation.[3] Priority was given to securities markets legislation in order to achieve an integrated securities market by 2003. The FSAP's strategic aim is to create fully integrated wholesale banking and capital markets, to develop open and secure markets for retail financial services, and ensure state-of-the-art prudential rules. Several initiatives are already under way to

3 For a detailed overview of the initiatives, see European Commission (1999).

pursue these objectives. Many important initiatives have already been launched with a view of achieving these objectives. In order to assist the Commission in its work on the FSAP, a Financial Services Policy Group, composed of representatives of ministries of finance and chaired by the Commission, was created (see next section).

Before the FSAP, the European Commission had already launched a wide-ranging initiative to promote the development of a pan-European risk capital market. This Risk Capital Action Plan (RCAP) was adopted in 1998 and later, it was agreed that the plan should be completed by 2003. The Plan identifies six types of barriers holding back European risk capital markets, i.e. market fragmentation, institutional and regulatory barriers, taxation, paucity of high-tech SMEs (small and medium-sized enterprises) in the EU, human resources and cultural barriers. The RCAP further lists the elements to remove these barriers. The euro and the Stability and Growth Pact were additional catalysts for the creation of an integrated risk capital market, *inter alia* by removing currency matching requirements for institutional investors and diminished borrowing by public authorities on capital markets. The initiatives proposed in the RCAP directly related to financial services legislation were taken up in the FSAP.

In the context of the Financial Services Action Plan (FSAP), especially the adoption of the Pension Funds Directive and the Directive on Prospectuses in 2003 have to be mentioned as contributions to the development of the market for risk capital. The first one introduces the principle of home-country control in the area of institutions for occupational retirement provision (IORPs) and allows them to operate in a more liberal environment, including the possibility to invest a significant amount of their resources in risk-capital markets. As a result, pension funds may become more important sources of risk capital funds, as is currently the case in the US. The second Directive upgrades the existing prospectus rules in order to achieve effective mutual recognition of equity offering prospectuses, which should facilitate the cross-border raising of risk capital.

As the legislative phase for the FSAP draws to a close, the Commission has taken the initiative to undertake a systematic assessment of the state of integration of European financial markets. This post FSAP work is not the prelude to a new comprehensive legal package, but is rather an effort to identify specific areas where carefully targeted legislation might be further required. In the autumn of 2004, the Commission is expected to publish its conclusions resulting from a wide consultation process.

EU Institutions Involved in the Work on Financial Integration

The European Parliament, Council, Commission and Court of Justice

There are four major EU institutions which derive their powers from Treaties and that are directly involved, among other things, in issues of financial integration: the European Parliament, the Council of the European Union, the European Commission and the European Court of Justice. These institutions have been created by one of the European Community Treaties to carry out the tasks entrusted to them.

The *European Parliament* is an assembly that is democratically elected by the EU citizens. It has three main roles: (i) the power to legislate, which it shares with the

Council; (ii) the democratic supervision over all EU institutions, and in particular the Commission; (iii) the exercise of authority over the EU budget, which it shares with the Council. The legislative power is especially important in the process of financial integration.

The *Council of the European Union* is composed of one minister for each Member State government and for each subject area. For example, in the area of economic and financial affairs it is the ECOFIN Council, which is composed of the Member States' Finance and Economic Affairs Ministers. If the Council meets at the level of the presidents and prime ministers to decide on the major policy guidelines, it is called the European Council. The Council is the main decision-making body in the EU and takes most of its decisions by qualified majority, meaning that a minimum number of votes is required for a proposal to be adopted, although unanimity is still required for some areas like taxation. Under the so-called 'co-decision procedure' (see below), the Council lays down, together with the European Parliament, the EU rules in the area of the single market.

The *European Commission* consists of twenty-five Commissioners that are appointed by the Member States, but once appointed they act independently of them. The Commission makes proposals for EU legislation, where it has the sole right of initiative (except for certain policy areas unrelated to the internal market). It further makes sure that EU decisions are properly implemented, supervises the way EU funds are spent and oversees the EU common policy. In fact, the Commission is involved in much of the day-to-day work related to the EU. For this purpose, each Commissioner heads an administration dealing with a particular subject matter, for example internal market issues or competition policy.

Finally, the *Court of Justice of the European Communities* is the supreme court of the EU. It ensures that EU treaties and legislation are interpreted and applied correctly by other EU institutions and by the Member States. Judgements of the Court in the field of EC law are binding on EU institutions, Member States, national courts, companies, and private citizens, and they overrule those of national courts.

The ECB, ESCB and Eurosystem

Apart from these main institutions, the role of the central bank community should be highlighted since a major impetus for further financial integration came with the introduction of the single currency. The institutional structure of the ECB, ESCB and Eurosystem is discussed more in detail in Chapter 2. In this section, the focus is on why they are interested in financial integration and how they contribute to it.

The interest of the ECB, and its support for integration initiatives, can be interpreted in the light of Article 105 of the EC Treaty, which states that without prejudice to the objective of price stability, the ESCB shall support the general economic policies in the Community. In addition, the ECB has a particular interest in the further integration of Europe's financial system as the latter is central to a smooth and effective transmission of monetary policy. Another reason relates to the ESCB's task to promote the smooth operation of payment systems. Integration, in particular at the level of infrastructure, may be instrumental in facilitating the pursuit of this objective. Finally, financial integration is related to financial stability, and the ESCB has a responsibility to contribute to the smooth conduct of policies pursued by the competent authorities relating to this area. A larger and more diversified financial system will be better able to absorb economic shocks than financial systems in individual countries. On the other hand, high integration may also increase the risk of cross-border contagion.

The ECB provides active support to financial integration, which can take the form of (i) direct action, (ii) acting as a catalyst for collective action and (iii) contributing to raising the awareness of the need for integration. Direct action is undertaken in the areas where the ECB has an immediate competence. The establishment of TARGET (the EU-wide large-value payment system operated by the ESCB), for example, was instrumental in the integration of the unsecured money market.

Owing to its particular institutional position, being both a public authority with a pan-European scope and a market participant, the ECB is well positioned to complement and support the action of other parties to promote financial integration. In this regard, the advisory role entrusted by the EC Treaty to the ECB is particularly noteworthy, as the ECB's advice can contribute to the integration of financial markets, in particular from a regulatory and legal point of view. In some instances, the EC Treaty or the ESCB Statute provide explicitly for a mission of harmonization and/or integration. This is for example the case for statistics in the areas that fall within the ECB's field of competence.

The action of the ECB to foster financial integration is equally channelled through its participation in a number of EU committees such as those discussed below. Beyond its cooperation with other public authorities, the ECB also acts in partnership with the private sector to foster collective action. An illustration of this is the development of the EONIA (euro overnight index average) interest rate and the neutral role the ECB plays in fixing this rate as a service to the banking sector.

The forums in which the ECB cooperates with third parties to raise awareness of issues related to financial integration extend to the academic sector. For example, a research network was established in cooperation with academia in order to stimulate policy-relevant research that aims to contribute towards understanding the current and future integration and structure of the financial system in Europe.[4]

Other Entities

The EC Treaty provided for the establishment of the Economic and Financial Committee (EFC) at the start of Stage Three of EMU. The EFC, whose predecessor body was the Monetary Committee, is a special consultative Community body (in particular to the ECOFIN Council) in which the Member States, the European Commission and the ECB are represented. Its tasks include reviewing the economic and financial situation of the Member States and of the EU. More recently, the EFC has been more frequently involved in issues relating to financial integration and supervision in the EU.

In 2003, the ECOFIN Council replaced the Financial Services Policy Group with the Financial Services Committee (FSC). The FSC continues to consist of senior finance ministry officials, but is now chaired by a Member State representative. The

4 ECB-CFS Financial Research Network http://www.eu-financial-system.org/ecbcfs.html.

ECB and the relevant Community committees of regulators (see below) have an observer status. The FSC's function is to provide advice and oversight for the ECOFIN Council and the Commission on the medium- and long-term strategy for financial market issues. This includes a range of matters, such as those relating to the implementation of the FSAP.

Legislative Tools and their Implementation

Types of Legislative Tools

Community law is composed of three different – but interdependent – types of legislation: primary legislation, secondary legislation and case-law. Together they form the so-called *acquis communautaire*. Primary legislation is agreed by direct negotiation between Member State governments. It consists foremost of the Treaties establishing the European Communities, which have been revised several times (see second section of this chapter). Secondary legislation is based on the Treaties and can take the form of regulations, directives, decisions, recommendations and opinions. They can be adopted by (i) the European Parliament acting together with the Council, (ii) the Council separately, and (iii) the Commission separately. Finally, the case-law includes judgements of the European Court of Justice and of the more recently established European Court of First Instance.

Of the secondary legislation, regulations and directives have in principle general legal validity. Regulations are binding in their entirety, and are directly applicable in the Member States so they do not require a transposition into national law. Regulations do not allow for amendment or supplementation by a Member State's legislature. Directives, on the other hand, are binding upon the Member States in terms of the results to be achieved, but Member States are free to choose the best forms and methods for implementation. Decisions are binding upon those to whom they are addressed – Member States, natural and/or legal persons. Recommendations and opinions are advisory in nature and are not legally binding.

The Legislative Process

At the EU level, the Commission has the power to initiate legislative measures. Originally, these were adopted by the Council, with the European Parliament having initially only an advisory role. The Maastricht Treaty introduced the co-decision procedure, whose scope of application was later extended. It has now become by far the most important element in the legislative process. Under the co-decision procedure, the legislative power is shared between the Council and the European Parliament, with the intervention of a conciliation committee in the event of disagreement between the two institutions. Only instruments of general validity, i.e. regulations and directives, are subject to the co-decision procedure. It further applies to certain policy areas, in particular (but not only) to the single market.

Under the EC Treaty, the Commission has the responsibility for implementing legislation at Community level. In this process, it may neither amend nor supplement the Council instrument. Compliance is assured through the intervention of committees ("comitology' procedure), as is explained further below. When the European Parliament has been involved in the adoption of a legislative instrument through the co-decision procedure, it can intervene in the implementation process through reasoned opinions if the planned implementation measure exceeds the scope of the instrument.

In practice, each legislative instrument specifies the scope of the implementing powers granted to the Commission and how these are to be used. Frequently, the instrument will also make provision for the Commission to be assisted by a committee in accordance with a procedure known as 'comitology'. The committees, which consist of representatives from Member States, enable the Commission to establish a dialogue with national administrations before adopting implementing measures. Procedures which govern relations between the Commission and these committees are based on models set out in a Council decision. The committees can act in an advisory, management or regulatory capacity. Advisory committees give their opinions to the Commission which must take the utmost account of them, without being bound. By contrast, when the intervention of a regulatory committee is provided for, the Commission can adopt implementing measures only if it obtains the approval by this committee. In the absence of such support, the proposed measure is referred back to the Council which takes a decision by qualified majority. However, if the Council does not take a decision, the Commission finally adopts the implementing measure provided that the Council does not object. As discussed more in detail below, these committees play an important role in the financial regulatory process.

Major Regulatory Measures to Support Financial Integration

Over the past years, many European regulatory measures were taken to foster financial integration in the areas of banking, securities and insurance. Without aiming to be comprehensive, the main initiatives are here briefly mentioned.

In banking, a major step was taken with the Second Banking Directive (1988), which developed for the banking sector the principles of a single licence, home country control and mutual recognition. This directive has now been integrated into the Directive relating to the Taking-up and Pursuit of the Business of Credit Institutions, also called the codified Banking Directive (2000). This latter directive, which forms the cornerstone for European banking regulation, incorporates also a number of other directives, in particular:

- the First Banking Directive (1977), harmonizing the authorization criteria for a credit institution;
- the Own Funds Directive (1989), harmonizing the definition of own funds that can be used to meet regulatory solvency requirements;
- the Solvency Directive (1989), harmonizing solvency requirements for banks;
- the Banking Consolidation Directive (1992), introducing supervision on a consolidated basis for banking groups;
- the Large Exposures Directive (1992), limiting bank exposures to individual or related counterparties.

Also in 1988, the Capital Account Liberalization Directive was adopted so that exchange controls or other forms of interference with capital mobility could no longer create obstacles to cross-border banking. Other important measurers in the banking area are the Directive on Deposit-Guarantee Schemes (1994), introducing minimum harmonization conditions for such schemes, and the Banking Winding-Up Directive (2001), creating a mutual recognition regime regarding insolvency proceedings for credit institutions.

In the securities area, there is foremost the Investment Services Directive or ISD (1993). The ISD can be considered as the equivalent of the Second Banking Directive as it introduces a single licence, minimum harmonization and mutual recognition for investment firms. Minimum rules for investor-compensation schemes were adopted in 1997 in order to protect investors following the failure of such a firm. A common framework for the operation and pan-European marketing of investment funds was established with the so-called UCITS Directive (1985), where the acronym UCITS stands for 'undertakings for collective investment in transferable securities'. The framework was later updated by extending the set of UCITS that can be sold on a cross-border basis (UCITS II Directive, 2001) and by establishing simplified prospectus rules and a single passport for managers of UCITS (UCITS III Directive, 2001). Several initiatives were also taken to harmonize the conditions for the admission of securities to official stock exchange listing and on information to be published; the existing measures were later coordinated and codified in one directive (2001).

For the insurance business, there were until recently six major directives, three for life insurance (1979, 1990, 1992) and three for non-life insurance (1973, 1988, 1992). The three directives in each area correspond to a different stage in the development of an internal market in insurance (Cecchini et al., 2003). In the first stage, insurance undertakings were allowed to open up subsidiaries and branches across the EU but were subject to the control of the authority of the host country. In the second stage, insurance business could be performed on a cross-border basis without the need to have a branch or subsidiary. For most activities, the host country control continued to exist. In the third stage, the principles of the single licence, minimum harmonization and home country control were generally established and price and product regulations were abolished. With the recent adoption of the Life Directive (2002), the rules set out in the three previous Life Directives have been consolidated. In addition, there are a number of other important insurance directives, including the Insurance Groups Directive (1998), the Insurance Winding-Up Directive (2001) and the Insurance Mediation Directive (2002).

Finally, some Directives have a cross-sectoral dimension, such as:

- the Anti-Money Laundering Directive (1991), adopted to prevent the financial system being used for the purpose of money laundering;
- the Post-BCCI Directive (1995), addressing corporate structures in regulated firms that may impede the consolidated supervision;
- the Capital Adequacy Directives (1993, 1998), dealing with capital requirements for market risk incurred by both banks and investment firms;
- the Financial Conglomerates Directive (2002), introducing a supplementary supervisory regime for groups that combine banking/investment services and insurance.

Prudential Regulation and Supervision

Before Adoption of the 'Lamfalussy (2001)' Framework

Although from an economic point of view European financial markets and institutions have become more integrated and inter-linked, the actual supervision of financial institutions and markets is still the prerogative of national authorities. In particular, the divergence in national rules and supervisory practices can cause a major cost burden and hamper integration.[5] In order to remove potential obstacles of a regulatory and supervisory nature to further financial integration, several institutional arrangements were set in place to promote information exchange and co-operation between national authorities. Table 4.1 provides an overview of the committee structure prevailing in the financial sector before the implementation of the so-called Lamfalussy approach.[6] Some of these committees, such as the Banking Advisory Committee, perform an advisory and/or regulatory function under the 'comitology' procedure (see fourth section of this chapter).

Table 4.1 Institutional arrangements for regulation and supervision (pre-Lamfalussy)

Banking	Securities and UCITS	Insurance and occupational pensions	Financial conglomerates
• Banking Advisory Committee (BAC) • Groupe de Contact • The ESCB's Banking Supervision Committee (BSC)	• High Level Securities Supervisors Committee • Forum of European Securities Commissions (FESCO) • Securities Contact Committee • UCITS Contact Committee	• Insurance Committee (IC) • Conference of Insurance Supervisors (CIS)	• Mixed Technical Group (MTG)

5 The dispersion of the supervisory structures also raises issues regarding maintaining financial stability through adequate cross-border cooperation, but these issues fall beyond the scope of this chapter (see e.g. Padoa-Schioppa, 2002 and Kremers et al., 2003).

6 See Committee of Wise Men's Final Report on the regulation of European Securities Markets delivered to the ECOFIN council in 2001.

The 'Lamfalussy (2001)' Framework

A comprehensive review of the EU arrangements for financial regulation, supervision and stability has been carried out in the recent past. The review, which will rationalize the EU institutional financial architecture, was initially triggered by the report of the 'Lamfalussy' Committee (also called 'Committee of Wise Men") on the regulation of European securities markets (see footnote 6). The aim of the Lamfalussy report's recommendations was to increase the speed and efficiency of the European regulatory and supervisory system in order for it to remain effective, and to reduce the burden caused by national divergences.

In order to achieve these aims, a four-level approach to regulation and supervision is introduced. The first level is comprised of high-level legal principles to be laid down in European directives or regulations. The second level covers implementation measures to be adopted by the Commission with the assistance of regulatory committees so that the time-consuming process of the first level can be avoided for issues that are of a technical nature. Under the third level, more intensive cooperation between authorities is organized through separate supervisory committees. These committees have to ensure a timely and consistent implementation of the measures agreed upon, and work on convergence of supervisory practices. Finally, the fourth level entails an increased monitoring of Member States' implementation of Community law and related enforcement by the European Commission. As a follow-up to the recommendations, the European Securities Committee (ESC) and the Committee of European Securities Regulators (CESR) were created as Level 2 and Level 3 committees.

At the end of 2002, the ECOFIN Council decided that the proposals made in the Lamfalussy report should be extended to other financial sectors, i.e. banking, insurance and pensions funds, and financial conglomerates. Work is now underway to put this new European set-up in place for the different financial sectors, which *inter alia* implies the creation of sectoral Level 2 and Level 3 committees in which the national authorities will be represented. These committees will have to deal with a number of important regulatory developments that are underway, such as the revision of the capital framework for banks and investment firms, the insurance 'Solvency II' project and the proposal for a directive on reinsurance supervision. Table 4.2 gives an overview of the new committee set-up, whereas Table 4.3 compares the sectoral regulatory and supervisory committees on the basis of some key elements.

The success of the new framework will also depend on the appropriate institutional balance between the Council and the European Parliament. The present 'comitology' framework, as presented above, only gives a 'call back' possibility to the Council. Since internal market measures are adopted under the 'co-decision procedure' which requires also the involvement of the European Parliament, the latter insists on having a similar 'call back' possibility as the Council. This, however, would require a Treaty change to deal with the implementation powers of the Commission. This issue will also have to be addressed in the context of the discussions that are now taking place on a Constitution for Europe.

Table 4.2 Institutional arrangements for regulation and supervision (post-Lamfalussy)

	Banking	Securities and UCITS	Insurance and occupational pensions	Financial conglomerates
Level 2 committee	European Banking Committee (EBC)	European Securities Committee (ESC)	European Insurance and Occupational Pensions Committee (EIOPC)	European Financial Conglomerates Committee (EFCC)
Level 3 committee	Committee of European Banking Supervisors (CEBS)	Committee of European Securities Regulators (CESR)	Committee of European Insurance and Occupational Pensions Supervisors (CEIOPS)	

Table 4.3 Key characteristics of the new regulatory and supervisory committees

	Level 2 Committee	Level 3 Committee
Nature of work	Political, regulatory	Technical, supervisory
Chair	European Commission	National supervisor
Members	Ministry representatives	• National supervisors • Only banking: ECB + non-supervisory national central banks (non-voting)
Tasks	• Regulation ('comitology') • Advice to the Commission	• Information exchange • Supervisory convergence • Supervisory best practices • Advice to the Commission

A Possible Future: A Single Supervisory Authority for Financial Services in Europe?

For an outsider, the sectoral and cross-sectoral arrangements for regulation and supervision in Europe may seem overly complex, and could raise the question whether it would not be more efficient to establish a single European supervisor. Commentators in the private sector and the academia have pleaded for such a set-up, and even in its final report the Lamfalussy Committee did not exclude the need to establish such an authority if the new framework it proposed should prove to be unsuccessful. It should be noted that the EC Treaty already provides for a simplified procedure to confer upon the ECB specific tasks concerning policies relating to the prudential supervision of credit institutions and other financial institutions with the exception of insurance undertakings. A single European supervisor could take different forms, depending *inter alia* on its area of competence (e.g. only the securities sector or all financial sectors; all firms or only firms with an important cross-border activity), its relationship with the central bank (inside or outside the ECB), its organizational structure (e.g. one central institution or ESCB type of set-up), etc.

Different pros and cons have been advanced in the debate. Pros have included, the improved supervision of pan-European groups, as well as the increased efficiency, economies of scale and lower costs for supervised firms (e.g. in terms of reporting requirements, compliance). A pan-European authority is also likely to be less receptive to lobbying by firms on purely national grounds. Cons relate to the willingness of national authorities to accept decisions by a pan-European authority whose decisions may have an important effect in their country, but which they are not able to influence. Moreover, there is still no pan-European fiscal authority to intervene in case of solvency problems in a firm supervised under such a regime. It has been pointed out that first more harmonization is required in the area of civil and criminal enforcement measurers. Finally, many practical problems would need to be resolved, such as the structure of the new authority, its relationship with other European institutions, and its accountability.

All in all, the establishment of a single European regulator seems to be a step too far and would also clash with the subsidiarity principle enshrined in the EC Treaty, i.e. the notion that decisions have to be made at the lowest possible level and consistent with efficiency and coherence for the EU as a whole. In any case, the new regulatory and supervisory set-up under the Lamfalussy framework will have to prove its efficiency and in due time it will be reviewed.

Competition Policy

Overview

Competition policy, which targets anti-competitive behaviour of undertakings as well as Member States, is an essential element in the creation of a single European market for financial services. The EC Treaty requires Member States to adopt an economic policy conducted in accordance with the principle of an open market economy with free competition and it also contains a number of provisions that deal explicitly with competition policy. Further rules are provided by European regulations in specific areas, for example merger control and anti-trust enforcement. The European Commission, under the control of the European Court of Justice, is the responsible authority to deal with competition matters at the EU level. Community competition law, however, is only activated when the trade between Member States may be affected. Purely domestic competition problems continue to be dealt with by national authorities.

The three main areas of EU competition policy are anti-trust and cartels control, merger control, and state aid control. Under the EC Treaty, anti-competitive agreements, both horizontal (i.e. between competitors) and vertical (with customers or suppliers) are prohibited. Examples include agreements to divide up markets into territories, price-fixing and tie-in arrangements. Any abuse of a dominant position by one or more undertakings, such as predatory pricing or the refusal to supply services, is furthermore prohibited. The merger control requires any mergers with a Community dimension to be notified to the European Commission and a prior approval must be obtained. Finally, the Treaty also prohibits Member States' authorities from granting state aid which distorts competition and trade. This prohibition covers direct as well as indirect state assistance, such as capital injections and state guarantees. Potential cases of state aid should be notified to the European Commission for clearance. Recently, reforms in all the three areas of competition policy were launched with the aim of modernizing existing rules.

Merger and State Aid Control

In so far as financial services are concerned, especially the merger and state aid control have attracted attention through some widely-published cases. In 2001, the European Commission indicated that it had concerns about the planned merger between SE Banken and FöreningsSparbanken (Swedbank), two of the major banks in Sweden, which would result in the largest financial group in the Nordic region. Reportedly, the Commission's concerns were an important element in the ultimate decision of the two institutions to abandon the project. This case also raises the question of how to define the relevant market and assess dominance. Concerns have been voiced that in some countries national markets are very small so that mergers would quickly lead to market dominance, thus hampering the development of 'national champions'. On the other hand, growing financial integration justifies to take a wider perspective than only the strict national one to assess market dominance, especially when services to large corporate customers are concerned.

Another widely publicized case is the Champalimaud affair. In 1999, the Portuguese authorities blocked the Spanish Banco Santander Central Hispano (BSCH) from acquiring a controlling interest in the Portuguese Champalimaud group, active in both banking and insurance. In response the European Commission opened a formal infringement procedure against Portugal, *inter alia* arguing that the European Merger Regulation had been violated. This regulation states that no Member State shall apply its national competition legislation to any concentration that has a Community dimension unless justified on prudential grounds. The case was in the end resolved by a new, more limited merger replacing the one initially planned.

At several occasions, the European Commission has confirmed that the competition rules related to state aid apply in their entirety to the banking sector. This implies that in principle the 'market investor principle' applies, which stipulates that for a capital injection using public resources not to be considered as state aid, one must be able to demonstrate that a private investor would have behaved in the same way. However, the Commission also acknowledges the special nature of the banking sector, which relates to the fact that it is prone to 'systemic risk' and subject to prudential rules and supervision. Thus, public assistance may in some cases be an acceptable and even a necessary tool to avoid any future injection of a potentially larger amount of public funds to ward off a widespread banking crisis.

This argument, for example, was put forward in relation to the state aid granted to Crédit Lyonnais.

Four types of state aid can be distinguished: (i) ad hoc aid to ailing banks, (ii) investment aid, (iii) operating aid, and (iv) aid to compensate extra costs of services in the public interest. In the 1990s most of the cases related to ad hoc state aid provided to ailing French and Italian banks. The Commission subsequently extended its focus to investment aid to banks that needed to reinforce their capital, although they were not in financial distress. Recently, the Commission has also addressed operating aid in the form of public guarantees. The prime example here are the German 'Landesbanken' that benefit from a guarantee by their public owners. The Commission has also acted against the overcompensation for banking services provided in the public interest, as demonstrated by the recent 'Crédit Mutuel–Livret Bleu' case.[7]

More Recent Regulatory Initiatives

The new Lamfalussy approach discussed earlier has already been used in the securities field to put forward three directive proposals to support further integration, and that have been recently approved: one on market abuse, one on prospectuses and one on markets in financial instruments. In 2003, the Directive on the activities and supervision for occupational retirement provision (the so-called Pension Funds Directive) was adopted, which extends the 'home country control' principle to pension funds. This creates the potential for increased cross-border activity. It also gives pension funds more flexibility in their investment strategy. An updating of the Investment Service Directive is underway, which will constitute the core of a securities rule-book for the EU, governing the main types of investment services and the activities of exchanges.

Very few truly cross-border firm structures exist at present, but this may change following the adoption in 2001 of a regulation on the establishment of a European Company Statute, better known by its Latin name of 'Societas Europae' (SE). This regulation will give companies, including financial services groups operating in more than one Member State, the option of being established as a single company under Community Law and operating on the basis of one set of rules throughout the EU. The SE form will equally facilitate cross-border mergers. In 2003, the Nordic financial services group Nordea, disclosed its plans to be the first to adopt the status of European Company from 2005 onwards. For companies that want to enter into a cross-border merger without adopting the SE form, the Commission proposed in 2003 a separate directive on cross-border mergers.

The recently adopted regulation requiring listed companies (including financial firms) to prepare consolidated accounts in accordance with the International Accounting Standards (IAS) from 2005 onwards will result in more reliable and transparent accounts, thereby reducing barriers to cross-border trading. However, it is not yet clear whether the national implementation will extend beyond the consolidated accounts of listed companies. The proposed Transparency Directive will also

7 Moser et al. (2002).

increase the frequency and content of interim reporting by listed companies, thus increasing investor confidence and encouraging a more efficient allocation of resources.

Following the set of corporate scandals in the US as well as in Europe, the European Commission presented in 2003 a separate Action Plan on Company Law and Corporate Governance, as well as a review of EU rules on Statutory Audit. The Plan's aims are to strengthen shareholder rights, reinforce protection for employees and creditors and to increase the efficiency and competitiveness of business. Some of these initiatives represent a further extension of the original FSAP.

In the retail field, the FSAP recognized the lack of harmonization in the field of customer information and the lack of efficient procedures for solving cross-border disputes as major obstacles. Several initiatives were taken to address these concerns. For example, a proposal for a new directive on consumer credit was adopted (2002) with the aim to promote transparency and ensure harmonized conditions. In addition, an out-of-court complaints network for financial services has been set up. Similarly, a voluntary code of conduct has been concluded between the mortgage lending industry and consumer groups, which covers harmonized information to be made available to consumers. As e-commerce and e-finance become more widespread, an appropriate regulatory framework is necessary. An important step was taken with the recent adoption of the directive (2002) relating to the remote marketing of consumer financial services e.g. through the Internet. The high costs which banks charge for cross-border retail payments continue to act as a brake on the development of cross-border trade and e-commerce. Following failed attempts to bring these costs down, a regulation (2001) was adopted to oblige banks to charge the same amount for domestic and similar cross-border payments. As a result, the European banking sector agreed to take the necessary steps to establish a single payment area by no later than 2010.

References

Borchardt, K.D. (2000), *The ABC of Community law*, European Commission.

Cecchini, P., F. Heinemann, M. Jopp (eds.) (2003), *The incomplete European market for financial services*, ZEW Economic Studies, no. 19.

Corcoran, A.M. and T.L. Hart (2001), *The regulation of cross-border financial services in the EU internal market: a primer for third countries*, June.

European Central Bank (2003), *The integration of Europe's financial markets*, Monthly Bulletin, October.

European Commission (1999), *Implementing the framework for financial markets: action plan*, 11 May.

Gjersem, C. (2003), *Financial market integration in the euro area,* OECD, Economic department working paper.

Kremers, J.J.M., D. Schoenmaker and P.J. Wierts (2003). *Financial supervision in Europe.*

Moser, S., N. Pesaresi and K. Soukup (2002), *State guarantees to German public banks: a new step in the enforcement of State aid discipline to financial services in the Community*, Competition Policy Newsletter, no. 2, June.

Padoa-Schioppa, T. (2002), *Central banks and financial stability: exploring a land in between*, 25 October.

Raffan, M. (2003), *A practitioner's guide to EU financial services directives*, Freshfields Bruckhaus Deringer.

Part II
Changes in the Financial Structure

Chapter 5

How are Euro Area Financial Structures Changing?

Angela Maddaloni and Christoffer Kok Sørensen

Introduction

Central banks operate through the financial system, i.e. the banking system and financial markets. Hence, it is crucial for central banks to have a sound knowledge of how the financial system works and what its structures are and, not least, how they are developing over time. Indeed, financial structures are relevant for most functions of central banks, including payment systems design, the choice of monetary policy tools and implementation, contributions to financial stability and, in particular, to the monetary policy transmission mechanism.[1]

This chapter examines the developments of the financial structures in the euro area over the 1995–2002 period. It also compares the financial structures across the euro area member countries as well as vis-à-vis the financial structures of the two other major macro-regions (i.e. the US and Japan).[2]

The chapter highlights several salient features of the euro area's financial structures. First, in the euro area, the main financing flows are from households to non-financial corporations and governments. Capital flows in and out of the euro area have been relatively balanced over recent years. Financial intermediaries play a major role in collecting and allocating funds in the euro area. Second, the euro area financial system is well developed and diversified. Intermediated instruments, i.e. financial instruments offered by financial intermediaries, and non-intermediated ones, i.e. typical market instruments like shares and bonds, are equally important both as investments and as financing tools. Non-bank intermediated instruments and market-based instruments have become more important in the past decades. Third, among the financial intermediaries, monetary financial institutions (MFIs), which mainly consist of banks and money market funds, are the major collectors of funds, but other types of financial intermediaries, such as investment funds, insurance corporations and pension funds, have become more important in recent years. Fourth, euro area economies are generally dominated by small and medium-sized enterprises. Partly

1 See also Gaspar et al. (2003, p. 13). Indeed, Issing (2003, p. 120) notes that 'central banks and the financial system are inextricably linked. Central banks rely on the financial system for the transmission of monetary policy. The financial system relies on the central bank as the ultimate source of liquidity'.

2 See the *Report on Financial* Structures (ECB, 2002) for a detailed description of the financial structures in the individual euro area countries.

owing to this characteristic, non-quoted shares, other forms of private equity, and bank loans are extensively used as means of financing. Indeed, shares and other equity, which include both listed and non-listed shares, represent the largest liability item for non-financial corporations. At the same time, debt securities financing, which has historically played a minor role for euro area corporations, has become more important – especially relative to shares – since the start of Stage Three of Economic and Monetary Union.[3] Fifth, the bond market has undergone a series of structural changes over the past few years. Changes have been particularly pronounced with regard to market liquidity, tick sizes,[4] the behaviour of sovereign issuers, growth in the corporate bond market, more closely integrated pan-European trading possibilities and, finally, what seems to be a certain degree of specialization in some market segments (maturity, economic sector) among countries in the euro area. Finally, concerning most indicators the euro area financial system is positioned somewhere in-between the US financial system, which is somewhat more market-based, and the Japanese financial system, which is more reliant on banks.

This chapter is structured as follows: the next section provides an overview of the distribution of financial assets and liabilities among euro area resident sectors. In the third section, the financial intermediaries of the euro area are described and in the fourth section the structures and developments of the bond and stock markets are presented. The financing of the non-financial sectors of the euro area is described in the fifth section, which is followed by a conclusion.

Financial Assets and Liabilities in the Euro Area

The financial assets and liabilities of the euro area residents amounted to almost 7 times the size of the area's Gross Domestic Product (GDP) by the end of 2002 (see Table 5.1). Households are net savers in the euro area, having a net financial position of around 129 per cent of GDP. Through their investments households thereby finance the activities of non-financial corporations and governments who are net lenders. Financial corporations are prominent players in the financial system in the sense that, while having a largely balanced net financial position, they account for around half of all the gross financial assets and liabilities of the euro area.

The value of intermediated financial assets in the euro area financial system (such as banking products, mutual/investment funds and insurance and pension fund products) is bigger than the aggregate value of non-intermediated assets (such as bonds, commercial paper, listed and non-listed shares). This distribution of assets differs significantly across the non-financial sectors (see Table 5.2). For example, households mainly rely on financial intermediaries to deposit their savings and to finance their investments. Non-financial corporations and governments primarily allocate

3 The rapid development of the corporate debt market in the euro area was not alone in being driven by the introduction of the euro. Other factors, such as the massive corporate restructuring and the telecommunications industry liberalization, are likely to have affected the corporate bond market in a positive way, see Carnegie-Brown and King (2003).

4 Tick sizes are the increments by which prices move. They affect the magnitude of the bid-ask spread and hence the overall liquidity of the market.

Table 5.1 Financial position by sector *(amount outstanding end-2002; % of GDP)*

	Financial assets	Liabilities	Net financial position
Households	186.6	57.7	128.8
Non-financial corporations	127.5	202.0	–74.5
General government	25.8	80.4	–54.6
Financial corporations	358.7	356.5	2.2
Total	*698.6*	*696.7*	*1.9*

Source: ECB.

Table 5.2 Distribution of financial assets and liabilities between intermediated and non-intermediated instruments of the non-financial sectors in the euro area *(end-2002; % of GDP)*

	Financial assets		Liabilities	
	Intermediated	Non-intermediated	Intermediated	Non-intermediated
Households	132.3	50.2	52.5	0.0
Non-financial corporations	20.1	64.5	70.7	105.5
General government	6.6	8.1	18.4	58.3
Total	*159.0*	*122.8*	*141.6*	*163.8*

Source: ECB.

their savings in direct holding of shares and securities and also tend to tap the markets for finance instead of through intermediaries. However, it should be stressed that a large part of non-intermediated liabilities of non-financial corporations consists of private equity, which is typically non-marketable.

The euro area financial system has often been characterized as a predominantly bank-based system. While banks are the dominant players for the allocation of financial assets and for providing finance, they are not the only players in the financial system: other types of intermediaries as well as markets have a significant role. In fact, the features of the euro area financial system seem to be closer to the more market-oriented US financial system than the largely bank-dominated Japanese financial system (see Table 5.3).

Financial Intermediaries

Financial intermediaries have a crucial role in the euro area financial system. First of all, they provide important instruments for the non-financial sectors' allocation of

Table 5.3 Distribution of financial assets and liabilities between intermediated and non-intermediated instruments of the non-financial sectors in the euro area, the US and Japan *(end-2002; % of GDP; % of total asset/liabilities in parentheses)*

	Euro area	US*	Japan
Intermediated assets	159.0 (56%)	191.9 (58%)	343.1 (83%)
Non-intermediated assets	122.8 (44%)	140.7 (42%)	70.1 (17%)
Intermediated liabilities	141.6 (46%)	132.7 (46%)	206.6 (51%)
Non-intermediated liabilities	163.8 (54%)	159.0 (54%)	203.3 (49%)

Sources: ECB, Board of Governors of the Federal Reserve System and Bank of Japan.
*Assets do not include 'miscellaneous assets', which could include cross-shareholdings. Equities are included in liabilities at market value.

savings, such as bank deposits, investment/mutual funds as well as insurance reserves and pension funds. But they are also major actors in the financial markets in the form of investors, market makers, securities underwriters and derivative dealers, and as such are crucial for the functioning of these markets.

In this chapter, financial intermediaries are divided into three main groups:[5] monetary financial institutions (MFIs), which mainly consist of credit institutions and money market funds; insurance corporations and pension funds (ICPF); and finally other financial intermediaries (so-called OFIs), which mainly consist of investment (or mutual) funds.

In terms of ratios to GDP, the assets held with financial intermediaries by euro area residents increased from roughly 205 per cent of GDP in 1995 to more than 250 per cent of GDP by end-2002 corresponding to an increase of 22 per cent over the period (see Table 5.4). It is notable that euro area residents' holdings with OFIs and insurance corporations and pension funds have increased by 92 per cent and 40 per cent, respectively, between 1995 and 2002, whereas holdings with MFIs (such as traditional bank deposits) have only increased by 8 per cent in the same period. This development, however, is partly due to revaluation changes, which seem to have particularly affected the value of holdings with non-MFI intermediaries. Indeed transaction data, which are partly adjusted for revaluation changes, show that in the period 1995–2001 total average annual acquisitions of MFI assets have been roughly similar to acquisitions of non-MFI intermediated assets.

However, if only the acquisitions by the non-financial sectors are considered (that is, disregarding financial corporations), acquisitions with non-MFI intermediaries have superseded the amounts allocated with MFIs. The non-financial sectors annually acquired financial assets of OFIs (mainly investment fund shares) for a value amounting to around 2.5 per cent of GDP on average between 1995 and 2001. The acquisition of insurance technical reserves amounted to 3.8 per cent of GDP on an annual average over the same period. The sum of this (6.3 per cent of GDP) was thus

5 The definitions used correspond to the statistical framework drawn up according to the European System of Accounts 1995 (ESA 95).

Table 5.4 Financial assets (acquisitions and holdings) in the form of intermediated instruments by sector *(% of GDP)*

	Monetary financial institutions (MFIs)		Insurance corporations and pension funds (ICPFs)		Other financial intermediaries (OFIs)	
Average annual acquisitions	**1995–2001**	**2002**	**1995–2001**	**2002**	**1995–2001**	**2002**
Non-financial sectors	3.0	3.8	3.8	3.4	2.4	2.1
– Households	2.1	3.3	3.7	3.3	2.0	0.8
– Non-financial corporations	0.8	0.3	0.1	0.1	0.4	1.2
– General government	0.1	0.2	0.0	0.0	0.1	0.1
Financial corporations	4.5	5.5	0.1	0.0	1.7	1.5
Total	*7.5*	*9.2*	*3.8*	*3.4*	*4.1*	*3.6*
	Monetary financial institutions (MFIs)		**Insurance corporations and pension funds**		**Other financial intermediaries (OFIs)**	
Holdings (end-year)	**1995**	**2002**	**1995**	**2002**	**1995**	**2002**
Non-financial sectors	84.4	82.6	36.4	51.0	15.3	24.9
– Households	65.2	62.2	35.1	50.0	12.4	20.1
– Non-financial corporations	12.7	14.5	1.3	1.0	2.6	4.2
– General government	6.5	5.9	0.1	0.0	0.4	0.7
Financial corporations	62.5	76.7	1.0	1.5	5.0	13.9
Total	*146.9*	*159.3*	*37.5*	*52.5*	*20.2*	*38.8*

Source: ECB.

more than twice as large as the allocation of funds into MFIs (e.g. currency and deposits and money market funds), which reached 3.0 per cent of GDP.

Flows into insurance corporations and pension funds have been persistently strong between 1995 and 2002, which to a large extent reflects an increasing demand for private savings for old age owing to the demographic 'burden', while investments in OFIs were significant in the beginning of the period, but decreased in the most recent years (see Figure 5.1). The decline in flows into OFIs from 1998 onward may be considered as a 'normalization' following the strong growth of this industry in previous years. In addition, many investors may to an increasing extent have substituted placements in investment funds with direct holdings of shares in the period 1998–2000 prompted by rises in stock prices and the privatization activity carried out by some euro area governments.

Several factors may explain why the importance of MFIs has been diminishing vis-à-vis other types of intermediaries/instruments in recent years. In some countries, changes in tax regulations have changed the savings patterns. More generally, the low level of interest rates has led many investors to search for alternative investments

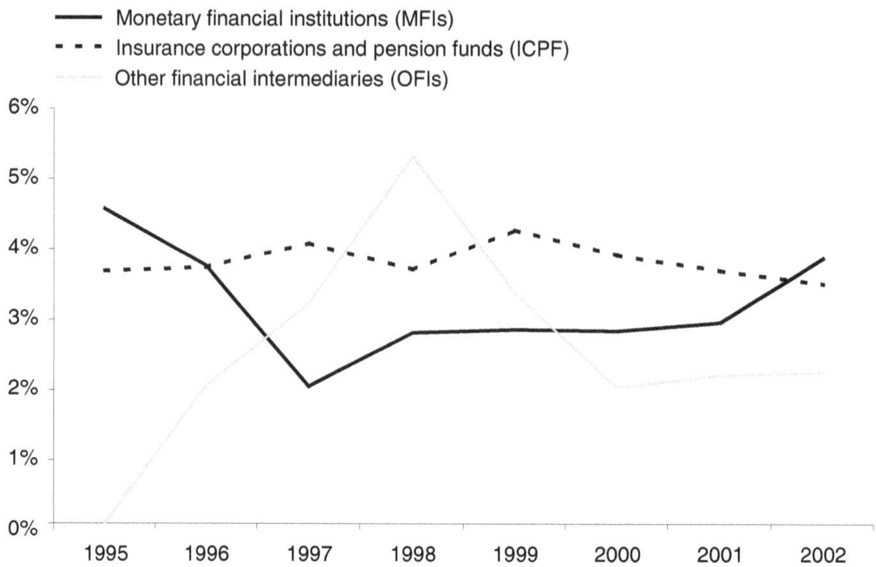

Figure 5.1 Financial investment in intermediated assets by non-financial sectors in the euro area, by type of intermediary *(% of GDP)*

Source: ECB.

with higher yields than traditional bank deposits. In addition, demographic developments have sparked a trend to invest in financial assets of a longer-term nature, such as pension fund shares.

The developments observed in recent years partly reversed during 2002. Due to the decline in stock prices and the rise in global risk aversion (especially after the terrorist attacks on 11 September 2001), many investors fled into safer assets such as bank deposits and money market funds. Thus, financial assets allocated with MFIs were larger in 2001 and 2002 than in previous years, although still somewhat lower than assets allocated with non-bank financial intermediaries.

Figure 5.2 shows that the relative distribution of intermediated assets held by the non-financial sectors overall is fairly similar across the member states and that the individual countries tend to cluster around the structure of the euro area as a whole. Hence, in all countries but the Netherlands, the majority of the holdings with intermediaries are held with MFIs, which thus remain the dominant type of intermediary in most countries and in the euro area as a whole. There are, however, discernible differences as well. Thus, MFIs are particularly important in countries like Belgium, Germany, Spain, Italy, Portugal, Austria and Finland. Insurance corporations and pension funds take up a large share in the Netherlands, in particular, but also in Germany, France and Finland, while other financial intermediaries (OFIs) are relatively important in Belgium, France and Italy.

In terms of the allocation of savings from non-financial sectors, the euro area lies somewhere in between the US and the Japanese financial system (see Figure 5.3). Both in the euro area and in Japan, most intermediated assets are held with monetary

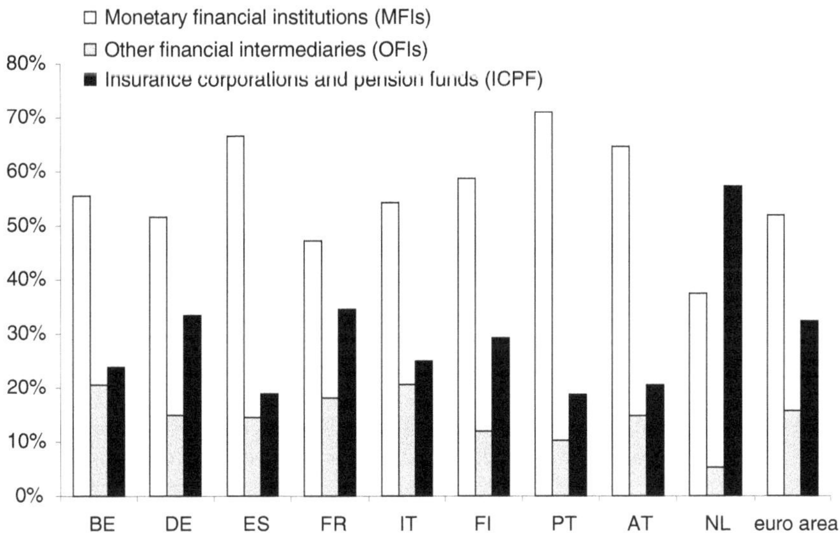

Figure 5.2 Relative distribution of intermediated assets held by non-financial sectors in the euro area countries *(end-2002, % of total)*

Source: ECB.
Note: Data for Portugal are amount outstanding at the end of 2001.

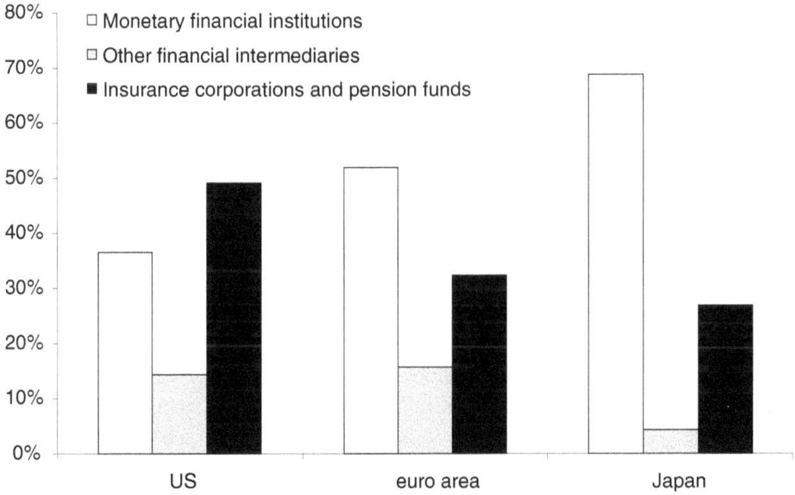

Figure 5.3 Relative distribution of intermediated assets held by non-financial sectors in the euro area, the US and Japan *(end-2002, % of total)*

Sources: ECB, Board of Governors of the Federal Reserve System and Bank of Japan.
Note: Japanese financial assets invested in 'other financial intermediaries' include 'securities investment trusts' and 'trust beneficiary rights'.

financial institutions, while in the US the most important intermediary in terms of the value of the assets outstanding are pension funds.

Monetary Financial Institutions (MFIs)

At the end of 1998 there were 9,844 MFIs (excluding central banks) in the euro area. By end-2002, this number had declined to 8,531, following a trend already started a couple of decades earlier. While the overall number of MFIs, which include credit institutions and money market funds, has declined in the period 1998–2002, the number of money market funds has by contrast increased significantly (by 7 per cent) over the same period. The importance of money market funds is, however, concentrated in only a few countries, such as France and Luxembourg, but overall accounts for only a small part of the total MFI sector (measured in terms of total MFI assets).

These developments reflect a continuing consolidation of the European banking sector, which has taken place in the form of mergers between (mainly) smaller credit institutions at both a regional and a national level. However, cross-border mergers among euro area countries have been relatively rare and have mostly involved larger institutions that have expanded on a regional basis, e.g. the Benelux and the Nordic/Baltic regions. At present, only a few MFIs operate on an euro area-wide scale, and then primarily with regard to wholesale activities. Retail business activities are still predominantly taking place on a regional/national level, although new technologies, such as internet banking, may eventually enable further cross-border expansions in relation to retail business. The speed of consolidation has decreased somewhat in recent years mainly due to the weakening of the stock market, which has made mergers and acquisitions (M&As) more difficult to finance as it became more costly to issue equity capital. The slowdown was most evident with regard to (cross-border) mergers involving major banks, while the process of consolidation has largely continued in relation to domestic mergers between small and medium-sized enterprises.[6]

Traditional banking activities, such as granting loans and taking deposits, still take up most of the aggregated MFI balance sheet (see Table 5.5). By the end of 2002, loans amounted to 70 per cent of total MFI assets (49 per cent, excluding euro area interbank loans) and deposits amounted to more than 65 per cent of total MFI liabilities (45 per cent, excluding euro area interbank funding). However, between 1998 and 2002, the share of loans to resident non-MFI in total assets declined by almost 4 per cent. Similarly over the same period, the share of deposits taken from resident non-MFI in total MFI liabilities declined by more than 8 per cent. These developments seem to some extent to reflect a shift in the nature of banking activities towards a larger degree of securitisation (see also Box 5.1). On the asset side, MFIs have increased their holdings of securities (including bonds, shares and money market papers) to 23 per cent of total assets by the end of 2002, representing an increase of almost 9 per cent since 1998. On the liability side, MFIs to an increasing extent fund

6 See for example ECB (2002) *Structural Analysis of the EU Banking Sector – Year 2001*.

Table 5.5 Aggregated balance sheet of the euro area MFIs, excluding the Eurosystem *(% of total assets/liabilities)*

ASSETS	**End-2002**	**Percentage change of share to total assets 1998–2002**
Cash	0.3	5.9
Loans	70.2	–2.5
– to resident MFIs	21.1	–4.0
– to other residents	39.9	–3.6
– to RoW	9.1	7.1
Securities other than shares	17.0	1.7
– to resident MFIs	6.2	7.7
– to other residents	7.9	–13.0
– to RoW	2.9	53.7
Money market papers	1.1	49.1
Shares and other equity	5.3	29.6
– to resident MFIs	1.4	17.7
– to other residents	3.0	20.5
– to RoW	0.9	112.5
Remaining assets	6.2	–1.3
Total assets	**100.0**	
LIABILITIES	**End-2002**	**Percentage change of share to total liabilities 1998–2002**
Deposits	65.1	–4.1
– to resident MFIs	21.6	–5.8
– to other residents	31.7	–8.4
– to RoW	11.9	13.5
Money market funds shares	3.7	121.4
Securities other than shares	17.9	6.5
Capital and reserves	5.8	10.6
Remaining liabilities	7.5	–10.6
Total liabilities	**100.0**	
Total assets as % of GDP	**269**	**13.2**

Source: ECB.
Note: The Eurosystem of Central Banks (ESCB) is composed by the ECB and the euro area national central banks.

their activities through the issuance of securities, such as subordinated debt and certificates of deposits, as a complement to traditional deposit financing.

Furthermore, the aggregated balance sheet of MFIs only reflects the on-balance sheet activities of banks and other credit institutions. It does not provide information about off-balance sheet activities, such as derivatives trading, financial guarantees, loan commitments (e.g. liquidity back-up lines and securities underwriting back-up lines), that have been growing in importance in recent decades. More generally, the technological developments and financial deregulation and innovation in the past decades have at the same time broadened the scope of banking activities and led to a more sophisticated risk management. This is also evidenced by the fact that banks' interest income has gradually been declining relative to their non-interest income.[7] Banking has hence been changing in many respects, but MFIs remained important players in the euro area financial system.

Insurance Corporations and Pension Funds

Due to their overriding function as saving vehicles for old age, ICPFs primarily invest in financial assets of a long-term nature, such as equity and long-term bonds (see Table 5.6). By the end of 2002 holdings of debt securities constituted 38 per cent of total main financial assets of ICPFs, while quoted shares amounted to 35 per cent of total main financial assets. While the overall share of securities to total assets has remained largely unchanged at around 70–75 per cent over the past five years, notable changes have occurred with respect to the relative importance of ICPFs' holdings of quoted shares vis-à-vis holdings of debt securities. During the stock market boom of

Table 5.6 Aggregated balance sheet of euro area insurance corporations and pension funds *(% of total assets/liabilities)*

ASSETS	**End-2002**	**Percentage change of share to total assets 1998–2002**
Deposits with MFIs	15.4	0.1
Loans	9.6	–22.0
Debt securities	38.3	1.2
Shares and other equity	34.9	8.5
– Quoted shares	17.9	–3.4
– Mutual fund shares	17.0	24.6
Money market fund shares	1.6	58.1
Insurance technical reserves	1.8	–21.0
Total assets	**100.0**	
LIABILITIES	**End-2002**	**Percentage change of share to total liabilities 1998–2002**
Insurance technical reserves	95.0	8.3
Quoted shares	3.3	–69.2
Remaining liabilities	1.7	8.7
Total liabilities	**100.0**	
Assets as % of GDP	**48.0**	**7.9**

Source: ECB.

7 See e.g., ECB (2000), *EU Banks' Income Structure.*

the late 1990s and early 2000, the value of shares holdings increased significantly, and hence the percentage of quoted shares to total assets peaked at 41 per cent by the end of 2000, where by contrast debt securities only constituted 33 per cent of total assets. The subsequent stock market correction in 2001 and 2002 reversed this trend, causing the combined value of quoted shares and mutual fund shares on the aggregated ICPF balance sheet to decrease significantly, while the share of debt securities had by end-2002 returned to its end-1998 level. Most of these changes were due to revaluation adjustments and only to a lesser extent to transactions.

On the liability side, 'insurance technical reserves', which insurance corporations are obliged by regulation to build up over the life of an insurance contract to take into account future claims, take up the major part of the funding of ICPFs. Furthermore, the sharp decline in stock prices and other problems facing insurance corporations in the past two years resulted in a marked decline in the value of the quoted shares issued by these corporations. While quoted shares accounted for 11 per cent of total liabilities at the end of 1998, the figure had fallen to 3 per cent by the end of 2002.

While public pension schemes have traditionally played a dominant role in household saving for old age in most euro area countries, demographic trends have in recent years heightened incentives to use complementary (private) pension schemes. Households have hence increasingly allocated long-term savings into insurance companies and pension funds. It should be noted that the ICPF sector varies significantly across the euro area countries, among other things reflecting 'country-specific factors with respect to mandatory funded pension schemes, the social security system and the tax treatment of voluntary pensions'(see ECB (2002) *Report on Financial Structures*, p. 26).

Other Financial Intermediaries (OFIs)

As noted above, over the last decade OFIs have become more important in the euro area financial system both as collectors of financial funds and as investors in the financial markets. Developments in the composition of assets and liabilities in OFIs' balance sheets changed during 2001 and 2002, reflecting the decline in stock prices and the rise in bond prices. The percentage of assets OFIs have invested in shares and other equity fell from 43 per cent by end-2000 to 30 per cent by end-2002 (see Table 5.7). At the same time, investments in securities other than shares, increased from around 39 per cent of total assets in 2000 to 47 per cent in 2002. The share of total assets of real estate funds and other funds also rose. This reflected the continued increase in real estate prices in some European countries and in the US as well as an increased incentive to diversify portfolios toward alternative sources of investments amid high capital market volatility.

The importance of OFIs still varies considerably across the euro area countries, with Germany, France and Luxembourg accounting for around 72 per cent of the total activity of the euro area OFIs at the end of 2001.[8] With respect to GDP, the size of OFIs was also above the euro area average in Belgium, Italy and Austria.

8 Statistics concerning the activity of 'other financial intermediaries' in Ireland, comparable with the other euro area countries, are not available. However, alternative sources suggest that investment funds in Ireland are important.

Table 5.7 Aggregated balance sheet of OFIs *(% of total assets/liabilities)*

ASSETS	End-2002	Percentage change of share to total assets 1998–2002
Deposits	8.4	13.1
Securities other than shares	46.6	10.8
Shares and other equity	29.8	–27.2
Mutual funds shares	6.6	74.4
Remaining assets	6.5	46.8
Total assets	**100.0**	
LIABILITIES	**End-2002**	**Percentage change of share to total liabilities 1998–2002**
Mutual funds shares	95.9	–0.3
Remaining liabilities	4.1	6.7
Total liabilities	**100.0**	
Assets as % of GDP	**41.0**	**–14.4**

Source: ECB.

Markets

Holdings of euro area residents in non-intermediated financial assets (shares and other securities) totalled 248 per cent of GDP at the end of 2002 (see Table 5.8). This corresponds to an increase of 41 per cent since 1995, although a major part of this increase was due to considerable revaluation changes, in particular reflecting the enormous rise in stock prices over most of this period. Thus, shares and other equity accounted for 55 per cent of non-intermediated financial assets whereas 45 per cent fell on other securities (mainly debt securities) by the end of 2002 compared to an almost equal distribution in 1995. At the end of 2002, non-financial corporations, partly reflecting the large use of cross-shareholdings and non-listed shares in the euro area held 42 per cent of the total outstanding amount of shares and other equity. At the same time, financial corporations held 73 per cent of the total outstanding amount of securities other than shares.

On average, between 1995 and 2001, non-financial sectors in the euro area annually acquired shares and other equity for a value of around 2.9 per cent of GDP, reflecting primarily acquisitions of non-financial corporations. Over the same period, the acquisition of other securities accounted for 0.8 per cent of GDP per year. Financial corporations were the main investors of non-intermediated assets between 1995 and 2001, accounting for 79 per cent of the total securities acquired in this period.

Due to the decline in equity prices, in 2001 and 2002 investments in shares were lower than in the previous years, reversing the increasing trend observed since 1995 (see Figure 5.4). Conversely, investment in securities other than shares increased in 2001. In 2002 it was comparable with investment in shares. In particular, from the second half of 2001, financial corporations reallocated their financial portfolios

Table 5.8 Financial assets (acquisitions and holdings) in the form of non-intermediated instruments by sector *(% of GDP)*

	Shares and other equity		Securities other than shares	
Average annual acquisitions	**1995–2001**	**2002**	**1995–2001**	**2002**
Non-financial sectors	2.9	1.4	0.8	1.4
– Households	0.4	–0.9	0.2	1.0
– Non-financial corporations	2.9	2.6	0.5	0.3
– General government	–0.4	–0.3	0.1	0.1
Financial corporations	3.5	2.2	10.7	2.6
Total	**6.5**	**3.7**	**11.5**	**4.0**
	Shares and other equity		**Securities other than shares**	
Holdings (end-year)	**1995**	**2002**	**1995**	**2002**
Non-financial sectors	67.4	93.1	29.9	29.7
– Households	27.6	29.7	23.5	20.4
– Non-financial corporations	31.6	56.8	4.7	7.8
– General government	8.2	6.6	1.7	1.5
Financial corporations	20.1	43.1	58.4	82.4
Total	**87.6**	**136.2**	**88.3**	**112.1**

Source: ECB.

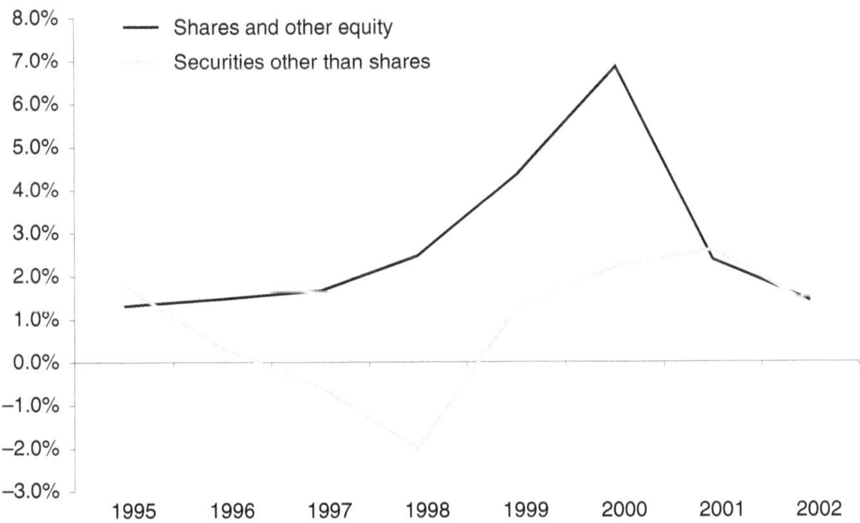

Figure 5.4 Financial investment in non-intermediated assets by non-financial sectors in the euro area, by instrument *(transactions; % of GDP)*

Source: ECB.

from equity to more secure financial assets. The decrease in equity investments of non-financial corporations also reflected the subdued merger and acquisitions activity during that period.

Compared with the US and the Japanese financial system, in the euro area the value of shares and other equity as a percentage of GDP is much higher (see Figure 5.5). This is likely to reflect the non-consolidation of euro area financial accounts and some double-counting of shares by non-financial corporations, a sector where the cross-shareholdings is particularly important. Non-quoted shares, which in some countries represent the large majority of the total, contribute also to this result. Conversely, the value of securities other than shares is much larger in the US than in the euro area and in Japan. This reflects the large size of the US fixed income market and in particular of the mortgage-related market.

The Debt Securities Markets

There has been substantial growth in the amount outstanding of debt securities in the euro area. The total amount outstanding of euro-denominated debt securities issued by euro area residents increased by an annual average of 6 per cent between 1998 and 2000. However, these growth rates differed significantly across issuing sectors. On account of fiscal prudence, between 1998 and 2000 the amount outstanding of debt

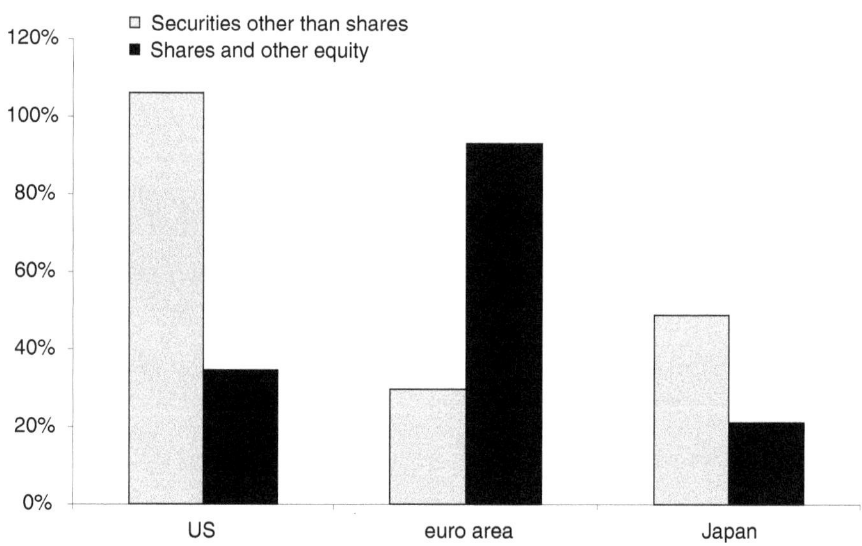

Figure 5.5 Holdings of non-intermediated assets by non-financial sectors in the euro area, the US and Japan by instrument *(amount outstanding end-2002; % of GDP)*

Sources: ECB, Board of Governors of the Federal Reserve System and Bank of Japan.
Note: US assets do not include 'miscellaneous assets' as reported in the balance sheet of non-financial corporations. This figure is likely to include cross-shareholding of the sector.

securities issued by central government only grew by 4 per cent a year. Over the same periods, corporate issuers stepped up the pace of their activities and the amount outstanding of corporate debt securities issued by non-MFIs increased at a rate of around 17 per cent a year.

In 2001 and in 2002, bond issuance trends partly reversed compared to the previous few years. There was a general decline in the issuance of the private sector and a rise in the general government sector, reflecting differences in the financing needs of these sectors at a time of weak economic growth.

The relative value of outstanding debt securities is lower in the euro area than in the other major developed economies (see Figure 5.6). The total amount outstanding of debt securities at the end of 2002 equalled around 105 per cent of GDP in the euro area, 154 per cent in the US and 160 per cent in Japan. Also these aggregate values hide significant differences in the sectoral composition. Both in the euro area and in Japan, government debt accounts for most of the outstanding securities. At the end of 2002, in the Japanese debt market government securities accounted for around 72 per cent of the total amount outstanding, while in the euro area government securities represented 51 per cent of the total debt outstanding. Conversely, in the US the most important issuers of debt securities are financial corporations and the total private sector (financial plus non-financial corporations) accounted for around 72 per cent of the total debt outstanding. In addition, in the euro area the large majority of corporate borrowing is done via loans, while in the US loans cover about half of corporations'

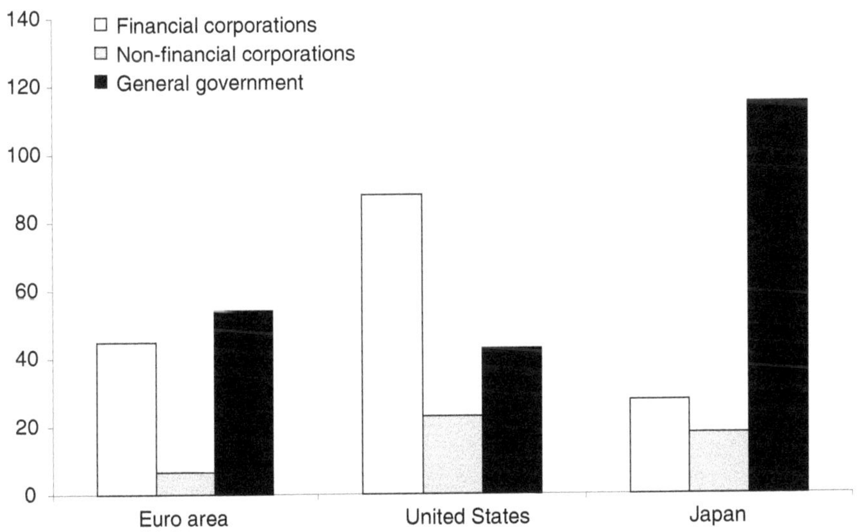

Figure 5.6 Amounts outstanding of debt securities denominated in national currency issued by residents in the euro area, the US and Japan *(end-2002; % of total)*

Sources: ECB, Board of Governors of the Federal Reserve System and Bank of Japan.

funding needs.[9] Thus there seems to be scope for further development of the corporate bond market in the euro area.

Trends in the Corporate Bond Market

In 2001 net bond issuance by non-MFIs (the sum of non-monetary financial corporations and non-financial corporations) was higher than the net issuance by banks. This represented a notable change in issuance activity compared with the recent past, as until the end of 2000 euro area MFIs were the primary net issuers of corporate bonds among euro area residents.

The start of Stage Three of Economic and Monetary Union led to a large increase in the use of bond issuance as a financing source by corporations (both financial and non-financial). However, the increase was also due to other, temporary factors, such as corporate restructuring and related merger and acquisition activity as well as telecommunication industry liberalization. The impact of these industry adjustments, which continued throughout 2001, seemed to diminish somewhat thereafter. Debt securities issuance from the private sector continued to grow in 2002, albeit at a lower pace, reflecting lower financing needs linked to sluggish economic activity.

In recent years, non-monetary financial corporations have been a driving force behind the issuance activity of the non-MFI sector. Between 1998 and 2002, the annual average rate of growth in the amount outstanding stood at around 34 per cent for non-monetary financial corporations and 12 per cent for non-financial corporations. The strong growth in the issuance activity of non-monetary financial corporations seems to reflect, in part, a shift from direct issuance by the non-financial corporate sector to indirect issuance via *special finance vehicles* (see Box 5.1).

Box 5.1 Securitization and the activity of special finance vehicles[10]

One of the most striking developments concerning debt securities issuance over recent years has been the remarkable increase in the amount of debt securities issued by non-monetary financial corporations in the euro area. This group includes insurance corporations and pension funds and other financial intermediaries (OFIs), but the bulk of its securities issuance stems from special finance vehicles. These are institutions which engage in financial activities and whose main purpose is to raise money on behalf of a third party, e.g. a non-financial corporation, a credit institution or an investment fund. Such vehicles can be legally owned by the companies to which they are providing funds or they can be without capital links to that company and can be established to facilitate a particular financial transaction. In the latter case they are known as *special purpose vehicles* (SPVs). SPVs act solely as a single purpose conduit for channeling funds from lenders to borrowers. They are precluded from engaging in activities other than the transaction for which

9 See Carnegie-Brown and King (2003).

10 See also the article 'Recent developments in financial structures of the euro area' in the *ECB Monthly Bulletin* October 2003, p. 39.

they were established and they immunise the investor against the potential bankruptcy of the original owner of the assets (the originator).

In the euro area these finance vehicles existed until very recently in only a few countries – particularly in the Netherlands, where they started their activity at the end of the 1970s.[11] Initially, they were typically established in that country by foreign multinationals and they were limited to collecting funds and lending or investing them within their own group. They were pure *holding companies* or companies managing licenses, patent or film rights. When the exchange controls on financing companies engaged exclusively in collecting funds and investing them abroad were relaxed, these special financial institutions were also able to raise money from non-resident investors external to their group.

More recently, the activity of special finance vehicles has been linked to the development of the securitisation market. The term securitisation refers to the transformation of non-marketable assets into marketable securities. Assets such as mortgage loans, which have traditionally been held in the loan portfolios of banks, can be packaged into securities and sold to investors. In this context, securitisation entails the sale of financial assets by the originator to a separate legal entity, the SPV. To finance its purchase, the SPV (in some cases through a trust, whose beneficiaries are investors in the securities) issues marketable securities usually known as *asset-backed securities* (see Chart A). The conveyance of assets from the originator to the SPV generally needs to be conducted in a manner that results in a 'true sale'. This is necessary to remove the assets from the bankruptcy or insolvency estate of the originator – the 'bankruptcy remote principle'. SPVs may, however, also be involved in so-called *synthetic securitisation* where the assets are *not* removed from the originator's balance sheet. That is, only the risk related to the underlying assets is being removed. In a synthetic securitisation involving an SPV the originator and the SPV typically engage in a credit default swap (CDS), in which the originator pays a swap premium to the SPV for protection and, should a credit event occur, would receive cash from the SPV. At the same time the SPV ranks the credit portfolio underlying the CDS by risk and issues several tranches of 'credit linked notes' (instead of asset-backed securities as in 'true sale' arrangements). The proceeds from these issues are then generally invested in high quality assets.

As a way of raising funds, securitisation brings several advantages for the originator. First, an SPV can generally obtain cheaper finance since it is typically assigned a higher credit rating than the originator. Since the assets are separated from the credit risk of the originator, the premium demanded by investors to lend money to that particular corporation is generally lower than it would be in traditional bank and debt capital markets. Depending upon the nature of the transaction and the assets involved, it may be necessary to enhance the credit quality of the asset pool by complementing it with one or more types of credit and/or liquidity support. These may be supplied from

11 See De Nederlandsche Bank, *Statistical Bulletin*, March 2000.

internal sources or, for a fee, by a third party. Second, institutions with a low rating, or no rating at all, can gain access to institutional investors, including banks, insurance companies and pension funds, which are often restricted to investment in high-rated bonds. Third, as an off-balance sheet funding technique, securitization also aims at reducing a company's leverage by selling assets and using the proceeds, for example, to repay more expensive long-term debt.

Chart A: Creation of an asset-backed security

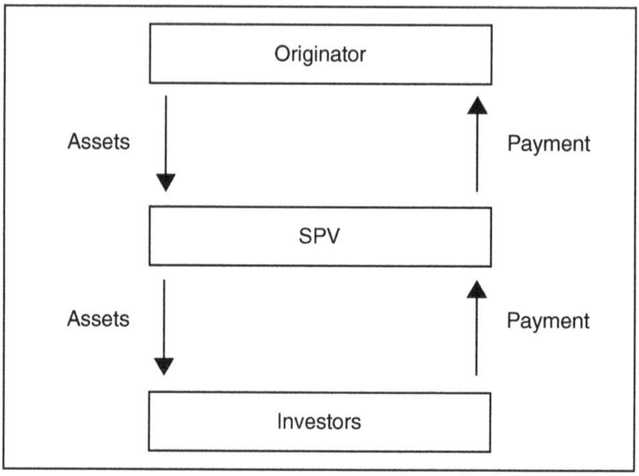

The issuance activity of special finance vehicles flourished in the last few years of the 1990s in parallel with the introduction of the euro. The bulk of the issuance of financial institutions legally established in the euro area countries is denominated in euros. Regulatory changes in several euro area countries also fuelled the increase in special finance vehicle activity, both in terms of the number of issues and issuance volume (see Chart B).

Finance vehicles are usually set up in jurisdictions which are more favourable in terms of the bankruptcy remote principle, the security arrangements provided for the investors and the tax treatment. In the euro area, a traditional jurisdiction in which to establish special finance vehicles has been the Netherlands, which on average between 1990 and 2002 was the jurisdiction for around 30 per cent of the total volume issued by such vehicles. Other common jurisdictions used for establishing special finance vehicles (in particular SPVs) are Ireland, Italy and Luxembourg. In addition, securitisation entities are established in the same jurisdictions as the originator in Spain, France and Italy (see Chart C).

Chart B: Issuance activities of special finance vehicles: volume (in €m) and number

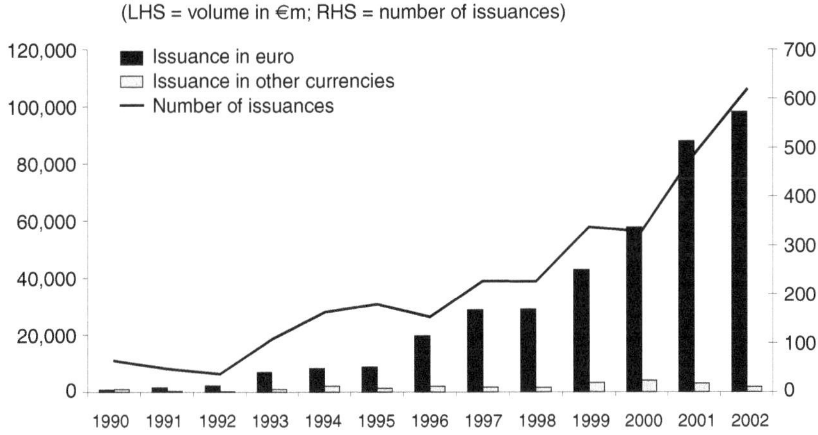

Source: Bondware Dealogic.

Chart C: Issuance activities of special finance vehicles by country of issuer – end-2002 *(% of total issuance)*

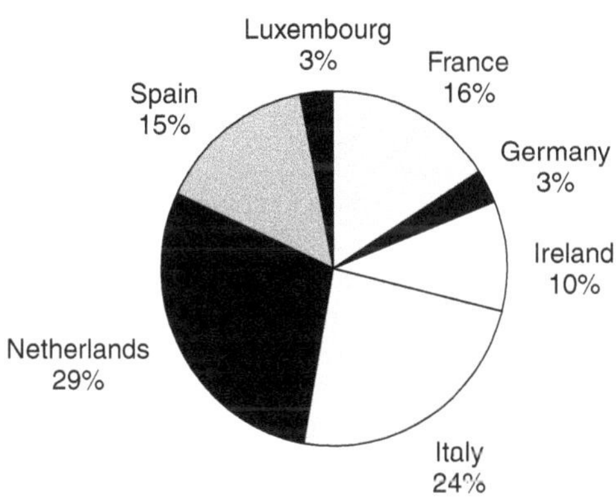

Source: Bondware Dealogic.

Trends in Government Debt Securities Market

Government debt securities represent the largest segment of the debt securities market. They amounted to 54 per cent of GDP at the end of 2002, having grown slowly between 1998 and 2000. During the 1990s the share of short-term government securities in total government debt declined steadily. Substantially lower long-term interest rates compared to the years prior to Stage Three of the Economic and Monetary Union and an environment of price stability created incentives for euro area governments to lengthen the average maturity of debt, taking advantage of the flatter yield curve. This adjustment process may have come to an end in the late 1990s as short-term government securities issuance rose again in 2001 and in 2002. This partly reflected the deterioration of economic activity and the consequent increase in government borrowing needs as well as the short-term budgetary benefits from the low level of short-term yields.

Government debt financing has undergone major changes in the last few years. The introduction of the single currency resulted in increased competition among government debt managers, fostering transparency and liquidity both in the primary and in the secondary market. At the same time, regulatory changes relaxed constraints on foreign holdings for certain categories of institutional investors, which were allowed to diversify their financial portfolios abroad. The disappearance of exchange rate risks in the euro area significantly reduced investors' 'home bias'. For example, domestic ownership of government debt in the euro area decreased from 73 per cent in 1998 to 63 per cent in 2002. Compared with the years prior to Stage Three, the volume of individual issues has generally increased, as governments are interested in providing high liquidity to the markets and accessing electronic trading platforms. The use of electronic trading systems for the secondary market has increased efficiency and liquidity, overall lowering financing costs for issuers.

There have been a number of important innovations in debt management. Increasingly, euro area debt managers use interest rate swaps, which give them more flexibility to actively manage their liabilities, without influencing volumes of issuance in the market. The involvement of governments in swap markets has had an impact on the market itself, due to the large size of the operations involved, and has tended to put a ceiling on euro swap spreads (see E. Remolona and P. D. Wooldridge, *BIS Quarterly Review*, March 2003).

Another important innovation has been the issuance of index-linked bonds. France has taken the lead in this market, starting in October 2001 to issue bonds linked to the euro area HICP excluding tobacco. (HICP stands for Harmonized Index of Consumer Prices.) The Greek government followed in March 2003 and the Italian government in September 2003. These financial instruments are of particular interest for insurance corporations and pension funds, as these financial intermediaries tend to have long-term liabilities linked to nominal price developments. Indeed, according to the French Treasury, insurance corporations and pension funds acquired around 18 per cent of the French index-linked bonds offered on the occasion of the first issuance.

More local and regional governments have issued bonds to meet their financing needs, seizing the opportunity to access a larger investor base. Regulatory changes in some countries also partly contributed to this development as did the less favourable budgetary developments and the resulting increased borrowing requirements of these public entities. Despite the strong growth in issuance of debt securities by local and regional governments in recent years, its importance remains relatively low – the overall amount outstanding accounted for only around 4 per cent of total government debt securities issuance in the euro area at end-2002 – and it largely remains limited to a small number of countries.

The Stock Market

The development in the amount outstanding of quoted shares in the euro area has broadly followed the upswings and subsequent downturns in share prices. The amount outstanding of quoted shares held by non-financial sectors was equivalent to 64 per cent of GDP at end-2001 and had declined to 49 per cent of GDP by end-2002. The non-financial sectors' holdings of quoted shares increased steadily between 1995 and 2000, amid favourable developments in stock prices. In 2001, however, this trend was reversed and the downtrend continued throughout 2002, as stock prices declined for their third consecutive year. This development resulted in a significant drop in quoted shares' holdings, while the holdings of mutual fund shares were almost unchanged.

The market capitalization of euro area stock exchanges was equivalent to 47 per cent of GDP at the end of 2002 (see Table 5.9), which should be compared with a peak of 88 per cent of GDP in 1999. The decline mainly reflects the decrease in stock prices, but also de-listing, as the total number of companies quoted on euro area stock exchanges fell by 2 per cent between end-2001 and end-2002.

Stock prices developments in 2001 and in 2002 made equity financing an expensive option for euro area corporations. Both capital increases and initial public offerings

Table 5.9 Characteristics and activity of the euro area stock market

	1998	1999	2000	2001	2002
Number of public companies listed	3,870	–	5,103	5,910	5,787
Number of newly listed companies	635	937	929	820	590
Market capitalization of listed domestic shares (€ billions)	3,625	5,430	5,646	4,942	3,324
Market capitalization of listed domestic shares (% of GDP)	61	88	87	72	47
Gross amount of capital raised by domestic companies through listed shares (€ billion)	120	186	277	144	73
Concentration (top ten companies' percentage share of total market capitalization)	62	68	67	62	59

Source: ECB (Report on Financial Structures), World Federation of Exchanges and Comisión Nacional del Mercado de Valores.

(IPOs) declined. The new capital raised by domestic companies through issuance of equities on regulated stock exchanges was in 2001 almost half of the volume raised in 2000 and it declined even further in 2002. This was also reflected in a significant drop of the number of euro area IPOs as well as their volume in 2001 and in 2002 compared to the previous years (see Box on 'Recent trends in equity issuance in the euro area' on the March 2003 ECB's *Monthly Bulletin*). Similar developments took place also in the primary equity markets in the US and in Japan (see Figure 5.7).

The diminished opportunities to raise capital in the equity market affected significantly the financing possibilities of companies belonging to the so-called 'new economy', which typically lack collateral to put forward as loan guarantee. The activity of the 'parallel markets' (mainly the new markets created between 1996 and 2000 to specialize in the trading of shares in technology or low capitalization firms), which were flourishing at the end of 2000, dropped significantly. The market capitalization on these parallel markets, which amounted to around 3 per cent of GDP at the end of 2000, fell by 78 per cent between end-2000 and end-2002. Over that period the new capital raised on these exchanges was virtually nil. The German Neuer Markt was, in fact, closed down at the beginning of 2003.

Since the early 1990s, several trends have had an impact on stock exchange activity. Alternative trading systems operating on networks (such as the internet) in parallel with traditional market places have emerged, offering advantages such as the possibility of cross-border trading and lower transaction costs. While specialization and segmentation of stock exchanges seemed to prevail after the introduction of the single currency, more recent developments seem to point more towards consolidation, probably due to the increased competition.

The globalization of financial markets and market operations also prompted important developments in the clearing and settlement business. Some consolidation in the clearing and settlement infrastructure of the euro area has taken place. However, there are still many different systems in use in Europe. The present structure seems to leave

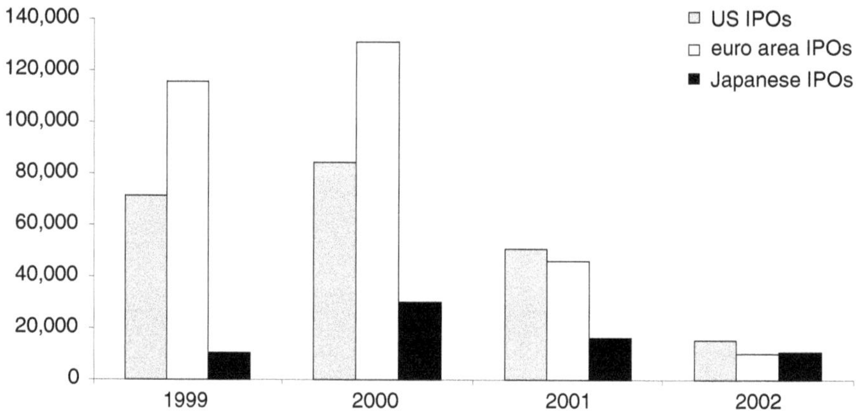

Figure 5.7 Volume of IPOs in the euro area, the US and Japan *(EUR millons)*

Source: Bondware Dealogic.

scope for further consolidation and harmonization, potentially generating substantial savings for end-users.

Financing of Non-financial Sectors

There are a number of common trends and characteristics with respect to the financing behaviour across the euro area. Above all, the private non-financial sectors in the euro area still to a large extent depend on bank intermediation for their financing, even taking into account the increasing use of securities financing for the corporate sector.

As regards non-financial corporations, the euro area economies are widely dominated by small and medium-sized enterprises, which generally, owing to informational barriers, only have limited possibilities to obtain funding directly from the financial markets and instead have to rely on intermediated finance. Loans and non-listed shares (including other equity) therefore remained the primary sources of finance for euro area firms during the period 1995–2002. Concerning the government sector, the process of consolidation in the latter half of the 1990s reduced the financing needs of euro area governments. At the same time, however, the creation of a more liquid government bond market following the introduction of the euro further moved government's preferences towards issuing bonds to the detriment of loan financing. Households' financing needs were primarily directed towards house purchases, partly reflecting historically low long-term interest rates as well as strong price increases in the property market in many countries.

Non-financial Corporations

The amount outstanding of total liabilities of non-financial corporations in the euro area amounted to 202 per cent of GDP by the end of 2002 (see Table 5.10). The net incurrence of liabilities increased considerably in the period between 1995 and 2002, as a result of both a high level of investment in a period of strong economic growth and low interest rates, and an unprecedented wave of mergers and acquisitions (see Figure 5.8).

By the end of 2001, the amounts outstanding of non-intermediated instruments of finance (i.e. securities other than shares and shares and other equity) accounted for 105 per cent of GDP, or 52 per cent of total external liabilities. A major part of the amounts outstanding of shares and other equity, however, takes the form of non-marketable/private equity.[12] This is due mainly to the particular industry structure of the euro area with many small and medium-sized enterprises the major part of which are generally not able to list their equity on public stock exchanges. By contrast, intermediated instruments (mainly MFI loans) accounted for around 67 per cent of GDP, or 33 per cent of the total.

12 A rough estimate based on a subset of the euro area countries indicates that around 60 per cent of the total of shares and other equity outstanding consist of non-listed shares or other private equity.

Table 5.10 Financing of non-financial corporations

	Average annual transactions (% of GDP)		Amounts outstanding (end-2002)	
	1995–2001	2002	% of total	% of GDP
Currency and deposits	0.0	0.0	0.0	0.0
Securities other than shares	0.3	0.2	4.1	8.2
Short-term	0.2	0.1	1.1	2.3
Long-term	0.1	0.2	2.7	5.5
Loans	4.2	3.2	33.0	66.7
Short-term	1.5	–0.4	10.7	21.7
Long-term	2.7	3.6	22.3	45.0
Shares and other equity	3.2	2.8	48.1	97.3
Insurance reserves	0.1	0.2	2.0	3.9
Other accounts payable	0.1	1.5	12.8	25.9
Trade credits and advances			7.7	15.6
Total	**9.1**	**7.9**	**100.0**	**202.0**

Source: ECB.

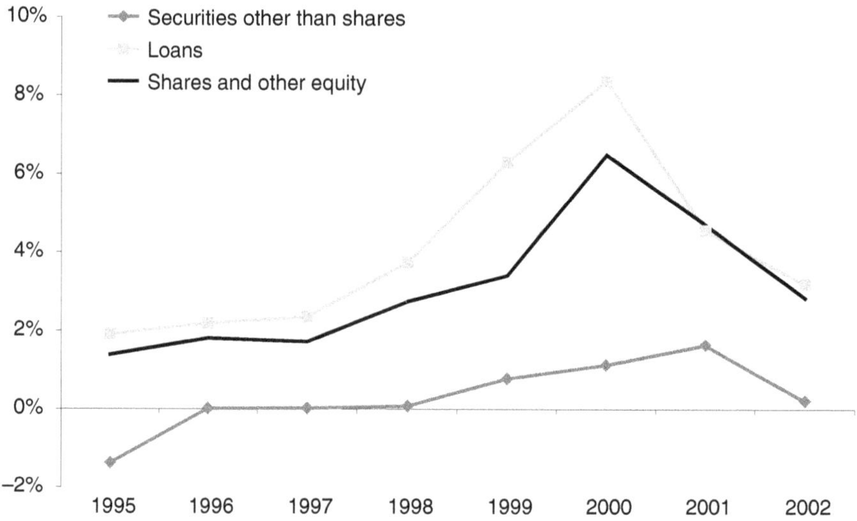

Figure 5.8 Financing of non-financial corporations broken down by instruments *(transactions; % of GDP)*

Source: ECB.

However, considering transaction data for the period 1995–2002 loan financing on average exceeded non-intermediated financing (such as bond and equity financing). In general, external financing increased considerably in the years 1998–2000 when corporate restructuring, the liberalization of the telecommunication sector and its subsequent large acquisitions of UMTS licences enhanced the financing needs of particularly large corporations in the euro area. The buoyant stock market in these years reduced the costs of raising equity capital, which provided cheap funding for the wave of mergers and acquisitions and a number of new listings. Following the correction of stock prices from mid-2000 onwards equity financing declined sharply. Alongside the introduction of the euro, which as noted above paved the way for a larger corporate bond market in the euro area, also the numerous mergers and acquisitions and the telecommunications industry liberalization contributed to increase euro area firms' reliance on funding through the issuance of bonds.

The issuance of corporate bonds and listings on public stock exchanges is, however, generally restricted to the larger companies, whereas the bulk of euro area non-financial corporations still heavily rely on bank loans. The strong use of loans in the period under consideration could nevertheless also be partly explained by the increasing use of syndicated loans, whereby a number of intermediaries provide funds under pre-specified conditions, giving firms faster and generally easier access to funds than traditional bank loans. It should also be mentioned that the growth in loan financing in the late 1990s and 2000 was closely linked with the growth of corporate bond financing through the provision of bridging loans.[13]

There are substantial differences across the euro area countries as regards the financing of non-financial corporations. These differences reflect both particular industry structures in the individual countries, such as the importance of small and medium-sized enterprises, and the relative size of the stock and bond markets. Indeed, in countries that are dominated by small and medium-sized enterprises the primary sources of financing would tend to be traditional bank loans, trade credit, non-listed shares and other forms of equity. In countries with relatively more large firms and more developed financial markets, corporate bonds and listed shares would tend to be important means of finance. Figure 5.9 illustrates the heterogeneous nature of non-financial corporate finance across the euro area.

In all countries except Austria, shares and other equity are the most important financing instrument. Loan financing is relatively important in Austria (in particular), Germany, the Netherlands and Portugal, whereas trade credit and other advances are relatively important in Spain and Portugal (and to a lesser extent in France and Italy). Finally, debt securities financing is mostly of limited size, although above the euro area average in France and Austria.

Non-financial corporations in the euro area and in Japan resort to loans to a much larger extent than US corporations (see Figure 5.10). Bonds represent a significant source of funding for US and Japanese non-financial corporations, while they are still

13 A bridge loan is typically a short-term loan that is used until a person or company can secure permanent financing. See for example de Bondt (2002) and the Box entitled 'The relationship between intermediated and debt securities financing of non-financial corporations in the euro area' on p. 12 of the October 2003 issue of the ECB's Monthly Bulletin on the substitution between bank loan financing and corporate bond financing.

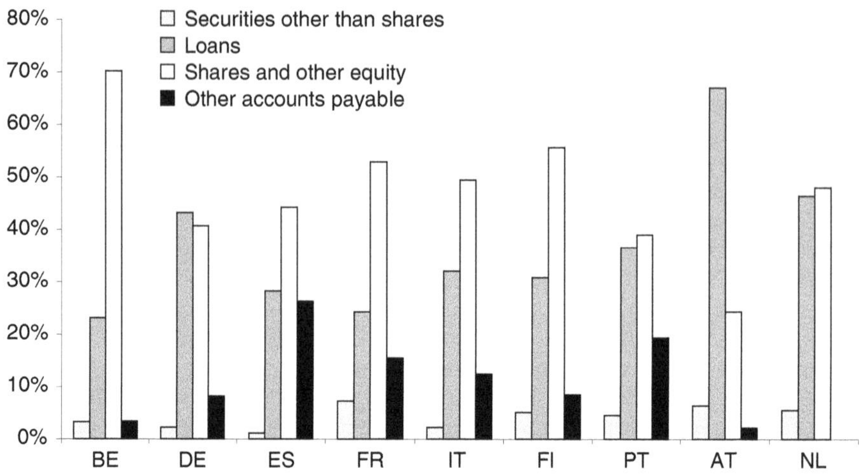

Figure 5.9 Distribution of means of non-financial corporate finance broken down by countries and instruments *(end-2002; % of total liabilities)*

Source: ECB.

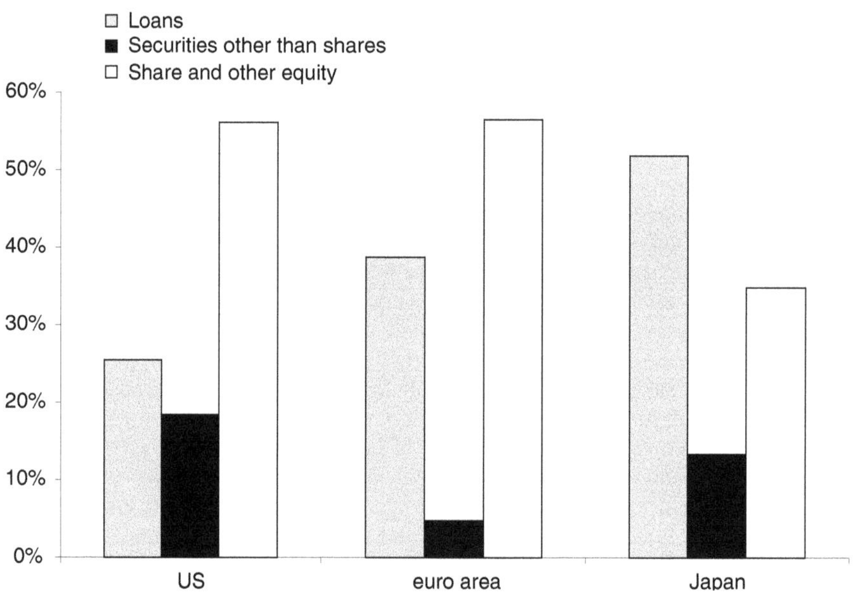

Figure 5.10 Financing of non-financial corporations in the euro area, the US and Japan *(end-2002; % of total external finance)*

Source: ECB, Board of Governors of the Federal Reserve System and Bank of Japan.
Note: Other accounts payable, currency and deposits and insurance technical reserves are excluded.

relatively unimportant in the euro area. The importance of private equity (unquoted shares) seems to be a peculiar characteristic of the euro area financial system, due to the fact that euro area economies have a relatively large proportion of small and medium-sized enterprises (SMEs). Indeed, 66 per cent of all employees in Europe are employed in SMEs, compared with 46 per cent in the US and 33 per cent in Japan.[14]

General Government

Total liabilities of euro area general governments amounted to around 80 per cent of GDP by the end of 2002, which is significantly more than in the US (63 per cent), but less than in Japan (91 per cent). There are, however, significant differences across the euro area Member States as regards the amount of government liabilities. Whereas the level of general government liabilities supersedes GDP in Belgium, Greece and Italy, all other countries are somewhat below the euro area average.

The general government sector in the euro area tends to rely on the issuance of debt securities in order to satisfy its financing needs (see Table 5.11). Thus, debt securities issued accounted for around 72 per cent of total external liabilities, whereas loans only accounted for little more than 17 per cent.

The general government sector's tendency to finance itself by issuing debt securities has been particularly marked in recent years, as confirmed by transaction data. In fact, debt securities issuance accounted for over 90 per cent of total financing in the

Table 5.11 Financing of general government

	Average annual transactions (% of GDP)		**Amounts outstanding (end-2002)**	
	1995–2001	2002	% of total	% of GDP
Currency and deposits	0.2	0.4	5.5	4.4
Securities other than shares	2.5	3.0	72.5	58.3
Short-term	–0.1	0.6	6.7	5.4
Long-term	2.6	2.4	65.9	53.0
Loans	–0.1	–0.1	17.5	14.0
Short-term	0.0	0.2	1.6	1.3
Long-term	–0.1	–0.3	15.8	12.7
Shares and other equity	0.0	0.0	0.0	0.0
Insurance reserves	0.0	0.0	0.0	0.0
Other accounts payable	0.1	0.0	4.5	3.6
Trade credits and advances			1.7	1.4
Total	**2.7**	**3.2**	**100.0**	**80.4**

Source: ECB.

14 European Commission (2002), 'SMEs in Europe, including a first glance at EU candidate countries,' Observatory of European SMEs.

period 1995–2002. More specifically, issuance of longer-term debt securities has been the dominant means of finance over the same period, which reflects the attempt of many euro area governments to lengthen the maturity of their debt. This was particularly evident in former high-inflation countries, such as Greece, Spain, Italy and Portugal. It should be mentioned, though, that despite the general tendency to lengthen the maturity of government debt, some governments have actually shortened the duration of their debt through swaps and other risk management instruments.

In general, the decreased reliance on bank loan financing and the increased use of longer-term debt financing seem to have been closely linked to the introduction of the euro and the process of fiscal consolidation leading up to it. The combination of reduced fiscal deficits, declining interest rates, lower inflation and a unified, more liquid government bond market reduced governments' use of bank financing and increased their reliance on debt securities issues. Arguably, the increased degree of 'securitization' has, *ceteris paribus*, allowed more cost-efficient government debt management.

Following the economic slowdown in 2001 and 2002 fiscal balances deteriorated, which led to an increase in external financing by euro area governments, thereby reversing somewhat the declining trend seen in the latter part of the 1990s and in 2000 (see Figure 5.11).

Households

The level of indebtedness, i.e. the value of their outstanding loans, of euro area households amounted to around 52 per cent of GDP by the end of 2002 (see Table 5.12). The household sector in the euro area was thus less indebted than in the US

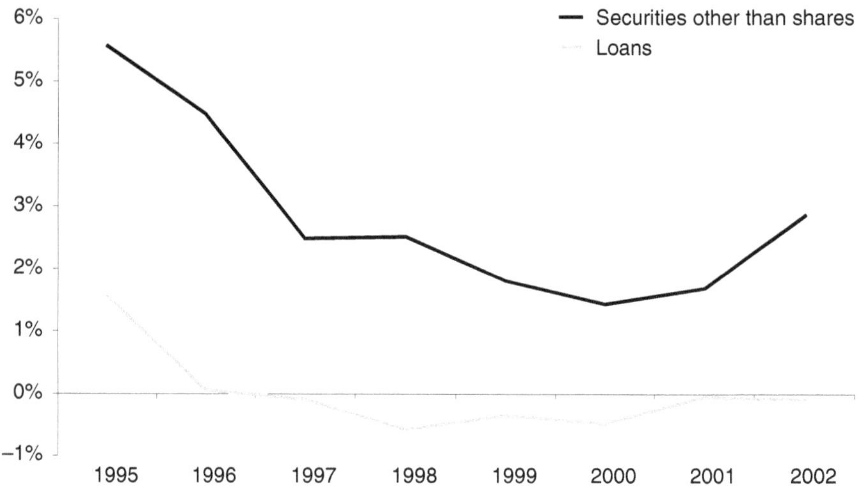

Figure 5.11 Financing of general government *(annual transactions as % of GDP)*

Source: ECB.

Table 5.12 Financing of households

	Average annual transactions (% of GDP)		Amounts outstanding (end-2002)	
	1995–2001	2002	% of total	% of GDP
Currency and deposits	0.0	0.0	0.0	0.0
Securities other than shares	0.0	0.0	0.0	0.0
Loans	2.8	3.1	90.3	52.1
Short-term	0.1	0.1	7.1	4.1
Long-term	2.7	3.0	83.1	48.0
Shares and other equity	0.0	0.0	0.0	0.0
Insurance reserves	0.0	0.0	0.7	0.4
Other accounts payable	0.4	0.0	9.1	5.2
Trade credit and advances			2.4	1.4
Total	**3.2**	**3.1**	**100.0**	**57.3**

Source: ECB.

(82 per cent) and in Japan (67 per cent). The relative importance of external finance of households varied, however, considerably across the euro area countries (see Figure 5.12). While the ratio of total liabilities to GDP was relatively high in Germany, Spain, the Netherlands and Portugal, it was far below average in countries such as Belgium, Italy and Finland where households to a larger extent rely on internal savings.

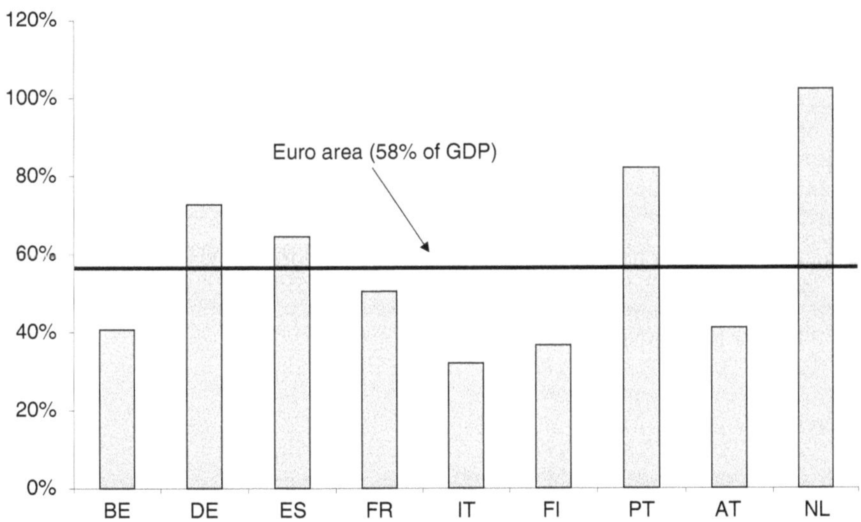

Figure 5.12 Household indebtedness across the euro area countries *(% of GDP)*

Source: ECB.

Of household liabilities, 90 per cent are in the form of loans, most of which are granted by euro area MFIs. Lending for house purchase constitute around two-thirds of all domestic MFI loans. Partly reflecting the historically low long-term interest rates and the boom in property markets in recent years the percentage share of loans for house purchase to total MFI loans has been increasing throughout the period. However, there have been notable differences across countries in this context, reflecting heterogeneous tax treatment and borrowing possibilities (e.g. the existence of a well-functioning mortgage financing market and differences in the business cycle). In addition, it should be mentioned that in some countries 'loans for house purchases' might be used for other purposes, such as consumption of goods, via the so-called equity withdrawal.

Conclusions

The euro area financial system is a well-developed system in which intermediated and non-intermediated instruments are more or less equally important. It therefore lies somewhere between the more market-oriented US financial system and the more bank-oriented Japanese financial system. Households can be regarded as the ultimate providers of funds for non-financial corporations and governments. The overall picture displaying households as financing the other two domestic, non-financial sectors and the position of the euro area vis-à-vis the rest of the world has been broadly stable since the mid 1990s.

Non-financial corporations in the euro area and in Japan resort to loans to a much larger extent than US corporations. The importance of private equity (unquoted shares) seems to be a peculiar characteristic of the euro area financial system, due to the fact that euro area economies have a relatively large proportion of small and medium-sized enterprises. Loans for house purchase constitute the lion's share of households' liabilities.

In the late 1990s, the euro area financial system started to rely less on traditional bank intermediation through loans and deposits, with other types of financial intermediaries developing, as investors allocated more funds to long-term savings products and direct securities holdings. Stock price increases at the end of the 1990s had a significant impact on the euro area financial system by reinforcing some of the general trends, e.g. towards increased household and corporate shareholdings. At the same time, the corporate bond market flourished, supported by several temporary factors. The bond market still continues to develop, as corporations are seizing the opportunity to issue bonds on a euro area-wide scale.

References

Bondt, G. de (2002), *Euro Area Corporate Debt Securities Market: First empirical evidence*, ECB Working Paper Series No. 164.

Carnegie-Brown, B. and M. King (2003), 'Development of European Bond Markets', in Gaspar, V., Hartmann, P. and Sleijpen, O (eds.) *The Transformation of the European Financial System*, Second ECB Central Banking Conference October 2002, ECB, May, pp. 247–262.

European Central Bank (2002), *Report on Financial Structures*, October.

Gaspar, V., Hartmann, P. and Sleijpen, O. (2003), 'Introduction', in Gaspar, V., Hartmann, P. and Sleijpen, O (eds.) *The Transformation of the European Financial System*, Second ECB Central Banking Conference October 2002, ECB, May, pp. 7–30.

Issing, O. (2003), 'Relationship Lending in the Euro Area', in Gaspar, V., Hartmann, P. and Sleijpen, O (eds.) *The Transformation of the European Financial System*, Second ECB Central Banking Conference October 2002, ECB, May, pp. 120–22.

Remolona, E. and P.D. Woodbridge, *BIS Quarterly Review*, March 2003.

Part III
Elements of Integration across Financial Services and Markets

Chapter 6

What Effects is EMU Having on the Integration of Financial Services?

Frank Dierick and Jukka Vesala[1]

Introduction

This Chapter focuses on capital market-related and retail financial services provided to firms and households. Several data sources are tapped to derive indicators of integration in these services in the euro area. While the focus of the study is on integration, the Chapter also comments on whether a simultaneous tendency towards increasing competition can be detected. In practice, it proves to be very difficult to disentangle, on the one hand, the effect of the single currency and, on the other hand, the effect of other measures that foster financial integration, such as a further harmonization in the regulatory framework. Hence, the discussion below takes sometimes a broader perspective by looking beyond the pure impact of EMU (see also Cabral et al., 2002).

The Chapter is organized in two major sections; one dealing with capital market-related financial services and one dealing with retail services. Each section investigates the different sub-markets in detail, in particular the market for corporate finance services, private equity and venture capital, securities trading, retail banking, asset management and insurance products. Both sections assess the degree of integration on the basis of price-based indicators as well as quantity-based indicators. The last section summarizes the evidence and discusses further obstacles to integration.

This chapter draws on the methodological framework set out in Chapter 3 when providing evidence of integration in financial services. In financial services, indirect quantity-based indicators come at the fore, because of the product heterogeneity and lack of comprehensive data. This also calls for particular caution in interpreting the indicators. The Chapter builds further on Chapter 4 where the policies and regulations to support financial integration are described. It also complements Chapters 7 and 8 by analysing the markets for underwriting and for other financial services in the capital markets area.

Capital Market-related Services

Capital market-related activities are associated with the allocation of savings to the users of long-term funds via marketable securities or lending. They include several

1 The chapter draws significantly on earlier work of the authors and Inês Cabral (Cabral et al., 2002).

corporate finance services, such as underwriting and other investment banking services, syndicated lending, corporate restructuring and investment, corporate advice, etc. This area also includes the part of asset management and trading relating to large-scale portfolios and institutional investors.

Highly specialized professional skills are required in these activities, and customers are often large financial or non-financial corporations, to whom several different financial products and services are offered at the same time. Hence, elements such as service quality, product bundling, distribution capacity and the financial intermediary's reputation are often very relevant. Because of these features, the law-of-one-price is more difficult to apply than in the case of wholesale activities, and it is relevant to look also at quantity-based indicators of integration.

Euro Area Capital Market Developments

As is explained in more detail in Chapter 8, capital markets in Europe have grown and deepened substantially over the past years, a process driven by macroeconomic, demographic, technological and financial innovation factors. Over the longer term, growth is likely to be stimulated by increased disposable income and wealth, a greater propensity to invest in securities, and the development of collective investment and supplementary pension schemes. In the euro area, the share of securities holdings in households' assets (including investment funds) now challenges the share of traditional bank deposits.

The introduction of the euro has given a major impetus to the growth and integration of capital markets. Before the introduction of the euro, the markets were largely segmented because of factors such as different risk-free yield curves, foreign exchange risk and currency matching rules, which restricted geographical diversification of investment by institutional investors and limited the size of the markets. Under the single currency conditions, these factors have been largely overcome.

The developments on the demand side and the emergence of a wider capital market in euros have opened up possibilities for especially the larger firms to diversify funding sources and to reduce funding costs. Especially the bond market grew very strongly, reflecting the increased trust in stable borrowing costs and the ability of firms to go beyond their domestic markets under the single currency. Likewise, a growing expansion of the lower-rated segment of the market could be observed, pointing towards a broadening of the set of firms that gained access to bond financing. However, the European market for high-yield bonds continues to be underdeveloped with a market size of approximately only one tenth of its US counterpart (see Galati and Tsatsaronis, 2001). Syndicated loans[2] and equity issuance also grew strongly, although at less impressive rates, and equity issuance suffered a setback in 2001 and into 2002 and 2003 due to poor market conditions.

The evolution depicted above is illustrative of the progress of disintermediation in Europe, i.e. the shift in the financial system away from the dominance of non-marketable bank loans towards an increasing role for marketable securities like in the

2 Syndicated loans are bank loans with several credit providers. Such loans can also be re-sold in the capital market, a practice, which seems to becoming more important.

US. All in all, such diversification should also contribute to a stabilization of the financing flows to the corporate sector. For banks, the development implies a growing demand for services in the areas of investment banking and asset management. Bond and also equity financing still represent a rather small share of European firms' overall financing, however (see Chapter 5).

Corporate Finance Services

Price-based indicators Signs of integration in corporate finance services can be seen in the convergence of intermediaries' fee levels, although it must be recognized that the exact content of the services provided strongly influences the fees charged. In order to investigate pricing developments separately for different size-classes of transactions, the available fee data were ranked according to the value of the transactions and then broken down into size-classes of quintiles (i.e. 20 per cent-segments).[3] For each of these segments, the weighted average fees were calculated as a percentage of the face value of the transactions (using transaction sizes as weights). In the following, information is presented for the largest and medium-sized transactions (the upper and median quintiles).[4]

There is evidence that integration has increased through enhanced cross-border competition. Gross fees[5] in the securities issues by euro area firms show a declining trend over the period 1995–2000 for both size-classes; this is particularly discernible in bond issues (Table 6.1). In 2000, fees for the largest bond transactions were less than one-third of their level five years earlier. Combined with the quantity-based evidence presented below, this evolution points to greater competition in a market

Table 6.1 Gross fees on securities issues and commitment fees on syndicated loans in euro (or euro legacy currencies) taken up by euro area resident non-financial firms *(% of face value or basis points)*

	Bonds		Equity		Syndicated loans	
	Upper quintile	Median quintile	Upper quintile	Median quintile	Upper quintile	Median quintile
1995	1.88	2.10	2.84	3.82	26.16	35.49
1998	2.05	1.65	2.22	4.02	12.25	13.47
1999	1.34	1.66	2.59	4.46	20.98	42.55
2000	0.56	1.08	2.37	2.99	17.85	53.99

Source: Bondware and Loanware. Commitment fees in syndicated loans (in basis points).

3 The analysis is based on data retrieved from comprehensive commercial databases. We focus on the instruments expressed in euro or euro legacy currencies.

4 The data are not sufficient to systematically evaluate the fees in small-value transactions.

5 Gross fees equal total commissions for managing, underwriting and selling a new issue, which is expressed as a percentage of the nominal face amount of the issue.

that is indeed integrated and operates on a European (or even global) basis. The downward pressure on fees has been somewhat more subdued in medium-sized transactions, but fees also decreased in this category to roughly half their level in 1995. As a result of the significant decline, underwriting fees in the euro segment are now to a level comparable to that of the US dollar segment (see also Galati and Tsatsaronis, 2001).

In equity issuance, the decline in fees has not been so strong, which may signal weaker integration and the greater importance of local factors. In addition, fees have been higher in equity than bond intermediation. As underwriting fees typically form a significant part of gross fees in the issuance of securities, this also reflects the different risk nature of the instruments when underwriting guarantees are provided.[6] Hence, local information is more valuable in underwriting equities than in the case of bonds, since the risks involved in equity are higher.

Commitment fees[7] in large syndicated loans have also declined, but less smoothly than in bond and equity issues. The upturn in fees in the late 1990s was probably to a large extent due to the financing of TMT (telecom, media, technology) sector companies, which were risky and therefore justified higher commitment fees.

There is some evidence (not presented here) that the variability of fees across countries and intermediaries increased over the period 1995 to 2000. However, this evolution cannot be taken as negative evidence of integration, since two different forces are at work. On the one hand, there is integration into a larger market, which leads to converging as well as declining fee levels as a result of increasing competition. On the other hand, the growth in capital market activity has occurred in higher-risk transactions in particular, leading to higher fee variability (since underwriting entails the intermediary bearing some of the risk).

Quantity-based indicators As discussed in Chapter 3, because of service heterogeneity and risk differences, as well as service charges intertwining with the pricing data, more unambiguous, albeit indirect, evidence of integration needs to be obtained from quantity-based indicators. The greater scope of capital markets could be expected to integrate the market for corporate finance services by expanding the use of financial intermediaries beyond the domestic sector. In a potentially larger market, international distribution capacity will carry a heavier weight, eroding the franchises that previous 'house banks' had in the distribution of securities of firms located in their own country. Hence, in an integrating market, the nationality of an intermediary, and in particular the fact that it is of the same nationality as the firm being financed, should become less important. In the following we will investigate the links between euro area issuers of bonds, equity and syndicated loans and their intermediaries.

In matching the firm-intermediary nationalities, the following approach was followed. The intermediaries were investigated on a group basis, i.e. all transactions involving intermediaries belonging to the same financial group were aggregated and grouped according to the nationality of the intermediary's controlling group. In this way, transactions performed by intermediaries based in the City of London (the most

6 I.e. there is a chance that the underwriting bank needs to absorb the instruments into its own portfolio.

7 A fee paid by a borrower on undrawn portions of a loan.

popular location for investment banks in Europe) will not be assigned to the UK but to their country of origin. This approach makes it possible to bypass the specific residential element of London that would otherwise bias the analysis of the nationality of the intermediary. The nationality for issuers is assigned on the basis of their residence and not on the basis of the country where their controlling shareholder is based, in order to analyse the financial services obtained by firms located in the euro area.

As regards bonds, the importance of bookrunners[8] having the same nationality as the issuer followed a decreasing trend between 1995 and 2000. The role of non-European (essentially US) intermediaries increased in parallel over the same period (Figure 6.1). This suggests significant integration within the euro area, as well as an ever-increasing global component in the competition in these markets. These two tendencies were evident in all size-classes, but foreign competition was most prevalent in the largest transactions. The role of domestic intermediaries eroded quite rapidly. In 1995, domestic intermediaries were always involved in large issues, while five years later they were involved in only 60 per cent of such transactions.[9] In 2000, a US bookrunner was already present in 80 per cent of the cases, demonstrating that US firms had made aggressive inroads into the European market.

There are no such clear trends in equity issuance, which is in line with the notion of more local equity markets (Figure 6.2). The involvement of domestic and US bookrunners in the upper segment of the transactions was more or less equal throughout the period covered. Thus, in spite of the introduction of the euro, bookrunners'

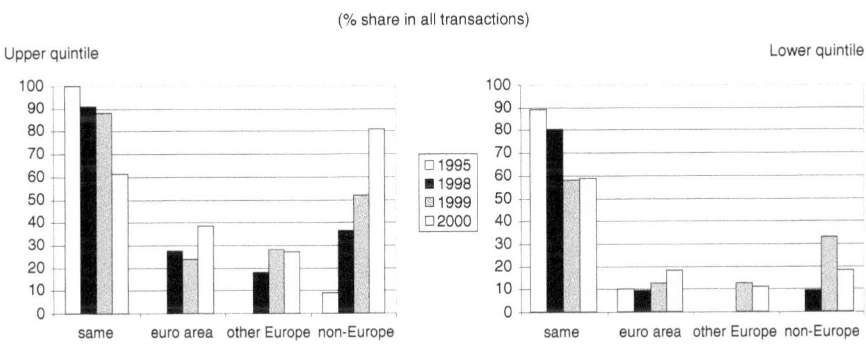

Figure 6.1 Bookrunners of euro area resident non-financial firms' bond issues *(% share in all transactions)*

Source: Bondware.
Note: Shares sum above 100 per cent, because single transactions can have several bookrunners.

8 Bookrunners are responsible for initiating the transaction with the borrower and for organizing the underwriting and placing of the issue in the primary capital market.

9 Since several intermediaries may be involved in each transaction, the shares do not total to 100 per cent.

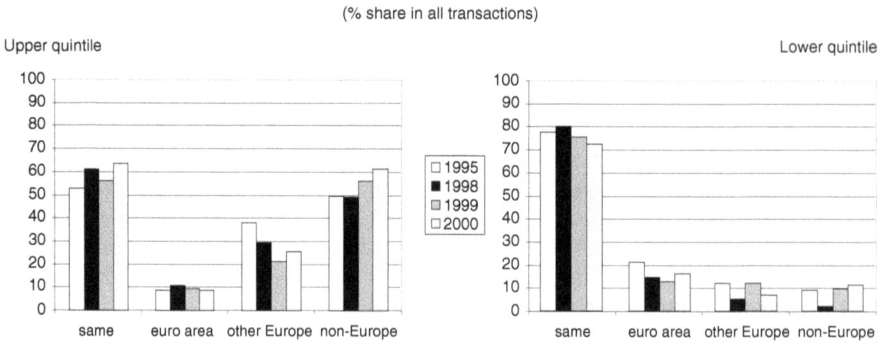

Figure 6.2 Bookrunners of euro area resident non-financial firms' equity issues *(% share in all transactions)*

Source: Bondware.
Note: Shares sum above 100 per cent, because single transactions can have several bookrunners.

national franchise for equity issuers has seemingly not yet been seriously affected, unlike in bond issuance.

Lastly, developments were even more different in syndicated loans (Figure 6.3). Non-domestic intermediaries have increased their presence in large transactions, especially banks from other euro area countries. In 1995, 15 per cent of large syndicated loans involved at least one non-domestic euro area arranger,[10] and in 2000 this

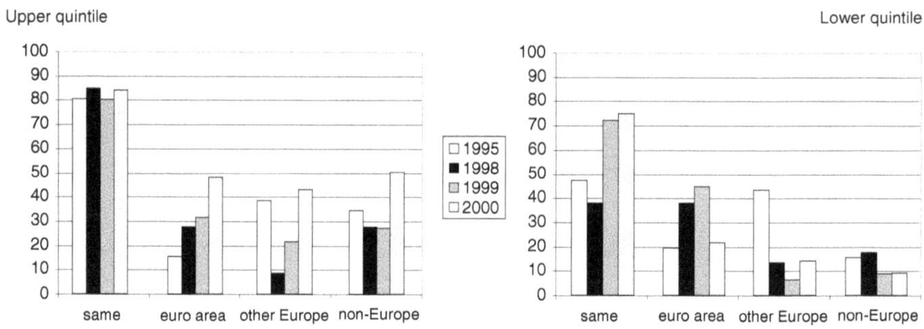

Figure 6.3 Arrangers in euro area resident non-financial firms' syndicated loans *(% share in all transactions)*

Source: Loanware.
Note: Shares sum above 100 per cent, because single transactions can have several bookrunners.

10 Arrangers are mandated banks responsible for originating, structuring and syndicating the loan transaction.

figure was over three times higher, indicating substantially increased cross-border lending. However, this evolution did not reduce the share of domestic banks, as they continued to be involved in 80 per cent of the transactions. In lending (as well as equity issuance) the need for local information and risk assessment seems to have endured. In smaller-sized transactions, the position of domestic intermediaries actually strengthened. This may reflect the fact that large internationalized intermediaries now show less appetite for smaller transactions, where the need for local information and the asymmetry in information about the creditworthiness of the borrower are high.

Tables 6.2, 6.3 and 6.4 provide summary information on the nationality distribution of the top 20 intermediaries of bonds, equities and syndicated loans issued by euro area firms between 1995 and 2002 in order to characterize the markets from a euro area-wide perspective. On the basis of the above evidence, the markets seem to be integrated on an area-wide scale, especially in the case of bonds. Since the top 20 lists cover the large majority of the markets for the three instrument categories, they give a good overview of the area-wide markets.

Euro area banks have been incurring fairly heavy losses in their market share in bond intermediation because of the aggressive inroads made by US banks. Euro area banks lost about half of their market share between 1995 and 2002. However, the rapidly increasing market size and the fact that several intermediaries (local and non-local) could be present in individual transactions tended also to increase the business volumes of the European intermediaries until the declines in capital market activity witnessed in 2001 and early 2002. In the period between 1995 and 2002, US players were able to increase their market share impressively, from 2 per cent to 30 per cent. To a certain extent, this may be linked with the use of the funds raised to finance

Table 6.2 Distribution of top 20 bookrunners in bonds in euro (or euro legacy currencies) issued by euro area resident non-financial firms and grouped according to nationality bookrunner *(% share in all transactions)*

		1995	2000	2001	2002
euro area		95.8	43.2	46.4	50.7
of which	DE	9.0	11.6	12.9	15.9
	FR	53.6	23.6	26.2	25.3
	NL	25.7	5.7	4.8	6.4
other Europe		1.0	10.6	14.2	11.2
of which	UK	0.0	4.1	6.1	8.3
	CH	1.0	6.5	8.1	2.9
rest of world		2.1	40.6	32.0	30.4
of which	US	2.1	40.6	32.0	30.4
	JP	0.0	0.0	0.0	0.0
Total top 20		98.9	94.4	92.6	92.3

Source: Bondware.

Table 6.3 Distribution of top 20 bookrunners in equities in euro (or euro legacy currencies) issued by euro area resident non-financial firms and grouped according to nationality bookrunner *(% share in all transactions)*

		1995	2000	2001	2002
euro-area		64.2	41.4	45.6	33.1
of which	DE	14.5	20.1	15.8	11.6
	FR	20.7	6.3	12.4	12.9
	NL	9.5	6.1	7.9	2.6
other Europe		20.3	10.6	15.1	13.2
of which	UK	0.0	0.0	0.0	5.4
	CH	20.3	10.6	14.0	7.8
rest of world		11.5	35.7	36.6	49.1
of which	US	10.8	35.7	36.6	49.1
	JP	0.0	0.0	0.0	0.0
Total top 20		96.0	87.7	97.3	95.4

Source: Bondware.

Table 6.4 Distribution of top 20 mandated arrangers in syndicated loans in euro (or euro legacy currencies) taken up by euro area resident non-financial firms and grouped according to nationality arranger *(% share in all transactions)*

		1995	2000	2001	2002
euro-area		61.0	47.2	53.3	47.4
of which	DE	26.2	10.0	25.0	17.9
	FR	10.8	18.6	15.4	16.4
	NL	7.6	13.7	5.7	6.4
other Europe		13.2	9.9	7.8	17.2
of which	UK	8.1	6.3	7.8	15.7
	CH	5.1	3.6	0.0	1.5
rest of world		10.7	29.6	21.4	18.9
of which	US	10.7	29.6	21.4	18.9
	JP	0.0	0.0	0.0	0.0
Total top 20		84.9	86.7	82.5	83.5

Source: Loanware.

acquisitions in the US. Galati and Tsatsaronis (2001) provide comparable figures for the US which show that for US firms borrowing in US dollars, by contrast, the fact that the bookrunner has the same nationality as the borrower continued to play a very important role. According to their figures, US bookrunners had for the period

1999–2000 a share of 79 per cent in such issues compared to 82 per cent in the period 1996–1998.

The intermediation of equity issues shows a similar pattern, albeit somewhat more subdued. Here too, euro area banks have been losing their market share to US firms. A comparison of bonds and equities reveals some differences across intermediaries, for example, the relatively strong position of the French banks in bond intermediation. The same picture emerges for mandated arrangers of syndicated loans, although changes in the market share of euro area and US banks are not as strong as in the case of bond and equity issues. In this area, euro area arrangers have tended to maintain a market share of around 50 per cent.

Tables 6.2, 6.3 and 6.4 also reveal a strong market concentration, even at the area-wide level. The largest 20 intermediaries (CR20) account for around 95 per cent of the markets in bond and equity intermediation and for roughly 85 per cent of syndicated lending. Indeed, economies of scale are extremely relevant in capital market-related activities under the single currency conditions (Dermine, 1999). Analysts are required to process industry-wide (rather than country-specific) information, which means monitoring a large number of European companies and requires a wide network of corporate contacts. In addition, the provision of underwriting and other investment banking services to large clients requires large scale on the part of intermediaries. Other concentration indicators also point to the considerable significance of the largest players in all three activities.[11] The top 10 firms (CR10) control between 60 and 70 per cent of the euro area market and the top three (CR3) between a quarter and a third. The market for syndicated loans appears somewhat less concentrated.

In the bond market, the relative importance of the top 10 and 20 bookrunners remained fairly stable over the period 1995–2000, while the top three as well as the top five lost around 10 to 15 per cent of their share. This indicates that the largest (domestic) players lost some of their market share to other intermediaries, confirming the picture of a strongly expanding market with an increasing role for non-domestic (US) players. A similar development can be identified in the syndicated loan market, while in the case of equities, the two concentration ratios have declined to a much lesser extent. These figures underscore the growing contestability of the markets, also reflected in the earlier identified downward trend in fee levels.

Private Equity and Venture Capital

Venture capital, or investments in unquoted companies for the launch, early development or expansion of a business, is considered to be crucial for job and wealth creation. In 2002, the European private equity and venture capital industry raised about €28 billion and invested approximately the same amount. This figure is markedly lower compared to the peak of €48 billion reached in 2000 at the height of the technology boom (Figure 6.4). The venture capital funding in Europe comes predominantly from banks, which account for more than a quarter of all funds, and to

11 A similar concentration of the market also applies in the case of corporate advice and restructuring services, e.g. based on the league tables published by Euromoney.

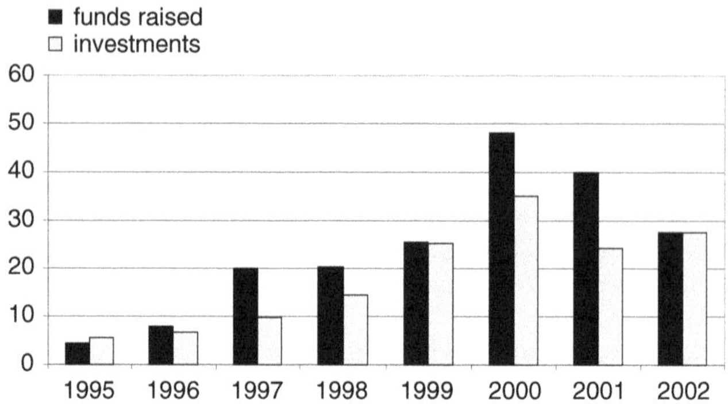

Figure 6.4 Venture capital activity in the EU *(€ billions)*

Source: European Private Equity and Venture Capital Association (EVCA).

a lesser extent also from pension funds, insurance companies, funds of funds and government agencies. Somewhat more than half of all the investments are used for buy-outs, an activity at the end phase of the venture capital cycle.

Although the venture capital industry grew quickly in the second half of the 1990s, it remains relatively small compared to the US. For example, venture capital investments to GDP are more than 2.5 times as high in the US as in Europe. This marked difference has been attributed to differences in the degree of entrepeneurship, risk aversion, regulation and tax treatment between the two geographical areas. Also the respective roles that banks and markets play in the economy, and in particular the existence of a mature stock market for high-growth companies, is an important explanatory factor (De la Dehesa, 2002).

The venture capital industry is unevenly developed across the EU so that in many European countries there continues to be a strong growth potential for risk capital. The private equity business remains a predominantly local activity, especially on the investment side. Private equity operators in Europe still obtain more than half of their funding from domestic sources and invest for about three quarters in domestic projects, with other European countries contributing about 20 per cent on both the funding and investment side. Nevertheless, there is a clear trend to diversify more internationally.

The existence of an efficient equity market is a key element in the development of venture capital as it allows smaller listed companies to raise capital and offers an exit route for private equity investors. Stock exchanges that cater specifically for the needs of young, fast-growing companies, such as the Nasdaq in the US, are seen as an essential element in fostering entrepreneurship and stimulating economic growth. In the wake of the boom of TMT stocks, various public equity markets were also created in Europe in the second half of the 1990s in order to accommodate small and young companies. In the UK, the Alternative Investment Market (AIM) was established (1995), later followed by Techmark (1999), a market tailored to technology stocks. Other exchanges followed suit, creating domestic markets for this type of companies. A number of these exchanges (Amsterdam, Brussels, Frankfurt, Milan,

Paris) entered into the pan-European network EURO.NM to promote the listing and trading on other member exchanges. Easdaq was established in Belgium (1996) as a pan-European market for small- and medium-sized growth companies, modelled on the Nasdaq in the US. The experience of these markets seems to be uneven, some attracting high-growth companies from a particular industry, others predominantly raising the interest of companies previously listed on the main market (Bottazzi and Da Rin 2002) (Table 6.5).

Some of these pan-European initiatives recently witnessed important changes, not at least as a result of the burst of the TMT bubble in 2000. Easdaq was acquired by Nasdaq as part of the latter's global strategy, and changed its name into Nasdaq Europe. The development of the market, however, continued to be hampered by its small scale and rather undiversified nature and the shareholders decided to close it down in the course of 2003. The EURO.NM initiative suffered from the different strategies of, on the one hand the exchanges of Paris, Amsterdam and Brussels which were merged into Euronext in 2000, and on the other hand Deutsche Börse which opted for a stand-alone strategy. Even the Neuer Market, at one point one of the largest of the 'new' markets in Europe, was badly hit by the very poor business environment and Deutsche Börse decided to close it down mid 2003, moving the companies still listed into other parts of its market. Tellingly, with the exception of Techmark and AIM, hardly any IPOs took place on these new markets in 2002 and also in 2003. Concluding, one can say that up to now no successful pan-European 'new' stock market has yet emerged.

Securities Trading

Asset management and trading have become an integral part of banking through two channels. First, banks account for the management of around 80 per cent of all mutual funds in the euro area (ECB, 1999). Second, large financial groups have emerged involving banks and securities firms (and occasionally also insurance companies). Asset management businesses have a capital market component, in which intermediaries trade assets in order to produce diversified products for final

Table 6.5 Key figures for some of the European 'New Exchanges', end-2002 *(€ millions)*

Exchange	New market	Listed companies	Market capitalization
London Stock Exchange	Techmark & AIM	914	391.4
Spanish Exchange (BME)	Nuevo Mercado	13	9.6
Deutsche Börse	Neuer Markt	240	9.3
Euronext		147	7.0
Italian Exchange	Nuovo Mercato	45	6.4
	Nasdaq Europe	40	3.0
	Nasdaq	3,725	2,007.2

Source: FESE, Nasdaq (end 10/02), Nasdaq Europe.

retail investors. This is distinct from the distribution of the products via retail networks.

Reliable figures for the different aspects of the asset management businesses are scarce. However, the supply of portfolio diversification services (i.e. the capital market part of the business) seems most affected by the introduction of the euro. Cross-border diversification has become less costly and risky, and free of any previously currency-based regulatory restrictions. There is also more diversification across asset classes, as funds are increasingly managed on an asset type and sectoral basis rather than a country basis (see also Chapter 8). These issues are discussed in the next section from the perspective of a retail investor being offered these diversification opportunities.

However, major obstacles to cross-border trading (and integration) continue to be the fragmented infrastructure for cross-border clearing and settlement of securities transactions as highlighted in the reports by groups led by A. Giovannini (2001, 2003). Another problem are differences in market practices, legislation, regulation and taxation. In the US, by contrast, the infrastructure for equities clearing and settlement is already organized on a national basis.[12] As a consequence, direct and indirect costs associated with trading can be several times higher in Europe than in the US (see for example Cruickshank, 2001). The importance of an efficient clearing and settlement infrastructure is well demonstrated by the successful integration of the money markets, in which operations involving unsecured instruments can be cleared and settled through the TARGET system. Thus, there is certainly room for a substantial consolidation of the securities settlement industry. There are also other market-related aspects hampering trading in capital markets, in particular differences in technical requirements and market practices.

Retail Financial Services

In the retail financial services area, financial institutions' counterparties are mainly households or small and medium-sized firms. Retail financial products include the traditional bank loan and deposit types, such as consumer credit, mortgages, small and medium-sized commercial loans, and demand and savings deposit accounts. Payment services are an integral part of the retail business associated with the deposit products. Asset management, in the form of investment accounts, investment advice, mutual funds, private pension schemes and life insurance, are also increasingly important components of retail financial services.

In these areas banking groups as well as financial conglomerates with insurance arms, increasingly compete with traditional specialized service providers. In general, the market landscape in the retail financial services sector is very diversified compared to wholesale and capital market-related services.

Retail services differ from those for wholesale and capital market-related services in one major respect. The proximity of financial institutions to customers is very important, because clients are scattered in geographic terms and typically have little

12 For a more detailed comparison between Europe and the US, see Corcoran et al. (2002).

mobility. Until electronic delivery techniques become widespread, physical distribution networks will continue to play a major role in the retail field. The local feature also means that there is limited scope in fostering integration through regulatory means (see Chapter 4). This implies that from the quantitative indicators of integration the ones relating to cross-border establishment are the most indicative, as one would not expect much cross-border acquisition of retail financial services.

While initial high expectations of the diffusion of e-finance have not been met, remote access options already exist for a wide range of retail banking services in many countries. Telephone banking developed first, but more recently banks have shifted their focus towards the Internet. There are also significant differences according to type of financial service. The current Internet penetration rates are significantly lower for lending than for savings-related products, and they seem to be the lowest in insurance products.[13] The penetration of online brokerage, by contrast, has been the fastest among financial services.

Retail Banking Services

With regard to the assessment of integration in retail banking services (and similar to other retail financial services), the major obstacle is that retail products are supplied by a variety of financial institutions in a very wide, and not always comparable, range. Price data are available at the national level at a very highly aggregated level, rather than for clearly defined individual products. Even if such data existed, differences across products would make cross-border comparisons difficult.

Moreover, the varying degree of indirect pricing of retail products is an obstacle to cross-country comparisons. Charging payment and account services implicitly to the deposit account holders in the interest margin on deposits (i.e. the opportunity return from money markets minus the deposit rate) has been the usual practice in many European countries (Humphrey et al., 1998). Although there is evidence for some countries that the direct pricing of payment and account-keeping services has become more important, this practice is apparently not yet very common in the EU countries (ECB, 1999 and 2000). For these reasons, the law-of-one-price benchmark is not easily applicable in the retail area and quantity-based indicators of integration play an important role.

Price-based indicators Broad aggregated retail interest rate data are available from the ECB and can be used as an indication of pricing developments, despite embracing a wide range of different products. In order to abstract from short-term fluctuations, the monthly retail interest rate data on household lending, corporate lending and deposit accounts were averaged over one-year periods from 1998 to 1999 and from 2001 to 2002. Then banks' respective margins vis-à-vis market interest rates were calculated, corresponding to the average maturities behind the retail interest

13 For deposit-related services, the average market penetration rates in Europe are less than 5 per cent on average (compared with estimates of 15 per cent in the US). In the Nordic countries Internet banking entered the rapid diffusion phase, reaching above 50 per cent of banks' retail customers in Finland and above 20 per cent in Sweden, according to existing estimates.

rate aggregates. The overall intermediation margin equals the average total lending rate minus the average deposit rate.

The retail interest rate levels reflect both macro and microeconomic factors. The macro-factors refer to market interest rate levels. The micro-factors include banks' risk premia, market power, and other pricing features, such as the cross-subsidization of payment or other services. By contrast, margins mostly represent the micro-factors, once one abstracts from the very short-term fluctuation stemming from the variability of the market interest rates. Thus, after abstracting from the short-term volatility, banks' margins are more reliable indicators for assessing integration or competition than the interest rate levels in an international comparison. Convergence in the margins (as measured by standard deviation) can be taken as a reasonable indicator of integration, and a decline in the margins may mean increased competition.

Between 1998–99 and 2001–02 differences across countries in household and corporate lending rates and deposit rates declined sharply in the euro area (Tables 6.6 and 6.7). However, this development seems to be mainly due to convergence in the macro-level monetary conditions brought about by the introduction of the euro. That is, the variability in banks' margins has diminished to a much smaller extent, which suggests that differences in the micro-factors have persisted. Household lending margins have tended to converge most significantly: standard deviation across countries decreased 50 per cent between 1998–99 and 2001–02. The variability of corporate lending and deposits diminished less visibly. Thus, while emerging convergence can be observed, the significant discrepancies in margins seem to imply that retail markets are still segmented across the euro area countries.

In countries such as Italy and Germany, regional differences in deposit and lending rates can be significant and attain sometimes levels similar to those across countries in the euro area. Such facts support the idea that retail markets have tended to be local even within countries. As retail customers choose banks close to their own location, banks have been able to exert local market power in retail pricing.

The margin data can also be indicative of changes in competition, while on the lending side changes in banks' average risk premia can also affect the margins. Comparing the two time periods, household-lending margins have fallen most significantly, on average by almost 1 percentage point between 1998–99 and 2001–02. In household lending, risk premia play a smaller role than in corporate lending. Corporate lending margins have decreased somewhat possibly signalling increased competition. By contrast, deposit margins have even tended to increase.

Another indicator of integration is 'sigma-convergence', which has been typically applied to financial market prices.[14] Sigma-convergence occurs if the cross-sectional (here cross-country) distribution of a variable decreases over time. If the cross-sectional sigma-convergence falls to zero, full integration is achieved.

In terms of lending to enterprises in the euro area, convergence seems to have taken place to some extent, comparing 2000–2002 figures to those for 1996–1998, but a reversal in the trend in convergence in both short and long-term bank loans took place in early-2001 (Figures 6.5 and 6.6). In the euro area household lending, since 1996–1998,

14 The value for sigma-convergence is obtained by running regressions with the cross-country standard deviation of the interest rate considered as the dependent variable and the linear time trend as the explanatory variable.

Table 6.6 Lending retail interest rates *(%-points)*

	Household lending rates				Corporate lending rates			
	Average Rate	(May 98–May 99) Lending Margin	Average Rate	(May 01–May 02) Lending margin	Average Rate	(May 98–May 99) Lending margin	Average Rate	(May 01–May 02) Lending margin
Austria	6.33	2.35	6.42	1.70	6.11	2.69	6.07	2.21
Belgium	5.36	1.38	6.37	1.65	4.98	1.57	5.64	1.78
Germany	6.25	2.27	6.74	2.03	6.23	2.83	7.05	3.19
Finland	5.24	1.25	5.24	0.53	4.31	0.89	4.71	0.85
France	7.16	3.18	7.23	2.52	4.52	1.12	5.31	1.45
Greece	12.56[1]	6.55[1]	7.65	2.94	16.44	5.61	8.09	4.23
Ireland	7.49	3.43	6.84	2.12	8.68	5.28	8.67	4.81
Italy	6.71	2.67	6.31	1.60	6.13	2.50	5.64	1.77
Luxembourg	5.18	1.19	5.12	0.40	–	–	–	–
The Netherlands	5.29	1.31	5.81	1.09	3.67	0.29	4.35	0.49
Portugal	6.36	2.34	6.09	1.38	6.36	2.83	5.51	1.65
Spain	5.85	1.83	5.78	1.06	6.06	2.53	6.20	2.34
Euro area	**6.65**	**2.48**	**6.30**	**1.58**	**6.68**	**2.56**	**6.11**	**2.25**
Standard deviation	**2.01**	**1.48**	**0.76**	**0.76**	**3.50**	**1.67**	**1.34**	**1.34**

Source: ECB and Datastream.

Note: Retail bank interest rates should be used with caution since national interest rates are not harmonized in terms of their coverage, the nature of the data (nominal or effective) or the compilation method. Margins were calculated as the difference between average retail interest rates (using ECB monthly adjusted country weights) and a reference market rate (obtained from Datastream), corresponding to the maturity distribution of the recorded retail business. Reported averages are unweighted. [1]Jan 99–May 99.

Table 6.7 Deposit retail interest rate and overall margin *(%-points)*

	Average (May 1998–May 1999)			Average (May 2001–May 2002)		
	Rate	Deposit margin	Overall margin	Rate	Deposit margin	Overall margin
Austria	2.18	1.24	4.04	2.17	1.69	4.09
Belgium	2.31	1.10	2.81	2.37	1.49	3.57
Germany	2.46	0.94	3.78	2.49	1.37	4.39
Finland	1.20	2.21	3.60	1.59	2.27	3.40
France	2.65	0.75	3.04	2.68	1.18	3.48
Greece	8.48	2.35	7.77	2.06	1.80	5.89
Italy	2.26	1.37	3.94	1.72	2.14	4.02
Luxembourg	2.50	0.91	2.67	2.54	1.32	2.58
The Netherlands	2.33	1.06	2.55	2.32	1.55	3.18
Portugal	2.44	1.08	3.91	2.45	1.41	3.33
Spain	2.08	1.46	3.89	2.32	1.54	3.68
Euro area	**2.81**	**1.32**	**3.82**	**2.25**	**1.61**	**3.78**
Std. dev.	**1.92**	**0.52**	**1.42**	**0.34**	**0.34**	**0.85**

Source: ECB and Datastream.

Note: Retail bank interest rates should be used with caution since national interest rates are not harmonized in terms of their coverage, the nature of the data (nominal or effective) or the compilation method. Deposit margins calculated as a difference between average retail interest rates (using ECB monthly adjusted country weights) and a reference market rate (obtained from Datastream), corresponding to the maturity distribution of the recorded retail business. The overall margin is the difference between average lending and deposit rates. Ireland is excluded due to the very small coverage of the provided deposit rate. Reported averages are unweighted.

convergence has occurred most clearly in the markets for mortgage loans (Figure 6.7). As changes are not much observable for consumer loans (Figure 6.8), the convergence in household margins discussed above is mostly explained by mortgage loans.

All in all, considering all the above indicators, integration tendencies seem to have emerged in varying degrees in the markets for retail banking products. It seems that household mortgage markets have witnessed most convergence since the introduction of the euro. Nevertheless, convergence in the respective rates clearly falls short of the full convergence (i.e. complete integration) in the euro area money markets right after the launch of the single currency in January 1999 (Figure 6.9).

Systematic data on other retail prices are very scarcely available. However, certain survey information exists which also points towards local pricing and a lack of integration. For instance, the existing inquiries indicate that major differences have persisted in the service charges levied on cross-border payment services, indicating lack of integration.[15] According to the 2001 survey by IEIC, the average cost of a €100 credit transfer varied from less than €10 in Luxembourg to €45 in Greece.

15 IEIC studies for DG SANCO (1999 and 2001), covering the Eurozone countries (EU–11) and studies for DG MARKT (1993 and 1994) covering 12 and (2001) 15 Member States, respectively.

Figure 6.5 Rates for short-term loans to enterprises
Source: ECB.

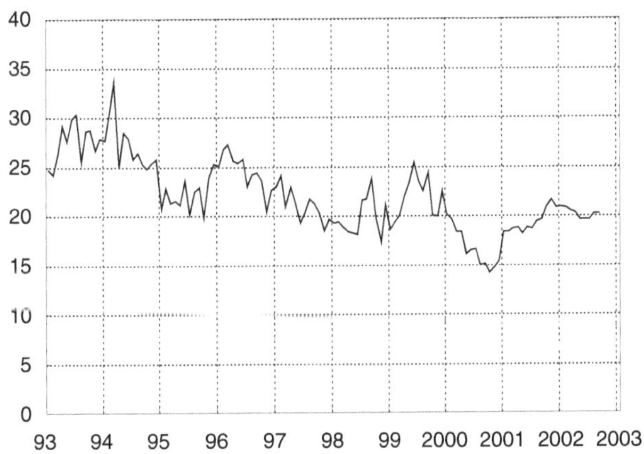

Figure 6.6 Rates for long-term loans to enterprises
Source: ECB.

Figure 6.7 Mortgage rates for mortgage loans to households

Source: ECB.

Figure 6.8 Rates for consumer loans to households

Source: ECB.

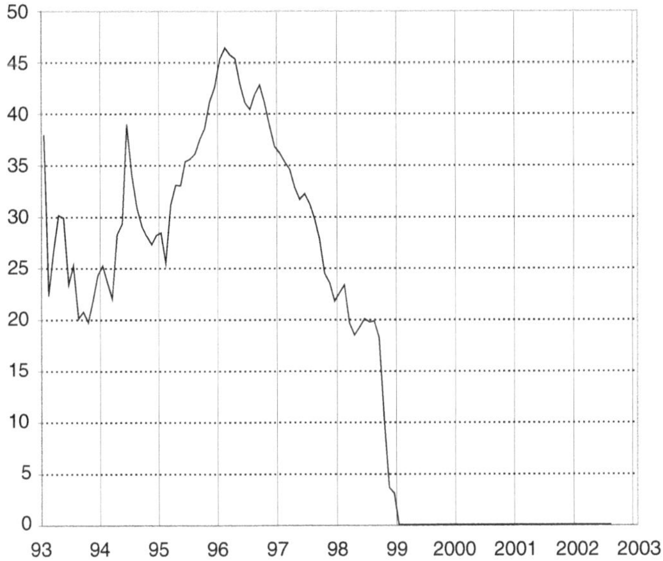

Figure 6.9 3-month money market rates

Source: ECB.

Figures 6.5–6.9 Sigma-convergence in retail bank interest rates in the euro area

It is also clear that the cost of cross-border payments is much higher than the cost of domestic payments, which are in general free of charge or only a couple of euro cents in most EU countries (while there are some exceptions). The most expensive cross-border transaction is a credit transfer, compared to ATM or manual cash withdrawals or debit card payments (Table 6.8). This cost constitutes a major obstacle to the cross-border acquisition of financial services and thus integration, as further discussed below. In order to remedy the situation, the EU regulation of December 2002 required the cost for cross-border card payments and ATM withdrawals to be

Table 6.8 Average cross-border payment charges in the EU *(in €)*

	Amount	Cost
Debit card payments*	25	0.19
ATM withdrawals*	100	3.84
Manual exchanges at a bank counter*	100	3.33
Cross-border credit transers**	100	24.09

Note: Results from the IEIC study on Banking fees of 2000* and the Retail Banking Research of 2001.**

the same as for domestic transactions and the cost for cross-border credit transfers to be brought to the level of domestic ones by 1 July 2003.

Quantity-based indicators As regards 'demand-side' quantity-based indicators of integration, anecdotal evidence suggests that cross-border flows are still negligible in retail loans and deposits. The statistics collected by the ECB on banks' assets and liabilities on a local (unconsolidated) basis confirm this picture. On the basis of March 2002 data (Table 6.9), banks in the euro area still relate to domestic customers in the case of 89 per cent of their loans and 84 per cent of their deposit base. Growth in cross-border activities has picked up, but it is likely that this is primarily due to customers other than banks' retail clients.

Another way of depicting the domestic orientation in banks' assets and liabilities is to look at the share of, for instance, domestic loans to the size of the domestic credit market. This indicator suggest a rather stable and high amount of 'home bias' in bank lending. For eight euro area countries this indicator has remained since 1999 between around 70 and 85 per cent. For four countries the share is below 60 per cent, Ireland and especially Luxembourg having the most diversified banking systems in terms of cross-border lending (which is probably due to tax reasons).

Remote banking, especially through the Internet, could be used to acquire customers across borders without establishment in the local market and could, thus, break the proximity requirement. However, Internet banking has mostly been offered by established banks, and as an integrated part of the existing delivery strategy ('multi-channel strategy') (ECB, 2002). Only a few banks have so far started to use this method to break into foreign markets by offering products at competitive prices.

Looking first at the internationalization of European banks within the euro area via the establishment of branches, one can see a clear increase between 1997 and 2000 (Table 6.10). A particularly strong increase took place in France, mainly due to the acquisition of CCF by the French branch of HSCB. However, in terms of the market share in the target country, branches from other euro area or EU countries hold a relatively minor position of less than 3 or 5 per cent of the total local banking assets respectively. Only in the case of Luxembourg and Ireland is the market share of branches of EU banks above 10 per cent (around 17 per cent in Luxembourg). One can also observe increased relevance of foreign branches of euro area banks in the EU market between 1997 and 2000 (Table 6.11). On average, euro area banks' branches in the EU account for 6.6 per cent of their assets (on a consolidated basis).

Foreign bank branches often concentrate on corporate finance services, trading activities and private banking, rather than retail activities. Retail businesses are much more difficult to enter; domestic banks enjoy substantial competitive advantages because of their widespread branch distribution networks. Thus, the most effective way of gaining access to the retail sector has been to merge with or acquire an existing local bank.

In the euro area between 1990 and 2001, 70 per cent of merger and acquisition (M&A) transactions involving banks occurred after 1998, as measured by transaction values (Table 6.12). Also the sharp increase in the average size of transactions after 1999 indicates that banks are concerned with becoming large players, which is essential in order to effectively participate in area-wide wholesale and capital

Table 6.9 Domestic and cross-border on-balance-sheet activities of euro area credit institutions *(€ billions)*

	Dec. 1997	Dec. 1998	Dec. 1999	Dec. 2000	Dec. 2001	Mar. 2002
Total interbank assets[1]	*4,649*	*4,979*	*5,369*	*5,719*	*6,274*	*6,308*
Loans to OMFIs	3,859	4,079	4,298	4,478	4,880	4,835
domestic business (%)	60.1	61.4	62.5	61.2	59.3	59.2
business with other euro area countries (%)	15.3	16.7	17.7	17.9	18.3	18.6
business with the rest of the world (%)	24.6	21.9	19.8	20.9	22.4	22.2
Other claims on OMFIs (securities, money market paper)	790	900	1,071	1,241	1,395	1,474
domestic business (%)	80.5	77.6	71.4	67.4	63.8	62.5
business with other euro area countries (%)	12.7	14.5	18.2	19.2	19.5	20.2
business with the rest of the world (%)	6.8	7.9	10.4	13.4	16.7	17.3
Total loans to non-banks[2]	*5,905*	*6,349*	*6,867*	*7,491*	*7,952*	*8,046*
domestic business (%)	91.6	91.6	90.4	89.9	88.9	88.7
business with other euro area countries (%)	2.2	2.6	3.0	3.2	3.4	3.6
business with the rest of the world (%)	6.2	5.8	6.6	6.9	7.7	7.7
Fixed income securities issued by non-banks[2]	*1,380*	*1,522*	*1,592*	*1,550*	*1,686*	*1,745*
domestic business (%)	72.5	68.0	62.1	57.0	53.0	52.6
business with other euro area countries (%)	15.6	18.9	23.7	25.7	29.3	30.5
business with the rest of the world (%)	11.9	13.1	14.2	17.3	17.7	16.9
Equity holdings	*380*	*588*	*753*	*903*	*972*	*984*
Other	1,069	953	1,120	1,234	1,332	1,231
Total	***13,383***	***14,390***	***15,700***	***16,898***	***18,217***	***18,314***
Total interbank deposits	*4,057*	*4,468*	*4,909*	*5,232*	*5,521*	*5,534*
domestic business (%)	59.5	58.3	57.3	55.0	52.9	52.6
business with other euro area countries (%)	14.6	15.9	16.1	15.5	16.4	16.4
business with the rest of the world (%)	25.9	25.8	26.6	29.5	30.7	31.0
Total deposits from non-banks[2]	*5,104*	*5,444*	*5,740*	*6,090*	*6,576*	*6,586*
domestic business (%)	88.0	87.8	86.2	85.1	84.3	83.7
business with other euro area countries (%)	5.4	5.5	5.3	5.2	5.0	5.2
business with the rest of the world (%)	6.6	6.7	8.5	9.7	10.7	11.1
Fixed income securities[3]	*2,064*	*2,262*	*2,604*	*2,826*	*3,030*	*3,117*
Capital and reserves	*688.42*	*765.09*	*867.46*	*959.98*	*1043.2*	*1054.18*
Other liabilities	*1,470*	*1,450*	*1,579*	*1,790*	*2,047*	*2,022*
Total liabilities	***13,383***	***14,390***	***15,700***	***16,898***	***18,217***	***18,314***

Source: ECB.

Notes: [1]These items do not include shares. OMFIs: Other monetary financial institutions. [2]Including general government. [3]The item includes money market paper.

Table 6.10 Inward branching of banks from EU countries into euro area

	Number of branches from				Assets of foreign branches as a % of total unconsolidated assets of host country			
	Euro area		EU 15		Euro area		EU 15	
Host country	**1997**	**2000**	**1997**	**2000**	**1997**	**2000**	**1997**	**2000**
Austria	4	12	6	15	0.6	–	0.7	0.8
Belgium	23	28	25	34	–	–	8.5	5.7
Finland	1	0	9	0	0	–	0	7.3
France	36	73	52	93	–	–	2.6	3.3
Germany	90	113	118	145	0.7	1.0	1.0	1.3
Greece	9	9	14	13	5.3	4.2	9.0	6.4
Ireland	–	–	–	–	–	–	–	13.5
Italy	27	32	34	41	3.0	3.0	3.4	3.5
Luxembourg	55	47	62	55	–	–	17.9	16.6
The Netherlands	6	0	9	0	–	–	2.1	2.7
Portugal	13	18	15	22	–	–	4.0	4.2
Spain	28	33	34	41	4.0	2.8	4.7	3.4
Euro area average	**27**	**33**	**34**	**42**	**2.3**	**2.8**	**4.9**	**5.7**

Source: Eurostat and ECB.
Note: Data in italics refer to branches from EEA countries and were calculated based on comparable figures from the 'Structural analysis of the EU banking sector: Year 2001', (2002), ECB.

market-related banking operations (Table 6.13). This suggests that large banks increasingly became involved in merger activity towards the year 2000. Merger transactions in the early 1990s mostly involved smaller banks (often savings and cooperative banks) and typically had cost-saving objectives. Cross-border transactions involving euro area banks as targets have been fairly strongly European. In 90 per cent (60 per cent) of the M&As between 1990 and 2001 the acquirer was from another EU (euro area) country, according to Thompson Financial data.

In addition to the wholesale and capital market-related objectives, cross-border bank M&As have been pursued in Europe (and elsewhere) as a strategy for internationalization in the retail field (see Group of Ten, 2001). Throughout the decade, M&As involving euro area targets were predominantly domestic. Over the entire period, domestic transactions accounted for 78 per cent of the total transaction value.

Table 6.11 Outward branching of banks from euro area countries into EU

	Number of foreign branches from				Assets of foreign branches as % of total Consolidated assets of home country[1]			
	Euro area		EU 15		Euro area		EU 15	
Home country	**1997**	**2000**	**1997**	**2000**	**1997**	**2000**	**1997**	**2000**
Austria	9	14	13	17	0.2	0.3	0.2	3.5
Belgium	19	23	24	28	0.6	0.4	0.6	5.0
Finland	0	1	4	2	0	0	0.4	0
France	61	68	72	83	2.5	2.0	2.6	7.4
Germany	64	83	78	109	0.2	0.4	0.2	15.1
Greece	3	6	7	11	0.2	0.3	0.2	9.9
Ireland	1	7	10	16	0.9	0.2	0.9	9.0
Italy	35	41	48	57	1.0	0.9	1.0	5.6
Luxembourg	35	39	38	40	0.1	0.0	0.1	0.0
The Netherlands	24	35	29	44	2.6	1.6	2.9	16.6
Portugal	10	12	14	16	0.9	0.4	0.9	3.0
Spain	31	36	37	42	1.9	2.2	1.9	4.3
Euro area average	**24**	**30**	**31**	**39**	**0.9**	**0.7**	**1.0**	**6.6**

Source: Eurostat and ECB.
Note: [1]Eurostat data concerning host countries available only for: AT, BE, DE, GR, IT, SP, SE, UK.

However, a clear increase in cross-border banking M&As can be observed for 1999 and 2000, when such transactions reached 42 per cent of the total value of the M&A activity. In Austria, France, Ireland, Luxembourg, the Netherlands and Finland, cross-border transactions accounted for more than half of the transactions in the period 1998–2001, while in Greece and Italy, M&A activity was still predominantly domestic. In 2002, bank M&A activity has slowed down, but cross-border transactions have continued to increase their share according to Thomson Financial data.

Cross-border bank M&As have led to an increase in the number of subsidiaries of euro area and EU banks in euro area countries. In some cases, the foreign component in the domestic banking system has significantly increased. Systematic data on the assets of EU banks' subsidiaries are not available, but in Austria, for example, the assets increased from €5 billion to €126 billion in 2000 on account of the merger between Bank Austria and the German HypoVereinsbank. In France and Portugal

Table 6.12 Value of mergers and acquisitions involving banks in the euro area *(€ billions)*

	Total value	% total	Within industry (%) Domestic	Within industry (%) Cross-border	Across industry (%) Domestic	Across industry (%) Cross-border
1990	15.35	5	45	7	45	3
1991	8.66	3	76	2	10	12
1992	5.16	2	16	4	19	60
1993	12.02	4	22	3	17	58
1994	6.06	2	73	5	22	0
1995	11.02	3	39	25	32	3
1996	6.44	2	74	1	6	18
1997	27.86	9	74	2	5	19
1998	72.43	23	70	3	18	10
1999	70.87	22	79	13	3	4
2000	49.74	16	38	42	11	8
August 2001	31.33	10	31	0	67	1
1990–2001	**316.94**	**100**	**60**	**11**	**18**	**11**

Source: Thomson Financial.
Notes: Percentages are rounded. Within industry = M&A among banks. Across industry = banks merging with securities firms or insurance companies.

Table 6.13 Average size of M&A deals in the euro area involving banks *(€ millions)*

	1990–1997	1998–2001 (August)	1990–2001 (August)
Average size	273.5	1,116.9	549.6
of which: Domestic/Within industry	315.4	1,279.5	648.8
Domestic/Cross-industry	205.8	1,075.3	413.5
Cross border/Within industry	163.6	1,011.7	456.8
Cross border/Cross-industry	38.5	575.2	429.5

Source: Thomson Financial.

these assets more than doubled in 2000. In France this was due to the restructuring of the Dexia Group and the acquisition of CCF, and in Portugal to the acquisition of the banks of the Champalimaud group by the Spanish BSCH. In the Nordic countries, the creation of Nordea has led to a major increase in foreign ownership.

In order to present an overview of the importance of foreign banks in the euro area banking markets, the amount of capital held by foreign entities in 2000 was calculated. Banks in which more than half of total capital is owned by foreign institutions constitute subsidiaries, while lower stakes represent other cross-border participations (Table 6.14).

Table 6.14 Capital of euro area banks owned by foreign residents end-2000
(as % of total equity capital)

Country of the participations	Country of the owners															
	BE	DK	DE	GR	ES	FR	IT	LU	NL	PT	SE	GB	JP	US	Other	*Total*
BE		0.00	1.11	0.00	0.23	0.47	0.00	0.04	27.04	0.00	0.00	0.00	0.00	0.24	0.37	**29.5**
DE	0.00	0.00		0.00	0.66	0.38	0.86	0.06	1.98	0.00	0.03	0.00	0.02	0.49	0.68	**5.2**
GR	0.00	0.00	0.00		0.00	1.16	0.00	0.00	0.00	0.00	0.00	0.96	0.00	1.25	2.72	**6.1**
ES	0.00	0.00	2.87	0.00		1.26	1.92	0.00	0.00	1.18	0.00	2.29	0.00	0.00	0.00	**9.5**
FR	6.17	0.00	2.54	0.00	1.44		1.09	0.19	0.58	0.02	0.00	1.56	0.67	0.00	0.00	**14.3**
FI	0.00	0.00	0.00	0.00	0.00	0.00	0.00	0.00	0.00	0.00	37.64	0.00	0.00	2.81	0.22	**40.7**
IE	2.88	0.00	26.30	0.00	0.00	0.00	2.79	0.91	5.82	0.00	0.00	1.14	0.00	0.01	0.38	**40.2**
IT	0.09	0.00	1.74	0.00	1.12	2.59		0.28	0.67	0.00	0.00	0.11	0.00	0.00	3.68	**10.3**
LU	18.40	2.17	47.30	0.32	0.00	9.80	4.28		1.49	0.00	0.27	0.79	0.00	0.00	1.02	**85.8**
NL	1.23	0.00	1.65	0.00	0.00	0.00	0.00	0.00		0.00	0.00	0.00	0.59	3.10	0.10	**6.7**
AT	1.01	0.00	9.03	0.00	0.00	0.02	0.11	0.00	0.00	0.00	0.00	0.00	0.00	0.00	0.00	**10.2**
PT	0.86	0.00	2.02	0.73	0.99	0.78	3.19	2.82	1.83		0.00	0.25	0.00	3.10	0.10	**16.7**
Average	**2.79**	**0.18**	**8.60**	**0.10**	**0.40**	**1.50**	**1.29**	**0.39**	**3.58**	**0.11**	**3.16**	**0.59**	**0.11**	**0.92**	**0.77**	**22.9**

Source: Fitch IBCA Bankscope.

Notes: Includes 570 euro area banks for which data are available. Includes all types of owners and participations (also minority holdings). The columns include the countries that appear as owners. Columns of Ireland and Finland were excluded given that there are no participations abroad.

The data point to a much greater degree of internationalization than the branching figures alone, as the average foreign ownership is 23 per cent of total banking capital. Other euro area country banks largely hold these ownership stakes. The role of other EU country banks and, in particular, that of Japanese and US banks is significantly smaller. Luxembourg constitutes the extreme case, as its banks are to a great extent owned by foreign, mostly German, banks. Ireland and Finland have 40 per cent of their banking systems controlled by foreign owners, and Belgium 30 per cent. At the lower end are Germany, the Netherlands and Greece, where no more than 6 per cent of banks' capital is in foreign possession.

The significant amount of foreign ownership reflects tangible links between local banking markets in the euro area. However, these linkages might not be definite indicators of integration, as pricing may also remain unaffected after a change in ownership. To recall, also the analysis of the margins suggested that, as far as the retail markets are concerned, a significant amount of segmentation persists in the euro area, while only gradual convergence in pricing was observed.

Finally, it is interesting to look at how different euro area countries are building up the cross-border links in the banking sector and whether some regions could exhibit a greater degree of integration than the euro area as a whole. This is best measured by the distribution of consolidated assets, including the assets held by foreign subsidiaries. As regards bilateral foreign exposures, the strongest linkages in absolute terms are found between large countries (Table 6.15). In addition, some euro countries have virtually no cross-border exposure when measured by consolidated claims, even when the originating or the target country is a large one. Spain and Italy, for example, show relatively low bilateral links when their size is taken into account.

Moreover, some of the highest bilateral exposures involve relatively small countries, e.g. the exposure of German banks towards Austria, or of Belgian banks against the Netherlands. Finally, there appears to be a bias in consolidated foreign claims towards

Table 6.15 Total consolidated foreign claims of euro area banks on other euro area countries *($ billions)*

	AT	BE	FI	FR	DE	IE	IT	NL	PT	ES
AT		5.0	0.1	5.6	106.9	6.7	–	5.4	0.5	1.7
BE	0.3		0.3	34.4	41.2	3.0	12.1	69.9	0.8	8.0
FI	0.4	1.9		5.6	9.3	2.3	0.3	2.3	0.1	0.7
FR	1.6	46.7	1.6		126.2	12.6	30.8	26.1	4.6	15.1
DE	11.9	40.3	1.0	103.5		125.0	26.9	107.2	2.4	26.7
GR	1.1	6.5	0.1	12.4	25.2	–	–	8.3	0.6	1.3
IE	2.6	24.0	0.3	12.9	42.6		7.9	10.2	1.6	2.4
IT	3.0	41.0	0.6	91.2	122.8	22.1		42.3	1.2	16.1
LU	1.5	24.7	0.2	14.0	64.9	1.3	21.4	13.6	2.0	2.2
NL	2.5	85.2	1.1	38.9	97.6	3.0	–		1.8	10.8
PT	0.6	6.2	0.0	5.6	23.4	–	7.2	5.3		33.1
ES	0.6	18.6	0.0	36.6	63.7	13.1	7.3	32.1	5.2	

Source: BIS consolidated foreign claims.
Notes: Columns represent the originating country, and rows the target countries.

countries of geographic proximity. The Nordic countries tend to define their home banking market as comprising Denmark, Sweden, Norway and Finland. In continental Europe, Belgium, the Netherlands, Luxembourg and to some extent France are becoming closely interlinked and are thus approaching a 'home market' status.

Beyond these linkages at the aggregated country level, individual banks may view their involvement in other countries as belonging to their core activities, even if these are not captured at the country aggregate level. Overall, banks have started to define their home markets across borders and have thus started to consider activities outside the country of incorporation as core activities.

Asset Management and Brokerage Services

Over a longer term, asset management services referring to securities market investment products, i.e. other than traditional deposits, have much increased in importance. Since retail investors can access securities markets more effectively though collective investment vehicles, such as mutual funds or pension funds, than directly purchasing individual securities, the collective investment business has had the fastest growth. According to FEFSI data, assets of European UCITS[16] tripled from €1.2 trillion in 1995 to €3.6 trillion in 2000. Reflecting this tendency, the investment in shares alone (either directly or indirectly) bypassed the deposit holdings of euro area non-financial sectors (households and firms) in 1999 (Table 6.16).

Table 6.16 Main financial assets of the euro area non-financial sector, fourth quarter figures *(€ billions)*

Year	Main financial assets (amounts outstanding) of the euro area non-financial sector							
	Currency	Deposits with non-MFI	Deposits with MFI		Securities		Insurance technical reserves	
			By other than central govt.	By central govt.	Other than shares	Shares	Net equity of household in reserves	Prepayment of insurance premiums
1998	323	141	4.211	149	1.532	3.762	2.353	277
1999	350	152	4.215	142	1.595	4.822	2.648	294
2000	348	155	4.361	164	1.777	4.867	2.885	307
2001	239	167	4.816	139	1.948	4.384	3.049	323
2002	341	181*	4.963	136	2.108*	3.480*	3.116*	339*

Source: ECB (Monthly Bulletin, April 2003, Table 6.1).
* Represents Q3 data, prepayments of premiums includes reserves for outstanding claims.

16 UCITS stands for 'Undertakings for Collective Investment in Transferable Securities' as defined in the EU Directive 85/611/EEC, which covers the regulated funds offered to the general public.

Price-based indicators Statistics are not available to compare fees and commissions in asset management and brokerage in the euro area and not obtainable from intermediaries' Internet sites in most cases. Schüler (2003) has made a comparison of the charges of specific online brokers with subsidiaries in different euro area countries. This is an interesting test for integration since, first, online brokerage is the most advanced form of electronic financial services, and, second, clients are not tied to their local brokers and can compare charges on the Internet. Hence, one could expect this area to exhibit the greatest degree of integration of all retail asset management and brokerage services.

Schüler (2003) compared the charges of four leading European online brokers in their home countries and in foreign countries and the charges demanded in the various markets. He found out that there are major differences in the prices charged by the parent company and their foreign subsidiaries in other countries. The foreign subsidiaries are in most cases more aligned with foreign market leaders, even though there is typically some price undercutting. Compared to the situation in the US, the price variance in this market is also found to be much larger in the euro area.

Since in this area quality differences could be of relatively minor significance, the findings indicate that there are substantial pricing differences across countries, even if the brokers have the same parent company. This variety suggests that the markets for online brokerage in the euro area are more fragmented than integrated. One could presume that the same holds for other retail services, which could be *a priori* be expected to be more rooted to local markets.

Quantity-based indicators The supply of portfolio diversification services has been much affected since the introduction of the euro, as cross-border diversification has become less costly and risky under single currency conditions. This follows from the removal of foreign exchange risks and greater market liquidity reducing transaction costs. The benefits of cross-border diversification can be demonstrated by, for instance, Sharpe ratios for German and French securities investors (Table 6.17).[17] By this measure, domestic investment is an inferior solution to European diversification for equity and bond portfolios. The relative value of cross-border diversification is, however, falling over time due to the convergence in the economic development in the euro area. Hence, there could be benefits from also diversifying across asset classes and industries, as many funds are increasingly doing.

Existing data show that there is increasing portfolio diversification of mutual funds across borders within the single currency area. To take the most significant example, (open-ended) mutual funds sold to euro area residents are already fairly diversified geographically. In the case of equity funds, the share of domestic equities was around 28 per cent on average in March 2002, while the share of non-domestic European equities and non-European equities reached 25 per cent and 46 per cent respectively (Table 6.18). At end-1997, the share of domestic equity was still almost 50 per cent. In the case of bond funds (for which data are less comprehensive), the

17 The higher the Sharpe ratio (for formula see Table 6.17), the higher the premium for one unit of risk and the greater the performance of the portfolio. Unhedged diversification at the world level does not bring along an increase in the Sharpe ratio due to the simultaneously increased foreign exchange risk (Schröder, 2003).

Table 6.17 Sharpe ratios for German and French holders of security portfolios

'German investor'	
Equities Europe	0.149
Equities Germany	0.085
Bonds Europe	0.150
Bonds Germany	0.063
'French investor'	
Equities Europe	0.127
Equities France	0.112
Bonds Europe	0.067
Bonds France	0.042

Source: Schröder (2003).
Note: Calculated from market data January 1997–June 2001. Sharpe ratio: (portfolio return – risk-free interest rate)/portfolio standard deviation.

respective shares were 30 per cent, 50 per cent and 20 per cent in March 2002. Also the percentage of assets invested in funds that are managed with a Europe-wide investment strategy has increased dramatically, in particular for money market and bond market funds (Adam et al., 2002).

Looking at all UCITS, the similar tendency of a greater share of non-residential assets can be observed for all euro area countries in the OECD data, except Greece and Portugal, for which data are available (Table 6.19). Finally, also banks' cross-border holdings of securities expressed as a percentage of the respective domestic holdings increased in the period 1997–2001 from 15 per cent to 35 per cent for securities issued by banks and from 20 per cent to 60 per cent for securities issued by non-banks (Hartmann et al., 2003). Data on pension funds is scarcely available, but the available OECD data point to increasing cross-border diversification also in these investments (Table 6.20). Figures for insurance companies and pension funds show a similar reversal in investment strategy (see the next section).

While it is clear that mutual and pension fund investments are becoming well diversified across borders in the euro area, which is a positive development from the effective risk reduction and portfolio management perspective, the retail interface with the final investor still seems to remain largely local. Retail investors access any investments, also the geographically diversified ones, through their local intermediaries.

The cross-border provision of mutual fund products by euro area financial institutions is still quite rare, as is evident from the number of notifications of foreign operations made by euro area UCITS (Figure 6.10).[18] Also the data on foreign funds' market shares in euro area countries is consistent with this segmented picture. In 2001, European Funds Services (2001) or Moody's (2000) have estimated the share to be less than 10 per cent in Germany and Italy and less than 5 per cent in France and Spain.

18 Such notifications are required by the respective EU UCITS Directive.

Table 6.18 Breakdown of the assets of the equity mutual funds operating in the euro area countries *(% of total funds; split into domestic and foreign according to whether investments are made in domestic or foreign markets)*

	% Domestic	% Total European	% Non European	Total value (€ *millions*)
March 2002				
Belgium	10	47	43	47.612
Germany	23	27	50	125.099
Greece[1]	91	0	9	4.913
Spain	31	20	48	48.683
France	50	16	34	215.500
Ireland	–	–	–	
Italy	16	34	51	111.564
Luxembourg	–	–	–	332.595
The Netherlands	14	17	68	55.200
Austria	2	34	64	13.160
Portugal	33	41	26	2.253
Finland	18	41	41	6.754
Total euro area[2]	**28**	**25**	**46**	**963.333**
End-1997				
Belgium	41	32	27	
Germany	50	17	33	
Spain	77	–	23	
France	59	–	41	
Ireland	–	–	–	
Italy	49	15	36	
The Netherlands	22	–	78	
Austria	6	75	19	
Portugal	80	–	20	
Finland	44	36	20	
Total euro area[2]	**49**	**10**	**41**	

Source: European Federation of Investment Funds and Companies (FEFSI).
Notes: [1]GR equity is only split between domestic and foreign.
[2]Weighted average for the countries for which data exist.

Even though the actual numbers can differ to some extent depending on the source, all other available data suggest that foreign funds play a relatively minor role in euro area countries and that there is limited integration in the markets for retail asset management services. Since funds costs fall with size (Heinemann, 2003), in particular for smaller countries, large foreign funds could bring about efficiency gains and lower prices. The main obstacles to the cross-border provision of funds seem to be related to the burden of registration in the target markets, specific market costs

Table 6.19 Share of non-residential assets of euro area UCITS (%)

	1991	1995	1999	2000
Belgium	51.30	53.18	53.13	–
Germany	33.85	20.35	42.63	48.54
Greece	9.52	3.07	1.84	–
Spain	0.99	2.81	30.96	42.62
France	–	–	–	–
Ireland	–	–	–	–
Italy	14.66	24.37	49.09	52.99
Luxembourg	–	–	–	–
The Netherlands	43.98	33.89	54.62	53.08
Austria	19.04	30.38	49.71	–
Portugal	–	17.44	9.96	13.14
Finland	7.20	11.74	44.47	61.09

Source: OECD, Institutional Investors' Statistical Yearbook.

(translation etc.) and potentially discriminatory tax rules against foreign funds. Limitation of the extra costs for foreign funds could bring about further cross-border activity, but market penetration could still be difficult for foreign funds if customers prefer the more familiar local funds.

Data on the cross-border acquisition of asset management or brokerage services do not seem to be available. However, a survey among leading European online brokers conducted in the fall of 2001 revealed that almost no broker had clients outside the national markets where they operate (Schüler, 2003). No growth in this activity was expected either and all firms planned to continue the strategy of establishment (of web-sites) in different local markets.

Table 6.20 Share of non-residential assets of euro area pension funds (%)

	1991	1995	1999	2000
Belgium	0.75	3.08	43.35	16.45
Germany	–	–	–	–
Greece	–	–	–	–
Spain	–	–	–	–
France	–	–	–	–
Ireland	–	–	–	–
Italy	–	–	0.68	–
Luxembourg	–	–	–	–
The Netherlands	12.50	21.52	55.92	61.88
Austria	–	2.78	0.45	–
Portugal	–	–	–	–
Finland	0.02	1.56	22.14	40.40

Source: OECD, Institutional Investors' Statistical Yearbook.

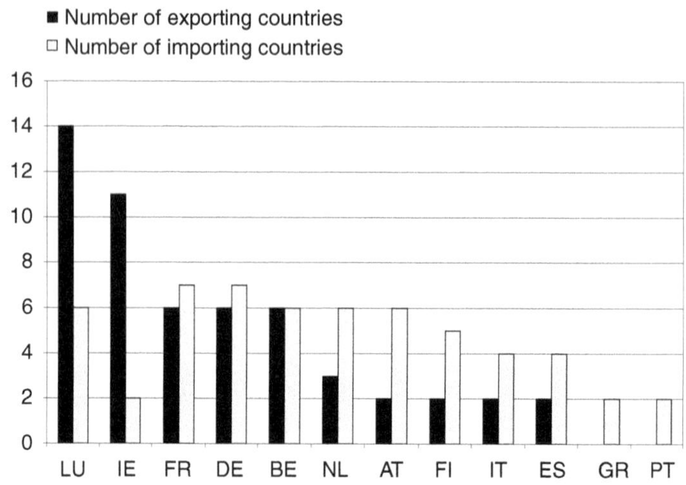

Figure 6.10 Exporting and importing of mutual funds in the euro area, number of cross-border notifications by 2001

Source: Heinemann (2003).
Note: Cross-border notifications obtained from European Fund Services.

Since the Internet can make the location of the supplier irrelevant, there must be other factors which hamper integration in this area. The main obstacles for the cross-border investment and fund acquisition activity are the high costs of cross-border credit transfers and the fragmented infrastructure for cross-border clearing and settlement of securities transactions. Unless these costs associated with the 'physical' settlement of transactions are reduced, the Internet does not seem to significantly boost integration.

Insurance Products

Data do not seem to be available to construct price-based indicators of integration for insurance products. Like UCITS and pension funds, insurance companies are also major institutional investors. The existing data generally indicate an increase in euro area life insurance companies' foreign asset holdings (i.e. diversification), while this is not so clear-cut for non-life insurance companies (Tables 6.21 and 6.22). Interestingly, one can observe especially in the case of life-insurance firms a major increase in foreign asset holdings in 1999 and thereafter, as the introduction of the euro made any previous regulations limiting the investment of insurance companies in foreign currency-denominated assets redundant. For life insurance companies data are available for the US as well, and the US firms seem much more oriented to domestic investments than the euro area firms, which actually partly reflects the greater diversification possibilities within the US, as well as the greater depth of the US financial markets.

Table 6.21 Share of non-residential assets of euro area life insurance companies *(%)*

	1991	1995	1999	2000
Belgium	3.01	7.22	22.78	–
Germany	–	–	–	–
Greece	–	–	–	–
Spain	0.87	1.92	9.93	13.75
France	–	–	–	–
Ireland	–	–	–	–
Italy	–	10.08	21.46	23.56
Luxembourg	–	–	–	–
The Netherlands	5.59	11.33	21.38	22.64
Austria	2.60	3.64	16.55	–
Portugal	0.55	–	–	–
Finland	–	2.13	14.34	29.45
US	3.24	6.15	5.18	5.39

Source: OECD, Institutional Investors' Statistical Yearbook.

Table 6.22 Share of non-residential assets of euro area non-life insurance companies *(%)*

	1991	1995	1999	2000
Belgium	3.10	7.09	22.77	–
Germany	–	–	–	–
Greece	–	–	–	–
Spain	–	–	–	–
France	–	–	–	–
Ireland	–	–	–	–
Italy	–	14.97	9.80	11.15
Luxembourg	–	–	–	–
The Netherlands	6.62	7.33	23.13	–
Austria	–	6.30	3.74	–
Portugal	–	–	–	–
Finland	10.95	5.76	7.28	20.10

Source: OECD, Institutional Investors' Statistical Yearbook.

Maybe the most suitable database for our purposes here is the OECD Statistical Yearbook, since it contains an indicator of the local insurance markets covered by foreign-controlled insurance firms. This indicator represents a measure of foreign penetration in insurance products on a gross premium basis. It appears that the foreign share is lower in life than in non-life insurance products. This might be attributed to factors such as tax rules and the long-term nature of life insurance decisions.

The high degree of consumer sensitivity in life insurance is evident from the typically very low penetration of remote selling of life insurance contracts. Anyhow, the differences across countries are quite high in both segments of the insurance business.

Among the countries for which these data are available, the share of foreign-controlled firms varies from 12 per cent in Germany to close to 50 per cent in Austria in non-life products, and from 8 per cent in Portugal to 32 per cent in Austria in life products (Figure 6.11).[19] Hence, the level that foreign control in non-life insurance reaches is higher and is on average above the one observed in banking, while in life insurance the levels appear to be smaller in comparative terms. The figures indicate rather substantial links across markets, in particular in non-life insurance, but (as in banking) changes in pricing behaviour are not guaranteed through foreign penetration. In insurance markets, the share of foreign control has since the early-1990s been more stable than in banking, even though typically crawling upwards. This could suggest that any changes in market conditions have occurred at a slower pace in the insurance field than in banking.

As noted, there has been a significant move towards the creation of financial conglomerates involving banks, insurance companies and securities firms. Over the entire period of 1999–2001, 30 per cent of the total M&A value involving euro area banks was due to cross-sector transactions. Such transactions were most prominent

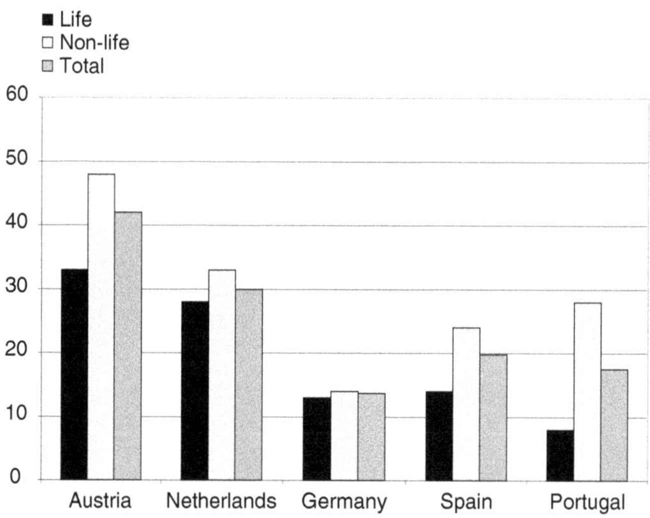

Figure 6.11 Share of foreign controlled companies in insurance markets of certain euro area countries, 1999 *(% of gross premium income)*

Source: OECD, Insurance Statistics Yearbook.

19 For comparison, the share of foreign insurance companies in the total US market was 14.5 per cent in 1999, up from 9 per cent in 1992 (source: OECD, Insurance Statistics Yearbook).

in Belgium, Germany, Finland and Ireland (Table 6.12). This conglomeration trend has also been relevant for the emergence of cross-border links. Looking at the M&A data, cross-border cross-industry transactions were already fairly prominent in the early-1990s. Looking at all financial sector transactions, cross-border deals involving insurance companies have been more evenly spread over time since the early-1990s. Hence, a clear boost in the cross-border activity at the end-1990s, like in banking, cannot be identified.

As regards consolidation across sectors, the costs of maintaining close proximity to retail customers may be spread over an increasing range of retail products, which generates economies of scope – for example, between traditional banking, asset management and insurance products. For this reason, the conglomeration process leading to the establishment of financial groups active in banking, securities and insurance, has very often focused on retail services. Many of these groups operate in several countries and represent major European financial institutions, as is evident from the above figures on foreign control in the insurance field. But it should be noted that European banks and insurance companies have also conducted alternative strategies to the pure cross-border acquisitions, such as alliances and joint ventures.

Competition and Efficiency Considerations

The increased M&A activity in the financial sector discussed earlier has resulted in a reduction in the number of EU credit institutions and insurance companies. Since the largest part of the activity has so far taken place within the domestic markets, many national markets are now dominated by only a handful of companies. In the smaller euro area countries, five major banks or insurance companies has a market share (CR5 concentration ratio) exceeding 80 per cent (in terms of total assets or gross premium income). The average banking concentration, CR5, in the euro area rose from 49 per cent in 1990 to 55 per cent in 2001. In insurance, average CR5 has risen to over 60 per cent (up from around 50 per cent in mid-1990s, according to Thomson Financial data). The increased involvement of the largest financial institutions in the M&A activity accelerated the concentration tendency.

As domestic concentration levels have increased, so has the vigilance of competition authorities, watchful that individual transactions do not lead to abuse of the market position. Individual transactions can be motivated by offensive (market penetration, diversification) and defensive (cost saving) objectives. Both types of motives can be socially beneficial. Offensive mergers may result in greater competition as a result of firms striving to gain higher market shares. Defensive mergers may result in reduced excess capacity and lower prices. However, if the merged partners are able to increase their market power via a strong market position, customers are likely to be worse off, and the merger partners will be able to increase their profits.

Research on the impact of bank M&As has mostly looked into the cost implications. Studies in the US have generally been inconclusive, and some studies have been quite sceptical about the realization of cost-efficiency gains (Berger et al., 2000). The few existing studies on European bank mergers seem to conclude that there are often significant efficiency gains, which also result in better conditions for customers. Huizinga et al. (2001) analyse 52 major mergers among European banks between 1994 and 1998, which are found to be largely socially beneficial. Cost-efficiency typically improved after mergers and there was some evidence of increased profits, although there was a tendency for deposit rates to increase. However, a previous study conducted by Vander Vennet (1996) on European bank mergers between 1988 and 1993 pointed more convincingly to profit increases following mergers. These contrasting results may be due to increasing banking market contestability throughout the last decade.

In addition, bank M&As seem to have been associated with capacity reductions, even though several other important factors such as business volume expansion, technological developments or changes in the business mix of universal banks are also relevant. Indeed, since the early 1990s, the largest reductions in bank branches have taken place in the countries with the greatest increases in concentration due to M&As (Belgium, Finland, the Netherlands and, in the EU context, Denmark and Sweden) (Table 6.23). The number of bank employees has also declined significantly in these countries (except in the Netherlands) (Table 6.24). In most other countries, the increased sophistication of banking services, with a greater demand for – for example – advice, has tended to maintain the level of bank employees, despite labour-saving technological improvements (ECB, 2000).

All in all, economic literature and evidence on capacity reductions in banking suggest that M&As can indeed perform a disciplining function against cost-inefficiency and excess capacity and support market contestability. It would appear that this disciplining force is increasingly at work on a cross-border basis, because of the clear increase in cross-border M&As (as well as in cross-border branching and the establishment of subsidiaries). Studies on the impact of M&As in the insurance or securities firm sectors do not seem to be available.

Table 6.23 Number of bank branches per 1,000 capita

	1990	1995	1999	2000	2001	%-change 1990–2001
Austria	0.81	0.76	0.68	0.64	0.60	–26
Belgium	0.62	0.64	0.71	0.69	0.66	6
Germany	0.19	0.23	0.26	0.27	0.28	47
Spain	0.87	0.93	0.99	0.98	0.97	11
Finland	0.45	0.44	0.43	0.43	0.44	–2
France	0.27	0.29	0.28	–	–	4
Greece	0.31	0.41	0.47	0.49	0.51	65
Ireland	0.78	0.85	0.71	0.68	–	–13
Italy	0.53	0.43	0.39	0.37	0.33	–38
Luxembourg	0.58	0.58	0.57	0.56	0.56	–3
The Netherlands	0.20	0.35	0.53	0.55	0.69	245
Portugal	0.66	0.38	0.23	0.23	–	–65
Euro area average	**0.52**	**0.52**	**0.52**	**0.54**	**0.56**	**7**

Source: ECB.
Note: Averages are unweighted and calculated for available data only.

Table 6.24 Number of bank employees per 1,000 capita

	1990	**1995**	**1999**	**2000**	**2001**	**%-change 1990–2001**
Austria	7.73	7.51	7.45	7.44	7.41	–4.14
Belgium	8.88	9.65	9.83	9.85	9.77	10.02
Germany	4.58	5.06	5.55	5.69	5.65	23.36
Spain	6.75	6.61	6.47	6.46	6.50	–3.70
Finland	7.59	7.19	7.06	–	–	*–6.98*
France	4.97	6.09	–	–	–	*22.54*
Greece	6.00	6.31	5.90	5.95	–	*–0.83*
Ireland	41.22	43.50	48.65	52.20	54.14	31.34
Italy	7.64	6.71	7.84	8.09	7.96	4.19
Luxembourg	9.60	9.47	9.07	9.07	9.19	–4.27
The Netherlands	6.23	6.09	6.02	5.67	5.47	–12.20
Portugal	10.01	6.28	4.66	4.86	–	*–51.45*
Euro area average	**10.10**	**10.04**	**10.77**	**11.53**	**13.26**	**31.30**

Source: ECB.

Notes: Averages are unweighted and calculated for available data only. When the figure for 2001 is not available, changes are calculated using the *most recent available year.*

Concluding Remarks

Summary of the Evidence

The purpose of this Chapter was to assess integration in financial services in the euro area in line with the methodological framework set out in Chapter 3. As this Chapter relied much on quantity-based indicators, special attention to the caveats raised in that Chapter have been paid in order not to over- (or under)interpret the evidence.

As regards capital market-related services, the evidence points to a transformation of previously segmented national currency-based markets into a significantly integrated area-wide market, in particular in the case of intermediating bond issues. This may be concluded from the replacement of the leading role of domestic intermediaries by international ones. US investment banks, in particular, have significantly increased their share of the euro area market, be it to a large extent via their establishments in London. Even though a similar increase in integration was observed for equity issuance and syndicated loans, these two segments present clear differences. Activity here has remained more local, probably because of the greater need for local information than in the case of bonds. Despite some efforts, a pan-European venture capital market has not yet emerged.

Market segmentation remains strongest in the retail area because of the need of the service providers to locate close to their customers. For instance, discrepancies in lending and deposit margins across the euro area indicate that integrated retail banking markets are not yet in place. Nevertheless, some convergence in margins can be observed, in particular in household lending. Moreover, the substantial links across local markets which have evolved through cross-border acquisitions and the establishment of subsidiaries, as well as through strategic alliances, could, over time, promote greater integration. In addition, a wider use of remote banking (such as Internet banking) could constitute a 'shortcut' to integration. By and large, these same conclusions hold for insurance services, which continue to remain quite local. However, in insurance the establishment of the cross-border institutional links has been less momentous over the recent period, while it started already in early 1990s.

Institutional investors have tended to strongly increase the geographical diversification of their investment, in particular after the introduction of the euro. This has made portfolios more efficient in terms of risk reduction. However, the retail interface with investors continues to be strictly local. There are very few mutual funds sold in foreign countries. Even online brokerage activity, which is the most widespread form of e-finance, continues to be a local, rather than a cross-border activity.

Thus, the general picture is that integration has progressed fastest in the areas where professional market participants have the resources to overcome the existing obstacles to integration (i.e. in the wholesale and capital market area). By contrast, retail clients do not usually have such resources, the outcome being a slower pace of integration. Retail financial services are still very much local activities, which necessitates the location of the suppliers close to their customers and integration can be mainly achieved by the foreign establishment by financial institutions.

The Chapter also surveyed some developments in competition in addition to the indicators of integration. Within corporate finance services, a remarkable reduction in bond intermediation fees in all transaction sizes was identified, but especially in the case of the largest bond issues. There is evidence which suggests that the fees are approaching the levels charged for issuers in the US market. In equity intermediation, the decline in fees has been tangible, but not as large. Fees have also declined significantly in syndicated lending, but margins and fees on undrawn credits increasingly reflect risk differentiation across borrowers. The most visible reductions in price levels in the retail field seem to have taken place in household lending. The evidence presented on the banking consolidation process would appear to signal positive developments from a consumer perspective: gradual efficiency increases and greater market contestability.

Finally, the Chapter highlighted the impact of the euro in fostering integration. This has been particularly relevant in the capital market field. In these areas, the common risk-free yield curve and access to central bank liquidity under the single currency conditions have supported the creation of integrated money and capital markets, replacing the previous national markets in the constituent currencies. This has also paved the way for the operation of financial intermediaries at the European level. In the retail field, the introduction of the euro does not appear to be having such an impact, and markets have continued to operate at the national level. The present study has also touched upon other forces which may influence the markets for banking services (economic, demographic, technological and financial innovation factors) and facilitate an understanding of the pace of integration and other changes in the markets.

Obstacles to Further Integration

There still remain a number of important obstacles to fully achieve the benefits of financial integration. Most of them can be grouped into two categories, i.e. (i) regulation, legislation and tax, and (ii) sub-optimal coordination and insufficient expression of the competition forces.

Many of the regulatory and legal obstacles in the capital markets field are identified in the FSAP and could be removed within the scheduled deadlines. However, important challenges remain. The draft Directive on takeover bids did not receive the European Parliament's approval. The lack of minimum harmonized rules on takeovers continues to act as a brake on the cross-border consolidation process, also in the financial services industry. According to the current Merger Regulation, Member States can take appropriate measures in order to protect certain legitimate interests (such as public security or prudential rules), which is sometimes too broadly interpreted. National competition authorities may also favour domestic consolidation and discourage acquisitions by foreign banks.

Other constraints continue to hamper bank customers and investors in diversifying across borders. For example, host countries may require compliance with national regulations intended to protect the public interest (such as consumers' interests). The creation of a single market may have been eroded by a too broad interpretation of this exception to the 'home country' rule. Divergent taxation rules remain a significant hurdle to further integration, but the most critical part of this area, the taxation of savings income, has been tackled by way of a Directive adopted in 2003. In addition, the process of establishing harmonization in consumer information and procedures for solving disputes with financial services providers is still incomplete. The result is that it is difficult to acquire services abroad, and financial services firms need to develop products separately for the different local markets.

But not all obstacles to integration originate from the legal and regulatory side. Some are due to sub-optimal coordination within the private sector or an insufficient expression of the forces of competition. This is perhaps the clearest illustrated in the area of clearing and settlement infrastructure. Here, the so-called 'Giovannini Group', which advises the European Commission, has found that the clear majority of barriers to efficient and integrated clearing and settlement arrangements relate to technical requirements and/or market practices, i.e. issues that can potentially be solved by market participants through coordinated action.

Finally, it should be realized that even if all regulatory and legal obstacles were to be removed and an integrated financial infrastructure to be established, there will continue to be natural obstacles that prevent financial integration to be fully accomplished, particularly in the retail area. Such natural obstacles relate to culture, language, the preference of customers for local structures and established distribution channels, etc. In the retail field, also the existing extensive capacity put in place by domestic service providers can represent a major obstacle as well, at least until e-finance becomes widespread.

References

Adam, K., T. Jappelli, A. Menichini, M. Padula and M. Pagano (2002), *Analyse, compare and apply alternative indicators and monitoring methodologies to measure the evolution of capital market integration in the European Union,* University of Salerno, Centre for Studies in Economics and Finance, January.

Berger, A.N., R. DeYoung, H. Genay and G.F. Udell (2000), *Globalization of financial institutions: evidence from cross-border performance*, Federal Reserve Board.

Bottazzi, L. and M. Da Rin (2002), *Europe's 'new' stock markets*, CEPR Discussion paper.

Cabral, I., F. Dierick and J. Vesala (2002), *Banking integration in the euro area*, European Central Bank, Occasional Paper, December.

Cecchini, P., F. Heinemann and M. Jopp (2003), *The incomplete European market for financial services*, Zentrum für Europäische Wirtschaftsforschung (ZEW), Heidelberg.

Cruickshank, D. (2001), *Clearing and settlement – the barrier to a pan-European capital market*, speech delivered at the Royal Institute for International Affairs.

Degryse, H. and S. Ongena (2002), *Distance, lending relationships and competition*, Tilburg University, Center for Economic Research, Discussion Paper.

De la Dehesa, G. (2002), *Venture capital in the US and Europe*, Group of Thirty, Occasional Paper.

Dermine, J. (1999), *European capital markets with a single currency*, Oxford University Press, Oxford.

European Central Bank (2003), *Structural analysis of the EU banking sector – year 2002*, November.

European Central Bank (2002), *Structural analysis of the EU banking sector – year 2001*, November.

European Central Bank (2000), *EU banks' margins and credit standards*, December.

European Central Bank (1999), *Possible effects of EMU on the EU banking systems in the medium to long run*, February.

Galati, G. and K. Tsatsaronis (2001), *The impact of the euro on Europe's financial markets*, BIS Working Paper, July.

Giovannini Group (2003), *Second report on EU clearing and settlement arrangements*, April.

Giovannini Group (2001), *Cross-border clearing and settlement arrangements in the European Union*, November.

Group of Ten (2001), *Report on consolidation in the financial sector ('Ferguson report')*, January.

Hartmann, P., A. Maddaloni and S. Manganelli (2003), *The euro area financial system: structure, integration and policy initiatives*, Oxford Review of Economic Policy, Spring 2003, Vol. 9 (1), pp. 180–213. Also published as ECB Working Paper No. 230.

Heinemann, F. (2003), *The Benefits of creating an integrated EU market for investment funds*, Zentrum für Europäische Wirtschaftsforschung (ZEW).

Huizinga, H., J. Nelissen and R. Vander Vennet (2001), *Efficiency effects of bank mergers and acquisitions in Europe*, Tinbergen Institute Discussion Paper.

Humphrey, D.M. Kim and B. Vale (1998), *Realizing the gains from electronic payments: costs, pricing and payment choice*, Norges Bank, Arbeitsnotat.

Schröder, M. (2003), *Benefits of diversification and integration for international equity and bond portfolios*, Zentrum für Europäische Wirtschaftsforschung (ZEW).

Schüler, M. (2003), *Integration of the European market for e-finance: evidence from on-line brokerage*, Zentrum für Europäische Wirtschaftsforschung (ZEW).

Vander Vennet, R. (1996), *The effect of mergers and acquisitions on the efficiency and profitability of EC credit institutions*, Journal of Banking and Finance, November, pp. 1531–1558.

Chapter 7

Integration of the Money Market in the Euro Area

Tom Bernhardsen and Steen Ejerskov

Introduction

The money market has perhaps experienced the most direct impact of the introduction of the euro among financial markets in the euro area. Funds traded between banks in the individual legacy currencies became a homogenous good literally overnight on 1 January 1999 with prices in the market represented by a single yield curve for the entire euro area anchored by one short-term monetary policy rate. Previously diverse procedures of the national central banks for implementing monetary policy and supplying reserves in the money market were substituted by a single operational framework.

The remarkable convergence of national money market rates before the introduction of the euro is illustrated in Figure 7.1, showing all national three-month deposit rates prior to 1999 and the three-month EURIBOR (euro inter-bank offered rate) from 1999. Interest rate differentials narrowed during the second half of the 1990s as the countries prepared for the currency union, with convergence of long-term interest rates being one of the criteria for participation.

This chapter presents some stylized facts about the euro area money market and provides an assessment of its development and degree of integration since the introduction of the euro. Also in order to put the structures of the euro money market into perspective, we provide some international comparisons, primarily from the US money market.

Three main conclusions emerge. First, the euro money market is generally characterized by a high degree of efficiency and integration, both in the primary and secondary markets. Second, prevailing evidence suggests that the money market is currently reinforcing its *implicit two-tiered structure* with a tier of large wholesaling banks specializing in primary market participation and cross-border trading and a second tier of smaller banks with primarily local business. Third, money market structures still exhibit some national heterogeneity. In the repo market, in particular, despite important improvements in recent years, country-specific legislation, collateral, payment systems and traditions still present some barriers to a fully integrated market. Current work on further development of the market infrastructure, such as common payment and settlement systems, may provide a boost to the cross-border activity.

This chapter is organized as follows. The ultimate source of supply of reserves in the money market is the central bank. Thus, in the first section, we describe the

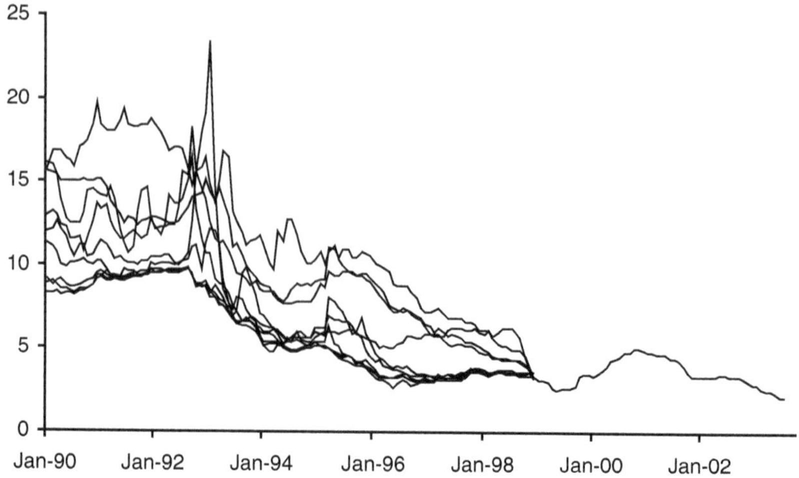

Figure 7.1 Three-month deposit rates in euro area countries (monthly data, per cent)

Source: BIS and Reuters.

operational framework of the ECB and its supply of reserves to the money market through open market operations (the primary market). The design of the central bank procedures has an important impact on the development of an integrated money market. Hence, we will provide an overview of the choice of the operational framework of the ECB and its impact on the dynamics of the euro money market. In the second section, we discuss the inter-bank market in the euro area (also referred to as the secondary market). We focus our attention on the main segments of the secondary market; the unsecured market, the secured (repo) market (which together form the cash market), the markets for short-term interest rate derivatives, and the market for short-term securities. Finally, the third section provides conclusions.

The Implementation of Monetary Policy and the Money Market

A well-functioning and integrated money market is of fundamental importance to the implementation of monetary policy and a smooth transmission of monetary impulses to the rest of the economy. Moreover, the procedures and instruments to implement monetary policy exert significant influence on the structure and development of the money market.

In this section we first describe the broad set of monetary policy instruments and procedures applied by the ECB and discuss their role in shaping the money market. Subsequently, we present evidence on the degree of integration in the open market operations of the ECB, which constitute the primary money market in the euro area. A comprehensive presentation of the operational framework is contained in ECB (2004a) and (2004b).

The Operational Framework of the ECB

The ECB operates in the money market in order to ensure that short-term interest rates are in line with the level deemed appropriate to achieve its primary objective of price stability. By virtue of its monopoly in issuing banknotes and bank reserves, the central bank can manage the liquidity conditions in the money market and guide money market interest rates.

The choice of the framework and consequences for the market structure The design of an operational framework should, as a key requirement, respect the principles of an open market economy, thereby fostering an integrated and deep money market contributing to an efficient allocation of liquid resources. For the ECB, this requirement is explicit in the Treaty of the European Union. In addition, the framework should be efficient in transmitting monetary policy decisions and signals precisely and quickly to the money market. This consideration comprises the aim of ensuring generally stable market conditions with low volatility of interest rates.

There may also be other requirements for a successful operational framework. For instance, simplicity and transparency may ensure that the monetary policy motivations behind the operations are correctly understood. This may facilitate the access to the primary market for a wide range of banks. It could also reduce the need for ad hoc communication on the operations, which bears the risk of being perceived differently among banks in different countries with different traditions.

These requirements, which to a large extent are mutually supportive, were considered in the choice of the operational framework of the ECB.

As a result, the framework includes three main elements. First, regular refinancing is provided to the banks from the ECB through *open market operations* (see Table 7.1 for an overview of the monetary policy operations). This helps banks meet their liquidity needs. The weekly main refinancing operation is a key element in the monetary policy implementation of the ECB. The main refinancing rate signals the stance of the monetary policy decided by the Governing Council of the ECB. Second, *two standing facilities*, a marginal lending and a deposit facility, are offered to the banks to allow overnight loans or deposits in exceptional circumstances. The facilities are available to banks at their discretion. Third, *reserve requirements* with averaging provisions of around one month are used mainly as a buffer against temporary liquidity shocks in the money market to reduce the volatility of short-term interest rates, but also as a means to adjust the structural liquidity deficit of the banking sector.

An overriding feature of the framework is the reliance on a self-regulating market with infrequent presence of the central bank (described as a 'European model' in Issing et al., 2001). The interventions of the central bank are generally limited to the main refinancing operations once a week and much smaller longer-term refinancing operations once a month. The framework has encountered a very low need for extraordinary fine-tuning operations. Until the end of June 2003, the ECB had only conducted an average of around two fine-tuning operations per year to cater for exceptional circumstances. For instance, one fine-tuning operation was conducted in January 2000 to drain the excess liquidity provided for the turn of the millennium and two operations were conducted to provide extra liquidity and support the normal

Table 7.1 Monetary policy operations

	Maturity	Frequency
Open market operations[1]		
Main refinancing operations	One week[2]	Weekly
Longer-term refinancing operations	Three months	Monthly
Fine-tuning operations	Non-standardized	Non-regular
Standing facilities		
Marginal lending facility	Overnight	Access at the
Deposit facility		discretion of banks

Notes: [1] The ECB can also conduct *structural operations* to adjust the structural reserve position of the banking system (the amount of reserves in the market over the longer term). By the end of 2003, the ECB had not conducted any such operations aimed at influencing the structural reserve position of the banking system.
[2] As of 10 March 2004. Prior to that date, two weeks.

functioning of the financial markets in the days following the terrorist attacks in the US on 11 September 2001.

Open market operations The open market operations, the first element of the framework, are conducted as auctions in a decentralized manner. While the ECB coordinates the operations, the transactions are carried out by the national central banks. This distinct choice should be seen together with the very broad criteria for counterparty eligibility in the ECB operations: in principle, all credit institutions located in the euro area are potentially eligible counterparties of the ECB. Any bank may choose to become counterparty if it is subject to the ECB reserve requirements, is financially sound, and fulfils specified operational criteria enabling it to transact with the ECB. Together, the broad counterparty criteria and the decentralized operations are formulated to ensure equal treatment for all institutions across the euro area to participate in the operations of the ECB and are conducive to an integrated primary money market. At the end of June 2003, there were 6,776 credit institutions located in the euro area.[1] Of these, 2,243 institutions were counterparties in the open market operations of the ECB. However, only a subset of these has chosen to participate in the operations. For example, in the period from June 2000 to June 2001, 1,200 different banks participated in the main refinancing operations of the ECB (Nyborg et al., 2002). During that year the average bank participated in 25 main refinancing operations, that is in every second operation on average, and received reserves in 20 operations.

Due to the large number of potential counterparties, the main refinancing operations of the ECB involve an extended procedure, generally with announcement of the

1 Credit institutions are a subset of monetary and financial institutions (MFIs), of which there were 8,474 in the euro area at the end of June 2003. The group of MFIs which are not credit institutions consists predominantly of money market funds. Credit institutions are subject to reserve requirements and can chose to become counterparties in the open market operations of the ECB.

operation on Monday afternoons, bid submission and allotment on Tuesday mornings and settlement of the transactions on Wednesdays.

A different choice was made, for instance, in the US (see for example Meulendyke, 1998). The Federal Reserve Bank conducts centralized open market operations exclusively from 'the Desk' – the Markets Group at the Federal Reserve Bank of New York – with a small set of around 20 selected 'primary dealers'. These counterparties are investment banks actively dealing in US government bonds and having a need to finance their inventory of bonds. The primary dealers, located in New York, re-lend reserves obtained in the primary market to banks in the secondary market, known as the federal funds market.[2] This structure of the money market in the US could be described as an *explicit two-tiered system.* A somewhat similar system is applied in the UK, where the Bank of England operates with 15–25 counterparties in its open market operations, however, the size of the money market is considerably smaller than in the US and the euro area. In Japan, the counterparties are also selected by the central bank from a pool of banks, securities companies and money market dealers (Tanshi), which are particularly active in the market. The number of counterparties eligible for participation in the open market operations of the Bank of Japan is currently around 150.

The transactions of the ECB are conducted as repurchase agreements (repos) or as collateralized loans. In both cases, reserves are provided against adequate collateral. The range of eligible collateral in the operations is very wide, including for example also private sector securities, to ensure an equally abundant collateral base for counterparties across euro area countries. Moreover, eligible assets can be used across borders. Counterparties can use assets located in Central Securities Depositories in any euro area country. The share of such cross-border use of collateral in the ECB's operations has increased from around 10 per cent of total collateral used in early 1999 to around 30 per cent at the end of 2002. The possibility of cross-border use of collateral has facilitated the consolidation of liquidity management in multinational banks (ECB, 2002c and 2002e). However, some banks might still prefer to access the collateral on a local basis due to the cost of transfers.

The main feature of the collateral framework of the ECB is a two-tiered system of eligible assets. The tier one list of assets, the main share of eligible assets, is uniform across the euro area countries, consisting of liquid debt securities of a high credit standing (e.g. government bonds). The second tier is defined by each national central bank to pay due attention to continuity of earlier national practices and to ensure a sufficiently large collateral base in all countries. This list includes marketable assets, such as bonds and equities, or non-marketable assets such as bank loans.

Although counterparties can use collateral from cross-border Central Securities Depositories, the two-tiered collateral framework entails some heterogeneity between countries. This implies that the opportunity cost of collateral, depending for example on the liquidity value of the asset, may not be identical across countries. It is likely that in countries with a higher marginal cost of raising collateral, the cost of collateral would be an important consideration for participation in the primary

2 In the federal funds market, banks obtain reserves to hold on their account with the Federal Reserve to meet their reserve requirement. In contrast to the banks, the primary dealers do not have current accounts with the Federal Reserve.

market. Scalia and Ordine (2003) test the relevance of the cost of collateral across the euro area and find that its importance as a determinant for the bids in the ECB's main refinancing operations varies substantially. It is a much more important determinant in countries such as Spain, France and Italy than in other euro area countries. To reduce the heterogeneity, the ECB is seeking ways to gradually merge the two tiers into a single list (see also ECB, 2003a).

The open market operations of the ECB are organized as auctions to ensure a transparent and efficient distribution of reserves in the primary market. On the day preceding the weekly tender, the ECB publishes its forecast of liquidity needs of the banking system in the following week. This enhances the transparency of the money market conditions and assists the banks in preparing their bids in the tender. The auctions were conducted as fixed rate tenders from January 1999. However, in a period of pronounced expectations of increases in the key ECB interest rates in late 1999 and early 2000, banks were eager to secure reserves early in the reserve maintenance periods prior to potential interest rate increases. The strategy led to escalating overbidding in the weekly fixed rate tenders. The overbidding culminated in Spring 2000 with bids exceeding allotments by a factor of hundred and led the ECB to switch to variable rate tenders with a pre-announced minimum bid rate in June 2000. In the variable rate tenders, banks can submit a range of bids (up to ten pairs of price and quantity). The average number of bids submitted per bidder in the period from June 2000 to June 2001 was 2.4 (Nyborg et al., 2002).

The minimum bid rate has the important monetary policy signalling role previously assumed by the fixed tender rate. Apart from providing a strong interest rate signal, applying a minimum bid rate (or previously a fixed tender rate) might also be explained by a political economy argument of balancing the interest rate steering power in a decentralized system. A procedure of pure variable rate tenders could potentially leave the hub with more discretion in the implementation of monetary policy.

In conclusion, the open market operations of the ECB constitute a primary market, which is generally highly standardized and easily accessible for all banks regardless of their location, thus providing a good starting point for integration and efficiency in the money market as a whole.

Standing facilities and reserve requirements The two major instruments complementing the open market operations (the standing facilities and the reserve requirements) are applied mainly to contain volatility in short-term money market rates. They are devised to support the market mechanism.

The rates on the standing facilities are, under normal circumstances, significantly less attractive than the inter-bank market rates (+/– one percentage point from the main refinancing rate). This gives banks an important incentive to transact in the market and only use the standing facilities when market alternatives are exhausted. At the same time, the rates on the two standing facilities provide a ceiling and a floor by market arbitrage for the overnight market interest rate (the EONIA).[3] This adds an

3 The euro overnight index average (EONIA) is disseminated by the European Banking Federation (EBF). It is the weighted average of all uncollateralized overnight loans made by a panel of the banks most active in the money market.

important structure to the money market which limits the volatility of very short-term market rates.

The reserve requirement system specifies banks' required minimum current account holdings with their national central bank. Compliance is determined on the basis of the average of the daily balances over a maintenance period of around one month. The system is also characterized by a lag from the reserve base computation day to the related reserve maintenance period. Furthermore, end-of-day overdrafts of current accounts are not possible. Negative end-of-day balances are automatically considered as a request to take recourse to the marginal lending facility.

The averaging mechanism provides inter-temporal flexibility to banks in managing the reserves across the reserve maintenance period. Temporary liquidity imbalances do not need to be covered immediately and volatility in the overnight interest rate can be smoothed out. If, for instance, the overnight rate is higher than the expected rate later in the reserve maintenance period, banks can make an expected profit from lending in the market and postponing the fulfilment of required reserve holdings until later in the period (inter-temporal substitution). This adjustment of the daily demand for reserves helps stabilizing interest rates.

The holdings of required reserves are remunerated at the average tender rate in the main refinancing operations over a maintenance period, a rate virtually identical to the average inter-bank market rate at the same maturity. Reserves held at the banks' current accounts in excess of the monthly requirement are not remunerated. Hence, the average cost of reserve holdings is zero whereas the marginal cost is positive. This ensures an incentive for banks to manage their reserves actively in the market and at the same time avoids that the reserve requirement imposes a burden on banks or hampers the efficient allocation of financial resources. It also avoids a distorting wedge between banks' lending and deposit rates and underlines that the reserve requirement is not used to exert control over monetary aggregates. The reserve requirement of a bank is determined as a fraction of its reserve base, a set of liabilities on its balance sheet (deposits, debt securities and money market papers with a maturity below two years).

The required reserves act as a buffer against liquidity shocks and thus, contribute to a low need for fine-tuning operations. The emergency nature of fine-tuning operations implies a need for a rapid procedure (a 'quick tender procedure'). Fine-tuning operations only take one hour from their announcement to the communication of the tender results as opposed to the main refinancing operations, which normally span three days. To ensure a rapid execution, only short-lists of counterparties selected by the national central banks are involved in the fine-tuning operations. However, restricting primary market access to only a subset of banks entails the risk of leaving these banks in a preferential position in the secondary market that could possibly be exploited.

Adjustment of the operational framework from March 2004 In the past, during a few periods of strong expectations of changes in the key ECB rates, interest rate speculation led to very volatile bids in the main refinancing operations. These episodes were also referred to as overbidding, as explained above, and underbidding, that is occasions where bids fell short of the amount needed to ensure a smooth fulfilment of reserve requirements. To provide banks with closed monthly cycles of liquidity management with stable conditions, the ECB decided to change the timing of the reserve maintenance periods and to shorten the maturity of the main refinancing operations to one week (ECB, 2003b). The decision established a direct link between the monetary policy meeting of the ECB Governing Council and the start of the maintenance period ensuring that, as a rule, there would be no expectations of changes to the key ECB rates occurring during a maintenance period. Thus it was decided that, with effect from March 2004, reserve maintenance periods would start on the settlement day of the first main refinancing operation following the monetary policy setting meeting of the ECB's Governing Council. They would end on the day preceding the similar settlement day of the following month.

Development of cross-border market infrastructure The creation of cross-border market infrastructure provided significant support for the development of an integrated money market at an early stage. In particular, the payment system TARGET (Trans-European automated real-time gross settlement express transfer system) was created for the cross-border and domestic inter-bank transactions, settlement of ECB's open market operations and other large-value euro payments. It provides continuous intra-day settlements (finality) and collateralized intra-day overdrafts on banks' current accounts thus limiting systemic risks and ensuring smooth money market transactions. Cross-border TARGET payments are transferred via the national real-time gross settlement systems (RTGS) and exchanged on a bilateral basis between national central banks.

However, further improvements are needed. The national RTGS systems were harmonized only to the extent necessary to ensure uniformity in the implementation of the monetary policy and a level playing field for credit institutions. In 2003, work on a more integrated payment system, TARGET2, was intensified (see also ECB, 2002d). It was acknowledged that the payment system should provide a more harmonized service and contain a single price structure. TARGET2 will be a significant step towards integration of the payment infrastructure compared to the original TARGET system, in which all countries maintained their national RTGS platforms. Also in view of the enlargement of the EU, maintaining a national RTGS system for each country in the common payment system could become an increasing impediment to market efficiency and integration (all EU countries are linked to the TARGET system, not only euro area countries).

In addition to the work on payment systems, cross-border clearing and settlement needs to be significantly improved to support further integration, in particular in the repo markets. Inefficiencies in clearing and settlement are probably the most important barriers to fully integrated financial markets in Europe (Giovannini Group, 2002). The settlement and clearing systems were fragmented during the first years following the introduction of the euro, with currently around 20 national clearing and settlement institutions, and costs have been significantly higher in the euro area than, for example, in the US. The costs of cross-border transactions are particularly high. Market participants estimate that the income per transaction of the international Central Securities Depositories is more than ten times higher than the income of the national Central Securities Depositories. In previous reports, the Giovannini Group urged infrastructure providers to standardize systems and public authorities to harmonize the tax and legal treatment of, for example, repos (Giovannini Group, 1999). The ECB has been active in setting standards and promoting an integrated regulatory and oversight framework, however, it has chosen not to be directly active in providing clearing and settlement services, unlike other central banks. The ECB has thus, so far, relying on a market-driven solution with private operators.

The Impact of the Operational Framework on the Money Market

Overview The operational framework for monetary policy has a significant impact on the structure of the money market and thus an important role in providing the basis for an efficient and integrated money market. In fact, the empirical features of the day-to-day behaviour of short-term interest rates seem to be more strongly influenced by the choices for the operational framework than by extensively researched market frictions (Prati et al., 2003). The influence of the central bank instruments on the money market in the euro area is illustrated in Figure 7.2. The figure shows the development of the key ECB interest rates since the introduction of the euro. The role of the rates on the standing facilities as a corridor for the movements of the EONIA is apparent from the figure. Also, it can be seen that the EONIA has generally been very close to the rate on the main refinancing operations, illustrating the importance of these operations as a key element for implementation of the monetary policy of the ECB. Moreover, the figure also shows that the EONIA exhibits a pattern of occasional spikes. These spikes mainly occur on the last day of the monthly reserve maintenance periods. Within the maintenance period, the EONIA is generally very stable indicating that the averaging

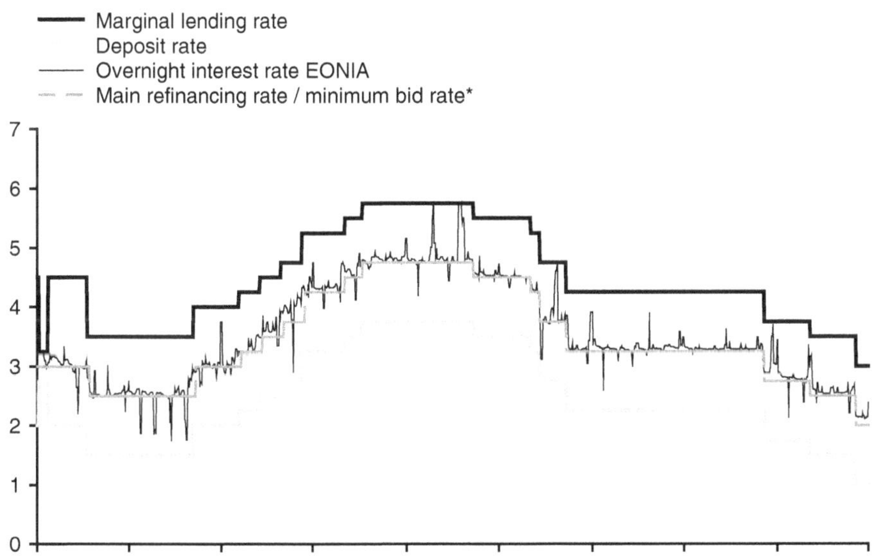

Figure 7.2 Key ECB interest rates and the EONIA (daily data, per cent)

*Prior to June 2000, the fixed tender rate.
Source: Reuters and ECB.

mechanism is working well. The picture of a generally stable development in the overnight rate in the euro area is confirmed when examining its average volatility. Table 7.2 shows that the volatility of the daily changes of the EONIA, normalized by the level of the interest rate, has been low during the first years following the introduction of the euro, also on an international standard.

Another indication that the market mechanism is working efficiently is the relatively low use of the standing facilities, as can be seen in Figure 7.3. The recourse to the standing facilities is well below €0.5 billion per day on average. In general, banks exploit the inter-bank money market while recourse to the standing facilities, at the penalty rates, is only taken in rare cases. Moreover, there are only few occasions of simultaneous use of the facilities. This would otherwise indicate important frictions in the market mechanism since banks experiencing contrasting liquidity imbalances would have benefited from transacting in the market. The notable occasions of larger recourses to the marginal lending facility are related to the first maintenance period of 1999 after the introduction of the euro and to the months around the cash changeover in January 2002. Also, the periods at year-ends (in particular the turn of the millennium) exhibit higher use of the standing facilities as well as a few occasions of underbidding in the market operations in Spring 2001 and subsequent liquidity shortfall. Within a maintenance period, the recourse to the standing facilities is normally limited to the last calendar day of the month and the last day of the maintenance period, while the use on other days is negligible. Moreover, the use of the standing facilities has diminished gradually since the introduction of the euro, indicating some learning process but also suggesting that the market functioning has advanced.

Table 7.2 Volatility of the overnight interest rates (percentage points, standard deviation of daily changes)

		Euro area	US	UK	Japan
Average volatility	1999	0.16	0.19	0.31	0.01
	2000	0.14	0.15	0.43	0.02
	2001	0.15	0.18	0.44	0.05
	2002	0.11	0.07	0.53	0.004
	2003	0.14	0.07	0.49	0.000
Average level	1999	2.74	4.99	5.22	0.05
	2000	4.12	6.26	5.85	0.11
	2001	4.39	3.88	5.04	0.05
	2002	3.29	1.67	3.92	0.001
	2003	2.36	1.15	3.60	0.001
Volatility divided by the level	1999	0.059	0.038	0.059	0.2
	2000	0.034	0.024	0.074	0.18
	2001	0.033	0.046	0.087	1.25
	2002	0.035	0.041	0.134	2.97
	2003	0.059	0.059	0.136	0.39

Note: The respective overnight rates are the EONIA, the fed funds rate, SONIA and Mutan.
Source: Reuters and own calculations.

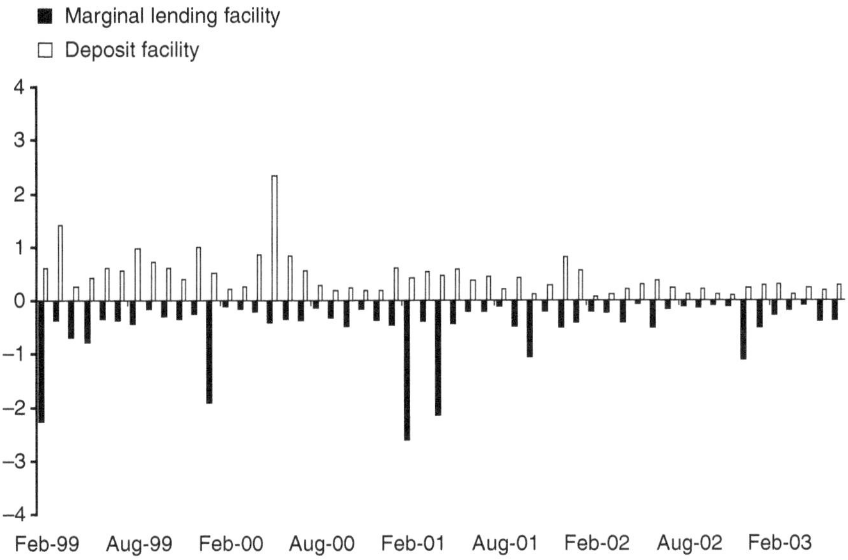

Figure 7.3 Recourse to the standing facilities 1999–2003 (averages of daily positions over the maintenance period, € billions)

Source: ECB.

Patterns within a maintenance period in the euro area and the US Taking a closer look at the market functioning within a reserve maintenance period, Panel A of Figure 7.4 illustrates the average EONIA and daily 'excess' reserve holdings, that is the daily reserve holdings minus the daily average of the total reserve requirement. It should be noted that the excess reserves, calculated as *accumulated* reserve holdings in excess of the total reserve requirement, are normally only generated in the last few days of the maintenance period (see also Bindseil et al., 2003). For comparison, a similar graph is depicted in Panel B for the US money market. The overnight spread is the spread between the overnight rate and the main refinancing rate in the euro area (the federal funds target for the US).

In both panels, the effect of the averaging provision of the reserve requirement is apparent. The average volatility of the overnight rate is relatively low during most of the maintenance period whereas it increases on the last few days of the period when reserve requirements have to be fulfilled. This can be seen from the widening of the dispersion bands illustrated by the dotted lines (see also Cassola and Morana, 2003). In the euro area, the reserve requirement is binding on the last day of the period and the demand curve for reserves becomes vertical. There is no carry-over provision between maintenance periods in the euro area.

The similarity in the dispersion of rates on the last day of the maintenance period in the euro area and the US is noteworthy given the difference in instruments and procedures. In the euro area, the corridor is an important instrument in containing spikes in the overnight rate on this day while in the US a corridor did not exist in the

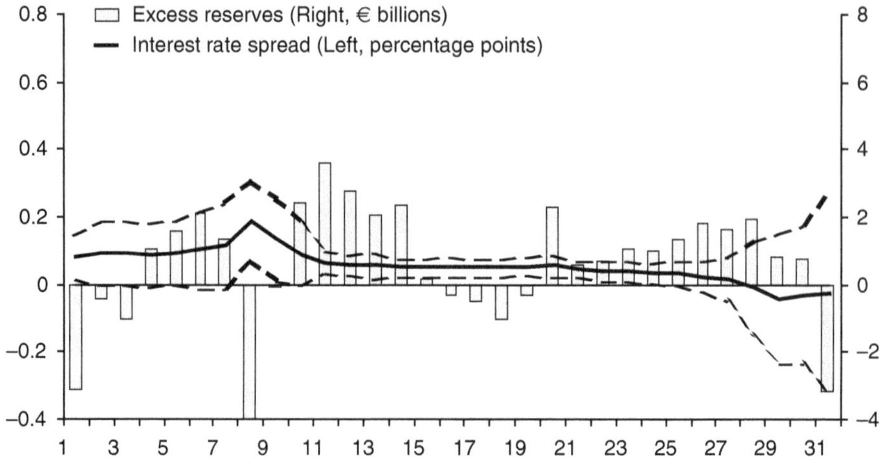

(A) The euro area

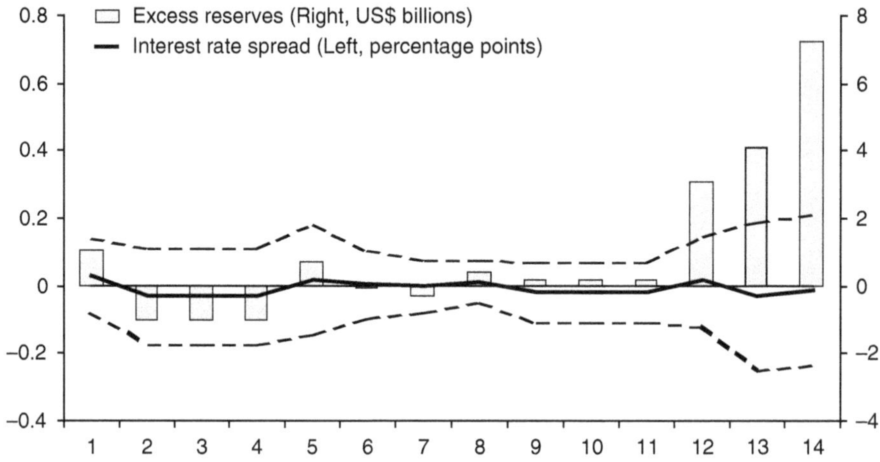

(B) The US

Figure 7.4 Excess reserves and overnight rates 2000–2002 (daily averages on each day of the reserve maintenance period)

Note: Dotted lines are +/– one standard deviation. End-of-year periods are omitted both for the euro area and the US. For the euro area, the maintenance periods in which underbidding occurred are omitted and for the US, the period from 11 September to 17 October 2001 is also omitted. Reserve maintenance periods in the euro area started on the 24th calendar day of one month and ended on the 23rd day of the following month in the period considered. In the US, reserve maintenance periods start on a Thursday and end on the Wednesday two weeks later. Weekend days are included.
Source: Bloomberg, ECB and the Federal Reserve Bank of New York.

period covered in Figure 7.4.[4] However, the Federal Reserve typically intervenes in the US money market on this day to affect money market conditions whereas the ECB generally does not. Also, to alleviate pressure on the overnight rate on the last day of the maintenance period, the US system contains carry-over provisions, implying a non-vertical demand curve on the last day of the period. The similarity of volatility on the last day of the maintenance period in the euro area and the US is also found in the study by Bartolini and Prati (2003). In contrast, average volatility on the days *before* the last day of the period appears to be significantly lower in the euro area compared with the US. Bartolini and Prati (2003) find that the average volatility on the days before the last day is less than one-tenth of its level on the last day in the euro area while around half of its level on the last day in the US.

For both panels of Figure 7.4, the average of the daily excess reserves over the maintenance period is positive, amounting to around €0.65 billion in the euro area and US$ 1 billion in the US. Excess reserves could perhaps be expected to be lower in the euro area where banks have the remunerated alternative of taking recourse to the deposit facility, unlike in the US. Hence, it might indicate some degree of inefficiency of the market mechanism towards the end of the last day of the reserve maintenance periods. However, it might also to some extent reflect that banks in general see high non-pecuniary costs associated with non-compliance and therefore use excess reserves as an insurance against late payments or liquidity management mistakes on the last day of the period.

The pattern of excess reserves chosen by banks is to some extent affected by the seasonality of autonomous factors – items beyond the control of the central bank or items normally not related to the monetary policy operations. Banknotes in circulation and government deposits with the national central banks are the most prominent autonomous factors in terms of size and volatility. The link between banks' daily excess reserves holdings and the autonomous factors was apparent, for instance, on the last day of the maintenance period for the euro area in Panel A of Figure 7.4: on this day, autonomous factors were €2 billion higher, that is more liquidity draining, than the daily average (mainly due to a drain caused by the monthly tax collections in Italy). This compares to the €3 billion average reserve deficit on this day in the period, as seen in Panel A of Figure 7.4. Also, in the first week of the maintenance period, autonomous factors were generally liquidity draining. In particular, on the last day of the calendar month (day 8 in the figure), autonomous factors were €8 billion more liquidity draining than the average. Mirroring this in part, banks had an average reserve shortfall of €4 billion on this day.

The pattern of the reserve holdings can also change with business and interest rate cycles. For instance, in periods of strong expectations of interest rate cuts, banks tended to delay reserve fulfilment in the period covered, and vice versa in periods of interest rate hike expectations. For instance, during 2001, the ECB and the Federal

4 The discount window of the Federal Reserve was reformed on 9 January 2003 and now resembles the marginal lending facility of the ECB. A rate of one percentage point above the federal funds target rate is applied. There is no marginal deposit facility, as is the case in the euro area, hence, the lower bound of the interest rate corridor for the overnight rate in the US is zero per cent.

Reserve reduced the monetary policy rates significantly and banks had a slight tendency for back-loading their reserve fulfilment. Following the change of the timing of reserve maintenance periods and the shortening of the maturity of the ECB's main refinancing operations as of March 2004 the future impact from interest rate change expectations is expected to be significantly reduced in the euro area.

The market mechanism and the martingale One way to gain insight into the functioning of the market mechanism is to assess whether the overnight interest rate follows a martingale process. The martingale property entails that, in the absence of market frictions, the prevailing overnight rate should equal the expected future rate, in particular, the rate on the last day of the maintenance period in a framework with a minimum reserve system. Deviations from this should be eliminated by inter-temporal substitution if the market mechanism is efficient. In other words, the pattern of the overnight rate over the maintenance period should not be predictable. Violations of the martingale property would allow for 'liquidity effects', that is changes in interest rates stemming from variability in day-to-day liquidity conditions.

Does the martingale hypothesis hold? In practice, it is a strong assumption and it is usually only met in approximate terms. In the euro area, there is a higher average overnight rate around the calendar month-end as can be seen in Figure 7.4 (day 8 in Panel A). On this day, banks are reluctant to lend reserves due to window dressing. Banks trim balance sheets for performance presentation and capital adequacy rules by increasing the relative cash holdings. The effect is largest at the end-of-quarter, end-of-semester and, in particular, at the turn of the year. The effect is also significant in the US at these frequencies (Prati et al., 2003). The month end is not visible in Panel B of Figure 7.4 for the US since it falls on different weekdays across maintenance periods, which start on a Thursday and end on a Wednesday two weeks later. Apart from the month-end effect, no predictable pattern of the level of the overnight rate is evident in the euro money market. Generally, a liquidity effect is not found in the euro area until the last few days of the maintenance period (Ejerskov et al., 2003; Würtz, 2003; and Bindseil and Seitz, 2001). However, there is also scant evidence of the opposite, for instance in the study of Angelini (2002). In addition, past holdings of liquidity are significant for the bidding in the ECB's main refinancing operations, in the sense that banks seek to roll over their maturing amount from an earlier operation. This is consistent with the hypothesis that a significant number of banks have a target level of end-of-day reserves for settlement purposes (Scalia and Ordine, 2003). Moreover, it would be consistent with a preference for a smooth fulfilment of reserve requirements. Both elements would leave some scope for imperfect averaging and liquidity effects also before the last main refinancing operation of the maintenance period. A survey on the martingale property for the euro area is provided for instance by Pérez Quirós and Mendizábal (2001).

In the US, banks normally back-load their reserve compliance to some extent regardless of their interest rate change expectations as can be seen from Panel B of Figure 7.4. The generally late fulfilment of reserve requirements in the US might be due to a tendency for 'soft' ends of the maintenance periods, that is ample liquidity and low rates in the second half of the maintenance period. The provision of particularly high levels of reserves resulting in soft interest rates on the last days of the maintenance period appears to be a recent achievement of the Federal Reserve. A similar conclusion is reached in the recent study of Bartolini and Prati (2003), whereas previous studies have found a tendency for high rates on the last days of the maintenance period (for example Hamilton, 1996). The figure also points to a few other characteristics of the maintenance period pattern in the US money market. For instance, reserve holdings and the overnight rate on Fridays are typically low as banks seek to avoid the cost of weekend holdings. Conversely, holdings are generally higher on the Mondays and the overnight rate increases. In addition, on days with high payment flows, for example to or from the Treasury account, pressure can build on the overnight rate. Several of these effects have also been identified in previous studies, for instance in Prati et al. (2002). The presence of the effects may partly be due to the relatively low level of required reserves, which implies that the risk of individual overnight overdrafts is a relevant concern. Overall, there appears to be some patterns for the overnight rate during the maintenance period in the US. However, the identification of liquidity effects in the federal funds market is not unambiguous. For opposite views on the existence of a liquidity effect in the US case, see Hamilton (1996) and Thornton (2001a, 2001b).

In conclusion, the martingale property may not be perfectly met in practice, neither in the euro area nor in the US. This conclusion has been reached by several researchers, for instance Pérez Quirós and Mendizábal (2001), Prati et al. (2002), Würtz (2003), and particularly for the US, Hamilton (1996) and Balduzzi et al. (1998). However, the departure from the martingale appears economically minor in the euro area, lending support to the stabilizing effect of the reserve requirement system, as also noted by Bartolini and Prati (2003). It suggests, therefore, that the system of instruments and procedures chosen by the ECB has provided a good underpinning for an efficient and integrated money market (see also Pérez Quirós and Mendizábal, 2001).

A hands-off and a hands-on system The average volatility has been fairly similar in the euro area and the US money markets in recent years, as was also apparent from Table 7.2. However, the result is reached through different choices of framework and does not necessarily provide conclusions for the degree of market efficiency and integration. For instance, an important difference between the ECB and the Federal Reserve is that the Federal Reserve has an explicit target for the overnight rate, the federal funds target rate, which is decided by the Federal Open Market Committee (the operational target). In the euro area, the overnight rate is not a target *per se*. Rather, the monetary policy stance is signalled through the rate on the main refinancing operations and the rates on the standing facilities.

The minimum reserve systems have some important differences. Compared to the euro area, the level of effective reserve balances, that is including clearing balances but excluding vault cash, is only around one tenth in the US and required reserve holdings are not remunerated (voluntary clearing balances provide credit to pay for Federal Reserve services). Furthermore, the reserve maintenance period is two weeks in the US, around half the length of the one in the euro area (around one month).

Overall, the averaging provision has a less important role in stabilizing the overnight rate in the US. Instead, as the level of required reserve balances in the US has declined over the past decade, the Federal Reserve has significantly increased the frequency of interventions (Bartolini and Prati, 2003). Central bank interventions are generally conducted daily in the US as opposed to weekly in the euro area. The system in the euro area has been characterized as a 'hands-off' approach (Bartolini and Prati, 2003), or as being consistent with a scheme between the 'dealing rate model' and an 'open mouth approach' (Manna et al., 2001). In contrast, the system in the US has been characterized as a 'hands-on' approach (Bartolini and Prati, 2003). The hands-off approach by the ECB, and the absence of an explicit target for the overnight rate, has been reflected in the reserve policy. The ECB has generally provided reserves to the money market in a smooth and neutral (quantity-oriented) way with only few deviations from benchmark allotments to guide short-term interest rates (Ejerskov et al., 2003; ECB, 2002a; Välimäki, 2002). Notable exceptions from the neutral reserve allotments were around the episodes of underbidding in the open market operations, which gave rise to complex non-convex allotment trade-offs between quantity and price smoothing (see Ewerhart et al., 2003).

Evidence of Integration in the Primary Money Market

Following the description of the instruments and procedures of the ECB and their impact on the money market structure, we will in this section assess the level of efficiency and integration in the primary money market of the euro area, that is the open market operations of the ECB.

Bid rates in the ECB main refinancing operations conducted as variable rate tenders with a pre-announced minimum bid rate are normally highly concentrated around the inter-bank market rates at the same maturity (ECB, 2001). The dispersion of bids may, for instance, be measured by the difference between the marginal and the weighted average rates of the tenders. These have usually been very close to each other, with a median of one basis point in the period from June 2000 to June 2003. However, there have been deterministic spikes in the spread between the marginal and the weighted average rates around year-ends of up to 10 basis points. There have also been rare smaller spikes related to exceptional events, e.g. very tight liquidity conditions following a few incidents of underbidding. The high concentration of bid rates may suggest that the primary market is transparent and relatively well integrated.

The concentration of allotments among banks in the main refinancing operations can be illustrated by the share of allotments of the three, ten and twenty largest bidders, as depicted in Figure 7.5. The ten largest bidders received less than 50 per cent of the allotted amounts in 2002 and 2003, indicating that the primary euro money market is generally very competitive. The bidders are generally small compared to the overall size of the open market operations. In a study of the period June 2000 to June 2001, the largest bidder received on average 7 per cent of the allotments and the average bank bid for 0.4 per cent of the operation (Nyborg et al., 2002). In this period, the 50 largest bidders received on average 72 per cent of the allotment in each operation.

Since the introduction of the euro in January 1999, the largest bidders have received a modestly increasing share of the total allotments. This development has occurred in conjunction with a decline in the number of bids and bidders, which is shown in Figure 7.6. The figure illustrates the declining trend in the number of bidders, in particular after the switch from fixed rate to variable rate tenders in June

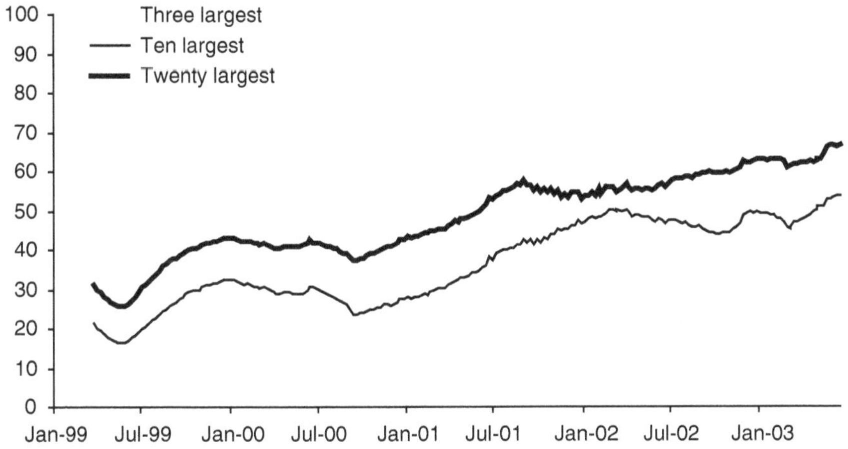

Figure 7.5 The largest bidders' share of the overall allotments (three-month moving average, per cent)

Source: ECB.

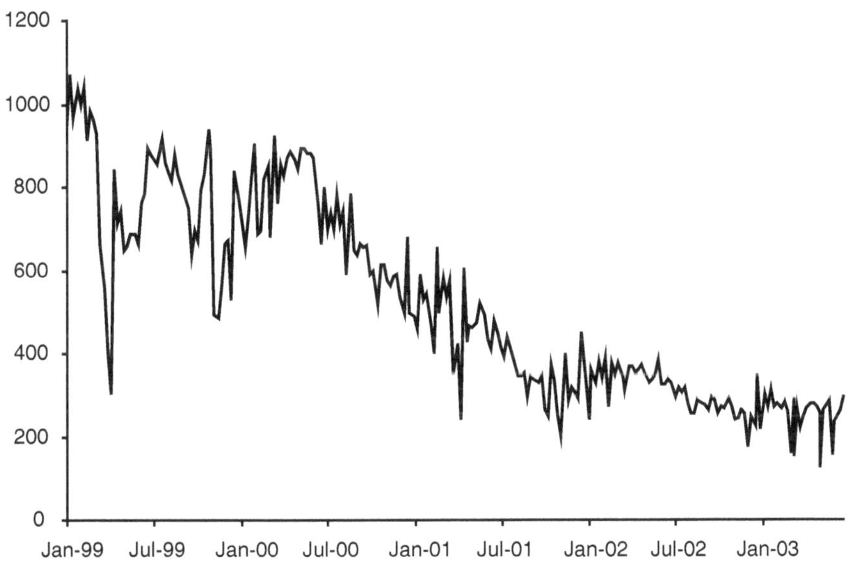

Figure 7.6 Number of bidders in the main refinancing operations

Source: ECB.

2000. In 2002 and 2003, the number of bidders in the operations was relatively stable, hovering around 300. Part of the decline in the number of bidders and the increase in the allotment share of large bidders after the change of the tender procedure might reflect that it is more complicated to bid in variable rate tenders than fixed rate tenders. In the variable rate tenders, there is some interest rate uncertainty. This may in particular discourage small or local banks from participating. In fact, in the variable rate tender period, the large bidders were submitting more successful bids compared to smaller bidders (ECB, 2001). Furthermore, the main refinancing rate is lower than the inter-bank market rates when there are neutral or increasing interest rate expectations. Conversely, in protracted periods of declining interest rates, which has generally characterized the variable rate tender period, the open market operations with a *minimum* bid rate may be less attractive. The decline in the number of bidders may also to some extent reflect the changing structures of the European banking sector and money market. First, it is likely to be a mirror of the consolidation in the European banking sector experienced in the period since 1999, including the growing importance of liquidity management at the group level in cooperative banks (ECB, 2002e). Second, the introduction of the single money market may have enhanced the possibilities for the specialization of banks' activities in the money market. For instance, some banks might increasingly specialize in acquiring reserves from the central bank in the primary market and distribute it in the secondary money market (large wholesaling banks). This could be described as an *implicit two-tiered money market* with some similarities to the explicit two-tiered market in the US, although the number of participants in the primary market in the euro area still is ten times higher than in the US.

Elements of an implicit two-tiered money market structure Larger banks, well-established in cross-border credit assessment and transactions, have an absolute advantage in dealing with banks in other countries over smaller banks who have predominantly local business. The larger banks might exploit their advantage and specialize in cross-border trading, arbitraging liquidity and interest rate imbalances across euro area countries. Smaller banks with mainly local interests and a less developed infrastructure for cross-border transactions may then use the wholesaling banks with origin in their country as intermediaries. The large wholesaling banks might also have an advantage in the primary market, as evidenced from the higher proportion of successful bids in the variable rate tenders. The cross-border interface of a specialized group of wholesaling banks is outlined in Figure 7.7 in a pure version, that is with no cross-border interaction between the smaller local banks. In practice, there is also some cross-border activity of the smaller banks. The two-tiered structure might partly be explained by historical bank-to-bank relationships within countries and, for mainly large banks, across borders (Ciampolini and Rohde, 2000). Relationships and some reciprocal credit lines were already in place prior to the introduction of the euro between larger banks across different countries. The advantage of the large wholesaling banks possibly stems from a more sophisticated formation of expectations of liquidity and interest rate conditions and a large collateral base with more extensive use of cross-border collateral. In addition, the large banks have the capacity to transact in large volumes and they may have a better credit assessment of banks in other countries coming from their international experience

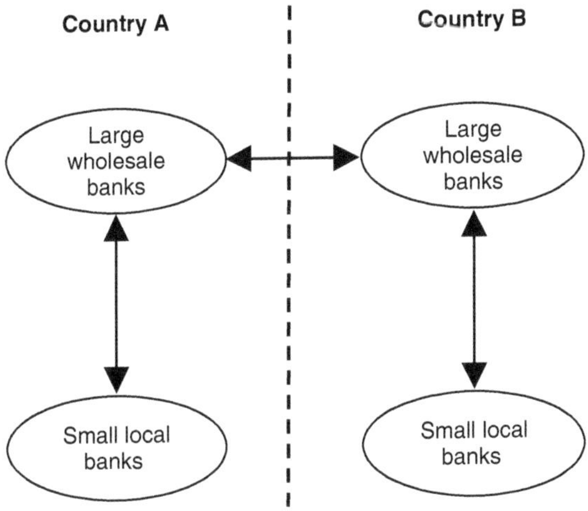

Figure 7.7 Simple model of a pure two-tiered money market structure

and more elaborate risk management systems. Furthermore, large banks tend to manage their reserves in a more sophisticated manner compared to smaller banks. Freixas and Holthausen (2001) formulated the two-tiered structure as the 'transnational bank hypothesis'. Their analysis shows that if banks have asymmetric information on the credit risk of their counterparties, a full integration of the euro money market might not materialize. However, they also show that large wholesaling banks with access to information in several countries may perform cross-border arbitrage and liquidity smoothing, thus counteracting the welfare-reducing effects of information asymmetries. The authors argue that cross-border dissemination of information is essential for an integrated inter-bank market to develop. They put forward the hypothesis that, in the longer term, information should become more evenly spread across the euro area which would be conducive to an integrated equilibrium in which also small banks could actively participate in cross-border transactions. The prediction that the introduction of the euro will be a catalyst to increased competition in the banking sector in the euro area and induce structural adjustments is shared by a number of studies (for example also De Bandt and Davis, 1999, and Ehrmann et al., 2001).

Some indications of a two-tiered money market are evident from primary money market data. Figure 7.8 shows the share of the allotments in the main refinancing operations of each country (relative to respective sizes of the banking sector measured by the reserve requirement). The share in the primary market of banks located in Luxembourg has increased significantly over the period and the share of banks located in Germany has remained high. This suggests that some banks in the financial centres play an important, and slightly increasing, role in the primary market and thus in re-distributing the reserves in the secondary market (see also Abildgren, 2002). Since the introduction of the euro, it is no longer necessary for banks to borrow reserves directly from their national central bank or from the inter-bank

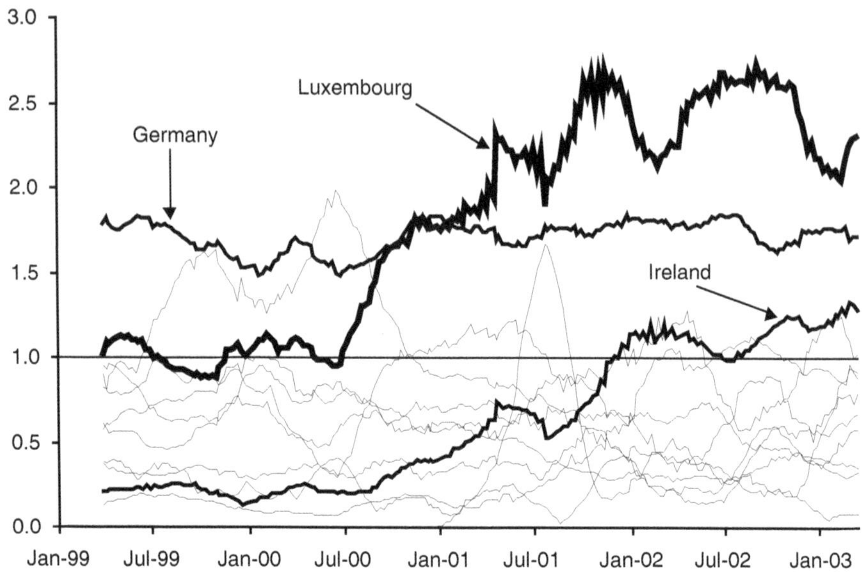

Figure 7.8 Share of the allotments in the main refinancing operations (three-month moving average)

Note: Shares are relative to the respective sizes of the banking sectors in each country measured by the reserve requirements. For instance, a factor of 1.0 implies that the country receives a share of the allotments equal to its share of the total euro area banking system.
Source: ECB.

market in their own country. This may also be consistent with the increasing tendency of the largest bidders' share of the allotments as seen in Figure 7.5 and the declining number of bidders in the main refinancing operations seen in Figure 7.6. Another point to note is that the share of banks located in Ireland has increased from very low levels in 1999 to share above their relative size in 2003, reflecting the significant increase in the market for international financial services in Ireland in recent years.

Further evidence on the level of integration of the primary money market in the euro area is provided by the panel study of Scalia and Ordine (2003). They focus on three main issues: effects from (i) bank size, (ii) participation in multinational bank groups and (iii) country of origin.

First, they find that the size of the bidder is important in determining its bidding behaviour in the main refinancing operations supporting the description of a two-tiered money market structure. Also, they find evidence supporting the hypothesis that large bidders have an absolute advantage in participating in the primary market. Large bidders appear to obtain lower rates than small bidders, primarily by making more extensive use of the possibility to submit multiple bids. In addition, larger banks are more active in the primary market and submit larger bids compared to smaller banks. Larger banks also seem to be typically less risk averse than smaller banks and their bidding is more efficient. Their demand is more elastic to the interest rate conditions, both at the short and long end of the yield curve. In contrast, smaller banks are more likely to have a daily target for the level of reserves implying an inefficient use of the averaging provision of the reserve requirement. Furthermore, when money market volatility increases, the large bidders reduce the bid amount and raise their bid rates less than the smaller bidders. They are also more likely to participate and bid for larger amounts of reserves when the forecast of the reserve need over the coming week increases. Finally, there are also signs that the collateral management, including the cross-border use of collateral, of the large banks is more sophisticated.

Second, bidders that participate in a multinational banking group (with minimum two bidders and maximum six), regardless of their size, resemble the bidding behaviour of the large bidders. Thus, these banks generally do not have a target level of reserves and are exploiting the averaging provision. Also, they do not react to the liquidity conditions specific to their country and they are more likely to bid in the open market operations of the ECB when the volatility of money market conditions is high.

Third, some country specific effects are also still important. For instance, German banks have a higher likelihood of participating in the primary market. Scalia and Ordine interpret the finding of more funding from the central bank as a sign of lower efficiency of the participation in the secondary money market for banks located in Germany due to the special structure of the banking sector with a very high number of small credit institutions (for instance, the importance of the savings banks). A more important reason explaining the higher participation in the primary market might, however, be the sign of some increased specialization of German banks in tapping money from the primary market and distributing it further within and across borders in the secondary market (wholesaling), as suggested by Abildgren (2002). Differences between countries also exist regarding the effect from the banks' size on the participation in the primary market. For instance, in Luxembourg the largest bidders do not necessarily have the largest liability base and reserve requirement. However, this might be consistent with the fact that Luxembourg is a centre for money market dealers, of which a significant number are owned by foreign banks, with a relatively small liability base. The finding that banks' bidding behaviour to some degree depends on its size and country of origin appears also to be true in the less frequent longer-term refinancing operations of the ECB (Linzert et al., 2003).

Overall, the evidence from Scalia and Ordine (2003) suggesting that the size and international profile of a bank matters for its participation in the primary money market lends some support to the description of the euro money market as an implicit two-tiered system.

Concluding remarks on the operational framework and the primary market The choice of the instruments and procedures of the ECB were made to support the development of an integrated and competitive money market. Harmonized rules and procedures ensure that there are no barriers, which discriminate banks in their access to the primary market. The decentralized implementation has supported a broad access to the primary market.

The prevailing evidence suggests that bidding in the main refinancing operations is generally competitive and efficient. What is more, the evolution of the degree of concentration of bids and allotments among bidders, reflecting some consolidation in the European banking sector but also still significant competition, indicates a well-integrated primary market. However, there are also signs that some country-specific effects are still prevailing, for instance as found in the study by Scalia and Ordine (2003) regarding bidding behaviour in the main refinancing operations. It is likely though that as the infrastructure for cross-border transactions is enhanced and information gets more easily disseminated across the euro area some of the heterogeneity will vanish. Yet, an equilibrium in which also small banks participate extensively in cross-border transactions is not imminent. Rather, when looking at the prevailing evidence, an implicit two-tiered money market structure, with some similarities to the explicit two-tiered system in the US, seems to exist. If, by making use of an absolute advantage, benefits of specialization are important, this might even be the most efficient equilibrium.

Efficiency and Integration in the Secondary Money Market

Following the assessment of the integration in the euro area primary money market and its impact on the structure of the secondary money market, we now turn our focus to the evidence of integration in the different segments of the secondary money market of the euro area.

The secondary money market is commonly divided into three parts: the cash market, the market for short-term interest rate derivatives and the market for short-term securities. We elaborate mainly on the cash market and the market for derivatives, as they are by far the most important segments of the euro area money market. The cash market consists of (i) the unsecured deposit market, in which banks exchange short-term liquidity without the guarantee of collateral, (ii) the repo market, in which participants exchange short-term liquidity against collateral, and (iii) foreign exchange swaps. The segments of the cash market will be discussed in the following section.

The Cash Market

The recent development of activity in the main segments Figure 7.9 shows the activity in the unsecured market, the repo market and the market for foreign exchange swaps as a share of the total cash market. In recent years, while the share of the activity in the repo market has increased, the share of the unsecured market has slightly declined. In fact, the trading volume of repos grew at their fastest rate in the two years up to 2002. In 2003 the unsecured market, the repo market and the currency swap market accounted for 32 per cent, 49 per cent and 19 per cent, respectively, of total cash market activities (ECB, 2004c). Hence the repo market has now become the largest segment of the cash market in the euro area.

The market for unsecured and repo transactions is mainly used for the management of cash positions, determined by, for example, banks' customer flows and the need to fulfil minimum reserve requirements, which leads to a very high concentration of activity in the short-term maturities from overnight and up to a week (see Figure 7.10). In money markets in other countries a relevant concern for banks is also

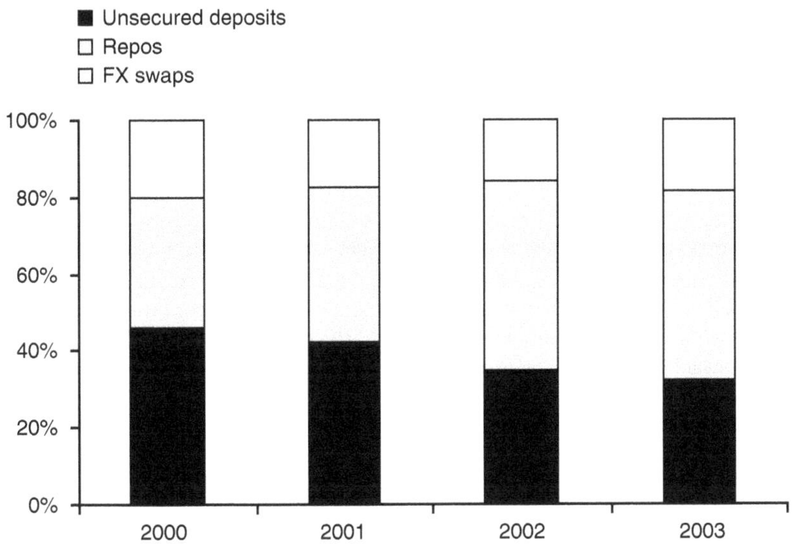

Figure 7.9 Unsecured deposits, repos and foreign exchange swaps as a share of total activity in the cash market

Source: ECB.

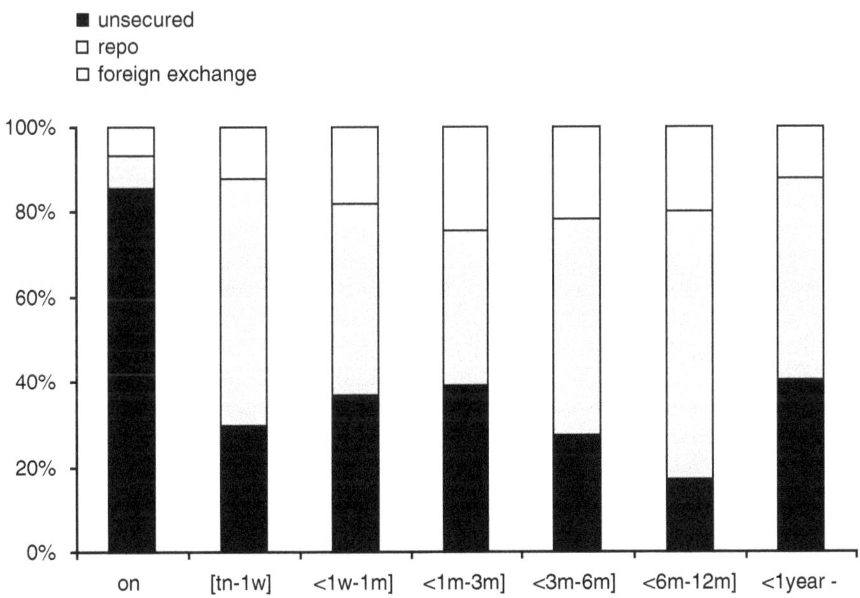

Figure 7.10 Euro cash market, breakdown by maturities

Source: ECB.

to avoid impermissible overdrafts on their current accounts at the central bank. However, in the euro money market, this is very rarely a consideration due to the high level of reserve requirements (fully remunerated). The breakdown by maturities in each cash market segment shows that unsecured deposit transactions remain predominant in the overnight maturity, as securities used as collateral in the repos are not normally settled spot, that is on the same day as the trade is agreed. Moreover, credit risk is perceived to be of limited relevance for this very short-term maturity.

For maturities beyond the overnight segment, however, repo operations are preferred to unsecured transactions as they provide better protection against credit risk.[5] Hence, there is a high degree of activity in the repo market for maturities up to 12 months. Though currency swaps constitute a noteworthy share of total activity for maturities between one month and 12 months, they are dominated by unsecured and secured transactions for all maturities.

The inter-bank *cross-border* lending, aggregated for all segments, has significantly increased since the introduction of the euro. From 1990 to 1998, cross-border lending in the euro area countries rose at an annual rate of around 10 per cent whereas the annual growth rates were close to 20 per cent in the three following years with the bulk of the increase being inside the euro area (Galati and Tsatsaronis, 2001; Gaspar et al., 2003). The relative share of euro area banks' cross-border claims also rose significantly in 1998 and 1999.

As regards the market organization, multiple forms co-exist in the secondary money market of the euro area: over-the-counter (OTC), voice brokers, electronic markets and market makers. National traditions still prevail in the market organization, which might prevent perfect and continuous homogeneity of market conditions. For example, OTC trading dominates in Germany, France and the Netherlands whereas Italy (e-MID) and Spain (voice brokers) are mainly characterized by brokerage.

We now take a closer look at the individual segments of the cash market.

The unsecured market As mentioned earlier, the ECB provides reserves in the primary market to euro area credit institutions on the basis of the refinancing needs of the whole euro area. The unsecured deposit market assumes the important role of redistributing reserves among credit institutions within countries and across borders. This segment has become highly liquid and deep and has achieved a high degree of standardization since the introduction of the euro. In fact, in a survey among 20 banks in the euro area, 16 of them expressed the view that market liquidity improved after the introduction of the euro in 1999 (Ciampolini and Rohde, 2000). Of the 20 banks surveyed, seven banks pointed out that liquidity had improved significantly. Only one expressed dissatisfaction with the degree of integration in the unsecured market. Furthermore, in a study of the development of bid-ask spreads in the unsecured market, Galati and Tsatsaronis (2001) find that spreads across countries converged after 1999 whereas differences had been significant prior to the introduction of the euro.

5 It is noteworthy that also in the tomorrow-next and the spot-next segments the repo market dominates the unsecured market. However, as the data on foreign currency swap transactions include tomorrow-next, spot-next and one-week transactions in one single group, it is not possible to depict these details in the figure.

Immediately after the introduction of the single currency, the euro area unsecured deposit market increased substantially with a 40 per cent jump in the overnight segment (Baele et al., 2004). However, between 2001 and 2002 total unsecured money market activity declined by 14 per cent (ECB, 2003c). The decline in the unsecured money market activity was mainly due to developments in the short-term segment, notably overnight transactions, which is still by far the most important segment of total unsecured money market activity. In fact, since 2000 unsecured transactions with maturities larger than one month have not reached 10 per cent of total activity, either on the lending or on the borrowing side of the market.

Integration in the overnight unsecured market At the starting point of the yield curve, the overnight rate (the EONIA) has a key role in the transmission mechanism of monetary policy impulses and a low dispersion across countries is therefore particularly important. The average overnight rate for each euro area country (for the EONIA panel banks) is shown in Figure 7.11. The dispersion of the overnight rates between countries has been negligible since early 1999, with overnight rates in different countries appearing as practically one line in Figure 7.11. The minor differences are partly stemming from, for example, different timings of transactions over the day in the different countries. Also, to the extent that a two-tiered money market exists, with some large international banks providing wholesaling services to smaller local banks, some price discrimination would be justified to cover for the cost of information and allowance for risk.

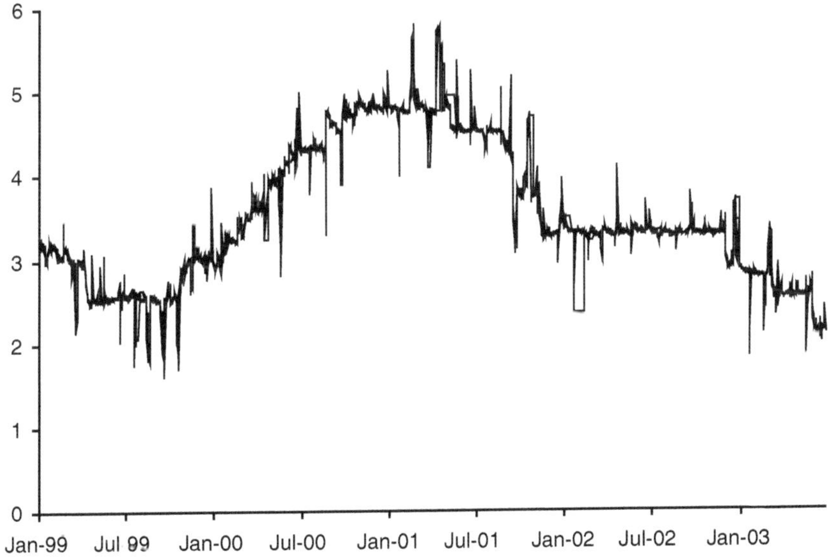

Figure 7.11 Overnight rates for some selected euro area countries (daily data, per cent)

Source: European Banking Federation.

One measure of integration can be obtained by examining whether differences *between* country rates are larger than the dispersion among banks *within* each member state. In a fully integrated market, cross-country dispersion should be of the same magnitude as the dispersion within countries. Figure 7.12 shows the average dispersion of lending rates across countries relative to the average dispersion of rates within countries at each point in time. The chart indicates a practically full integration in the overnight segment, as the ratio generally has been very close to one since the introduction of the euro. Moreover, it suggests that there are practically no barriers to cross-border arbitrage of instantaneous interest rate disparities. However, as a caveat it should be noted that the around 50 prime banks participating in the panel are among the most active in the money market. In a larger sample of banks also including smaller and less active banks, the rate dispersion would probably increase slightly.

In a study of transaction rates of banks located in the euro area and the UK, Hartmann et al. (2001) find that cross-border rate differentials were already very small soon after the introduction of the euro. However, examining the overnight rate together with daily reserve holdings across euro area countries, Angelini (2002) detects some minor differences between countries. Although generally very similar, he finds that the daily demand for reserves shows small differences in the degree of interest rate elasticity across countries.

In conclusion, the results support the view of a very high degree of integration in the unsecured overnight segment in the euro area. Although minor country-specific effects also can be detected, overnight deposits in different countries of the euro area are very close to being perfect substitutes.

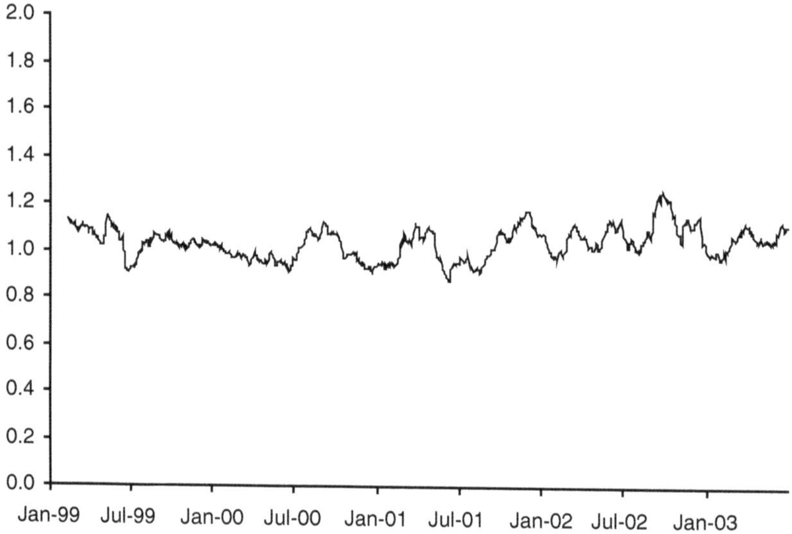

Figure 7.12 Ratio of average cross-country EONIA rate deviation to average within-country deviation (daily data, 30-day moving average)

Source: European Banking Federation and Baele et al. (2004). Work by Peter Galos in organizing the data is gratefully acknowledged.

Longer maturities of the unsecured market Turning to the unsecured inter-bank money market at longer maturities, Figure 7.13 shows interest rates at one-month and twelve-month maturity for approximately 50 individual banks participating in the

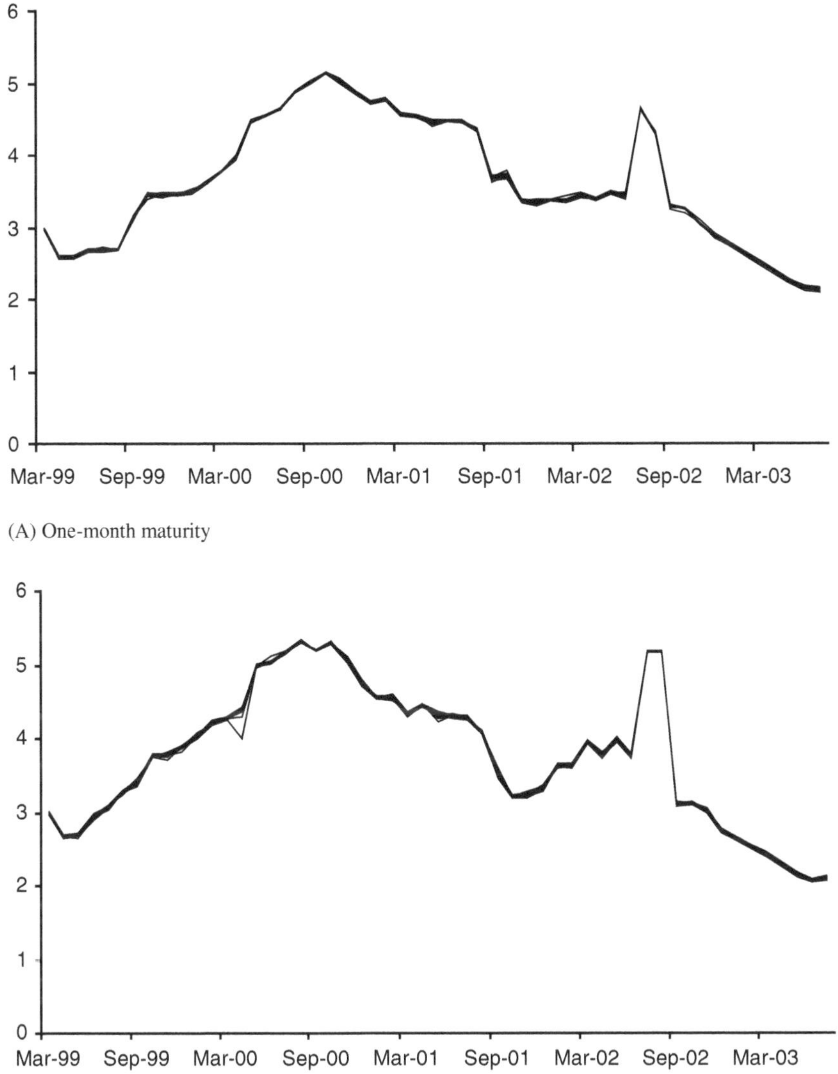

(A) One-month maturity

(B) Twelve-month maturity

Figure 7.13 Unsecured rates for close to 50 individual banks participating in the EURIBOR panel (end-of-month data, per cent)

Source: European Banking Federation.

EURIBOR panel. For both maturities the degree of dispersion between individual bank rates is very low and the individual bank series almost coincide in one single line. Furthermore, conducting a similar exercise as for the overnight rate above, Figure 7.14 shows the degree of cross-country dispersion vis-à-vis the degree of within-country variation with daily data. The ratio between cross-country variation and within-country variation has been very close to one since the introduction of the euro.

In addition, Adam et al. (2002) study the cross-country variation of three-month deposit rates over time and find that the standard deviation of cross-country rates already significantly declined in the period before the introduction of the euro. After the introduction, the variation of the three-month rates converged fully.

Overall, the evidence indicates a very high degree of integration in the unsecured euro area money market following the introduction of the euro and the common monetary policy framework. The unsecured segments quickly converged to a pan-euro area market with a single yield curve. The need to redistribute central bank liquidity among euro area countries enhanced the evolution of cross-border transactions in the unsecured money market. One reason for this development was the success of the euro area money market reference rates, the EONIA and the EURIBOR, and the efficient functioning of the wholesale payment system (TARGET). Moreover, cross-border transactions were simplified by the disappearance of costs associated with foreign currency settlements, and as opposed to repo transactions, unsecured trades involved no cost of collateral settlement. We now turn to the secured segment of the cash market.

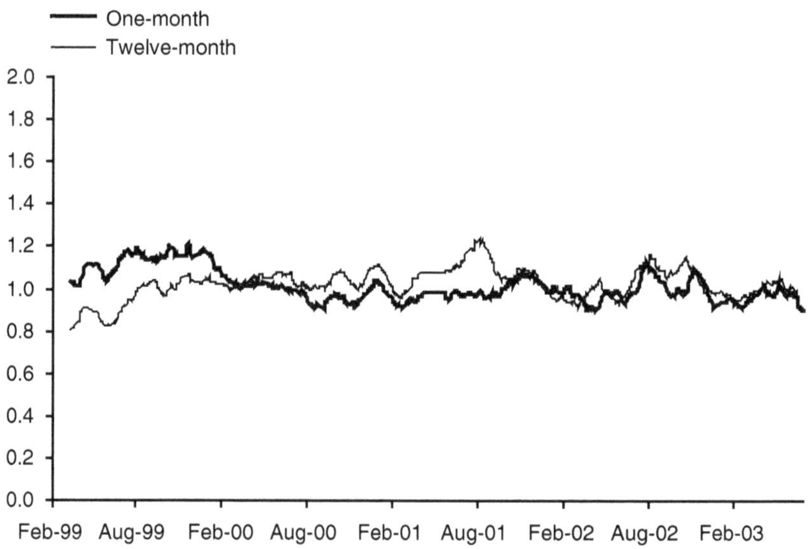

Figure 7.14 Ratio of average cross-country EURIBOR rate deviation to average within-country deviation (daily data, 30-day moving average)

Source: European Banking Federation and Baele et al. (2004).

The repo market A repo is a sale and repurchase agreement, which involves a sale of securities with an agreement to repurchase those securities at a specified price on a predetermined date in the future. Hence a repo transaction is basically a loan of cash secured by collateral. As opposed to the unsecured market, where the lender of cash is exposed to the credit risk of the borrower, in a repo transaction the lender faces a much lower risk. Conditions like the interest rate and the date of repurchase of the securities are agreed in advance.

Repos can be either 'cash-driven', in which case transactions are triggered by the borrowing or lending of cash with securities serving as collateral, or 'securities-driven', where transactions are triggered by the desire of borrowing or lending a specific security. In the cash-driven segment, the characteristics of the securities serving as collateral are of secondary importance and transactions are usually conducted against 'general collateral', consisting mainly of bonds and bills issued by euro area governments. The repo rate is normally slightly lower than the unsecured inter-bank rate. This reflects the lower risk for the cash lender. Seen from the other side of the trade, because the cash taker provides collateral, this institution can obtain cash at a better rate than in the unsecured market. The cash demand in the repo market originates *inter alia* from some institutions needing to finance the carrying of an asset portfolio temporarily in their balance sheet.

The securities-driven segment of the repo market is composed of specific securities that are in high demand. The motivation for the securities borrower (the cash provider) could be the need to cover short positions in the security, to cover a settlement failure or for delivery on a futures contract settlement. The securities provider (the cash taker) can, for example, either fund longer securities positions or reinvest the cash obtained in other markets with a higher yield.

As opposed to the unsecured inter-bank market, which is normally accessed only by banks, there is a wide spectrum of market participants involved in the repo market. Several market participants who cannot obtain unsecured inter-bank funding, either because they do not have access to the unsecured inter-bank market or because of poor credit standing, may raise cash against collateral on the repo market. It has thus been extended from regular money market participants, mainly bank treasurers, to other financial market participants like fund managers, insurance companies and corporations.

Ciampolini and Rohde (2000), surveying the repo activity of banks operating in Europe, report that after the introduction of the euro, cross-border repo transactions rose substantially in France, Germany, Benelux and Italy, while they declined somewhat in Spain. Domestic transactions were less affected, with, however, slight declines in activity in Benelux and France and a small increase in Germany, Italy and Spain. For all these countries, except Spain, the number of counterparties in cross-border transactions increased. Hence the introduction of the euro seems to have contributed to higher activity in the repo market, and as noted above, in 2002 the activity in the repo market surpassed that of the unsecured market. Interestingly, Ciampolini and Rohde (2000) also report that both domestic and, in particular, cross-border repo activity was boosted in the UK in 1999 following the introduction of the euro. As regards interest rates, they report some dispersion across euro area countries. For example, one- and three-month general collateral repos were traded at an interest rate 4–5 basis points higher than repos in Germany.

As the economic convergence and the introduction of the euro led to more homogenous euro-denominated collateral, the market needed a representative benchmark for secured transactions. To contribute to standardization in the repo market across the euro area, the representative benchmark EUREPO was introduced in March 2002, supplementing the existing reference rates for unsecured business, the EONIA and the EURIBOR. The index was created by the European Repo Council and the European Banking Federation. The EUREPO is the rate at which prime banks offer funds in euro to other prime banks against EUREPO general collateral, which mainly includes government bonds and bills denominated in euro or guaranteed by any of the euro area governments. The maturity ranges from tomorrow-next to twelve months. For a given maturity the EUREPO index is the average of the rates provided by EUREPO panel banks. This panel is not identical to the EONIA/EURIBOR panel.

The banks in the EUREPO panel adhere to a Code of Conduct, which ensures a transparent and efficient management of the panel. A Steering Committee oversees compliance with the Code of Conduct and monitors market developments. The committee periodically reviews the list of banks participating in the panel. The EUREPO market is highly standardized as all banks in the panel must provide quotes for all maturities to the screen service provider on a daily basis.

Taking a closer look at the repo rates at the one- and twelve-month maturities, Figure 7.15 shows the rates for all euro area countries, where the rate for each country is the average over its banks participating in the EUREPO panel using daily data. For both maturities the dispersion across countries is low. Figure 7.16 shows the degree of cross-country dispersion compared to the degree of within-country variation, also using daily data. This measure of integration has tended to deviate more from one than in the case of the EONIA and the EURIBOR rates. Hence the degree of integration in the repo market seems to be somewhat lower than in these other segments. In particular, for the longer twelve-month maturity, cross-country variation is larger than the within-country variation, indicated by the ratio being larger than one. Most of the trading in the repo market is concentrated at short maturities, albeit less than in the unsecured money market, and the liquidity is markedly lower at the twelve-month maturity.

It should be noted, however, that while the EUREPO segments are highly standardized, other parts of the repo market are less so and would be expected to be less integrated. The reasons are, among other things, related to country-specific differences in the type of securities serving as collateral. In particular, as government bonds frequently serve as collateral in repo transactions, different credit, liquidity and tax conditions of the different government bonds in euro area countries make them imperfect substitutes, contributing to a still somewhat fragmented repo market in the euro area. Furthermore, the infrastructure for cross-border payment and settlement, as mentioned in the previous section, is not fully integrated, involving costs and inefficiencies for repo market participants. Last but not least, differences regarding legal treatment (different Master Agreements) and the diversity of market practices are also important challenges for further integration of the repo market. This notwithstanding, the cross-border repo activity has exhibited an increasing trend in recent years, mainly due to an increasing use of the links among the Central Securities Depositories (ECB, 2002c; Giovannini Group, 2002).

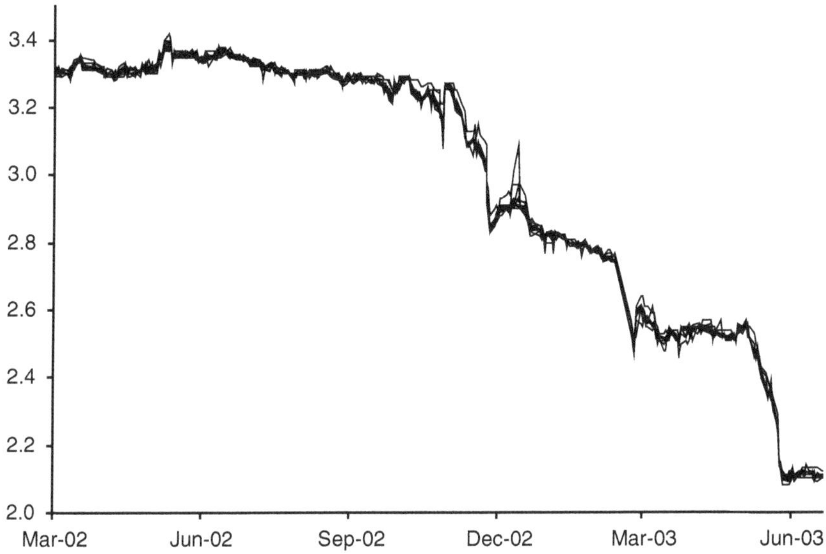

(A) One-month maturity

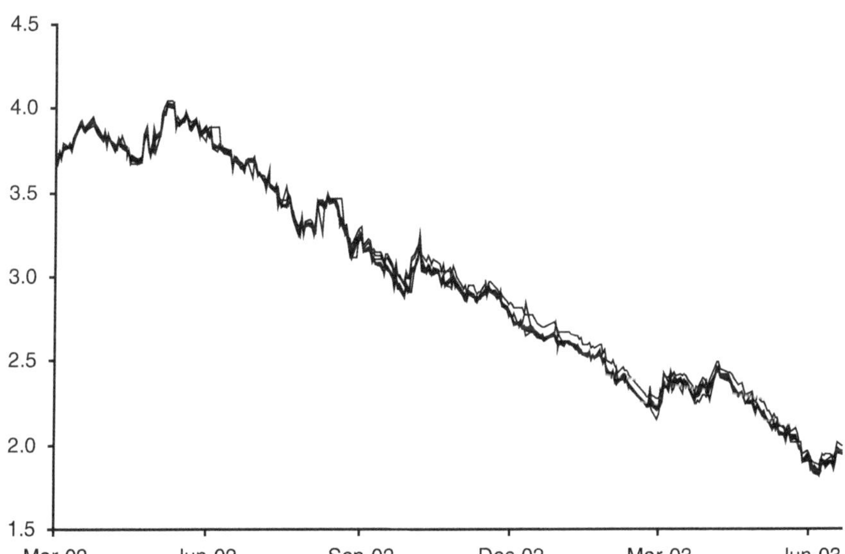

(B) Twelve-month maturity

Figure 7.15 Repo rates for individual euro area countries (daily data, per cent)

Note: Country average of EUREPO quotes by contributing banks.
Source: European Banking Federation and Baele et al. (2004).

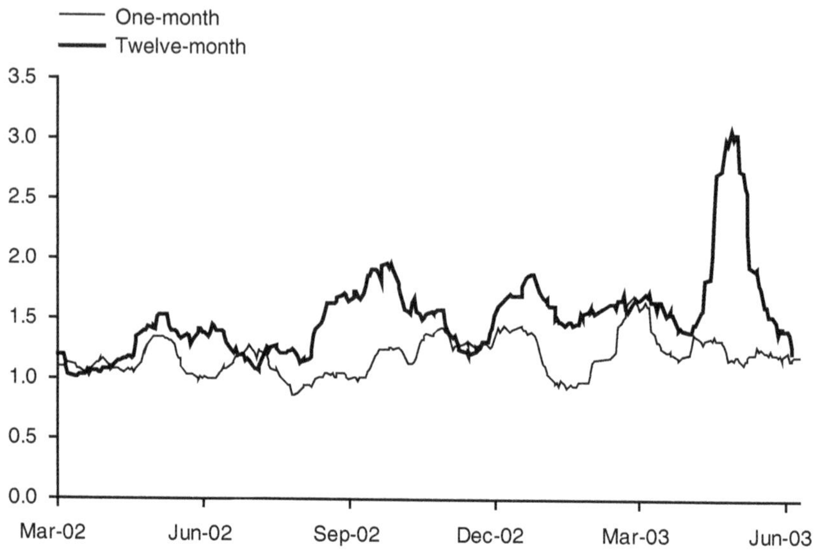

Figure 7.16 Ratio between average cross-country EUREPO rate deviations and average within-country deviations (15-day moving average, daily data)

Source: European Banking Federation and Baele et al. (2004).

Foreign exchange swaps Finally, we will briefly treat the last segment of the cash market, foreign exchange swaps, which is an agreement between two parties to exchange future payments in one currency for payments in another currency. These agreements are used to transform the currency denomination of assets or liabilities. After the introduction of the euro in 1999, in contrast to the traded volumes in the unsecured and repo markets, foreign currency swaps activity declined. This evolution was due to the disappearance of cross-currency trading among the euro legacy currencies (Santillan et al., 2000).

Foreign exchange swaps activity declined by around 20 per cent between 2000 and 2001, after which it remained broadly unchanged (ECB, 2003c). The lower activity since 2000 has mainly been due to a decrease in the segment with maturity up to one month, a segment still accounting for around 80 per cent of transactions in 2002. As noted above, the market for foreign exchange swaps is the smallest segment of the cash market with the share of total cash market activity declining from 23 per cent in 2000 to 17 per cent in 2001 and 2002. This development is linked to lower activity on the market for foreign exchange, a higher degree of market concentration, greater consolidation in the banking industry (leading to more in-house funding) and the existence of other, more flexible instruments for hedging and position taking on the interest rate market. Hence, the importance of foreign exchange swaps for managing interest rate positions appears to be gradually decreasing.

The Short-term Interest Rate Derivative Market

The market for short-term interest rate derivatives consists of (i) interest rate swaps, in which fixed interest rate payments are exchanged for floating interest rate payments, (ii) the market for futures, which is an agreement to buy or sell a specific quantity of a financial instrument at a pre-specified price on a stipulated date in the future and (iii) the options market, notably the options on futures contracts on the three-month EURIBOR.

The futures market The futures market is dominated by three-month EURIBOR futures linked to the three-month EURIBOR rate. This implies that the EURIBOR futures rates are mainly determined by market participants' expectations of the EURIBOR rates to prevail in the future. The contracts are mainly traded at the LIFFE exchange in London, and, albeit to a far lesser extent, at the German Eurex and the French Matif exchanges. The three-month EURIBOR futures market is highly standardized and has become very liquid and deep. Trading volumes, open interest, and the number of outstanding contracts at a given point in time, have increased substantially since 1999 (see Figure 7.17).

After the introduction of the euro, EURIBOR futures transactions rose rapidly and volumes traded in 2002 were three times greater than in 1999 (ECB, 2003c). However, the growth rate has slowed down in recent years with an annual rate of increase of 56 per cent in 2001 and 16 per cent in 2002. The deceleration in 2002 might be linked to market participants' expectations of unchanged official ECB rates during most of the year. EURIBOR futures are the most commonly traded short-term

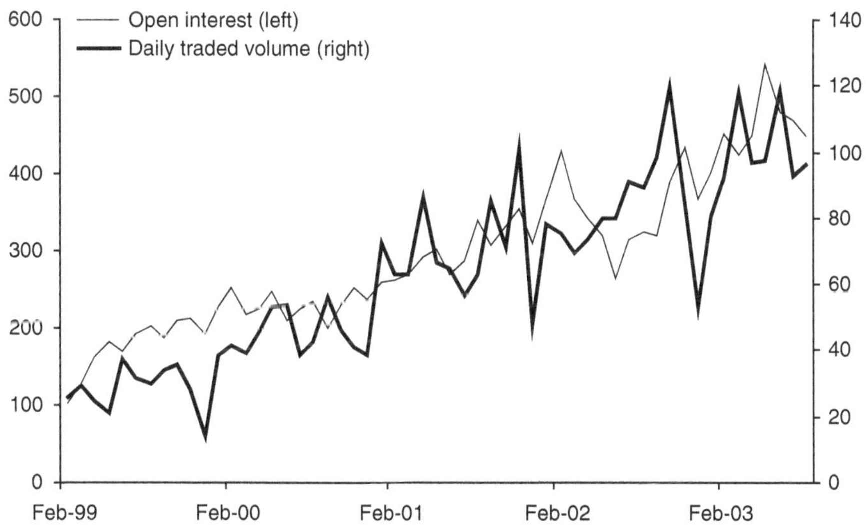

Figure 7.17 Volumes in EURIBOR futures since 1999 (thousands of contracts)

Source: Reuters and own calculations.

interest rate futures in Europe, with a share of 73 per cent of total short-term interest rate futures on LIFFE (while Sterling and Swiss Franc futures account for respectively 24 and 3 per cent).

Similar to the three-month EURIBOR futures, a forward rate agreement (FRA) is a forward contract where the parties agree that a certain interest rate will apply to a certain principal during a specified future time period. Hence as for the futures, FRAs also reflect market participants' expectations of future short-term interest rates. In contrast to the futures contracts, which are traded on an exchange and marked-to-market daily, FRAs are traded over-the-counter and the contracts are typically marked-to-market with exchange of residual value between the parties on the date of expiry. In 2002 FRA activity grew by 35 per cent compared to 2001, especially in the segment with maturity between six months and one year (ECB, 2003c). Around 45 per cent of total FRA trading takes place within the euro area and trading is highly concentrated. However, despite the significant increase in activity in 2002, FRAs still account for only a relatively small fraction of total over-the-counter derivative activity, which is by far dominated by EONIA interest rate swaps and foreign exchange swaps.

The options market An option on a EURIBOR futures contract gives one the right, without obligation, to enter into such a contract. While a call option gives the right to buy a futures contract at a pre-specified price, a put option gives the right to sell a futures contract at a specified price. The purpose of options on EURIBOR futures contracts is to hedge (or speculate) against movements in short-term interest rates, where the holder of a call option secures against lower interest rates and the holder of a put option secures against higher rates.

The price of the option depends, among other things, on the expected volatility of the underlying asset price, in this case, the price of the EURIBOR futures contract, that is, the future short-term interest rate. Implied interest rate volatility is an *ex ante* measure of the market's expected volatility of future short-term interest rates. Expected future short-term money market rates mainly depend on the expected future monetary policy rates and implied volatility therefore, to a large extent, indicates the degree of uncertainty the market attaches to the future path of the key monetary policy rates.

As for the futures, the EURIBOR options are also mainly traded on the LIFFE, where EURIBOR and Sterling options account for 82 and 18 per cent respectively of total short-term interest rate options trading. Although EURIBOR options transactions increased by 54 per cent in 2002, the growth slowed and was significantly lower than the large growth of 170 per cent in 2001 (ECB, 2003c).

The short-term interest rate swap market The euro area interest rate swap market has become increasingly liquid since the introduction of the euro. As early as the second quarter of 1999, average daily interest rate swap transactions rose by 72 per cent compared with 1998 (Santillan et al., 2000). The largest money market swap segment in the euro area is the EONIA swap market, in which the daily EONIA rate can be exchanged for fixed rates at horizons running from one week and up to a year (longer maturities exist but they are not frequently traded). The EONIA swap transactions have become very standardized in a very deep and liquid market. While individual country rates differed substantially in the 1990s, a single yield curve for the whole euro area emerged immediately after the introduction of the euro.

To illustratc, Figurc 7.18 shows thc EONIA swap ratcs at thc twclvc-month maturity for euro area countries (Greece adopted the euro in January 2001). Bid-ask spreads are generally very narrow at around one to two basis points. Banks mainly use the EONIA swaps for hedging short-term interest rate risks or to take speculative positions. The interest rate swap market is a pan-European market with cross-border transactions accounting for more than two-thirds of the overall transaction volumes. The participants are mainly large credit institutions located in the financial centres. The credit risk is relatively limited in an interest rate swap since the principal amounts are not exchanged. This has contributed to the relative success of the interest rate swap market.

Looking at the development over the past three years, while EONIA swap market activity rose by around 25 per cent in 2001 compared to a year earlier, activity declined slightly by 8 per cent in 2002 (ECB, 2003c). The same study also reports that banks participating in the survey perceive the interest rate swap market to be highly efficient and liquid. In 2002 around 75 per cent of all activity in the EONIA swap market took place within the euro area (domestic euro area or cross-border euro area).

Credit risk in the unsecured, secured and interest rate swap segments To compare the rates in different segments of the money market, Figure 7.19 shows the three-month EURIBOR and the three-month EONIA swap rate relative to the three-month REPO. Because of credit risk, the unsecured three-month EURIBOR is, on average, around ten basis points higher than the less risky three-month REPO, where contracts

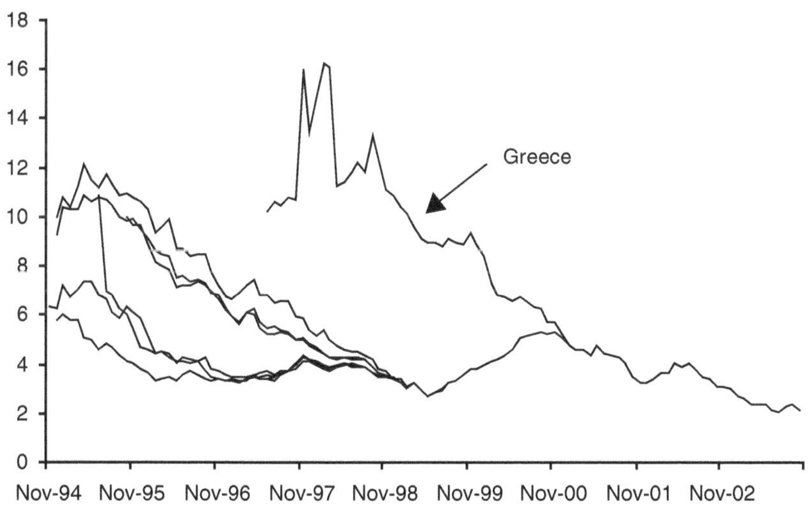

Figure 7.18 One-year interest rate swaps for euro area countries (per cent)

Source: Datastream.

Figure 7.19 Three-month EURIBOR and three-month EONIA swap rate relative to the three-month REPO rate (percentage points)

Source: Reuters.

are covered by collateral. Furthermore, the EURIBOR is, on average, also slightly higher than the three-month EONIA swap rate. The differential again reflects credit risk, since swap transactions, as opposed to unsecured inter-bank transactions, do not involve the exchange of the principal amount. Also, the underlying instrument in the EONIA swap is an overnight transaction. Credit concerns are limited at this maturity and this element is reflected in the price of the derivative.

The Market for Short-term Securities

The market for short-term securities consists of government securities (T-bills) and private securities, the latter being comprised mainly of commercial papers issued by non-financial corporations and certificates of deposits issued by banks. Though short-term securities activity remains far below volumes traded in other segments of the euro area money market, transactions have increased significantly in recent years. Looking at the primary market, Figure 7.20 shows the gross issuance of euro-denominated short-term securities by issuer sector. In 1999 gross issuance was boosted by the introduction of the single currency and the higher trend continued in the following years. Securities issued by monetary and financial institutions (MFIs) have in particular contributed to the higher growth.

Turning to the secondary market, the volume of transactions in short-term securities has increased substantially in the recent years. As illustrated in Figure 7.21, in 2003 total transactions were five times higher than in 2000. This has in particular been due to significantly higher trading activity in T-bills, which in 2003 accounted for around 50 per cent of total trading activity in short-term securities. Also trading

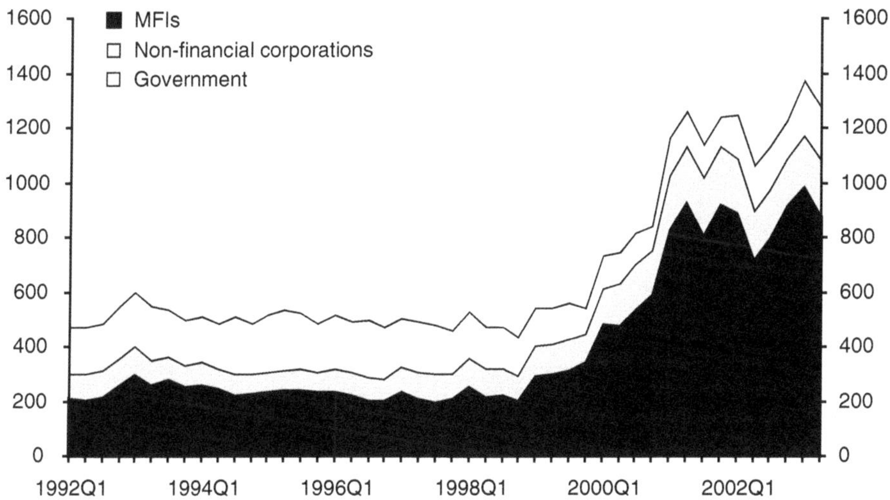

Figure 7.20 Gross issuance of euro-denominated short-term securities by issuer sector (quarterly data, € billions)

Source: ECB.

activity in securities issued by financial and non-financial entities rose by significantly over the period (accounting each for around a quarter of total trading in 2003).

With regard to the degree of efficiency and integration in the short-term securities market, a recent survey reveals that around 80 per cent of the market participants perceive the market as being sufficiently efficient (ECB, 2003c). A substantial share of around 55 per cent of total turnover takes place domestically in individual euro area countries, while around 20 per cent is executed across countries within the euro area. The high degree of concentration in activity within national markets indicates a somewhat lower degree of integration than in other segments of the euro area money market. Contributing to the national character of the short-term securities market are the heterogeneous legal treatment of the securities across euro area countries and the lack of integrated settlement systems. Furthermore, as opposed to other segments of the money market in which pricing is more directly linked to the single monetary policy (like the unsecured deposit market and the EONIA swap market), which ensured price convergence, the pricing of short-term securities depends on several other factors and heterogeneity has proven more persistent.

Integration in the secondary money market A very high degree of integration is particularly evident in the unsecured deposit market and the market for short-term interest rate derivatives, which have merged into practically fully integrated euro area-wide markets. The national money markets existing prior to the introduction of the euro have converged into one market and no barriers discriminate banks in their access to the market based on their location. The ECB Money Market Study 2002 reports that market participants were satisfied with the degree of efficiency and integration, in

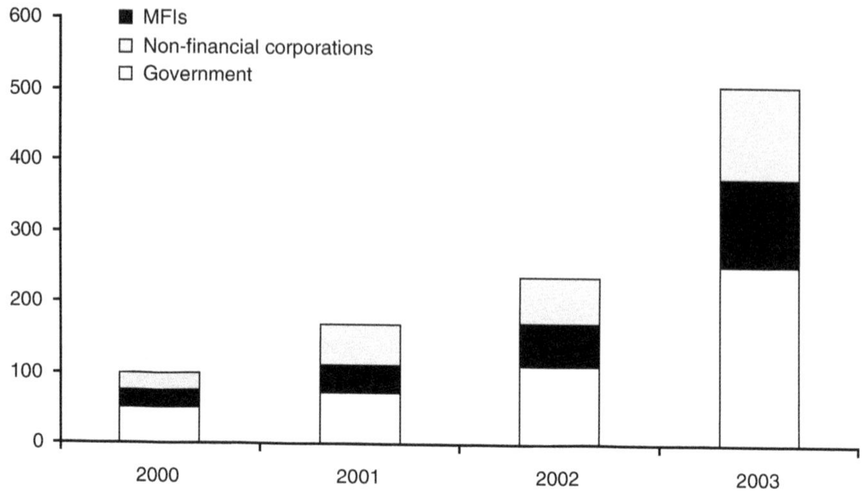

Figure 7.21 Outright transactions in euro-denominated short-term securities

Note: Indexed with the transactions volume in 2000 as base value 100.
Source: ECB (2003c).

particular in the unsecured deposit and derivative markets (ECB, 2003c). Although less integrated, the repo market has also become more integrated. Due to, *inter alia*, the links between Central Securities Depositories, cross-border repo activity has increased significantly in recent years. The issuance of short-term securities in the euro area was boosted by the introduction of the euro; however, this segment has remained more fragmented than the other segments of the secondary money market.

Conclusions

The introduction of the euro on 1 January 1999 transformed national money markets in the euro area countries into a single area-wide market. A common set of ECB monetary policy instruments and procedures, notably represented by a uniform monetary policy interest rate, provides identical conditions for transactions with the ECB for banks across the euro area. A salient characteristic of the operational framework for monetary policy is the reliance on a self-regulating market mechanism with only infrequent interventions of the central bank (a 'hands-off approach'). The open market operations of the ECB, forming the primary money market of the euro area, are implemented in a decentralized manner by the national central banks. The decentralized implementation of monetary policy, together with very broad counterparty eligibility criteria, has facilitated access to the primary market regardless of location and thus ensured equal treatment of banks. Some minor country-specific effects are found in the bidding data of the main and longer-term refinancing operations of the ECB, for example that the country of the bank can be a determinant for participation in the open market operations of the ECB. Overall, the prevailing evidence suggests that bidding in the open market operations of the ECB is competitive and efficient.

There are signs of an *implicit two-tiered structure* with a tier of large banks particularly active in cross-border arbitrage and primary market auctions and a tier of smaller local banks relying to some extent on wholesaling services. There were signs of the structure in the European money markets prior to the introduction of the euro and recent developments appear to reinforce it. Such a structure shares traits with the *explicit two-tiered structure* in other countries, for example in the US, UK and Japan.

The evidence from the secondary money market in the euro area suggests a high degree of integration and market efficiency. In the unsecured segment, reserves in different countries of the euro area are very close to being perfect substitutes and the evidence indicates that there are no barriers to cross-border arbitrage of interest rate disparities. The practically full integration which is particularly evident in the overnight market for reserves has been boosted by the area-wide wholesale payment system (TARGET). The co-existence of several forms of market organization (OTC, voice brokers, electronic markets and market makers) does not appear to have impeded integration in the unsecured and short-term interest rate derivative markets. Evidence suggests that the martingale property may not be perfectly met in practice in the euro area. However, this conclusion seems to be true to the money markets in other countries as well (for example in the US). The departure from the martingale appears economically minor in the euro area. This indicates that the operational framework of the ECB has provided a good underpinning for an efficient and integrated money market.

Integration in the repo segment has improved markedly in recent years. Cross-border activity has increased significantly as banks have made an extensive use of the links between Central Securities Depositories. However, there are still important impediments to further integration of the repo market (emphasized by the Giovannini Group, 1999 and 2002). The heterogeneity of collateral (for instance credit, liquidity and tax characteristics of government bonds) and legal treatment (for example different Master Agreements) are barriers which have proven difficult to change. In addition, the lack of integration in cross-border clearing and settlement systems imposes costs and inefficiencies on the repo and short-term securities segments of the money market. The market for short-term securities in the euro area is still fragmented with only around 20 per cent of transactions being cross-border trades.

Overall, the degree of integration in the euro money market is very high in most segments and progress is being made in the remaining areas. Initiatives are underway in several areas to improve the integration of the cross-border market infrastructure. For example, significant consolidation is foreseen in the further integration of euro area payment systems (TARGET2). Also, to reduce heterogeneity in the current collateral rules applied to the monetary policy operations, the ECB is seeking ways to gradually merge the two tiers of collateral into a single list.

References

Abildgren, K. (2002), 'Experience with the Eurosystem's Weekly Open Market Operations', *Monetary Review*, 4, Denmark's Nationalbank, pp. 29–50.

Adam, K., Japelli, T., Menichini, A., Padula, M. and Pagona, M. (2002), *Analyse, Compare, and Apply Alternative Indicators and Monitoring Methodologies to Measure the Evolution of Capital Market Integration in the European Union*, prepared by the Centre for Studies in Economics and Finance for the European Commission, Brussels, January.

Allen, L., Peristiani, S. and Saunders, A. (1989), 'Bank Size, Collateral, and Net Purchase Behavior in the Federal Funds Market: Empirical Evidence', *Journal of Business*, 62 (**4**) pp. 501–15.

Angelini, P. (2002), 'Liquidity and Announcement Effects in the Euro Area', *Banca d'Italia Temi di Discussione*, No. 451.

Baele, L., Ferrando, A., Hördahl, P., Krylova, E. and Monnet, C. (2004), *Measuring Financial Integration in the Euro Area*, ECB Occasional Paper Series, No. 14.

Balduzzi, P., Bertola, G., Foresi, S. and Klapper, L. (1998), 'Interest Rate Targeting and the Dynamics of Short-Term Rates', *Journal of Money, Credit, and Banking*, 30, pp. 26–50.

Bartolini, L. and Prati, A. (2003), 'The Execution of Monetary Policy: A Tale of Two Central Banks', *Economic Policy,* October, pp. 435–67.

Bindseil, U., Camba-Mendez, G, Hirsch, A. and Weller, B. (2003), 'Excess Reserves and the ECB's Implementation of Monetary Policy', paper presented at the conference 'Monetary Policy and the Money Market', Federal Reserve Bank of New York, June.

Bindseil, U. and Seitz, F. (2001), *The Supply and Demand for Eurosystem Deposits – the First 18 Months*, ECB Working Paper Series, No. 44.

Breitung, J. and Nautz, D. (2001), 'The Empirical performance of the ECB's Repo Auctions: Evidence from Aggregated and Individual Bidding Data', *Journal of International Money and Finance*, 20, pp. 839–56.

Cassola, N. and Morana, C. (2003), *Volatility of Interest Rates in the Euro Area: Evidence from High Frequency Data*, ECB Working Paper Series, No. 235.

Ciampolini, M. and Rohde, B. (2000), 'Money Market Integration: A Market Perspective', paper presented at the conference 'The Operational Framework of the Eurosystem and Financial Markets', European Central Bank, Frankfurt am Main, May.

De Bandt, O. and Davis, E. P. (1999), *A Cross-Country Comparison of Market Structures in European Banking*, ECB Working Paper Series, No. 7.

Ehrmann, M., Gambacorta, L., Martinez-Pages, J., Sevestre, P. and Worms, A. (2001), 'Financial Systems and the Role of Banks in Monetary Policy Transmission in the Euro Area', *Banca d'Italia Temi di Discussione*, No. 432.

Ejerskov, S., Martin Moss, C. and Stracca, L. (2003), *How Does the ECB Allot Liquidity in its Main Refinancing Operations? A Look at the Empirical Evidence*, ECB Working Paper Series, No. 244.

European Central Bank (2001), 'Bidding Behaviour of Counterparties in the Eurosystem's Regular Open Market Operations', *Monthly Bulletin*, October, pp. 51–63.

European Central Bank (2002a), 'The Liquidity Management of the ECB', *Monthly Bulletin*, May, pp. 41–53.

European Central Bank (2002b), 'Main Features of the Repo Market in the Euro Area', *Monthly Bulletin*, October, pp. 55–68.

European Central Bank (2002c), *The Euro Money Market Study 2001 (MOC)*, Frankfurt am Main.

European Central Bank (2002d), 'Public Consultation – TARGET2: Principles and Structure', Press Release, 16 December.

European Central Bank (2002e), *Developments in Banks' Liquidity Profile and Management*, Frankfurt am Main.

European Central Bank (2003a), 'Public Consultation: Measures to Improve the Collateral Framework of the Eurosystem', Press Release, 11 June.

European Central Bank (2003b), 'Changes to the Eurosystem's Operational Framework for Monetary Policy', *Monthly Bulletin*, August, pp. 41–54.

European Central Bank (2003c), *Money Market Study 2002*, Frankfurt am Main.

European Central Bank (2004a), *The Monetary Policy of the ECB*, Frankfurt am Main.

European Central Bank (2004b), *The Implementation of Monetary Policy in the Euro Area: General Documentation on Eurosystem Monetary Policy Instruments and Procedures*, Frankfurt am Main.

European Central Bank (2004c), *Money Market Study 2003*, Frankfurt am Main.

Ewerhart, C., Cassola, N., Ejerskov, S. and Valla, N. (2003), *Optimal Allotment Policy in the Eurosystem's Main Refinancing Operations*, ECB Working Paper Series, No. 295.

Freixas, X. and Holthausen, C. (2001), *Inter-bank Market Integration under Asymmetric Information*, ECB Working Paper Series, No. 74.

Galati, G. and Tsatsaronis, K. (2001), *The Impact of the Euro on Europe's Financial Markets*, BIS Working Paper Series, No. 100.

Gaspar, V., Hartmann, P. and Sleijpen, O. (eds) (2003), 'The Transformation of the European Financial System', proceedings of the 2nd ECB Central Banking Conference, European Central Bank, Frankfurt am Main.

Gaspar, V., Perez-Quiros, G. and Sicilia, J. (2001), *The ECB Monetary Policy Strategy and the Money Market*, ECB Working Paper Series, No. 69.

Giovannini Group (1999), 'The EU Repo Markets: Opportunities for Change', *European Commission, Euro Papers*, No. 35.

Giovannini Group (2002), 'Cross-Border Clearing and Settlement Arrangements in the European Union', *European Commission Economic Papers Series*, No. 163.

Hamilton, J.D. (1996), 'The Daily Market for Federal Funds', *Journal of Political Economy*, 104 (1), pp. 26–56.

Hamilton, J.D. (1997), 'Measuring the Liquidity Effect', *American Economic Review*, 87, pp. 80–97.

Hartmann, P., Maddaloni, A. and Manganelli, S. (2003), 'The Euro-Area Financial System: Structure, Integration, and Policy Initiatives', *Oxford Review of Economic Policy*, 19 (1), pp. 180–213.

Hartmann, P., Manna, M. and Manzanares, A. (2001), 'The Microstructure of the Euro Money Market', *Journal of International Money and Finance*, 20, pp. 895–948.

Issing, O., Gaspar, V., Angeloni, I. and Tristani, O. (2001), *Monetary Policy in the Euro Area: Strategy and Decision-Making at the European Central Bank*, Cambridge University Press, Cambridge.

Linzert, T., Nautz, D. and Bindseil, U. (2003), 'The Longer Term Repo Auctions of the European Central Bank', paper presented at the CFS Workshop 'Implementing Monetary Policy', 25 November 2003, Frankfurt am Main.

Meulendyke, A.-M. (1998), *U.S. Monetary Policy and Financial Markets*, Federal Reserve Bank of New York.

Nyborg, K.G., Bindseil, U. and Strebulaev, I.A. (2002), *Bidding and Performance in Repo Auctions: Evidence from ECB Open Market Operations*, ECB Working Paper Series, No. 157.

Pérez Quirós, G. and Mendizábal, H.R. (2001), *The Daily Market for Funds in Europe: Has Something Changed with the EMU?*, ECB Working Paper Series, No. 67.

Prati, A., Bartolini, L. and Bertola, G. (2002), 'The Overnight Inter-bank Market: Evidence From the G–7 and the Euro Zone', *Journal of Banking and Finance*, 27, pp. 2045–83.

Santillan, J., Bayle, M. and Thygesen, C. (2000), *The Impact of the Euro on Money and Bond Markets*, ECB Occasional Paper Series, No. 1.

Scalia, A. and Ordine, M. (2003), 'Banks' Participation in the Eurosystem Auctions and Money Market Integration', *EFA Annual Conference Paper*, No. 783.

Thornton, D.L. (2001a), 'Identifying the Liquidity Effect at the Daily Frequency', *Federal Reserve Bank of St. Louis*, July/August, pp. 59–78.

Thornton, D.L. (2001b), 'The Federal Reserve's Operating Procedure, Non-borrowed Reserves, Borrowed Reserves and the Liquidity Effect', *Journal of Banking and Finance*, 25, pp. 1717–39.
Välimäki, T. (2002), 'Variable Rate Liquidity Tenders', *Bank of Finland Discussion Papers*, No. 24.
Würtz, F.R. (2003), *A Comprehensive Model on the Euro Overnight Rate*, ECB Working Paper Series, No. 207.

Chapter 8

Bond and Equity Market Integration

Lieven Baele and Annalisa Ferrando

Introduction

This chapter examines the integration process of the different euro area bond and equity markets. Both markets have witnessed substantial growth over the last decade, not only in the total amounts outstanding, but also in the number of new issues and listings. In addition, evidence suggests that bonds and stocks are now more homogeneously priced than before. Moreover, after the introduction of the euro, investors gradually changed the composition of their portfolios as to include a higher percentage of non-domestic assets, hereby reducing the so-called home bias. On the other hand, integration has not been as quick and far-reaching across all market segments and countries, as some barriers (such as differences in the legal system, tax treatment, clearing and settlement systems) continue to exist.

The Bond Market

The Euro Area Bond Market

The government bond markets of the euro area are the main source of financing for central and local governments within the area. In addition, they play an important role in the functioning of the financial system. Not only do government bonds serve as the benchmark risk-free assets, they are also frequently used as collateral in various financial transactions.

Over the last years, euro area government bond markets have changed quite dramatically. With the introduction of the euro and the convergence in inflation expectations resulting from a common monetary policy, investors have started to focus more on credit and liquidity risk. At the same time, bond portfolios have become increasingly internationally diversified. In this more competitive environment, governments have put great effort in making their outstanding debt and new issues more attractive to international bond investors. To this end, they have engaged in a number of supply-side innovations, some of which were already described in Chapter 2. Overall, the evidence seems to suggest that euro government bond markets now exhibit a relatively high degree of integration.

This section is structured as follows. The next section provides an overview of recent development in the government bond market in the euro area. Second, we discuss the degrees of integration achieved in the market distinguishing among different maturity segments.

Recent Developments in the Government Bond Market

For descriptive purposes, we summarize the major changes that have taken place in the market, distinguishing between those that have been mainly supply-driven and those that have been demand-driven.[1] The section also includes a brief description of recent developments in the financial infrastructure of bond markets.

Supply-driven changes The literature distinguishes between two major forces behind recent changes in government debt financing. On the one hand, the fiscal consolidation and the constraints imposed by the Stability and Growth Pact have led governments to limit their debt exposures. On the other hand, with the introduction of the euro, government debt managers have been increasingly competing to access a common investor base. Numerous changes in the issuance of sovereign bonds, as regards issuance techniques and strategies, can be traced to this new competitive environment (Santillan et al., 2000).

First, competition has led to increasing liquidity of government securities, and larger volumes of outstanding issues. In this respect, issue sizes have become bigger and sovereign issuers, in particular small countries, have started to focus increasingly on creating benchmark issues. In addition, some governments have undertaken buyback programmes and carried out bond exchanges. Following a trend that started prior to the introduction of the euro, illiquid and/or short-dated instruments were targeted by those programmes.[2] In a similar vein, governments have also started to use trading systems for the secondary market in order to enhance efficiency and increase liquidity of their bonds.

Second, debt managers have also made issuance activity more regular and predictable with the introduction of pre-announced auction calendars, which has improved market transparency. They have also made greater use of primary dealers in order to secure a smooth and diversified placement of debts. At the same time, some of the small issuers (Finland and Portugal, for instance) have resorted to syndication to make the investor base broader.

Third, governments have tried to focus their efforts on 'niches' targeting particular investor needs. For instance, Spain and France have introduced constant-maturity bonds while France (followed by Greece) has taken the lead in the issuance of index-linked bonds.[3]

1 See Santillan et al. (2000) and ECB (2001) for a more detailed discussion of government bond market developments following the introduction of the euro.

2 The most prominent examples are Ireland, which in May 1999 completely restructured its outstanding debt into a few liquid benchmark issues, and Spain and the Netherlands which also introduced programmes to exchange old illiquid bonds for new benchmark bonds.

3 Insurance corporations and pension funds are among the biggest customers of this new instrument. They acquired around 18 per cent of the total supply of French index-linked bonds on the occasion of the first issuance in October 2001.

Fourth, the introduction of the euro has led to an expansion in the interest rate swap and derivatives market, which has given debt managers more flexibility to actively manage their liabilities without influencing issuance volumes in the bond market.

Notwithstanding the efforts to harmonize market practices, the decentralized management of the public debt market is one reason for the continued fragmentation of the market and the absence of a unique government bond yield curve. Indeed, the launch of the euro also triggered a search for a euro-denominated benchmark to replace benchmarks in the legacy currencies. As discussed in Chapter 4, market participants seem to have adopted the euro interest rate swap curve as such a reference, due to the homogeneity of swaps across countries, as well as the high degree of liquidity in this market.

Demand-driven changes The elimination of intra-euro area exchange rate risk as well as the efforts of debtors to make their issues more liquid induced investors to start taking a euro area-wide perspective rather than a national one when deciding their portfolio allocations. This is reflected in the considerable rise in the proportion of non-domestic bonds in the portfolios of many (institutional) investors. This may in part be explained by the introduction of the euro, which directly eliminated the currency matching rule, at least within the euro area. The latter restricted the foreign currency holdings of certain categories of institutional investors. Evidence suggests that institutional investors in smaller euro area countries diversified their portfolios quicker than investors in bigger countries, partly as a result of their relatively smaller choice of domestic assets.

Developments in financial infrastructure Trading in bond markets has historically taken place over the counter (OTC), where it was typically concentrated among a relatively small group of counterparts. Technological advances as well as the introduction of a broader euro-denominated market have reduced the advantages of this type of trading. At the same time, intensified competition among debt managers, intermediaries and investors has led to increased demand for efficiency, which had become feasible through technological innovation. As a result, several structured trading platforms have emerged in the euro area, which in turn seem to have had a positive impact on market integration.[4] The fact that traders have gained access to a common marketplace in which counterparts can be found rapidly has had a beneficial impact on liquidity, in particular in some of the smaller countries. Indeed, many investors, who earlier might not have found smaller government debt markets attractive enough to incur the costs of entering them, now invest in these markets through common, cross-border platforms.

4 The most successful example of these platforms is MTS (for the national markets in Italy, the Netherlands, France, Belgium and Portugal) and EuroMTS, based in London, for trading in benchmark government bonds of several euro area countries (Italy, Germany, Spain, Austria, the Netherlands, France, Belgium, Portugal and Finland). Other developments include Senaf in Spain and Eurex Bonds in Germany.

How Integrated is the Government Bond Market in the Euro Area?

The strongest measures of financial integration are those based on the law-of-one-price, which states that if assets in different regions have identical risks and returns, then they are priced identically. Insofar as government bonds are sufficiently homogeneous across the various euro area markets, one can directly test the law-of-one-price by comparing the yields on local government bonds across countries. If we assume that the degree of systematic risk is identical across countries, then risk premia should converge or, at the limit, be equal under perfect integration, hence yields on government bonds with the same maturity should converge or be identical as well. Of course, systematic risk may differ across countries, for example due to differences in credit risk or liquidity. In fact, the 'no bail-out' clause of the Treaty, which stipulates that neither the Community nor any Member State is liable for or can assume the debts incurred by any other Member State, shows that governments who accumulate excessive debt cannot eventually be bailed out. Hence, if the market perceives that a country conducts unsound fiscal policies, this will tend to lead to a higher risk premium for government debt of that country. In the following, however, we assume that such differences in risk are of a relatively small magnitude for the countries of the euro area,[5] and proceed to investigate the degree of integration by comparing yields directly. As a robustness check, however, we also compare – where possible – yields from countries with the same credit rating.

Ideally, to measure the degree of integration of a particular government bond market, one would calculate the difference between the local yield and the yield that would prevail in perfectly integrated markets. As the latter is not directly available, most studies use the yield on a benchmark government bond as a second-best alternative. For instance, to analyse the integration of the 10-year maturity segment, previous studies (such as Adam et al., 2002, Adjaouté and Danthine 2003, and, recently, Baele et al., 2004) have used German government bond yields (for bonds with identical maturity).

The reason for doing so is that previous research suggests that the 10-year German government bond market is very well integrated with world capital markets (see for example Barr and Priestley 2002). International investors are especially attracted by the high liquidity, as well as by the very well developed derivatives market linked to this market segment. As a result, the yield on German government bonds should be reasonably close to the one that would prevail in fully integrated markets. For shorter maturities, the French 2- and 5-year government bond yields are instead used as benchmark bonds.[6]

Figures 8.1, 8.2 and 8.3 plot the spread between yields in the various euro area government bond markets and in the corresponding benchmark country from January 1993 to April 2003.

---

5 A recent paper (Codogno et al., 2003) provides evidence that liquidity factors play a small role to explain movements in yield differentials between euro area government bonds while international risk factors are more important. Default risk explains a substantial part of changes in yields spreads in specific countries.

6 This follows, in part, the results of Dunne et al. (2002) which suggest that French and German bonds should be chosen as benchmarks for medium and long-term maturities.

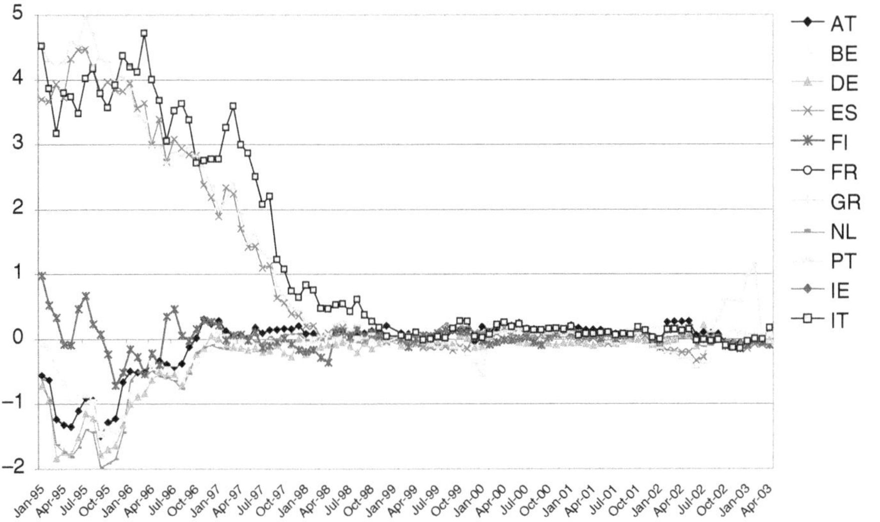

Figure 8.1 Yield spread for 2-year government bonds relative to France (percentage annual terms)

Source: ECB.

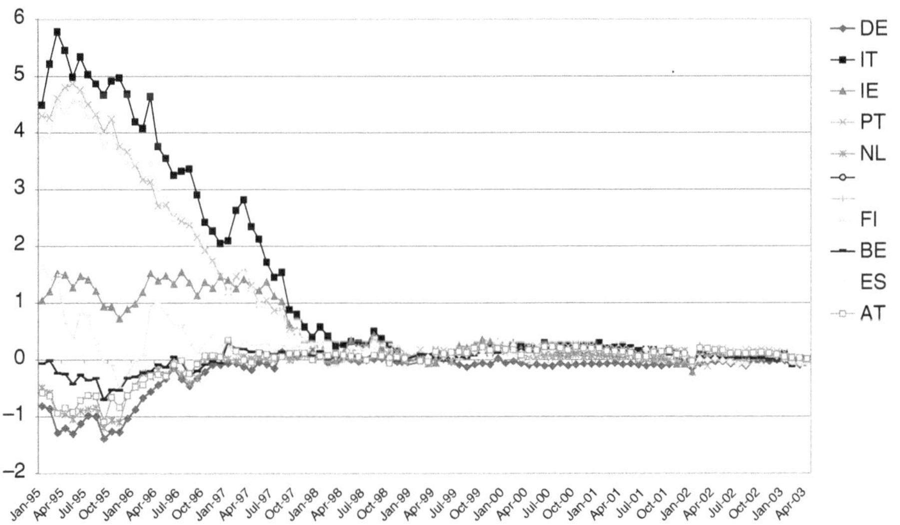

Figure 8.2 Yield spread for 5-year government bonds relative to France (percentage annual terms)

Source: ECB.

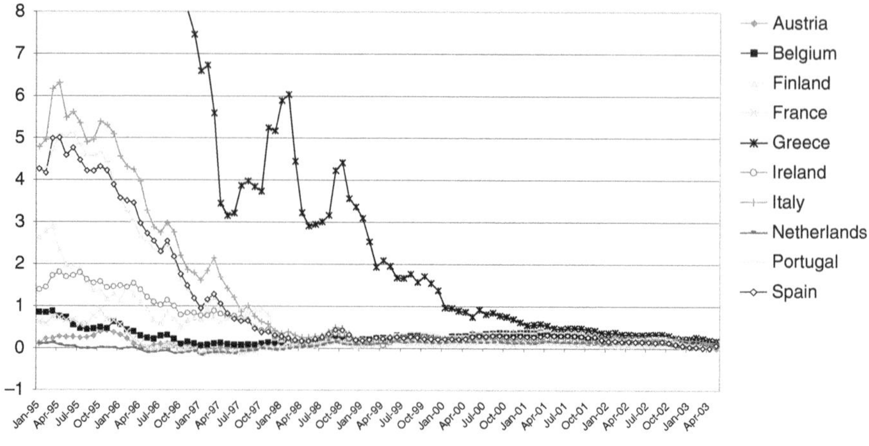

Figure 8.3 Yield spread for 10-year government bonds relative to Germany (percentage annual terms)

Source: ECB.

Except for Greece, government bond yield spreads have become very small since the beginning of 1998. The considerable convergence in government bond yields is to a large extent explained by a convergence in underlying fundamentals. First, exchange rate stability in the run-up to the single currency, and the eventual introduction of the euro, first decreased and then eliminated any possibility for exchange rate fluctuations among individual currencies. This removed one major discrepancy between yields on bonds issued by different countries in the euro area, by eliminating exchange rate risk premia. Second, restrictions on fiscal policies as outlined in the Stability and Growth Pact helped to keep perceived levels of credit risk relatively small, at least in the first years of its application. Last but not least, further economic convergence, as well as a unified monetary policy, has lead to a substantial convergence of inflation expectations across the euro area. Adjaouté and Danthine (2003) relate the strong convergence of government yields mainly to this convergence of fundamentals, but interpret the remaining yield differences as evidence against government bond markets being fully integrated.

In addition to yield spreads, it is useful also to analyse the cross-sectional standard deviation (dispersion) of yields. While this measure does not allow distinguishing between countries, it can serve as a composite measure for the degree of integration in the aggregate euro area government bond market. In line with the strong convergence in yields, Adam et al. (2002) find that dispersions of 10-year government bond yields have fallen substantially. Using this measure, Adjaouté and Danthine (2003) reported an average cross-sectional dispersion of 2.28 in the pre-euro period, compared to 0.16 since the introduction of the euro; a decrease of more than 90 per cent. These authors also show that in all countries the volatility of government bond yields has decreased substantially after the introduction of the euro, indicating that euro area bond markets now respond to a lesser extent to idiosyncratic local shocks.

Baele et al. (2004) report instead the cross-sectional dispersion in the spread relative to Germany. Their aim is to partly eliminate potential level effects, i.e. the empirical regularity that interest rate volatility tends to be positively related with the level of interest rates.

Following their approach, Figure 8.4 plots the cross-sectional dispersion in yield spreads for the 2-year, 5-year, and 10-year maturities. Greece is not taken into consideration in the calculation of this measure, because the convergence of the Greek government bond yields occurred mainly when Greece joined the monetary union in January 2001.

First we focus on the 10-year segment. Dispersions in monthly yields have fallen from an average of 2.1 in 1995 to 0.06 in 2002, or by more than 97 per cent. As was the case for spreads, dispersions decreased substantially as of 1998, but have stayed at roughly the same levels since then.

As for the other segment of the government bond market, overall the cross-sectional dispersion for the 2- and 5-year maturities closely follows the pattern observed for the 10-year maturity bonds. It is interesting to notice however that before 1998, the dispersion in 10-year government bond yield spreads was systematically lower compared to the other segments. While the degree of dispersion is comparably low for all maturities after the introduction of the single currency, no further decrease is observed after 1999.

The results indicate that the government bond market in the euro area has achieved a very high degree of integration. However, while the level of convergence in yields is impressive, yields of government bonds with similar, or in some cases identical,

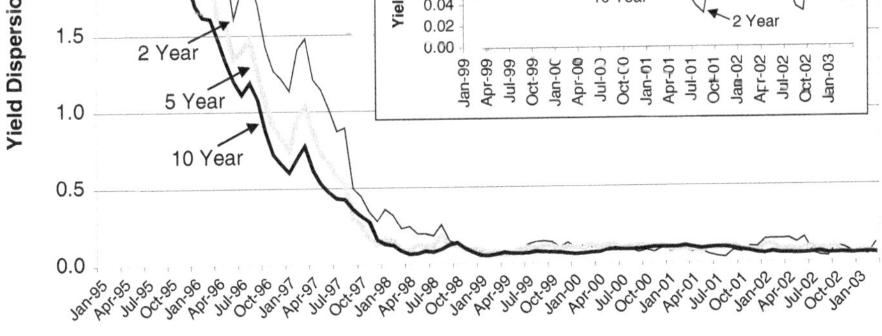

Figure 8.4 Dispersion in government bond yield spreads for 2, 5 and 10-year maturity

Source: ECB.

credit risk and maturity have not yet entirely converged. For instance, in the case of the 10-year government bond market, even though Austria, France, and the Netherlands all share the AAA credit rating with Germany, in 2002 their governments had to pay on average 16.8, 8.4, and 11.1 basis points more than Germany. Furthermore, remaining spreads have not converged any further since 1999. Differences in liquidity as well as in the availability of developed derivatives markets tied to the various individual bond markets may partly account for these spreads. Insofar as bond yields in different countries also reflect differences in perceived credit risks, this could explain why local factors continue to play a role in the pricing of government bonds. This is more so in the case of the 2- and 5-year maturity segments than of the market for 10-year government bonds.

The Euro Area Corporate Bond Market

The European corporate bond market is relatively young, certainly compared to the government bond market. Its development over the last years has, however, been spectacular. Before 1998, the market was dominated by debt issued by highly-rated (financial) corporations, whereas thereafter also industrial corporations have increasingly found their way to the corporate bond market. This is reflected in the dramatic growth in the lower-rated A and BBB market segments since then. Despite the impressive growth rates recorded over the last years, the euro area corporate bond market continues to be much smaller than in the US and Japan, both in terms of absolute value and relative to the size of the economy (see Chapter 2 for an international comparison).

This section is structured as follows. First, we discuss the main developments in the euro area corporate bond markets. We do so by looking respectively at the supply and demand side of this market. Second, we discuss the degree of integration in the market.

Recent Market Developments

A striking development in the euro area financial markets in the last years has been the rapid growth of the corporate debt securities markets. There are a number of reasons for the increased issuance of corporate debt, especially by industrial organizations. First, the introduction of the euro removed the currency risk component in corporate bonds. This significantly increased the pool of funds corporations have access to in order to finance their projects without currency risk. Second, coinciding with the introduction of the single currency, Europe was going through a period of considerable corporate restructuring. Carnegie-Brown and King (2003), for instance, show that the strong increase of corporate debt issuance in the euro area went hand in hand with increased M&A activity. This effect was strengthened by the need of telecommunication companies to finance UMTS licences as well as by some large Initial Public Offerings (IPOs). Third, more competition in the European business sector led corporate managers to focus more on their financial structure and optimal financing leverage. This may partly explain why large corporations – often with a better credit rating than their bank – began exploring alternative ways of financing, such as through the corporate bond market.

Figure 8.5 shows that the average annual rate of growth of the amount outstanding of euro-denominated debt securities issued by non-financial corporations has largely

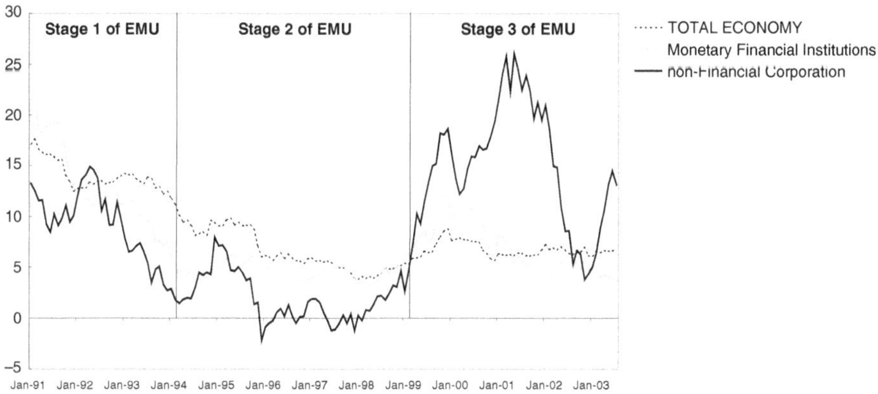

Figure 8.5 Annual growth rate of euro-denominated debt securities issued by euro area residents (annual percentage changes)

Source: ECB.

outpaced that of the total economy since the start of the Stage Three of Economic and Monetary Union (EMU). The amount outstanding of euro-denominated debt securities issued by non-financial corporations grew at an average annual rate of 14 per cent since January 1999, which is significantly higher than the average annual growth rate of 2 per cent during Stage Two of EMU.

Some of the reasons for the strong growth in corporate debt issuance outlined above, such as need to finance M&A, UMTS licences or IPOs, are of a temporary nature. Figure 8.6 shows, however, that while the net issuance of corporate debt by monetary and financial institutions (MFI) soared after 2000, it has remained at sustained levels for non-MFIs, which comprise non-financial corporations and non-monetary financial corporations.[7] This suggests that the strong growth in the euro corporate bond market is not only a temporary phenomenon.

Finally, it is worth noting that the euro area corporate bond market is, despite its substantial growth, still considerable smaller compared to the US and Japan. As already shown in Chapter 2, at the end of 2002 the euro area corporate debt securities represented less than 7 per cent of GDP, while they accounted for 23 per cent in the US and for 18 per cent in Japan.

To illustrate the structural changes that have shaped the euro area corporate bond market over the last few years, we report some statistics and results, recently proposed by Baele et al. (2004). They based their analysis on the bonds considered for the Merrill Lynch EMU corporate bond index over the last five years.[8]

7 See Chapter 2, Box 2.1 for a detailed analysis of the recent developments in the activity of non-monetary financial sector, in particular of special finance vehicles.

8 These are 2,215 individual bonds over the period April 1998–May 2003. While this index does not cover the entire euro area corporate bond market, it constitutes a very good approximation for it. For a more detailed description of the dataset see Baele et al. (2003).

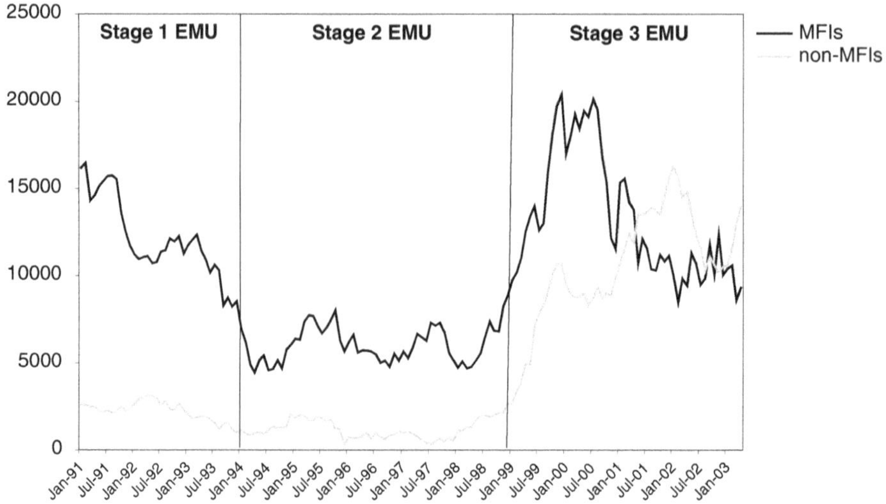

Figure 8.6 Net issuance of corporate bonds in the euro area by issuers (12-month moving average)

Source: ECB.

Figure 8.7 shows at each point in time the total outstanding value of all corporate bonds in the sample, per rating category. The total outstanding value has increased from about €180 billion at the beginning of 1998 to about €680 billion in April 2003, i.e. an increase of about 280 per cent. Looking at the separate rating categories, the substantial increase in the outstanding value of lower-rated bonds is noteworthy. The value of the A-rated segment increased from €30 billion in 1998 to €220 billion in 2003, or by more than 600 per cent. While the BBB-rated segment was almost non-existent in 1998 (about €3 billion), its total outstanding value in 2003 amounted to more than €182 billion. As a percentage of total outstanding value, the BBB segment increased from less than 2 per cent in 1998 to about 27 per cent in 2003.

The increase in the volume of lower-rated bonds is to a large extent explained by the increased participation of non-financial corporations. Baele et al. (2004) show that in 1998 financials constituted more than 85 per cent of the total value of outstanding corporate bonds, compared to 7 per cent and 6 per cent respectively for industrials and utilities. By 2003, however, the picture had changed markedly. While the share of utilities has remained more or less constant, the share of outstanding debt issued by industrials has increased substantially to about 38 per cent. This increase has come at the expense of the share of financials, which has decreased to 54 per cent.

The increasing importance of lower-rated bonds, typically issued by industrials, is not only reflected in a dramatic increase in their outstanding value, but also in the strong improvement in their overall liquidity. Based on the same sample, Van Landschoot (2003) found, for instance, that until the end of 1999 less than 30 per cent of BBB rated bonds were traded at least once a week, compared to about 90 per cent for higher rated bonds. The liquidity situation for BBB-rated bonds improved

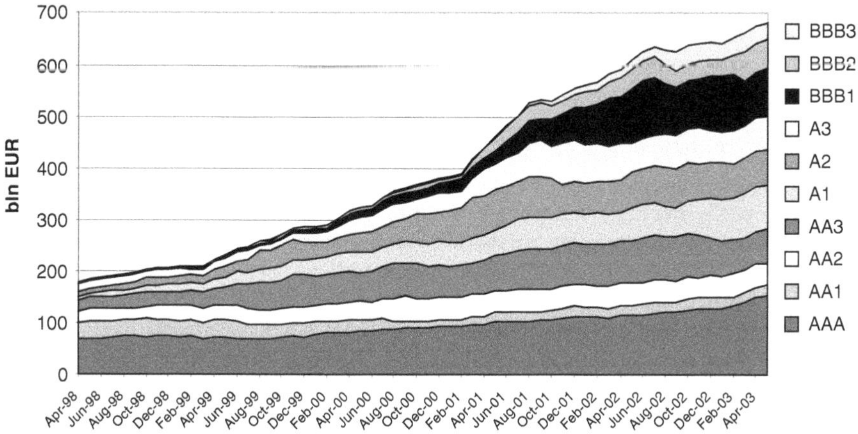

Figure 8.7 Euro area corporate bond outstanding values per rating category

Source: Baele et al. (2004).

dramatically in 2000, and has since then been comparable to the other rating categories (see Figure 8.8).

The demand for corporate bonds was further stimulated by a considerable increase in the supply, diversity, and liquidity of these bonds. The stronger interest in corporate

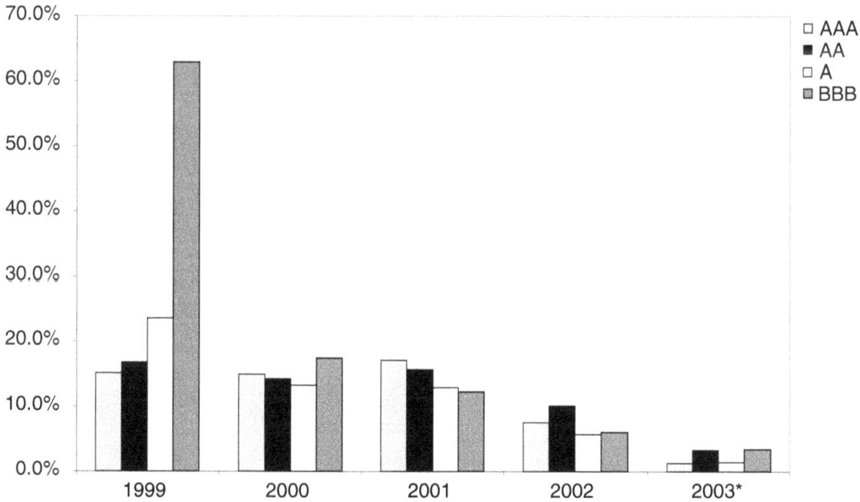

Figure 8.8 Proportion of corporate bonds that were not traded at least once a month

Source: Baele et al. (2004) and authors' calculations.

bonds has, however, not only been induced by a more developed corporate bond market, but also by other factors. First, with government bond yields reaching historically low levels, investors have increasingly been looking towards investment grade corporate bonds as an alternative. This effect was further strengthened by the developments in the equity market, especially in 2001 and 2002, which induced investors to shift their portfolio holdings to safer assets, such as corporate bonds. Second, because of reduced government bond debt in the late 1990s – related to the desire for sound fiscal balances – investors that were looking for long-term fixed income investments turned increasingly to corporate bonds. While this general trend of fiscal consolidation now seems to have been interrupted, it contributed to the demand of corporate bonds in the first years following the introduction of the euro. Third, the combination of an ageing population and large unfunded pension liabilities have greatly expanded the demand for long-term savings in general and for corporate bonds in particular.

How Integrated is the Corporate Bond Market in the Euro Area?

We have shown in the previous section that a way to measure the degree of government bond market integration is through the analysis of the differences between local and benchmark bond yields within a certain maturity class. Unfortunately, a direct comparison of corporate bond yields across countries does not serve as a good indicator of integration, as yield differences may reflect other factors, such as differences in pervasive risk, rather than a lack of integration.

The yield on a corporate bond typically depends on a number of factors, such as the bond's credit rating, time-to-maturity, liquidity as well as its cash-flow structure. For these reasons, Baele et al. (2004) suggest controlling risk-adjusted bond yields[9] for these factors in a regression analysis and then obtaining measures of corporate

Table 8.1 Average parameter estimates for cross-sectional regressions

Rating effect			**Country effect**		
AAA	–33.79	0.00	Austria	2.21	0.00
AA1	–23.09	0.00	Germany	–1.54	0.06
AA2	–21.74	0.00	Spain	3.86	0.00
AA3	–14.66	0.00	France	–7.64	0.00
A1	–2.55	0.21	Ireland	5.78	0.00
A2	17.94	0.00	The Netherlands	–0.57	0.01
A3	24.10	0.00			
BBB	69.46	0.00			
			Common effect	86.52	0.00
Sector effect			Maturity effect	1.88	0.00
Financial	–0.27	0.19	Coupon effect	4.17	0.00
Non-financial	0.31	0.38	Liquidity effect	–66.19	0.00

Source: Baele et al. (2004).

9 In order to calculate risk-adjusted bond yields they have subtracted from each corporate yield the zero-coupon yield on a German government bond with identical time to maturity.

bond market integration by investigating whether these risk-adjusted bond yields have a systematic country component or not.

Table 8.1 reports the average size and significance level of the various parameters. Under the hypothesis of full integration, the parameters related to the country dummies should not be statistically different from zero.

In every case, except Germany, the parameter related to the country dummy is statistically significant, but the country-specific spread is relatively small in economic terms. Spanish, Irish and Austrian corporations pay a country premium of about 4, 6 and 2 basis points, respectively, while French corporations get a premium of about 8 basis points less. The premium is close to zero for Germany and the Netherlands. These country premia are only slightly higher than for the government bond market and moreover not statistically significant for Germany.

Overall, the results indicate that the corporate bond market has achieved a rather good degree of integration. The level and evolution of corporate bond yield spreads is to a large extend determined by the credit rating while the country where a bond is issued has only marginal explanatory power for the cross-section of corporate bond yield spreads.

The Equity Market

At the beginning of the 1990s, the size of the various continental European equity markets was relatively small, especially compared to those in the UK and the US. Over the last decade however, European equity markets have recorded impressive growth rates, and have become a more important source of financing for European corporations. At the same time, investors seem to have developed an equity culture and have increased their holdings of equities, both directly and indirectly through pension and investment funds. While the recent market downturn may somehow have slowed down these trends, we expect the euro area equity markets to become increasingly important as a financing source for corporations, and as an investment alternative for households.

Further development and integration of euro area equity markets has large potential benefits. First, it is well documented that the cost of equity capital typically decreases as integration proceeds. Hardouvelis et al. (2002) for instance show that over the 1990s, further European integration resulted in a decrease in the cost of equity capital of between 0.5 and 3 per cent, depending on the sector being looked at. The lower cost of capital in integrated equity markets reflects the better possibilities international investors have to eliminate country-specific risks by diversifying their portfolios across countries. A lower cost of capital typically increases the number of productive investments, and contributes to more economic growth. According to a recent study by London Economics (2002), the reduction in the cost of equity capital may result in an absolute increase of 0.5 percentage points in the EU-wide level of GDP at constant prices. A second advantage of further equity market development is that corporations will have access to a much larger pool of funds, as they will no longer be restricted by the supply of financing in their domestic market. As a result, corporations benefit from further integration both by an increase in the supply and lower cost of equity financing. Third, from an investor's point of view, further integration greatly expands the possibilities to share risks across countries and regions. By doing so, households are able to immunize their consumption from adverse shocks to their local income. Recent evidence by Adam et al. (2002) and Adjaouté and Danthine (2003) shows that risk sharing opportunities are currently far from being fully exploited. This may prove especially important though in times of strong asymmetric shocks and further industrial specialization across countries. Finally, further integration may increase the competition between issuers, stock exchanges, and providers of clearance and settlements systems, leading to more transparency, more liquidity and lower transaction costs.

This section is structured as follows. In the first part, we discuss how equity prices and holdings are influenced by further economic, monetary, and financial integration. Second, we discuss some of the recent developments in the euro area equity markets. Finally, we investigate whether the rapid growth has also resulted in better integrated equity markets.

Further Integration and the Determinants of Equity Prices

Over the last two decades, Western Europe in general, and the euro area in specific, has witnessed a period of substantial economic, financial, and monetary integration. Further European integration did not take place in isolation though, but in a period of increasing globalization, in which most barriers to international trade and capital flows were gradually abolished. In this section, we briefly discuss the impact of further integration on the pricing of euro area equities.

According to the dividend discount model, the current stock price equals the net present value of all future dividends. In other words, equity prices incorporate expectations about both the future value of dividends, as well as about the relevant discount rate. The latter reflects in turn expectations about the risk-free rate and the equity premium. As a consequence, to investigate the impact of EMU and globalization on equity prices, one should focus on their effect on the discount rate and expected dividend payments.

The total discount rate consists of two parts, being the yield on a (quasi) risk-free bond, and the equity risk premium. For medium and long-term investors, the risk-free rate is most often proxied by the (nominal) yield on government bonds. As we have argued in the previous section, government bond yields have nearly fully converged. This is not only the result of the abolition of currency risk, which constituted an important 'wig' between government bonds from different countries, but especially of the strong convergence of inflation expectations resulting from a single monetary policy. The near convergence of government bond yields contributed to a convergence in the discount premium, and hence a more homogeneous valuation of euro area equities.

Apart from the risk-free rate, the discount rate consists also of an equity premium (EP), which compensates for the amount of systematic risk incorporated in a particular stock. The level of systematic risk, and hence the cost of capital that local corporations face, depends upon the possibilities investors have to diversify their portfolios internationally. Generally, the higher the degree of equity market integration, the easier it is for investors to reduce their systematic risk, and the lower the cost of equity capital will be. The reason why international portfolios have a lower amount of systematic risk is that cross-country equity market correlations are typically lower than one. This in part reflects the occurrence of non-synchronous economic shocks across countries. As a result, investors can insure against adverse country-specific shocks by investing abroad. Because this allows them to smooth consumption over the business cycle, they will typically require a lower risk premium in integrated rather than in segmented markets. To the extent that the euro area equity markets become more integrated, one should expect a convergence in the amount of systematic risk local investors have to bear, and hence a more homogeneous valuation of equities across countries.

Notice that also the abolition of intra-euro area exchange rate risk resulted in a further convergence of cross-country discount rates. Exchange rate risk premia – previously different across the various euro area countries – decreased substantially in the run-up to the euro, and disappeared completely within the euro area after 1999. Hardouvelis et al. (2002a) for instance estimate that, prior to the launch of the euro, intra-European currency risk contributed on average about 14 per cent to the total equity risk premium across countries. This indicates that with the introduction of the single currency, an important component of the equity risk premium disappeared, leading to a further convergence of cross-country discount rates.

Let us now focus on the likely effect of economic, monetary, and financial integration on (expected) dividends. First notice that in the long run, dividends are related to earnings, and hence to the overall performance of the economy. To the extent that EMU has resulted in a convergence of economic fundamentals, one expects, *ceteris paribus*, that corporate profits, dividends, and hence equity prices are driven more and more by common European factors. Recent evidence seems to support the hypothesis that European business cycles have become more alike (see e.g. Artis, Krolzig, and Toro (1999), Peersman and Smets (2001)). This trend does not only reflect economic integration, but also the strong convergence in monetary and fiscal policies. Furthermore, the strong increase in cross-country trade has made corporate profits increasingly dependent upon economic situation in other countries. To the extent that corporate profits are more and more determined by common factors, one would expect, *ceteris paribus*, a structural rise in cross-country equity return correlations.

Notice that the trend towards business cycle synchronization may to some extent be counteracted by increasing industry specialization at a country level. A removal of trade barriers may induce countries to specialize in the industries they have a comparative advantage in. If this occurs, the industry composition of country stock indices will become more and more dissimilar, resulting in decreasing cross-country correlations. This effect may be reinforced by financial integration, as investors themselves can reduce their industry-specific exposure by investing in other sectors in other countries, making it in this sense unnecessary for corporations or countries to diversify activities across industrial activities. As pointed out by Adjaouté and Danthine (2003), these structural changes in the European economy are slow and likely to be offset by the more immediate effects of macroeconomic policy convergence. It is however important to monitor these structural changes in the future.

Equity Market Linkages

To the extent that further economic, monetary, and financial integration has resulted in the convergence of the determinants of equity prices, one expects a structural increase in the degree of equity market co-movements.

A number of authors have investigated this by measuring the proportion of local equity returns that are driven by common news. In their seminal paper, Bekaert and Harvey (1997) estimated the sensitivity of a large number of emerging equity market returns to shocks in the world equity market portfolio. The latter are thought of being a condensed measure for news common to all investors. They find that countries react more strongly to world equity market news after important liberalization events. Similar results are obtained by Ng (2000) for a number of Pacific Basin countries. Two recent papers have applied this model to European equity markets. First, Fratzscher (2002) investigated whether the process towards EMU has influenced the sensitivities of local European equity markets to shocks in the aggregate European and US market. He finds that correlations between EMU markets have increased since 1996, and that this rise can mainly be explained by a reduction in exchange rate volatility and to some extent also by monetary policy convergence. Second, Baele (2004) allows the sensitivities of 13 European equity markets to aggregate European and US equity returns to be state dependent. He finds a structural increase in the intensity by which local European equity markets react to common European and US news. For most countries, the shift from a low to a high intensity state is situated at the end of the 1980s. The probability of being in the high spillover state appears to be strongly related to the reduction in inflation differentials (further monetary integration), as well as to measures of trade integration and equity market development.

These results are confirmed in recent work by Baele et al. (2004). They find a dramatic increase in the sensitivity of local euro area returns to both European and US shocks (see Table 8.2). The average sensitivity of the various euro area stock market returns to common European shocks increased from 0.40 in the period 1973–1985 to 0.83 during the period 1999–2003. The bulk of this increase appears to be concentrated in the second half of the 1980s and early 1990s. A similar albeit slightly smaller increase is observed for the sensitivities to US shocks. The strong increase in both European and US shock spillover intensities strongly suggests that euro area equity markets have become increasingly integrated with European and world equity markets.

Table 8.2 Average sensitivity of euro area equity markets to common European and US shocks

	73–85	**86–91**	**92–98**	**99–03**
EU Shocks	0.40	0.65	0.76	0.83
% change	–	63	17	10
US Shocks	0.26	0.37	0.37	0.46
% change	–	44	1	24

Source: Baele et al. (2004).

In Table 8.3, we report the proportion of variance of local European equity returns explained by common European and US shocks. While in the 1970s and the beginning of the 1980s on average 8 per cent of local equity variance was explained by common European news, this ratio has increased to about 24 per cent in the recent years. Notice moreover that while the US was the dominant source of news in the first period, common European news has taken the lead since the beginning of the 1990s.

Overall, the increasing importance of common news as a driver of euro area stock returns indicates a considerable increase in the degree of integration. In integrated markets, investors treat local news more and more as 'idiosyncratic', and hence diversifiable by investing internationally. In other words, it does not affect the rate at which local investors discount future cash flows, and stock returns will only react to local news to the extent that it affects earnings expectations. Common European and US news on the other hand reflects systematic risk. A rise (decrease) in the level of systematic risk will have a positive (negative) effect on the discount rate in all countries, and cross-country stock returns will move in tandem. As a result, the structural increase in cross-country correlations[10] observed in euro area equity markets suggest a considerable increase in the level of equity market integration.[11]

Country versus Sector Effects

The structural increase in cross-country equity market correlations would imply that the risk reduction potential of international diversification (at least within the euro area) has decreased. In fact, in a financially integrated area, one would expect that stock returns are gradually less and less determined by the country in which they are listed, and more and more by the sector to which they belong.

Practitioners seem to have reacted to this by drastically changing the way they construct portfolios. Until recently, the first step in the asset allocation process was

Table 8.3 Average proportion of local variance explained by European and US shocks

	73–85	86–91	92–98	99–03
EU Shocks	8%	13%	23%	24%
US Shocks	12%	14%	17%	20%

Source: Baele et al. (2004).

10 It is important to realize that we refer here to *structural* rather than *temporary* increases in cross-country correlations. Temporary increases may be due to an overall rise in market volatility, which clearly has nothing to do with variation in the degree of equity market integration.

11 Notice that part of the increase in cross-country correlations may also be related to a convergence in risk-free rates (government bond market integration) as well as in cross-country earnings expectations (further economic integration).

typically to decide upon an adequate geographical allocation. Thereafter, stocks were chosen according to some selection criteria within the pre-selected countries. Over the last years however, especially since the introduction of the single currency in 1999, more and more investors became convinced that, at least within the euro area, the country orientation in the first step should give way to an industry or sector orientation, and changed their asset allocation paradigm as such. This evolution is in part reflected in the dramatic increase in the number of sector funds and indices.

To investigate the relative merits of respectively country and sector allocation, Baele et al. (2004), following Roulet and Solnik (2000), and Adjaouté and Danthine (2003), calculate the cross-sectional dispersion in both sector[12] and country index returns to investigate the structure of cross-country and sector correlations over time. The cross-sectional dispersion, calculated as the cross-sectional standard deviation of all sector or country returns, is inversely related to the degree of correlation: the less equity returns are correlated, the more they will tend to drift apart, and the higher the dispersion will be. Similarly, a high degree of dispersion indicates large diversification opportunities.

Figure 8.9 plots the country and sector dispersions over time. In order to focus on the slowly moving components, we report Hodrick-Prescott filtered dispersion series. Over nearly the entire sample, country dispersion has been higher than sector

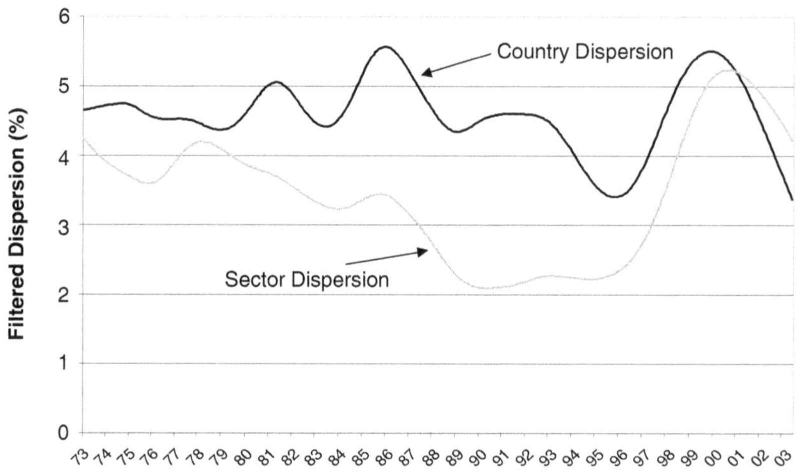

Figure 8.9 Hodrick-Prescott filtered country and global EMU sector dispersions

Source: Baele et al. (2004).

12 We use the EMU global sector indices provided by Datastream. Sector returns are calculated on a monthly basis over the period January 1997–July 2003, include (re-invested) dividends, and are denominated in euros. Monthly country returns are based upon Datastream's total market indices.

dispersion, implying that cross-country correlations were typically lower than cross-sector correlations. This confirms previous results that country diversification has been superior to sector diversification for most of the time.

Interestingly, the difference between sector and country dispersion was reduced in the second half of the 1990s. Moreover, our measure of sector dispersion surpassed country dispersion in 2000, consistent with a possible shift in the asset allocation paradigm from country- to sector-based strategies. These results support recent findings by Baca et al. (2000) and Cavaglia et al. (2000) that the potential of sector diversification is now larger than for geographic diversification. Similarly, using a mean-variance spanning test, Ehling and Ramos (2002) found that, while country diversification has been superior to sector diversification over most of the last three decades, both strategies yield nearly identical returns in the post euro period.

However, one should note that, given the large variation in dispersions, one has to be careful when interpreting the results in terms of the relative advantage of sector diversification compared to country diversification. In fact, not only sector but also country dispersion increased in the second half of the 1990s, suggesting that the potential of geographic diversification actually improved relative to the period 1990–1995. The rise in both country and sector dispersion indicates that diversifying across sectors and countries may result in portfolios with a lower risk than those constructed on a country or sector basis only. To analyse this, we use country-sector indices over the same period to calculate cross-sectional return dispersions.[13] The results are depicted in Figure 8.10. In line with the findings of Adjaouté and

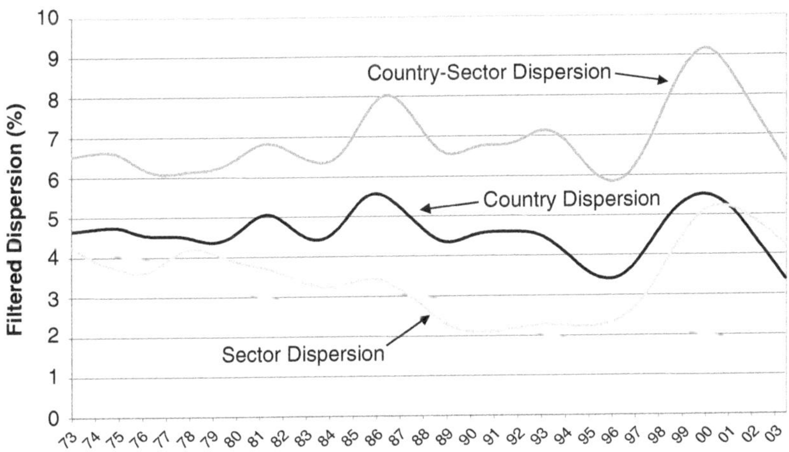

Figure 8.10 Hodrick-Prescott filtered country, global EMU sector and country-sector dispersions

Source: Baele et al. (2004).

13 Datastream provides for each country a number of sector indices. Here, we use the same sector classification as used in the previous graphs. In total, this yields us with 108 country-sector indices.

Danthine, we find that while the potential of sector diversification has increased considerably in the second half of the nineties, the largest risk reduction can be obtained from diversifying equity portfolios both across countries and sectors.

The relative rise in sector relative to country effects is consistent with an increase in the degree of euro area equity market integration. This is confirmed by the structural break in the portfolio allocation paradigm. While previously most managers favoured country allocation, after 1999, the balance seems to have shifted to sector diversification. However, as was shown here, there still seems to be an important role for cross-country diversification, especially if combined with sector diversification.

The Equity Home Bias

From the previous sections, it was clear that there are large benefits from diversifying equity portfolios across countries, sectors, or both. In reality however, investors seem to allocate a disproportionately large fraction of their equity holdings in domestic stocks. This finding, which has been widely studied and observed in nearly all countries, is denoted the 'equity home bias' (see e.g. Tesar and Werner (1992) and Lewis (1999).

Recent evidence indicates though that the equity home bias is decreasing, at least within the euro area. Adam et al. (2002) and Baele et al. (2004) use data collected by FEFSI[14] to calculate the percentage of assets in euro zone equity funds that is managed according to a Europe-wide investment strategy. They find that, over the period 1997–2002, this proportion increased substantially in nearly all countries, surpassing 50 per cent in most countries by the end of 2002. Similar evidence is provided in ECB (2002). All these studies use data from InterSec Research Corporation[15] to determine the percentage of foreign equity invested in pension funds in a number of European countries. They find that the proportion of foreign equity is constant over the period 1992–1998, but rises considerably after 1999. This suggests that the introduction of the euro had an important impact on the investment strategy of pension funds. They find a similar result for insurance companies, although the results differ more across countries.

In Figure 8.11, we investigate the size and evolution of the equity home bias in euro area insurance corporations, investment, and pension funds over the period 1995–2000. The data represent the proportion of euro area institutional investors that have a non-domestic investment strategy.

The share of investment funds with a non-domestic strategy has increased considerably, from about 40 per cent in 1995 to 67 per cent in 2000, indicating a strong reduction in the equity home bias of euro area investment funds. Note that the increase started already in 1997, well before the introduction of the euro. The proportion of foreign equity in pension funds stayed relatively constant over the period 1995–1998 at levels slightly below 40 per cent. Following the introduction of the euro, a considerable increase was observed, notably to 46 and 53 per cent in respectively 1999 and 2000. Anecdotal evidence suggests that the reduction in the home

14 Fédération Européenne des Fonds et Sociétés d'Investissement, see http://www.fefsi.com.

15 InterSec is a consultant company that advises pension funds and insurance companies; see http://www.intsec.com.

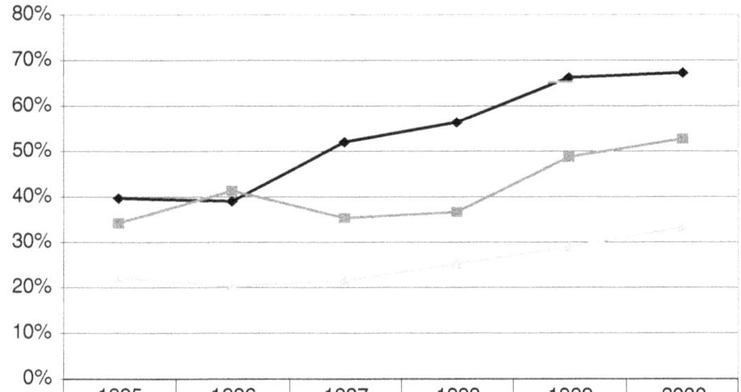

	1995	1996	1997	1998	1999	2000
Investment Funds	40%	39%	52%	56%	66%	67%
Pension Funds	34%	41%	35%	37%	49%	53%
Insurance Companies	22%	20%	22%	25%	29%	33%

Figure 8.11 Average proportion of non-domestic equity holdings in euro area investment funds, pension funds and insurance corporations

Source: FEFSI, Intersec Research Corporation, ECB calculations.

bias of pension funds was mainly the result of a gradual rebalancing of equities, while the internationalization of equity holdings of investment funds was merely the result of issuing new funds. This in part explains why the home bias decreased more slowly for pension than for investment funds. Similarly, until the actual introduction of the euro, pension funds were restricted by the currency matching rule, which seriously restricted the foreign currency composition of pension funds. While also the share of foreign equities in the portfolio of insurance corporations is gradually increasing, it is still at relatively low levels (33 per cent in 2000 relative to 22 per cent in 1995). The considerable differences in the internationalization of the equity holdings across institutional investors and countries suggest that there still exist a number of important barriers to full equity market integration.

A Changing Market Infrastructure

The heightened interest in cross-border equity trading has led euro area stock exchanges to expand across their national borders. Consolidation among exchanges has until now been limited to the relatively successful merger of the exchanges of Amsterdam, Brussels, and Paris in September 2000, which now constitute Euronext. The newly founded exchange expanded further in 2001, when it acquired LIFFE, the London derivatives trading platform, and agreed to integrate also the Portuguese exchanges of Lisbon and Porto. New entrants in the market are meanwhile attempting to create pan-European exchanges. For example, Virt-X, a joint venture of Tradepoint (a London-based electronic market) and the Swiss Stock Exchange, offers trading in all fully listed UK common stocks and in European blue-chip stocks. Before these two initiatives, merger talks between Deutsche Bourse and the London

Stock Exchange – to form iX (International Exchange) failed. The relatively low speed of consolidation in euro area equity markets is due to a number of factors, including the existence of cross-country and regulatory differences as well as the severe fragmentation of Europe's clearing and settlement systems. The latter is one of the main reasons why cross-border equity transaction costs remain considerably higher than for domestic transactions.

At a European level, there have been several efforts to increase the degree of European financial integration (for details, see Chapter 4 in this book). Both the Financial Services Action Plan (FSAP), the Lamfalussy report on the regulation of European securities markets, as well as the work of the Giovannini group identified a considerable number of barriers to full integration. These are related to differences in accounting rules, corporate governance practices, investment fund regulation, taxes, supervision, the speed of legislative processes, and last but not least market infrastructure. A large number of directives are issued in order to deal with most of these barriers. These are expected to give a considerable impetus for the degree of integration in European (equity) markets.

Conclusion

In this chapter, we have analysed the latest developments and integration of the euro area bond and equity markets.

In the first part, we focused on the euro area government bond markets. We showed that yields converged dramatically in the run-up to the single currency's introduction in January 1999. This largely reflects the similarly large convergence in economic fundamentals. Further economic and especially monetary integration resulted in a strong convergence of inflation expectations across the various euro area economies, while exchange rate risk, previously an important 'wig' between government bonds from different countries, vanished entirely with the introduction of the single currency in 1999. The results indicate that the government bond market in the euro area has achieved a very high degree of integration. However, while the level of convergence in yields is impressive, yields of government bonds with similar, or in some cases identical, credit risk and maturity have not yet entirely converged. Differences in liquidity as well as in the availability of developed derivatives markets tied to the various individual bond markets may partly account for these spreads.

The second section focused on the euro area corporate bond market. While this market is relatively young, its development over the last years has been spectacular. Before 1998, the market was dominated by debt issued by highly-rated (financial) corporations, whereas thereafter also industrial corporations have increasingly found their way to the corporate bond market. This is reflected in the dramatic growth in the lower-rated A and BBB market segments since then. Together with its development, also the liquidity of the market for lower rated bonds improved. Despite the impressive growth rates recorded over the last years, the euro area corporate bond market continues to be much smaller than in the US and Japan, both in terms of absolute value and relative to the size of the economy. Using a number of measures, we showed that – once corrected for pervasive risk – the country where a bond is issued has only marginal explanatory power for the cross-section of corporate bond yield spreads. This suggests that the corporate bond markets of the countries we analysed, i.e. Austria, France, Germany, Ireland, the Netherlands, and Spain, are reasonably well integrated with each other.

In the final section, we provided a number of measures for equity market integration. First, we discussed the channels through which economic, monetary, and financial integration may affect the pricing of euro area stocks. Further financial integration has mainly an effect on the cross-country equity premia, which are expected to converge to a lower level. Next, we reported three (indirect) measures for equity market integration, each of them suggesting that the euro area equity markets are now more integrated than before. First, we showed that since the end of 2000, the advantages of sector diversification have for the first time in the last 30 years surpassed those of geographical diversification. Second, equity returns in the various euro area equity markets appear to be more and more determined by common news factors. While in the first half of the 1980s less than 20 per cent of local return variance was explained by aggregate European shocks, this proportion had risen to more than 40 per cent in the post-euro period. Finally, we found strong evidence that the home bias in the equity holdings of insurance corporations as well as investment and pension funds has decreased considerably over the last few years. While integration has increased considerably, there still exist a number of important barriers to further integration. Examples include cross-country regulatory differences and the severe fragmentation of Europe's clearing and settlement systems. Further competition between stock exchanges and clearing and settlement corporations as well as the new policy initiatives part of the Financial Services Action Plan should give a renewed impetus for further integration in Europe's equity markets.

References

Adam, K., T. Jappelli, A. Menichini, M. Padula, and M. Pagano (2002), *Analyse, Compare, and Apply Alternative Indicators and Monitoring Methodologies to Measure the Evolution of Capital Market Integration in the European Union*, Centre for Studies in Economics and Finance (CSEF), University of Salerno.

Adjaouté, K. and J.-P. Danthine (2003), 'European Financial Integration and Equity Returns: A Theory-Based Assessment', in Gaspar V., Hartmann P. and Sleijpen O. (eds) *The Transformation of the European Financial System*, Frankfurt, pp. 186–245.

Artis, M.J., H.-M. Krolzig and J. Toro (1999), *The European Business Cycle*, CEPR Discussion Papers 2242.

Baca, S.P., B. Garbe and R.A. Weiss (2000), 'The Rise of Sector Effects in Major Equity Markets', *Financial Analysts Journal*, September/October, pp. 35–40.

Baele, L. (2004), 'Volatility Spillover Effects in European Equity Markets', *Journal of Financial and Quantitative Analysis*, Forthcoming.

Baele, L., A. Ferrando, P. Hordahl, E. Krylova and C. Monnet (2004), *Measuring the integration of euro area capital markets*, forthcoming Occasional Paper, European Central Bank.

Barr, David G. and Richard Priestley (2002), Expected Returns, Risk and the Integration of International Bond Markets, *Journal of International Money and Finance*, forthcoming.

Bekaert, G. and C.R. Harvey (1997), 'Emerging Equity Market Volatility', *Journal of Financial Economics* 43, pp. 29–77.

Brooks, R. and M. Del Negro (2002), 'Firm-Level Evidence on Globalization', Working Paper.

Carnegie-Brown and King (2003), 'The transformation of the European financial system', in Gaspar V., Hartmann P. and Sleijpen O. (eds) *The Transformation of the European Financial System*, Frankfurt, pp. 247–262.

Cavaglia, S., C. Brightman and M. Aked (2000), 'The Increasing Importance of Industry Factors', *Financial Analysts Journal*, September/October, pp. 41–54.

Codogno, L., C. Favero and A. Missale (2003), 'Government bond spreads', *Economic Policy*, October, pp. 503–532.

ECB (2001), *The Euro Bond Market*, July.

ECB (2002), *Report on Financial Structures.*

Dunne P., Moore M. and R. Portes (2002), *Defining benchmark status: an application using euro-area bonds*, CEPR Working Paper n. 3490.

Ehling, P. and S.B. Ramos (2002), 'Strategies of Asset Allocation: A Comparison in EMU and non-EMU countries', Working Paper.

Ferreira, M.A. and P.M. Gama (2002), 'The Developed Market's Stock Portfolio Volatility: An Investigation of Country and Sector Idiosyncratic Risk', Working Paper.

Fratzscher, M. (2001), 'Financial Market Integration in Europe: on the effects of EMU on Stock Markets', *International Journal of Finance and Economics*, forthcoming. Also published as ECB Working Paper 48.

Hardouvelis, G., D. Malliaropulos and R. Priestley (2000a), *EMU and European Stock Market Integration*, CEPR Discussion Paper No. 2124.

Hardouvelis, G., D. Malliaropulos and R. Priestley (2000b), 'The Impact of Globalization on the Equity Cost of Capital', Working Paper.

Lewis, K. (1999), 'Trying to Explain the Home Bias in Equities and Consumption', *Journal of Economic Literature*, Vol. 37, Nr. 2, pp. 571–608.

London Economics (2002), '*Quantification of the Macro-Economic Impact of Integration of EU Financial Markets*, Report for the European Commission's Directorate-General for the Internal Market.

Ng, A. (2000), 'Volatility Spillover Effects from Japan and the U.S. to the Pacific-Basin', *Journal of International Money and Finance*, 2000, Vol. 19, pp. 207–233.

Peersman G. and F. Smets (2002), 'Are the effects of monetary policy in the euro area greater in recessions than in booms?', in *Monetary transmission in diverse economies*, L. Mahadeva and P. Sinclair (eds), Cambridge University Press, pp. 28–48 (also European Central Bank Working Paper Series, No. 52).

Roulet, J. and B. Solnik (2000), 'Dispersion as Cross-Sectional Correlation', *Financial Analysts Journal*, January–February, pp. 54–61.

Santillan J., Bayle M. and Thygesen C. (2003), *The impact of the euro on money and bond markets*, ECB Occasional Paper no. 1.

Tesar, L. and I. Werner (1995), 'Home Bias and High Turnover', *Journal of International Money and Finance*, Vol. 14, no. 4, pp. 467–92.

Van Landschoot, Astrid (2003), *The term structure of credit spreads on euro corporate bonds*, Tilburg University, Center for Economic Research, Discussion Paper No. 46.

Part IV
A Case Study: The Integration of Transmission Processes

Chapter 9

External Finance Premia in the Euro Area: Stage Three of EMU versus Stage Two

Gabe de Bondt

Introduction

This chapter aims to shed light on whether the changes in the financial structure, banking system and the money, bond and equity markets in the euro area – as described in the previous chapters – have had an impact on the linkages between the price of debt finance and monetary policy. In this respect, Stage Three of EMU is compared with Stage Two. The perspective thus differs from the preceding chapters in the sense that this chapter analyses the effects of financial integration instead of aiming to measure it. The focus lies on the price of the two main forms of debt, namely loans – usually from banks – and publicly traded debt securities issued by non-financial corporations (see also discussion in Chapter 8 of this book).

This issue is important for two interrelated reasons. First, the price and availability of debt finance may play an important role in the monetary policy transmission process (ECB 2002, Angeloni et al., 2003). Monetary policy can influence private consumption and investment directly by altering the liquidity or financial constraints as well as indirectly via various channels, for instance via the pass-through of official interest rate changes to the prices of bank-based debt finance (de Bondt 2002a) or via a premium on external finance, the so-called balance sheet channel (de Bondt 1999b and 2004). Second, debt finance forms a crucial ingredient of the macro-financial structure of an economy and therefore can significantly affect economic growth. For instance, the extent to which firms have access to external sources of corporate finance other than bank loans may be important for economic activity. More generally, a well-developed financial structure should improve the efficiency of financing decisions, favouring a better allocation of resources and thereby economic growth.

The main message of this chapter – admittedly tentative given the short history of Stage Three of EMU, but shown to be robust across different empirical methods – is that the speed and nature of monetary policy transmission in the euro area through the external finance premia (EFP) seem to have changed since the single currency. The monetary policy transmission mechanisms in the euro area seem to have strengthened and deepened in Stage Three of EMU.

As regards the interest rate channel of monetary policy, it is found that euro area bank lending rates have adjusted quicker to market interest rate developments in the first three years of the single currency (1999–2001), compared with Stage Two of EMU (1994–1998). In other words, bank-based external finance premia (BBEFP), that is, the spread between bank lending rates and market interest rates with a comparable maturity, seem to have become less sticky since the single currency and therefore have strengthened monetary policy transmission. Likely reasons for the observed quicker adjustment speed of bank lending rates are, among others, an increase in the prevailing competitive forces in the different segments of the bank credit market in the euro area since January 1999, and an increase in non-deposit or market-based funding of bank loans. The latter, in turn, partly relates to an increase in the cross-border activity of the euro area inter-bank market. Assuming a national convergence of the adjustment speeds of bank lending rates in the different segments of the bank credit market to the fastest levels observed, some integration benefits have been achieved in the first years of Stage Three of EMU. At the same time however, integration for the relatively sticky bank rates on consumer credit is weak.

Turning to the balance sheet channel of monetary policy it is found that changes in monetary policy significantly affect the bank- and market-based external finance premia, which in turn have a significant impact on the real GDP growth. This finding suggests that the balance sheet channel of monetary policy is macroeconomically relevant and has deepened in Stage Three of EMU, since it no longer exclusively works via the banking sector, but also through the corporate bond market (de Bondt 2002b and 2004). The market-based external finance premium (MBEFP) has become of importance around the introduction of the euro and is approximated by the spread between long-term BBB-rated corporate bonds and government bonds with a comparable maturity. These empirical findings suggest that movements in official interest rates may have effects on real economic activity via a financial accelerator mechanism, as reflected in the EFP (external finance premium). They imply distributional monetary policy impacts across borrowers along the size of the EFP which highly depend on the net worth or balance sheet position of borrowers. With respect to the EFP, further integration benefits can be expected through a national convergence in the nature (bank-based versus market-based) and level (via the balance sheet position of borrowers) of bank- and market-based EFP. It is shown that a lower level of the premium on bank- and market-based debt finance results in higher economic activity.

External Finance Premium and Monetary Policy Transmission in Theory

Figure 9.1 presents the channels of monetary policy transmission in a simplified schematic form. Official interest rate changes are passed on to the real economy along a wide range of different channels. Two monetary policy channels particularly play a key role with respect to debt finance: interest rate and credit channel.

Interest Rate Channel

The interest rate channel works through the price of debt finance and deals with the issue of how policy-controlled interest rates affect the interest rates charged by banks and other financial intermediaries. Central banks exert a dominant influence on money market conditions and thereby steer money market interest rates (see Chapter 7

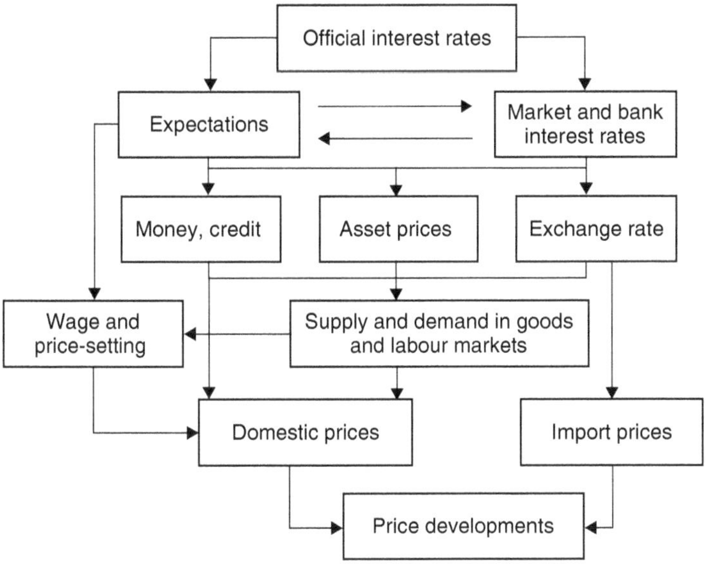

Figure 9.1 Transmission mechanism from official interest rates to prices

Source: Chart 3.1 in ECB (2004).

for a description of the money market). Changes in market interest rates, in turn, affect retail bank interest rates, albeit to varying degrees (de Bondt 2002a). A quicker pass-through of official and market interest rates to bank lending rates strengthens monetary policy transmission.

This section focuses on the pass-through of changes in market interest rates to bank lending interest rates. Market interest rates can be viewed as the best available proxy for the marginal funding costs of bank loans. Applying this idea to the price-setting of bank loans results in the following marginal cost pricing model equation (de Bondt 2002a and 2005a):

$$br = \gamma_0 + \gamma_1 mr \tag{9.1}$$

where *br* is the price set by banks, that is, the bank lending rate, parameter γ_0 is a constant markup and *mr* is the market interest rate.

In the textbook world of perfect competition with complete information, the price equals marginal cost, and the derivative of prices, with respect to marginal costs, equals one (γ_l=1). This derivative typically becomes less than one when loan demand is not fully elastic with respect to the bank lending rate, if banks have some degree of market power or asymmetric information costs exist. Market power may be related to the fact that the bank credit market is segmented and thus not fully integrated and asymmetric information costs to heterogeneous borrowers (credit risk).

As regards the latter, if banks increase their lending rates, they may attract riskier borrowers (adverse selection) or will give adverse incentives for borrowers to choose riskier projects (moral hazard) (Stiglitz and Weiss 1981). Consequently, banks' expected receipts may actually fall when they increase their lending rates. If the probability of default rises sufficiently, banks will set lending rates below the market clearing rates and ration the amount of credit supply accordingly. In this case of credit rationing, bank lending rates exhibit upward stickiness.

However, credit rationing is not the only outcome due to asymmetric information. Another outcome is that bank lending rates react in the first instance by more than one-to-one to changes in the market interest rate. Consider two broad classes of borrowers to which banks can lend. For the first class of loans, such as fully secured lending, the probability of default is zero, while for the second class of borrowers the probability of default is positive. This probability of default positively relates to the lending interest rate through adverse selection and moral hazard. Assume that banks can distinguish between the two borrower types, but not between customers within each class, and that banks are risk neutral. Given perfect competition, banks must earn the same expected return on both classes of loans, as formulated in equation (9.2):

$$br_1 = [1 - P(br_2)]br_2 = \gamma_0 + \gamma_1 mr \tag{9.2}$$

where br_1 is the rate charged by banks on the riskless loan, $P(\cdot)$ is the probability of default on the second class of loan and br_2 is the bank lending rate on these loans. In other words, the bank lending rate br_2 includes a credit risk or EFP, whereas br_1 is free of any risk premium.

For the first type of loans $\partial br_1/\partial mr = 1$, that is, changes in the marginal cost of funds get transmitted one for one into changes in the lending rate on the riskless loans. However, when banks are lending to the second borrower type, $\partial br_2/\partial mr > 1$, since $\partial P/\partial br_2$. For these loans banks must increase their lending rate by an amount greater than the increase in the market interest rate to compensate for the decrease in the probability of repayment. At some point banks will not be able to increase the interest rate sufficiently to compensate for this risk, and all lending will be made to the first type of borrower, that is, a flight to quality. This phenomenon closely relates to the financial accelerator mechanism, as described in the next section (Bernanke et al., 1994). However, until this happens, the interest rate should not be sticky on the risky loans. In fact, the reverse is true; the rate on these loans should be very sensitive to changes in the market interest rate.

Credit Channel: Bank Lending and Balance Sheet Channel

The second monetary transmission channel works in particular through the availability of debt finance, both indirectly from banks and other financial intermediaries, as well as directly from money and capital markets. This so-called credit channel of monetary transmission emphasizes the additional role that bank behaviour (bank lending channel) and debt market imperfections (balance sheet channel) may play in the monetary transmission mechanism (de Bondt 2000 and Trautwein 2000).

The bank lending channel The bank lending channel assumes that there are no perfect substitutes for bank loans, either on the asset side of bank balance sheets or on the liability side of borrowers. Another assumption is that monetary policy can affects the liability side of bank balance sheets. For instance, following a monetary tightening, which drains deposits from the banking system, banks have to readjust their asset portfolio to the same extent. Banks do so by changing loan supply, given the imperfect substitutability between loans and other assets. Implications of a bank lending channel are, among others, that monetary policy has distributional effects. For instance, monetary policy is expected to have a relatively strong impact on banks with a small buffer stock of liquid assets and on undercapitalized banks, because these banks are less able to offset a monetary policy tightening. At the same time, monetary policy will have a strong impact if firms and households are unable to resort to internal finance. In other words, firms which have limited access to the financial markets, typically characterized by small size and high financial leverage, should be more affected by monetary policy changes than firms which can easily tap money and capital markets. The potential relevance of the bank lending channel depends on the extent to which central bank actions determine bank behaviour with respect to loan supply and the degree of bank dependence in the economy.

As regards bank behaviour, several issues are important for a bank lending channel.[1] First, following a monetary policy tightening, banks may issue money market liabilities, such as large certificates of deposits, to offset any drop in (reservable) deposits. In particular large, capital-unconstrained and/or highly rated banks may have easier access to non-deposit funding sources. The second issue is that, if bank liabilities indeed decline after a monetary tightening, banks may sell liquid assets instead of reducing loan supply to realize the decline in total assets. In other words, monetary policy has typically a strong impact on less liquid banks, because these banks want to prevent their liquid asset ratio falling to an undesirable low level.

Turning to the bank dependence condition of the bank lending channel – the degree of bank financing versus debt security – equity and trade financing is important. Although only a limited number of (large) enterprises have access to financing sources based on debt securities or equity instead of loans, these firms may help those, without direct access to capital markets through trade credit. In other words, the financing flows between firms may weaken the degree of dependence on bank financing in an economy.

The balance sheet channel It emphasizes that debt market imperfections may make external finance more costly than internal financing and for borrowers more difficult to obtain in the event of a fall in the value of the assets pledged as collateral for debt. Firms and households pay additional costs for raising outside financing over and above internal sources. The size of the EFP depends on borrowers' balance sheet positions or net worth, which in turn is affected by changes in the stance of monetary policy.

1 See, among others, Romer and Romer (1990), Peek and Rosengren (1995a and 1995b), Kashyap and Stein (1995, 1997 and 2000), de Bondt (1999a), Favero et al. (1999), Fase and de Bondt (2000), Kishan and Opiela (2000) and Altunbaş et al. (2002).

According to the balance sheet channel theory, the EFP plays a key role in accelerating and amplifying monetary policy shocks.[2] The academic literature typically defines the EFP with respect to bank-based financing. However, firms also face an EFP on market-based debt. The financial accelerator mechanism contends that the EFP may amplify and propagate business cycles, since a shock to the EFP affects the financing decisions of borrowers and therefore their investment activities. A key element in the financial accelerator mechanism of a balance sheet channel of monetary policy is the financial condition of the borrower. The net worth of the borrower, for instance corporate credit ratings, is reflected in the size of the EFP. A change in the net worth of borrowers modifies the EFP and the overall terms of debt that firms and households face, and therefore investment and consumption.

Figure 9.2 illustrates for firms the financial accelerator mechanism of a balance sheet channel. The demand curve *D* represents the demand for funds by firms and is downward sloping: the higher the cost of funds, the lower the investment. The supply curve is horizontal up to point *W*, which denotes corporate net worth. As long as the amount of external finance is less than the firm's net worth, the external finance rate is close to the risk-free interest rate or the opportunity cost of internal finance. The firm's net worth position is closely linked to its credit rating. For instance, the yield on AAA-rated corporate bonds is close to that of government bond yields, resulting in a very small EFP. In a 'perfect' world without credit risk or market imperfections, the level of investment undertaken by firms equals I^P. However, in the presence of credit risk, markets can be more reluctant to provide firms with funding unless they

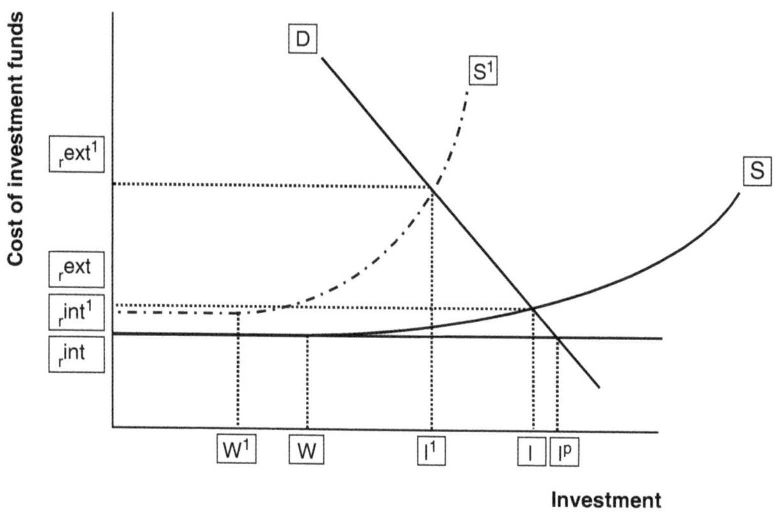

Figure 9.2 External finance premium and financial accelerator mechanism

2 See, among others, Bernanke and Gertler (1989), Gertler and Gilchrist (1993), Greenwald and Stiglitz (1993), Bernanke and Gertler (1995), Fisher (1997), Kiyotaki and Moore (1997) and Boissay (2001).

are adequately compensated. Thus the supply curve becomes upward sloping beyond *W*, leading to a lower equilibrium level of investment *I*.

This framework can also be employed to analyse the effect of a rise in the default risk-free interest rate due to a monetary policy tightening. Following an increase in the risk-free interest rate, default probabilities rise and firms' net worth or corporate credit ratings deteriorate, which causes a rise of the EFP. This leftward shift in the supply curve S^1 puts leveraged firms at even higher risk of default, which results in an increase in the EFP that is much larger than the rise in the risk-free interest rate. Thus, the initial shock to the default risk-free interest rate induced by monetary policy is magnified through its effect on the EFP. As such it has the potential to amplify the influence of monetary policy shocks on business cycles.

Developments in Euro Area External Finance Premia

A graphical examination of different EFP in the euro area shows, in accordance with the theory as described in the previous section, that credit risk considerations play an important role in the determination of the level of the EFP. However, one has to keep in mind that the euro area aggregated bank interest rates used in this chapter are based on non-harmonized national interest rate statistics, which are generally not fully comparable across countries. Monetary Financial Institutions (MFI) interest rate statistics produced on the basis of harmonized national definitions are only published since December 2003, starting from January 2003 onwards (ECB 2003b).

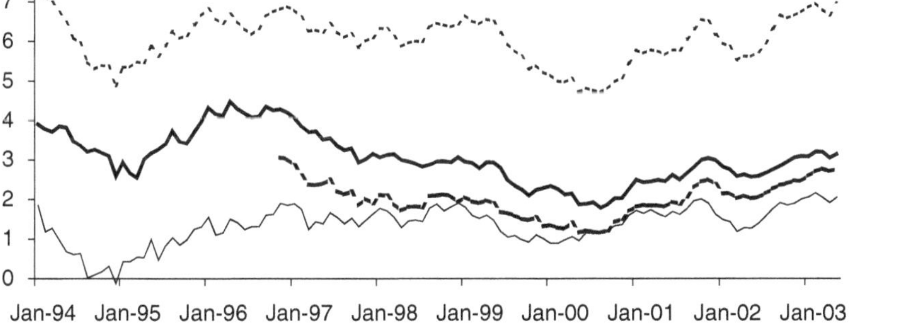

Figure 9.3 External finance premia in the different segments of the euro area bank credit market (percentages per annum; monthly averages)

Sources: ECB, Reuters, and author's calculations.

Table 9.1 Average bank-based external finance premium on bank loans in the euro area (basis points)

	Enterprises *of up to 1 year*	*of over 1 year*	**Households** *for consumer lending*	*for house purchase*
Stage Two	348	220	621	122
Stage Three*	258	191	587	150
Difference	–90	–28	–35	28

* Up to May 2003.

Sources: ECB, Reuters, and author's calculations.

Figure 9.3 plots the BBEFP defined as the spread between bank lending rates and market interest rates with a comparable maturity, in the different segments of the euro bank area credit market. Table 9.1 shows the average level of the different BBEFP in Stage Two and Three of EMU up to May 2003. The BBEFP are defined as the spreads between bank lending rates and market interest rates with a comparable maturity. The figure and table show that differences exist in the level of the different external finance premia. Among other factors, asymmetric information costs and credit risk considerations may explain these differences. In particular, the spread on consumer lending is high, compared with the other EFP, which suggests high asymmetric information costs and credit risk in this segment of the bank credit market in the euro area. The level of the mortgage finance premium is much lower, because of the typical lending practice against collateral. An explanation for the spread difference between short- and long-term loans to enterprises, besides differences in the collateral practice, might be an adverse selection bias due to the fact that borrowers with severe information asymmetries will borrow relatively more with a short maturity because of the larger information costs associated with long-term debt (de Bondt 1998).

Another observation of the figure is that the levels of the BBEFP in Stage Three of EMU show a tendency to decline over time, with the exception of one segment. The average level of the BBEFP is between 30 and 90 basis points lower in Stage Three of EMU than in Stage Two in three segments of the bank credit market (see Table 9.1). At the same time however, the fourth segment of the bank credit market shows a slight average increase of 25 basis points since the single currency. In other words, some financial integration benefits seem to have been reached in the first four years of the single currency, at least as reflected in lower BBEFP in some segments of the bank credit market. The levels of these EFP may, however, be positively related to the interest rate levels, which were lower in Stage Three of EMU than in Stage Two.

As regards the relative importance of the different BBEFP, the lending categories of loans to households for house purchase and loans to enterprises of over one year were the most important in terms of amounts outstanding (each amounted to around one-third of total MFI loans at the end of 2002). Loans to households for consumer lending and loans to enterprises of up to one year were of almost equal importance and together amounted to one-third of total MFI loans at the end of 2002. At the start of Stage Three of EMU these figures were fairly similar. The main difference is that, compared with the end of 1998, the share of loans to households for house purchase has increased by over 3 percentage points, whereas the share of consumer lending and short-term corporate loans show a corresponding decline. An aggregated BBEFP is constructed by taking a weighted average of the bank lending rate spreads as presented in Figure 9.3. Fixed weights on the basis of the amounts outstanding at the end of 2001 are used.

Turning to the MBEFP, it has been approximated by the spread between long-term corporate bonds and government bonds with a comparable maturity. Reliable euro area figures for this EFP are however only available for Stage Three of EMU, since the euro area corporate debt securities market has substantially broadened and deepened since the introduction of the euro (see Chapter 8, de Bondt 2002b and de Bondt and Lichtenberger 2003 and 2004). The corporate bond market in the euro area, broadly defined as long-term debt securities issued by non-financial and non-monetary financial corporations, amounted to around 6 per cent of GDP at the end of 1998 as opposed to 12 per cent of GDP at the end of 2002. Notwithstanding the increasing importance of corporate debt securities since the single currency, bank loans are still the most important debt finance source for the private sector in the euro area.

Figure 9.4 plots the BBEFP and MBEFP during Stage Three of EMU. It shows that the BBEFP has varied between 200 and 350 basis points in the period January 1999 and May 2003 and was all the time higher than the MBEFP, which has varied between 100 and 250 basis points. This level difference can, besides intermediation costs in the case of BBEFP, be explained by differences in asymmetric information costs and credit risk between firms which are solely dependent on bank financing and firms which tap the bond market themselves. The movements over time of both EFPs, albeit fairly similar, may vary.

All in all, it seems to be the case that some integration benefits, that is a lower premium on external finance in some but not all segments of the bank credit market, has occurred since the start of Stage Three of EMU. This conclusion is tentative and should be viewed with caution, since the level of the EFP may depend on the levels of the market interest rates, which were lower in Stage Three of EMU than in Stage Two. The next section takes in particular a closer look at the determination of the BBEFP over time.

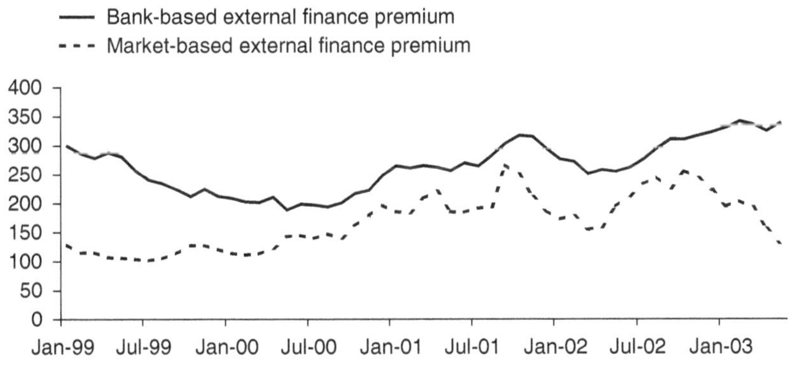

Figure 9.4 Bank-based and market-based external finance premia (basis points; monthly averages)

Sources: Bloomberg, ECB, Merrill Lynch, Reuters, and author's calculations.

Empirical Analysis: Stage Three versus Stage Two of EMU

This section empirically examines the linkages between EFP and monetary policy by looking at the interest rate channel and balance sheet channel of monetary policy. Readers who are interested in empirical evidence on the bank lending channel should have a look at Ehrmann et al. (2001) and Angeloni et al. (2003) and the literature cited there. The main overall finding of these bank-level studies, based on data prior to the start of Stage Three of EMU, is that the impact of monetary policy on bank lending behaviour in euro area countries depends on the degree of liquidity of bank assets. Broadly speaking, this is in line with an earlier European bank-level study by de Bondt (1999a) which empirically shows that the impact of monetary policy differs, particularly in Germany, along bank liquidity as well as bank size. In addition, Altunbaş et al. (2004) show that the monetary policy impact on bank lending might also depend on the degree of bank capitalization.

The effective sample period of the empirical analysis starts in January 1999 for the Stage Three sample and in January 1994 for the Stage Two sample. Results with respect to the BBEFP are presented for both samples to make a comparison possible between Stage Three and Two of EMU. The Stage Three sample period ends in 2001 to allow an out-of-sample forecasting exercise in order to test the stability of the results of the empirical bank-based debt pricing model. The sample periods are short, but have the advantage that structural changes due to the introduction of the euro are not part of the sample. However, it has the disadvantage of not covering several business cycles. Therefore, the empirical findings have to be interpreted with more than usual caution. In order to test the robustness of the results, more than one empirical method is applied.

Interest Rate Channel

In sum, an empirical examination of the interest rate channel shows that the co-movements between market interest rate changes and bank lending rates have become closer since the start of Stage Three of EMU. In addition it is found that the adjustment of bank lending rates to market interest rates has become quicker since January 1999. These findings suggest that market interest rate developments are quicker reflected in bank financing costs since the introduction of the single currency.

Correlation analysis Table 9.2 presents the highest correlations between bank lending rates and market interest rates with a comparable maturity for different lags of the market interest rates. A distinction is made between the correlations of the interest rate pairs in levels and in first differences (the change in the interest rate).

The correlation coefficients in level terms vary for the first three years of Stage Three of EMU between 0.96 and 0.98. This implies that bank and market rates move closely together. The lag with the highest correlation is six months for the interest rate on consumer lending and two months for the other bank lending rates. This suggests that bank lending rates do not collectively react by the same speed to market interest rate changes. The correlation coefficients, in terms of first differences, are lower with 0.57 for the interest rate on consumer lending and around 0.75 for the other bank lending rates and an 'optimal' lag between zero and three months. The

Table 9.2 Correlation analysis between bank lending and comparable market interest rates

Bank lending rate	Market interest rate	Level	Lag	Δ	Lag
		1994.1–1998.12*			
Up to 1 year to firms	6-month deposits	0.95	7	0.51	1
Over 1 year to firms	2-year government	0.78	3	0.36	1
Consumer lending	2-year government	0.97	4	0.36	5
House purchase	5-year government	0.99	1	0.76	1
		1999.1–2001.12			
Up to 1 year to firms	6-month deposits	0.98	2	0.73	1
Over 1 year to firms	2-year government	0.96	2	0.78	0
Consumer lending	2-year government	0.97	6	0.57	3
House purchase	5-year government	0.96	2	0.78	0

* Data for the interest rate on loans to enterprises with a maturity of over 1 year is available since November 1996.

Sources: ECB, Reuters, and author's calculations.

same qualitative picture emerges for Stage Two of EMU. However, a striking difference between the two samples is that the correlation coefficients for the sample starting in January 1999 are in all cases, except one, higher than for the years 1994–1998. This suggests that the co-movement between bank lending rates and market interest rates has become closer since the introduction of the euro, suggesting a quicker interest rate pass-through process since the start of Stage Three of EMU. The next subsections address this issue in more detail.

Regression analysis An appropriate way to empirically specify the adjustment of the price of bank-based debt *br* to changes in market interest rates *mr* is within an error-correction framework (Winker 1999 and de Bondt 2002a and 2005a). The main advantage of this empirical approach is that it takes into account both the short-term dynamics as well as the possibility of a co-integration or long-term equilibrium relationship between the two interest rate pairs. The estimated error-correction model equation reads as follows:

$$\Delta br_t = \alpha_1 + \alpha_2 \Delta mr_t - \beta_1 (br_{t-1} - \beta_2 mr_{t-1}) + \varepsilon_t \qquad (9.3)$$

The coefficient α_2 reflects the immediate or short-term pass-through, parameter β_2 the final or long-term pass-through, and $(1\text{-}\alpha_2)/\beta_1$ equals the mean adjustment lag at which market interest rates are fully passed through to bank interest rates (Hendry 1995). The existence of co-integration between bank lending rates and market interest rates can be directly tested by examining the significance of the coefficient of the error-correction term β_1 using the critical values as proposed by Kremers et al. (1992) and Boswijk (1994). As a robustness check the same model is also estimated within the Johansen and Juselius (1990) and Johansen (1991) vector error-correction modelling framework. Co-integration and lag exclusion tests suggest one co-integration relation and a lag order of one month, respectively.

Three conclusions, along the line of the three components of the interest rate pass-through process, emerge from the estimation results of a univariate and bivariate error-correction model, as summarized in Table 9.3.

First, the immediate pass-through of market interest rates to bank lending interest rates is in all cases found to be incomplete. The proportion of a given market interest rate change that is passed through within one month is found to be at most 30 per cent during Stage Two of EMU and 45 per cent in the first three years of Stage Three of EMU. The immediate pass-through is found to have significantly increased for the interest rate on loans to households for house purchase. This could be the result of a rise in the prevailing competitive forces, that is, market power and loan demand elasticity, and/or a fall in the asymmetric information costs in this segment of the debt market.

The second conclusion is that the final pass-through of market interest rates to bank lending rates is close to complete. The main exception is that the final pass-through with respect to the interest rate on loans to enterprises is clearly found to be above 100 per cent during Stage Two of EMU. An argument for this 'overshooting' is a move towards riskier borrowers, as described in the second section of this chapter.

Third, in all cases the adjustment speed has become quicker since the single currency, most notably for corporate bank lending rates. This may relate to an increase in the availability of alternative non-bank sources of finance, at least for enterprises. The commercial paper and corporate bond markets in the euro area have become more deep and liquid since the introduction of the euro and has opened up a viable alternative avenue of debt finance for corporations (de Bondt 2002b). The speed of adjustment of six to nine months, as found for the interest rates on consumer lending for the years 1999–2001, is much slower than for the other lending rates, which shows a mean adjustment speed of around three months.

This difference might be explained by the fact that the asymmetric information costs are relatively high for (unsecured) consumer lending and/or the degree of competition in the consumer credit market comparatively low, and that the interest rate elasticity with respect to consumer lending is relatively low. In all cases the adjustment coefficients are highly significant, which indicates that a long-term equilibrium relationship exists between the bank lending rate and the comparable market interest rate.

All in all, the estimation results of equation (9.3) show that bank lending interest rates adjust to changes in market interest rates incompletely in the short term. Bank lending rates more or less completely adjust to changes in market interest rates in the long term. The speed at which this adjustment takes place has, however, become quicker since January 1999. In other words, the rate on bank-based debt finance is observed to have become less sticky since the single currency, suggesting that some integration benefits have been achieved since the single currency. The results also suggest that integration is weak in the consumer credit market, given that the interest rate on consumer lending is found to be the most sluggish bank lending rate in Stage Three of EMU. The former follows from the reasoning that differences in the speed of interest rate pass-through may relate to differences in the degree of integration of the euro area bank credit market, as argued by Heinemann and Schüller (2002) and Kleimeier and Sander (2002).

Table 9.3 Overview bank lending interest rate pass-through based on error-correction framework

Bank lending rate	Immediate pass-through α_2	Final pass-through β_2	Adjustment speed[1] $(1-\alpha_2)/\beta_1$	Immediate pass-through α_2	Final pass-through β_2	Adjustment speed[1] $(1-\alpha_2)/\beta_1$
	Univariate error-correction model			Bivariate error-correction model		
Stage Two of EMU: 1994.1–1998.12[2]						
Up to 1 year to firms	0.04	1.33**	11.6**	0.13**	1.43**	17.1**
Over 1 year to firms	0.17	2.11**	8.2*	0.11	1.75**	7.3*
Consumer lending	0.10*	0.89**	9.3**	0.05	0.86**	8.9**
House purchase	0.18**	0.77**	3.0**	0.28**	0.80**	7.9*
Stage Three of EMU: 1999.1–2001.12						
Up to 1 year to firms	0.21**	0.89**	2.8**	0.04 0.89**	3.0**	
Over 1 year to firms	0.42**	0.95**	3.6**	0.24 0.95**	3.6**	
Consumer lending	0.08	0.78**	8.5**	0.05 0.71**	5.5**	
House purchase	0.44**	1.03**	2.4**	0.46**	1.14**	2.8**

Notes: ** and * denote significance at the 1 per cent and 5 per cent level, respectively.

[1]In months. [2]Data for the interest rate on loans to enterprises with a maturity of over one year is available since November 1996.

Sources: ECB, Reuters, and author's estimations.

Out-of-sample forecasts To further test the stability of the results, one-month-ahead out-of-sample forecasts for January 2002 up to March 2003 are performed on the basis of the estimated univariate error-correction model for the first three years of Stage Three of EMU (see Figure 9.5).

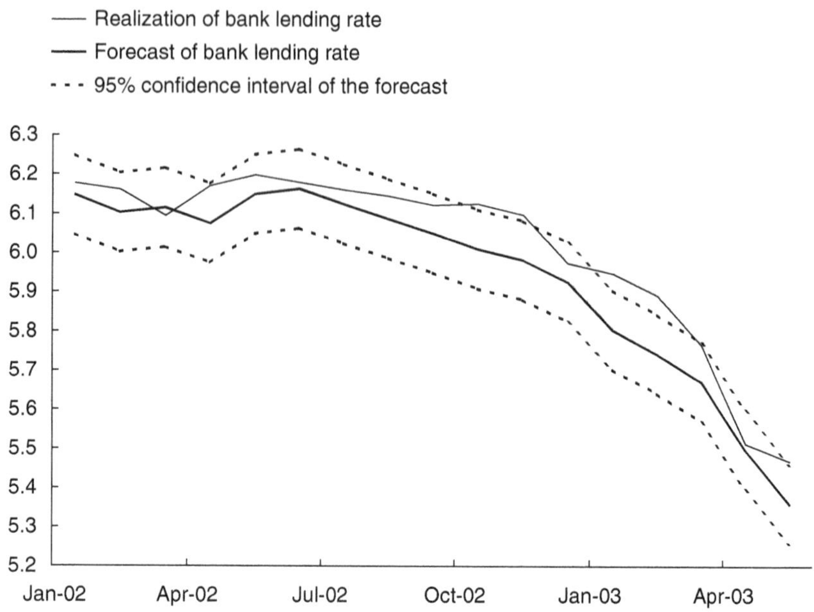

(A) Bank rate on loans to enterprises of up to 1 year

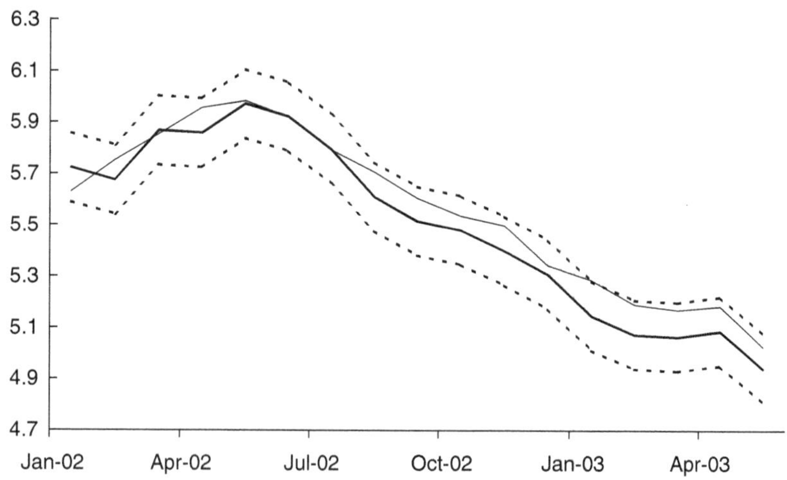

(B) Bank rate on loans to enterprises of over 1 year

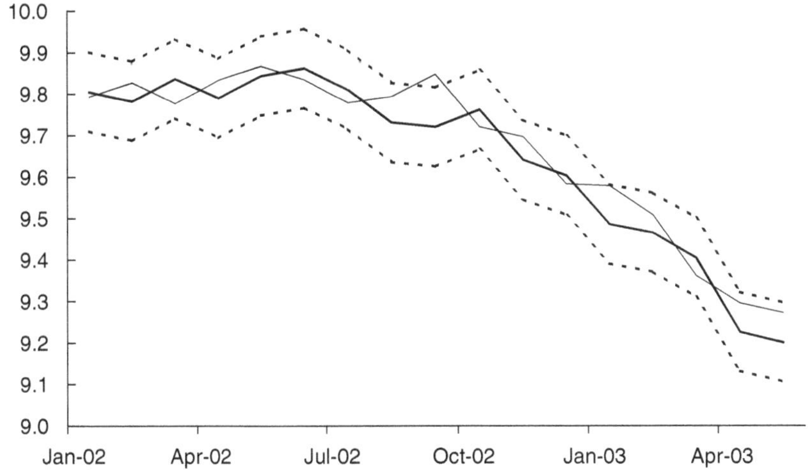

(C) Bank rate on loans to households for consumer lending

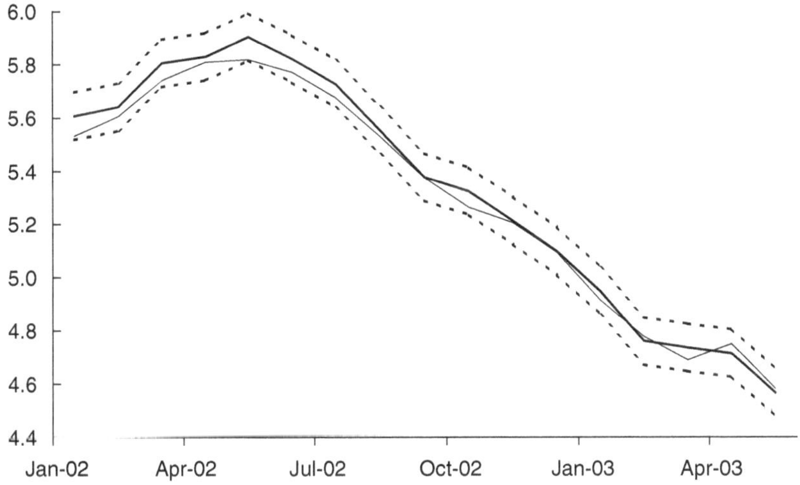

(D) Bank rate on loans to households for house purchase

Figure 9.5 Out-of-sample forecasts of bank lending rates for January 2002 up to May 2003 (percentages per annum; monthly averages)

Note: One-month ahead forecasts on the basis of a univariate error-correction model estimated for the first 3 years of Stage Three of EMU.

Sources: ECB, Reuters, and author's estimations.

Broadly speaking, bank lending rates have adjusted from January 2002 up to May 2003 in a typical way to changes in market interest rates with a comparable maturity. The main exception is that the interest rates on loans to enterprises were stickier since the summer of 2002 than models may have predicted on the basis of the first three years of the single currency. A likely explanation of the more than usual sluggish behaviour of corporate bank lending rates is credit risk considerations, as indicated by the high level of MBEFP during this period (see Figure 9.4). Qualitatively, the same picture emerges from a bank lending survey for the euro area in which banks report of a tightening of credit standards on loans to enterprises of 65 per cent and 46 per cent net in January and April 2003, respectively (ECB 2003a).[3]

Economic explanations of the quicker adjustment speed of bank lending rates
Prima facie, two likely explanations emerge for the observed change in the adjustment process since January 1999. First one could argue that the observed change around January 1999 relates to the reversal in the direction of the change in market interest rates and therefore is in favour of an asymmetric interest rate pass-through, that is, bank lending rates are more quickly adjusted upward in an environment of rising market interest rates than adjusted downward when market interest rates fall.

In the course of 1999 the declining pattern in market interest rates as observed since January 1994 reversed into a rise in market interest rates, which continued more or less up to the end of 2000, after which market interest rates started to decline again. Although the period of rising market interest rates is a substantial part of the Stage Three sample, an asymmetric pass-through argument can not explain why the speeding up is also found for deposit rates (de Bondt 2002a, de Bondt et al., 2002 and de Bondt 2003 and 2005a). Nevertheless, it can not be excluded that in some (national) segments of the bank credit market an asymmetric pass-through process might be observed in certain periods (de Bondt 2003).

The second and more likely economic explanation is that the prevailing competitive forces in most segments of the retail bank market have increased in the first years of Stage Three of EMU, both from a supply and from a demand perspective. The developments towards a rise in the prevailing competitive forces in the different segments of the bank credit market may in turn have been triggered by the introduction of the euro.

As regards the supply side, the ongoing restructuring of the banking sector seems to have promoted higher efficiency in the banking markets and more competitive pricing (see Chapter 6). A declining role of traditional banking, for example, granting long-term loans and funding them by short-dated deposits, as reflected in an increasing use by banks of non-deposit or market-based funding sources, is observed in Stage Three of EMU (see Figure 9.6). As regards the euro area inter-bank market, which plays an important role in the overall banking activity in the euro area, an increasing tendency of cross-border transactions vis-à-vis the domestic ones exists since the introduction of the euro (Hartmann et al., 2003). In addition, notwithstanding the steady decline in the number of credit institutions, new (foreign) players have

3 Studies for the US show that a high positive correlation exists between corporate bond spreads and the credit conditions as reported by the Federal Reserve Bank lending survey (Duca 1999, and Gertler and Lown 1999).

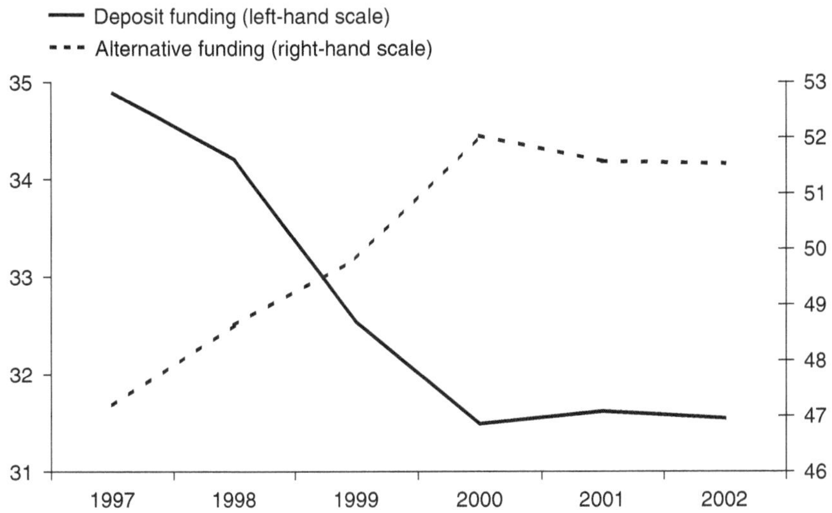

Figure 9.6 Deposit and alternative funding of MFI loans in the euro area (in percentage of balance sheet total)

Note: Alternative funding defined as deposits from resident MFIs and from non-residents (interbank and foreign deposits) and securities other than shares issued by MFIs.

become active in the retail bank credit market (see Chapter 6). Euro area banks also face more and more competition from other financial intermediaries such as insurance companies and pension funds (see Chapter 5).

Turning to the demand side, there are also indications that competition has increased as bank customers have become more sensitive to the interest rates on bank loans compared with those charged by other banks and by financial markets. This may be related to the higher stability of nominal interest rates in an environment of price stability, which facilitates the comparison of prices across different suppliers, and to an increase in the availability of alternative non-bank sources of finance, at least for some enterprises. For example, the commercial paper and corporate bond markets in the euro area have become deeper and more liquid since the introduction of the euro (see Chapter 8, de Bondt 2005b and de Bondt and Marqués Ibáñez 2005). Obviously, competition may differ across different segments of the bank lending market. While competition seems to be relatively high for household mortgages, the uncollateralized consumer credit market seems to be less competitive.

Balance Sheet Channel

This section examines whether monetary policy, approximated by the three-month money market rate, affects the EFP (existence of a balance sheet channel), and whether changes in the EFP affect real economic activity (macroeconomic relevance of a balance sheet channel).[4] In sum, the empirical results are supportive of the existence and relevance of the balance sheet channel of monetary policy.

Regression analysis Regressions results suggest that movements in the short-term interest rate precede those in the EFP. In turn, EFP developments precede real GDP growth. Furthermore, the EFP have marginal explanatory power for future real GDP growth, taking account of other monetary transmission variables.

The existence and macroeconomic relevance of a balance sheet channel is examined by performing pairwise Granger causality analyses between the change in the short-term interest rate and in the EFP, and between the change in the EFP and in the real GDP growth (see Table 9.4). A variable x Granger causes a variable y if the current value of y can be explained by past values of y and past values of x and the coefficients on the lagged x are statistically different from zero. In both sample periods, changes in the short-term interest rate Granger predict movements in the EFP. In other words, short-term interest rate movements significantly precede those in the EFP. In turn, movements in the EFP significantly precede those in the change in real GDP growth in the euro area, at the 10 per cent level for the BBEFP during the first three years of the single currency, and at the 1 per cent level in the other two cases.

The macroeconomic relevance of a balance sheet channel is further examined by estimating equations that explain real GDP growth by past movements in EFP and in

Table 9.4 Pairwise Granger causality tests of external finance premia (F-statistic)

Sample period	Bank-based EFP	Market-based EFP
	From short-term interest rate to EFP	
Stage Two of EMU: 1994.1–1998.12	6.2*	–
Stage Three of EMU: 1999.1–2001.12	4.8*	4.9*
	From EFP to short-term interest rate	
Stage Two of EMU: 1994.1–1998.12	0.5	–
Stage Three of EMU: 1999.1–2001.12	0.4	1.4
	From real GDP growth to EFP	
Stage Two of EMU: 1994.1–1998.12	2.3	–
Stage Three of EMU: 1999.1–2001.12	1.1	0.4
	From EFP to real GDP growth	
Stage Two of EMU: 1994.1–1998.12	10.6**	–
Stage Three of EMU: 1999.1–2001.12	3.2	9.1**

Notes: * and ** denote significance at the 1 per cent and 5 per cent level, respectively. F-statistic of a Wald test: $\alpha_1 + \alpha_2 = 0$ in $\Delta y_t = \alpha_0 + \alpha_1\Delta x_{t-1} + \alpha_2\Delta x_{t-2} + \beta_1\Delta y_{t-1} + \beta_2\Delta y_{t-2} + \varepsilon_t$. Lag order is reduced to 1 month if absolute t-values with a 2-month lag order are below one.

Sources: Bloomberg, ECB, Eurostat, Merrill Lynch, Reuters, and author's estimations.

4 The focus is here on the real GDP. Monthly data for GDP are obtained from interpolation. Fairly similar results are obtained for the industrial production.

other financial variables which capture the conventional interest rate and money channels of monetary policy: the short-term interest rate, the spread between the long and short-term interest rate, and M1 growth (see Table 9.5). The lag orders of the explanatory variables correspond with the lags of the highest correlation between the real GDP growth and the respective financial variable during the period under review. The regression results show that both EFP have significant marginal predictive power for the real GDP growth. An increase of 1 percentage point in both the BBEFP and the MBEFP results in a decline in the annual growth of real GDP by around 1 percentage point. An increase in the BBEFP leads up to one month to real GDP growth, while the MBEFP leads output with eight months. In addition, the short-term interest rate and M1 growth predicts real GDP growth with a lead of around ten months.

Impulse response analysis Impulse response functions, plotting the adjustment of variable *y* to a temporary and unexpected change in variable *x*, are also supportive of the existence and the macroeconomic relevance of a balance sheet channel. Following a monetary policy tightening, the EFP widens. An increase in the EFP, in turn, leads to a fall in the real GDP growth. The impulse responses as plotted in Figures 9.7 and 9.8 are based on bivariate vector autoregressive models with a lag order of two months.

As regards the existence of a balance sheet channel, Figure 9.7 shows that, following a 1 percentage point rise in the short-term interest rate, the EFP immediately

Table 9.5 Predictive power of external finance premia for the annual growth of real GDP

	1994.1–1998.12		**1999.1–2001.12**	
	Model[1]	**Model[2]**	**Model[1]**	**Model[2]**
Bank-based EFP	–0.66**	–0.50**	–0.66*	–0.54*
[Lag 0 and 1 month]	(0.12)	(0.10)	(0.24)	(0.25)
Market-based EFP	–	–	–0.32	–0.42*
[Lag – and 8 months]		(0.18)	(0.18)	
Short-term interest rate	–0.13*	–0.08	–0.42**	–0.68**
[Lag 10 and 11 months]	(0.07)	(0.06)	(0.12)	(0.11)
Term spread	–0.08	–0.11	–0.02	–0.01
[Lag 5 and 7 months]	(0.06)	(0.06)	(0.09)	(0.10)
M1 growth	0.14**	0.17**	0.11**	0.05
[Lag 10 and 10 months]	(0.04)	(0.03)	(0.02)	(0.03)
Constant	4.19**	3.27**	5.28**	6.73**
	(0.90)	(0.58)	(0.71)	(1.08)
R^2	0.79	0.80	0.97	0.98

Notes: ** and * denote significance at the 1 per cent and 5 per cent level, respectively. Absolute Newey-West corrected standard errors between parentheses. The lags of the explanatory factors of model[1] and [2] are between square brackets.

Sources: Bloomberg, ECB, Eurostat, Merrill Lynch, Reuters, and author's estimations.

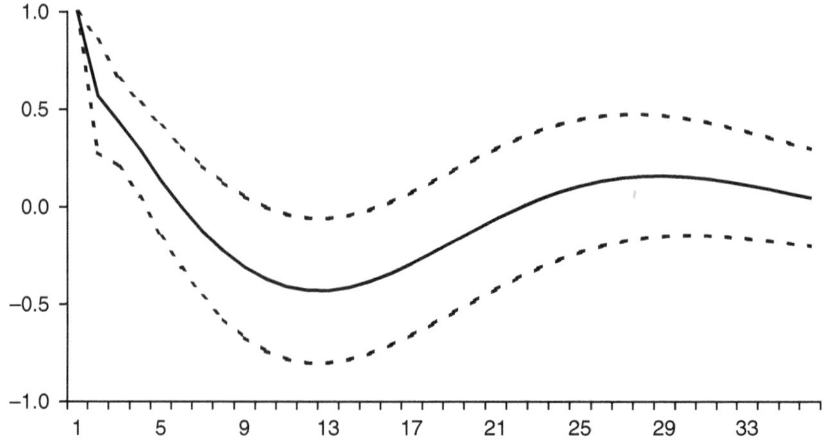

(A) Short-term interest rate, Stage Two of EMU

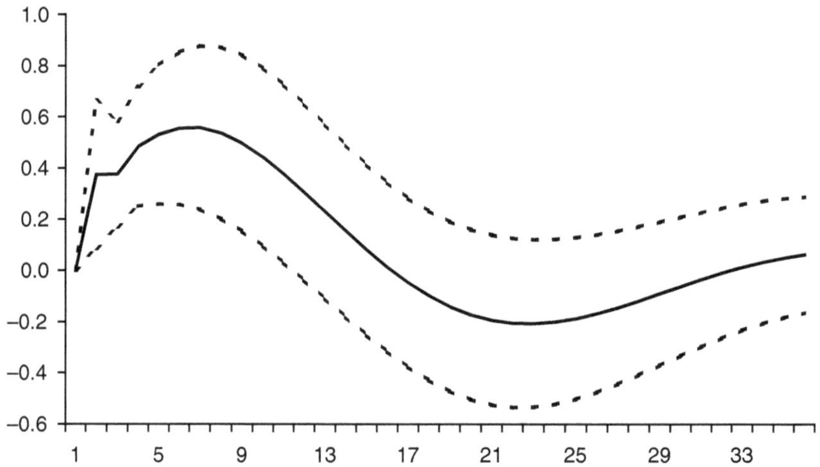

(B) Bank-based external finance premium, Stage Two of EMU

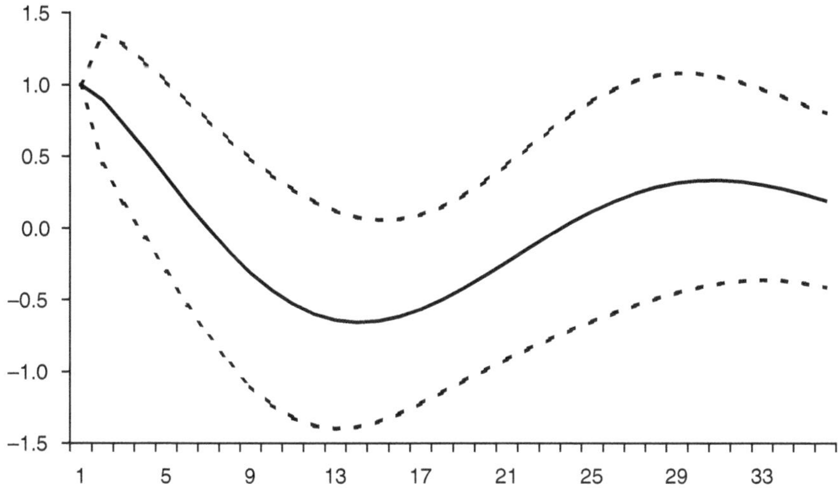

(C) Short-term interest rate, Stage Three of EMU

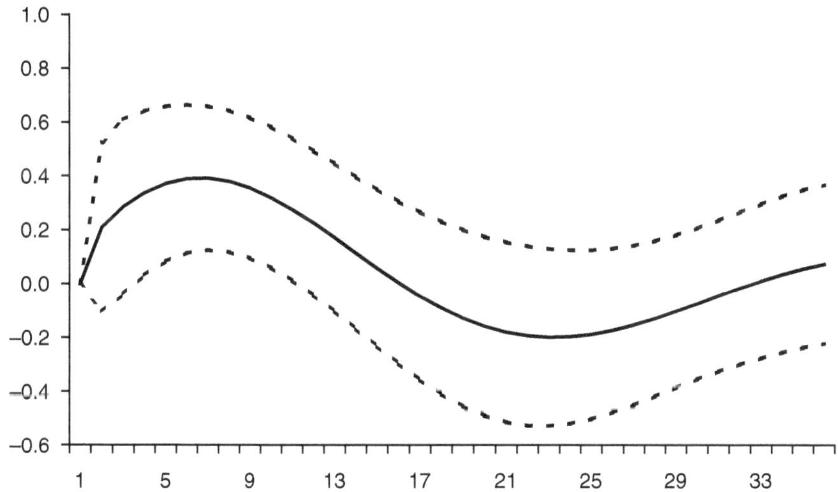

(D) Bank-based external finance premium, Stage Three of EMU

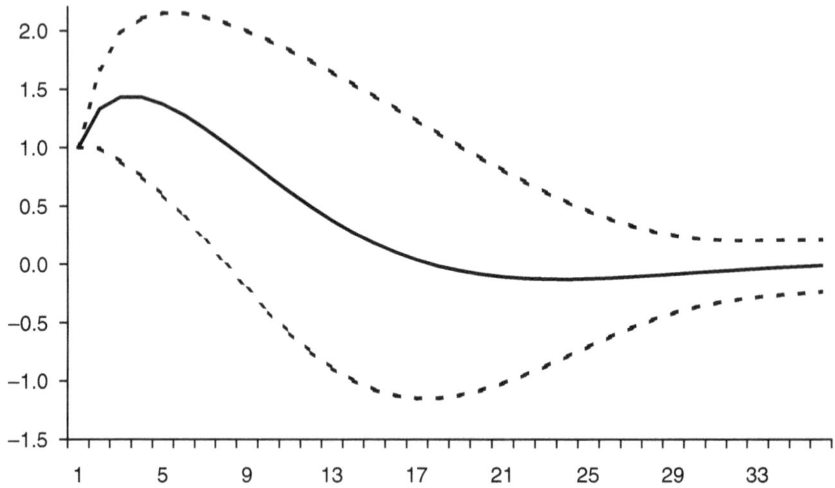

(E) Short-term interest rate, Stage Three of EMU

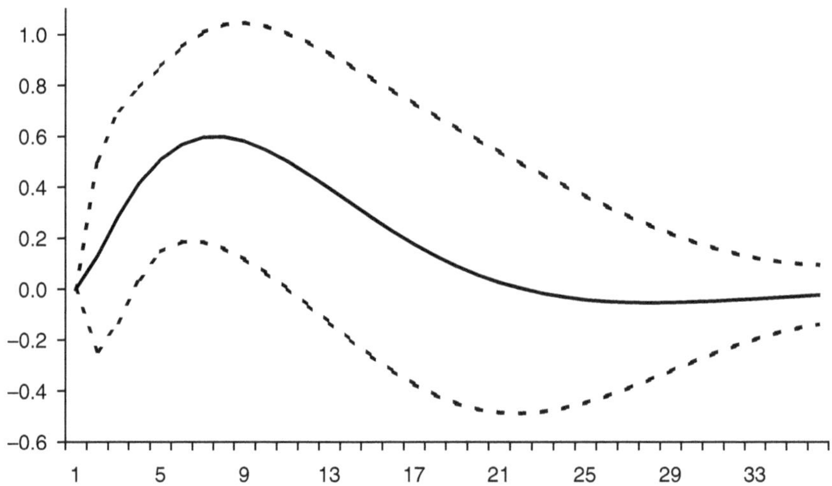

(F) Market-based external finance premium, Stage Three of EMU

Figure 9.7 Adjustment of the external finance premium to a temporary rise in the short-term interest rate of 1 percentage point (percentages per annum)

Note: Dotted lines denote 95 per cent confidence interval based on analytical standard errors.
Sources: Bloomberg, ECB, Merrill Lynch, Reuters, and author's estimations.

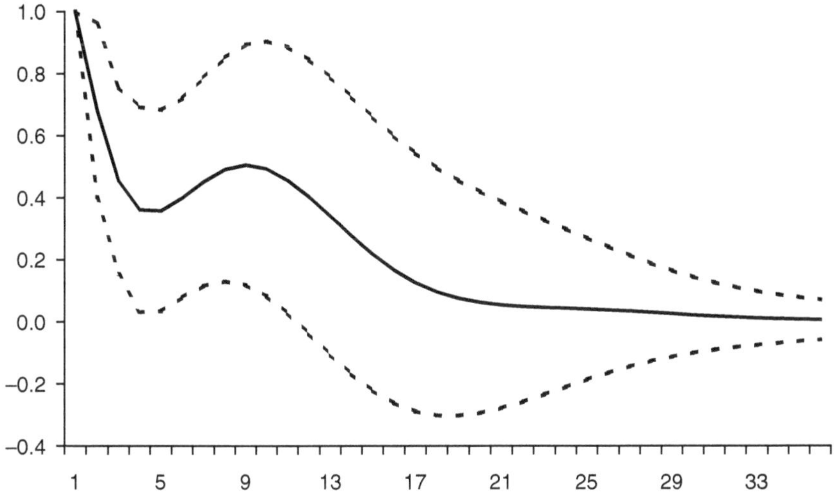

(A) Bank-based external finance premium, Stage Two of EMU

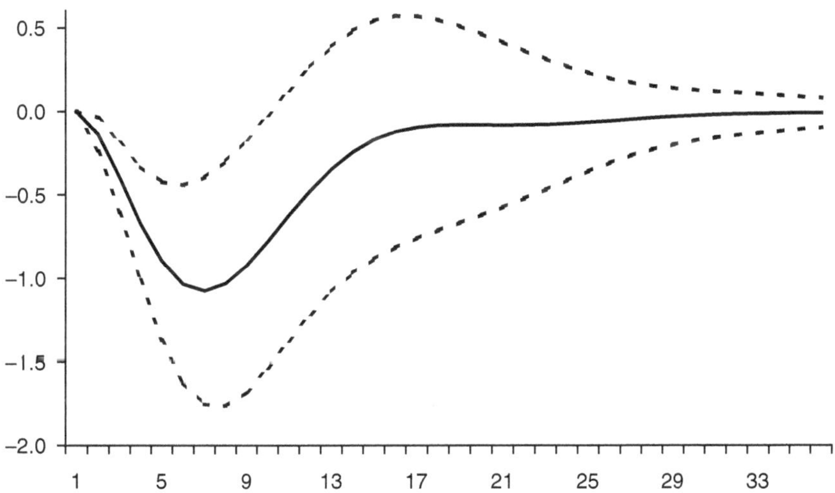

(B) Real GDP growth, Stage Two of EMU

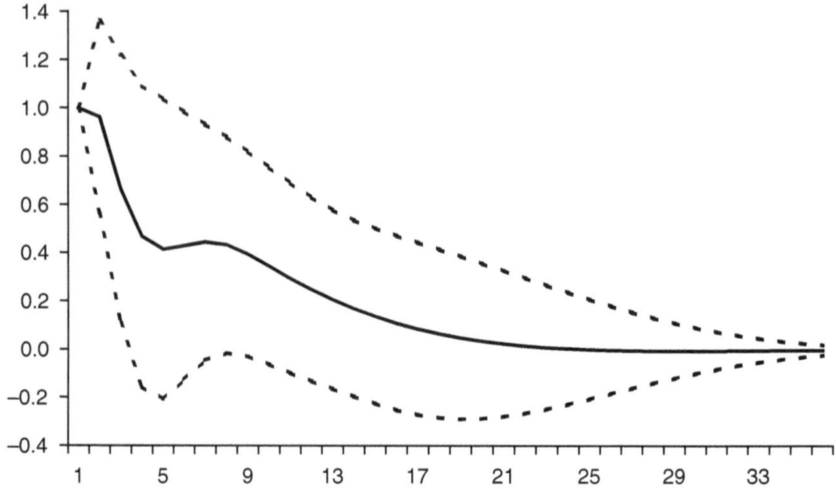

(C) Bank-based external finance premium, Stage Three of EMU

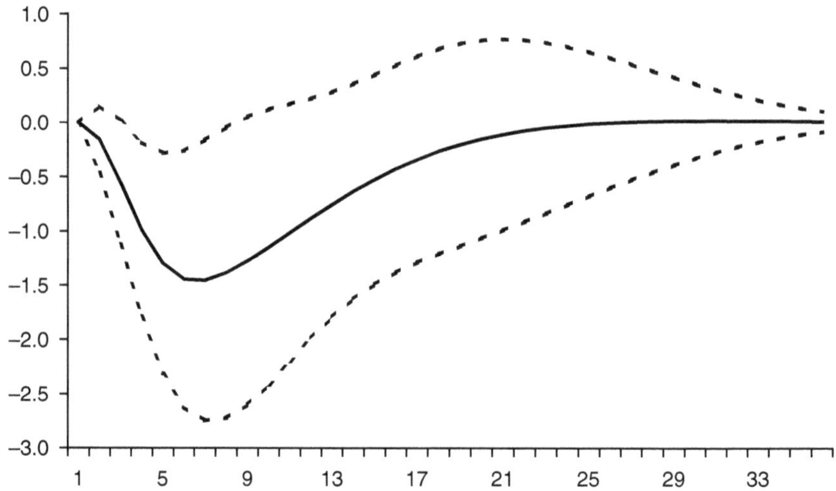

(D) Real GDP growth, Stage Three of EMU

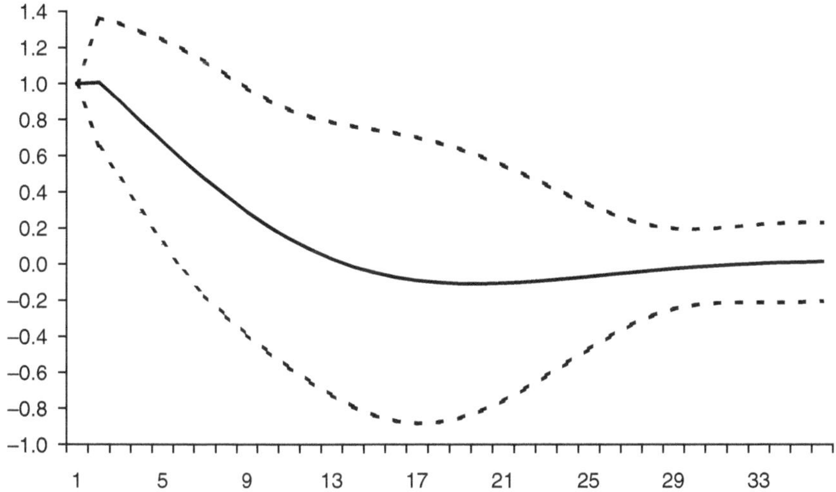

(E) Market-based external finance premium, Stage Three of EMU

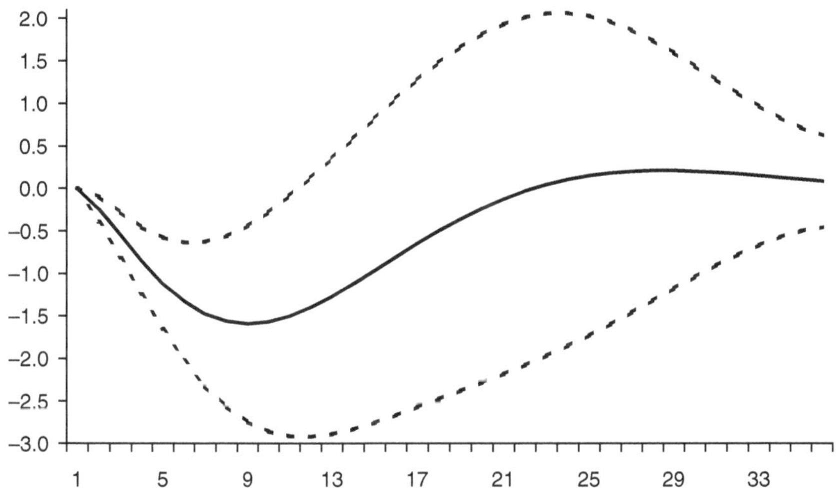

(F) Real GDP growth, Stage Three of EMU

Figure 9.8 Adjustment of real GDP growth to a temporary widening of the external finance premium of 1 percentage point (percentages per annum)

Note: Dotted lines denote 95 per cent confidence interval based on analytical standard errors.
Sources: Bloomberg, ECB, Eurostat, Merrill Lynch, Reuters, and author's estimations.

widens and peaks after seven months around 0.5 percentage points.[5] This increase is significant up to 11 months. The lagged response of the EFP may be related to a lagged effect of monetary policy on the creditworthiness of borrowers, for example firms' cash flow, the price of collateral and the burden of debt.

Turning to the macroeconomic relevance of a balance sheet channel, Figure 9.8 shows that the real GDP growth immediately declines following a temporary widening of the EFP. This decline is significant up to around ten months. A temporary widening of the EFP by 1 percentage point results in a significant decline in the real GDP growth of up to 1.5 percentage points.

The latter output effect is not negligible compared with the impact of the short-term interest rate found in models which neglect the possibility of a balance sheet channel. One should, however, keep in mind that on the basis of Figure 9.7, a widening of the EFP by 100 basis points broadly matches with an increase in the short-term interest rate by 200 basis points. Simulation results from large macroeconomic structural models reveal that, following a temporary increase in the short-term interest rate of 100 basis points for two years, real GDP growth in the euro area typically declines by between 0.2 to 0.4 percentage points in the first and second year (de Bondt et al., 1997, van Els et al., 2001 and McAdam and Morgan 2001). At the same time impulse response functions show for the euro area that an unexpected temporary rise in the short-term interest rate of about 100 basis points tends to be followed by a decline in output growth of up to 0.8 percentage points in the first two years (Mojon and Peersman 2001 and Peersman and Smets 2001). However, it can not be excluded that the BBEFP or the MBEFP captures the general degree of concern in the economy about credit risk. In other words, the EFP could be indicative of many debt factors at work in the business cycle.

Concluding Remarks

This chapter examines the linkages between the premium on debt finance and monetary policy in the euro area and whether these mechanisms have changed since the introduction of the single currency. The main overall finding is that the speed and nature of some linkages between the EFP and monetary policy at the euro area level seem to have changed since January 1999. A strengthening and deepening of the monetary policy transmission process has been observed since the introduction of the euro.

This finding is based on two main empirical conclusions, which are admittedly tentative given the short history of Stage Three of EMU and at the same time fairly robust across different empirical methods. The first conclusion is that the pass-through of changes in market interest rates to bank lending rates has changed since January 1999. A quicker adjustment of bank lending rates to market interest rate developments is observed since the single currency, suggesting a strengthening of monetary policy transmission. The second conclusion is that the balance sheet

5 The external finance premium with respect to mortgages in individual euro area countries shows a similar impulse response pattern, following a short-term interest rate shock (de Bondt 1999b).

channel of monetary policy has deepened since January 1999, in particular the monetary transmission channel working through the external finance premium as observed in the euro area corporate bond market. The empirical analysis reveals that following a rise in the short-term interest rate the bank- and market-based EFP significantly increase. A rise in EFP, in turn, significantly explains future growth in the real GDP. These findings are supportive of the existence and macroeconomic relevance of a balance sheet channel of monetary policy.

What are the implications of these findings for financial integration in the euro area? First, the empirical findings imply that market interest rate changes are more rapidly reflected in bank-based debt financing costs since January 1999. The observed quicker adjustment speed of bank lending rates suggests that in the first years of Stage Three of EMU probably some integration benefits have been achieved. However, further convergence of the adjustment speeds, in particular for consumer credit rates, to the fastest levels observed would imply some further integration benefits. This process may benefit from an increase in prevailing competitive forces in the different segments of the bank credit market, a more active behaviour of borrowers on interest rate changes and from improvements in the assessment of credit risk. Second, the finding of the existence and macroeconomic relevance of a balance sheet channel implies that movements in official interest rates may have effects on real economic activity via a financial accelerator mechanism working through the external finance premium. Consequently, monetary policy in the euro area may have a distributional impact across borrowers along the size of the EFP, which highly depend on the net worth or balance sheet position of borrowers. Further integration benefits can be expected through changes in the nature and level of bank- and market-based EFP. For instance, an increased use of market-based finance may positively affect the availability and price of bank-based debt or a strengthening of the balance sheet position of borrowers will result in lower EFP.

References

Altunbaş, Y., Bondt, G.J. de and Marqués, D. (2004), 'Bank Capital, Bank Lending, and Monetary Policy in the Euro Area', *Kredit und Kapital*, **37** (4), pp. 443–464.

Altunbaş, Y., Fazylov, O. and Molyneux, P. (2002), 'Evidence on the Bank Lending Channel in Europe', *Journal of Banking and Finance*, **26**(11), pp. 2093–110.

Angeloni, I., Kashyap, A. and Mojon, B. (2003), *Monetary Policy Transmission in the Euro Area*, Cambridge University Press, Cambridge, UK.

Bernanke, B.S. and Gertler, M. (1989), 'Agency Costs, Net Worth, and Business Fluctuations', *American Economic Review*, **79**(1), pp. 14–31.

Bernanke, B.S. and Gertler, M. (1995), 'Inside the Black Box: The Credit Channel of Monetary Policy Transmission', *Journal of Economic Perspectives*, **9**(1), pp. 27–48.

Bernanke, B., Gilchrist, S. and Gertler, M. (1994), *The Financial Accelerator and the Flight to Quality*, NBER Research Paper No. 4789, National Bureau of Economic Research.

Boissay, F. (2001), *Credit Rationing, Output Gap, and Business Cycles*, ECB Working Paper No. 87, European Central Bank.

Bondt, G.J. de (1998), 'Financial Structure: Theories and Stylized Facts for Six EU Countries', *De Economist*, **146**(2), pp. 271–301.

Bondt, G.J. de (1999a), 'Banks and Monetary Transmission in Europe: Empirical Evidence', *Banca Nazionale del Lavoro Quarterly Review*, **52**, pp. 149–68.

Bondt, G.J. de (1999b), *Credit Channels and Consumption in Europe: Empirical Evidence*, BIS Working Paper No. 69, Bank for International Settlements.
Bondt, G.J. de (2000), *Financial Structure and Monetary Transmission in Europe: A Cross-Country Study*, Edward Elgar, Cheltenham, UK and Northampton, MA, USA.
Bondt, G.J. de (2002a), *Retail Bank Interest Rate Pass-Through: New Evidence at the Euro Area Level*, ECB Working Paper No. 136, European Central Bank.
Bondt, G.J. de (2002b), *Euro Area Corporate Debt Securities Market: First Empirical Evidence*, ECB Working Paper No. 164, European Central Bank.
Bondt, G.J. de (2002c), 'Debt Finance and the ECB Monetary Policy: Where Do We Stand after the First Three Years?' (in Spanish), *Papeles de Economía Española*, **94**, pp. 66–90.
Bondt, G.J. de (2003), 'Has the Retail Bank Interest Rate Pass-Through Been Atypical in 2002?', *CESifo Forum*, **4**(1, Spring), pp. 42–6.
Bondt, G.J. de (2004a), 'The Balance Sheet Channel of Monetary Policy: First Empirical Evidence for the Euro Area Corporate Bond Market', *International Journal of Finance and Economics*, **9**, (3), pp. 219–228.
Bondt, G.J. de (2005a), 'Interest Rate Pass-Through: Empirical Results for the Euro Area', *German Economic Review*, **6**(1), pp. 37–38.
Bondt, G.J. de (2005b), 'Determinants of Corporate Debt Securities in the Euro Area', *European Journal of Finance*, **10**, pp. 1–19 (forthcoming).
Bondt, G.J. de, Els, P.J.A. van and Stokman, A.C.J. (1997), *EUROMON: A Macroeconometric Multi-Country Model for the EU*, DNB Staff Reports No. 17, De Nederlandsche Bank.
Bondt, G.J. de and Lichtenberger, J.-D. (2003), 'The Euro Area Corporate Bond Market: Where Do We Stand since the Introduction of the Euro?', *European Business Organization Law Review*, **4**(4), pp. 517–539.
Bondt, G.J. de and Lichtenberger, J.-D. (2004), 'Empirical Estimates of the Impact of the Euro on the Corporate Bond market in the Euro Area', *Applied Economics Letters*, **11**, pp. 675–678.
Bondt, G.J. de and Marqués Ibáñez, D. (2005), 'High-yield Bond Diffusion in the US, the UK, and the Euro Area', *Journal of Financial Services Research*, **27** (2), pp. 163–181.
Bondt, G.J. de, Mojon, B. and Valla, N. (2002), *Interest Rate Setting by Universal Banks and the Monetary Policy Transmission Mechanism in the Euro Area*, CEPR Conference Paper, Centre for Economic Policy Research conference entitled 'Will Universal Banking Dominate or Disappear? Consolidation, Restructuring and (Re)Regulation in the Banking Industry', Madrid, 15/16 November 2002.
Boswijk, H.P. (1994), 'Testing for an Unstable Root in Conditional and Structural Error Correction Models', *Journal of Econometrics*, **63**, pp. 37–60.
Duca, J.V. (1999), 'What Credit Market Indicators Tell Us', *Economic and Financial Review*, Third Quarter, pp. 2–13.
Ehrmann, M., Gambacorta, L., Martínez-Pagés, J., Sevestre, P. and Worms, A. (2001), *Financial Systems and the Role of Banks in Monetary Policy Transmission in the Euro Area*, ECB Working Paper No. 105, European Central Bank.
Els, P. van, Locarno, A., Morgan, J. and Villetelle, J.-P. (2001), *Monetary Policy Transmission in the Euro Area: What Do Aggregate and National Structural Models Tell Us?*, ECB Working Paper No. 94, European Central Bank.
European Central Bank (2002), 'Recent Findings on Monetary Policy Transmission in the Euro Area', *Monthly Bulletin*, October, pp. 43–53.
European Central Bank (2003a), 'First Results of the Bank Lending Survey for the Euro Area', *Monthly Bulletin*, May, Box 2, pp. 15–7.
European Central Bank (2003b), 'New ECB statistics on MFI interest rates', *Monthly Bulletin*, December, Box 2, pp. 23–5.
European Central Bank (2004), *The Monetary Policy of the ECB*, ECB, Frankfurt am Main.

Fase, M.M.G. and Bondt, G.J. de (2000), 'Institutional Environment and Monetary Transmission in the Euro Area: A Cross-Country View', *Revue de la Banque / Bank-en Financiewezen* **64**(2–3), pp. 149–55.

Favero, C.A., Giavazzi, F. and Flabbi, L. (1999), *The Transmission Mechanism of Monetary Policy in Europe: Evidence from Banks' Balance Sheets*, NBER Working Paper No. 7231, National Bureau of Economic Research.

Fisher, J. (1997), 'Credit Market Imperfections and the Heterogeneous Response of Firms to Monetary Shocks', *Journal of Money, Credit, and Banking*, **2**, pp. 187–211.

Gertler, M. and Gilchrist, S. (1993), 'The Role of Credit Market Imperfections in the Monetary Transmission Mechanism: Arguments and Evidence', *Scandinavian Journal of Economics* **109**(2), pp. 309–40.

Gertler, M. and Lown, C. (1999), 'The Information in the High-Yield Bond Spread for the Business Cycle: Evidence and some Implications', *Oxford Review of Economic Policy*, **15**(3), pp. 132–50.

Greenwald, B.C. and Stiglitz, J.E. (1993), 'Financial Market Imperfections and Business Cycles', *Quarterly Journal of Economics*, **108**(1), 77–114.

Hartmann, P., Maddaloni, A. and Manganelli, S. (2003), 'The Euro Area Financial System: Structure, Integration, and Policy Initiatives', *Oxford Review of Economic Policy*, **19**(1), pp. 180–213.

Heinemann F. and Schüler, M. (2002), *Integration Benefits on EU Retail Credit Markets – Evidence from Interest Rate Pass-through*, ZEW Discussion Paper No. 02–26, Zentrum für Europäische Wirtschaftsforschung.

Hendry, D.F. (1995), *Dynamic Econometrics*, Oxford University Press, Oxford.

Johansen, S. (1991), 'Estimation and Hypothesis Testing of Cointegration Vectors in Gaussian Vector Autoregressive Models', *Econometrica*, **59**, pp. 1551–80.

Johansen, S. and Juselius, K. (1990), 'Maximum Likelihood Estimation and Inference on Cointegration – with Applications to the Demand for Money', *Oxford Bulletin of Economics and Statistics*, **52**, pp. 169–210.

Kashyap, A.K. and Stein, J.C. (1995), 'The Impact of Monetary Policy on Bank Balance Sheets', *Carnegie-Rochester Conference Series on Public Policy*, **42**, pp. 151–95.

Kashyap, A.K. and Stein, J.C. (1997), 'The Role of Banks in Monetary Policy: A Survey with Implications for the European Monetary Union', *European Perspectives*, **21**, Federal Reserve Bank of Chicago, pp. 2–19.

Kashyap A.K. and Stein, J.C. (2000), 'What Do a Million Observations on Banks Have to Say About the Monetary Transmission Mechanism', *American Economic Review*, **90**(3), pp. 407–28.

Kishan, R.P. and Opiela, T.P. (2000), 'Bank Size, Bank Capital, and the Bank Lending Channel', *Journal of Money, Credit, and Banking*, **32**(1), pp. 121–41.

Kiyotaki, N. and Moore, J. (1997), 'Credit Cycles', *Journal of Political Economy*, **105**(2), pp. 211–48.

Kleimeier, S. and Sander, H. (2002), *Consumer Credit Rates in the Eurozone: Evidence on the Emergence of a Single Retail Banking Market*, ECRI Research Report No. 2 (January), European Credit Research Institute.

Kremers, J.J.M., Ericsson, N.R. and Dolado, J.J. (1992), 'The Power of Cointegration Tests', *Oxford Bulletin of Economics and Statistics*, **54**(3), pp. 325–48.

McAdam, P. and Morgan, J. (2001), *The Monetary Transmission Mechanism at the Euro-Area Level: Issues and Results Using Structural Macroeconomic Models*, European Central Bank Working Paper No. 93.

Mojon, B. and Peersman, G. (2001), *A VAR Description of the Effects of Monetary Policy in the Individual Countries of the Euro Area*, ECB Working Paper No. 92, European Central Bank.

Peek, J.B. and Rosengren, E.S., eds. (1995a), *Is Bank Lending Important for the Transmission of Monetary Policy?*, Federal Reserve Bank of Boston Conference Series, **39** (June).
Peek, J.B. and Rosengren, E.S. (1995b). 'The Captital Crunch: Neither a Borrower nor a Lender Be', *Journal of Money, Credit, and Banking*, **27**(3) pp. 625–38.
Peersman, G. and Smets, F. (2001), *The Monetary Transmission Mechanism in the Euro Area: More Evidence from VAR Analysis*, ECB Working Paper No. 91, European Central Bank.
Romer, C.D. and Romer, D.H. (1990), 'New Evidence on the Monetary Transmission Mechanism', *Brookings Papers on Economic Activity*, **1**, pp. 149–213.
Stiglitz, J.E. and Weiss, A. (1981), 'Credit Rationing in Markets with Imperfect Information', *American Economic Review*, **71**, pp. 393–410.
Trautwein, H.-M. (2000), 'The Credit View, Old and New', *Journal of Economic Surveys*, **14**(2), pp. 155–89.
Winker, P. (1999), 'Sluggish Adjustment of Interest Rates and Credit Rationing: An Application of Unit Root Testing and Error Correction Modelling', *Applied Economics*, **31**, pp. 267–77.

Index

www.ingramcontent.com/pod-product-compliance
Ingram Content Group UK Ltd.
Pitfield, Milton Keynes, MK11 3LW, UK
UKHW010956180926
475701UK00004B/406
* 9 7 8 1 1 3 8 6 1 9 5 5 5 *